Culture of the Baroque

Theory and History of Literature
Edited by Wlad Godzich and Jochen Schulte-Sasse

Culture of

the Baroque

Analysis of a

Historical Structure

José Antonio Maravall

Translation by Terry Cochran

Foreword by Wlad Godzich and Nicholas Spadaccini

Theory and History of Literature, Volume 25

University of Minnesota Press, Minneapolis

The University of Minnesota Press gratefully acknowledges trans-
lation and publication assistance provided for this book by the
Program for Cultural Cooperation Between Spain's Ministry of
Culture and North American Universities.

This book was originally published in Spain by Editorial Ariel as *La cultura
del Barroco*, copyright © 1975, 1980, and 1983 by José Antonio Maravall.

Published by the University of Minnesota Press
2037 University Avenue Southeast, Minneapolis MN 55414.
Published simultaneously in Canada
by Fitzhenry & Whiteside Limited, Markham.
Printed in the United States of America.

Library of Congress Cataloging-in-Publication Data
Maravall, José Antonio
       Culture of the baroque.
       (Theory and history of literature ; v. 25)
       Translation of: La cultura del barroco.
       Bibliography: p.
       Includes index.
       1. Spain — Intellectual life — 17th century.
2. Civilization, Baroque.   I. Title.   II. Series.
DP171.5.M3713   1986   306'.4'0946   85-28976
ISBN 0-8166-1443-1
ISBN 0-8166-1445-8 (pbk.)

Contents

Foreword
The Changing Face of History
Wlad Godzich and Nicholas Spadaccini

Once upon a time, it was possible to make an audience chuckle by saying that history is no longer what it used to be. Everyone understood this amphibological use of the term *history*, which was called upon to mean both the representation of past events and the actual course of these events; and, whereas it was generally accepted that differing and multiple representations are possible, perhaps even desirable, the actual course of past events could only be singular and have the immutability of a fate accomplished. Today, the same statement would no longer elicit similar mirth. Not only are we all too aware of the constant manipulation and rewriting of history that is one of the hallmarks of our age, whether for reasons that we may find as abhorrent as Orwell did, or, on the contrary, that we may approve of as in the new histories that no longer omit the fate and the feats of women: but we are also becoming more conscious of the determinant role played by the discourse of the historian upon the representation of history that results from this discourse. Among historians, the work of Hayden White is preeminently concerned with this problem, while among literary scholars, the poststructuralists have used it to challenge the very possibility of historical cognition.

History, as an academic enterprise, is being haunted with something that it thought it had exorcised at its very beginnings. For, as Arnaldo Momigliano reminded us recently, the oldest chairs of history in Europe were created in the sixteenth century when the chairs of letters at the universities of Göttingen and Leiden were split into two different chairs, reflecting and instituting the perceived difference between letters and history.[1] There is thus an irony, even a historical irony, in our present situation; but as with most ironies, what is at stake is not merely the discomfiture of some assertory discourse, in this instance the historical one, nor even the very setting of the distinction, which is the present institutional organization of knowledge as exemplified in the disciplinary structure of our universities, but rather our conception of what constitutes historical representation.

The discourse of the historian — to designate in the abstract singular what has been a plurality of concrete practices — has grown more remote from its original ground in letters, and it has done so by concentrating on one aspect of its formal communicational apparatus — the referent, or what historians have traditionally called the facts — at the expense of the others, and most notably of the addressee, who is the reader. History used to be read by cultured individuals almost as much, if not more, than fiction. That is the case much less today, though some forms of it, especially biography and so-called narrative history, seem to fare somewhat better. Some historians have come to believe that history must return to this traditional form of narrative to recapture its past audience or, more precisely, to move beyond the narrow readership of specialized historians. Such a conclusion is overly hasty inasmuch as it grants features exclusively to narrative that the latter shares with other forms of discourse: closure and finality. These features also happen to be the most vulnerable to an epistemological critique of a poststructuralist type, which has no difficulty in pointing out that the well-attested seductiveness of narrative is as operative in historical narratives as it is in fictional ones; but although the latter make no claim to veracity, the former do and thus may well find their claims to truthfulness to be at odds with the requirements of narrative tale-telling.

The dependency of the discourse of the historian upon narrative deserves some consideration in its own right. It may well appear quasi-natural to us that historical discourse should take narrative as its privileged mode, but there is no inherent necessity for it to do so. The frequently invoked lack of distinction between the words for *story* and *history* in a number of languages has further served to obfuscate the fact that the link between history and narrative is itself historical, that history developed as a discipline in the shadow of a system of signification that placed special value upon teleological explanations couched in emplotted forms. Salvational discourse in Christianity is narrative in nature, as is its messianic predecessor in Judaism. In both instances, events in the world result from divine intention or from mostly contrary human willfulness; in any case, however, they are part of a discourse of actions, as Aristotle calls it, or plot. And plot becomes significant if the actions it repertories achieve closure, for only within such a closure does their end become clear.

This dominant Western mode of historical discourse is understood more easily if one contrasts it with the descriptive imperative of, let us say, Ibn Khaldun's reflection upon history, which places greater importance upon a structural representation than upon a cause and effect account.[2] The model is still one of closure and finality, but both of these are conceived in relation to a structure rather than a historical movement. The specificity of the Western mode of historical discourse lies in the fact that it is concerned with the dimension of becoming as manifested in the past — that is, with the very movement of history, where the latter is conceived as a force or as a set of forces capable of effecting movement. Under such a conception, the paramount question is *why*, whereas in Ibn Khaldun's view it is *how*.

These two questions form the articulatory axes around which revolve the various practices of history at present, but, as the debate about the new narrative history demonstrates, their role is unequal. The older interrogation into causality may appear less sophisticated in its use of quantitative techniques, for example, but it does have the seductive power of narrative at its disposal and puts itself forward as a form of explanation. It benefits from the still powerful presence in our thought of the Enlightenment model of nature conceived as a system of ends, a model that was the successor to the sacred models of the world that dominated not only the Middle Ages but even early modern times. In the latter, time was conceived *sub specie aeternitatis*; thus, the end of human actions — their finality — was known beforehand, or at least there was in place a hermeneutics that permitted their rational calculation. The Enlightenment changed this conception of time, of course, but it reinscribed the closure of signification into nature. Nowhere is this clearer than in Kant's opuscula on history, in which he argues that the highest of human values, namely freedom, is first realized in a society governed under the best constitution, and that such a society is the means whereby nature itself accomplishes its own goals, fulfills its own ends.[3] For nature here is conceived of as a system of ends, and it is the task of the philosopher to determine speculatively what these goals are so that individual and specific human actions may be evaluated according to whether they contribute to the fulfillment of these ends or contravene them.

If the goals are known, then we are back within a structural approach of the Ibn Khaldun type, but we lose the sense of historical movement. This is one of the reasons why Kant's conception was critiqued by Hegel. Modern thought is characterized by the fact that humankind no longer thinks of itself as the emanation or creature of a superior being or as a part of an external nature, but rather as a becoming. In his *Philosophy of History*, Hegel emphatically rejects Rousseau's distinction between a state of nature and a social state, a distinction that presupposes that some form of human essence, pure, absolute, and immediate, is somehow apprehensible, and then that customs and social behaviors somehow graft themselves onto it. For Hegel, human beings have only historical existence and meaning, and one does not attain some ethereal dimension of the human by stripping away the layers of the historical, that is, by abstracting humankind from its historical heritage; rather, one defines the human by uncovering the law of historical constitution that makes humankind progressively what it is. The *why* has regained its preeminence.

But Hegel's conception of the law of historical constitution presupposes not only the prior acceptance of a law of historical progression, but also that all of humankind be conceived of as a totality — and a homogeneous one at that — undergoing the very same processes in the course of historical developments. Since the historian, even a Hegelian one, cannot ignore the empirical fact of difference among human societies, the postulate of homogeneity requires that, in practical terms, differences among human societies be explained as differences of temporality: an early nineteenth-century German Protestant industrialist and his contemporary Indian Hindu peasant farmer may well occupy the same chronological frame, but they represent different levels of accomplishment in the development of the spirit. Hegel's well-known distinction of the various stages of development of the spirit constitutes the privileged chronology against which all human achievements are measured, and their application serves to redistribute contemporaries and predecessors alike according to the logic of that chronology, with the paradoxical effect that people who live at the same time are no longer thought of as true contemporaries. This view has become so prevalent among us today that we are no longer conscious of its extraordinary mode of apportioning time. And, of course, the potential for the imposition of ethnocentric assumptions inherent in such a view hardly needs remarking.

Marxism has retained the Hegelian notion of stages of development, though no longer describing them as degrees in the disclosure (*Offenbarung*) of the spirit, but rather as steps in the complexity of modes of production. It has also attempted to address the question of "noncontemporaneous contemporaries" by describing the relations between two societies in terms of domination, though, of course, such an explanation is acceptable only in those instances where a direct relation between the societies in question can be established. Otherwise, the Hegelian formulation remains in effect as, for instance, in the vexed problem of the so-called Asiatic mode of production.

The specific problematic that has drawn us into this discussion is the question of how historical representation will account for change and for difference among human societies. Faithful to the Enlightenment belief in the continuity and homogeneity of humankind, Hegelians and Marxists deal with the problem of difference by rupturing time and supposing that one chronology accommodates itself to multiple temporalities. Those who rejected this view did so on the basis of a belief in inherent human differences, or racism. Racial characteristics would thus account for the differences in development between human societies. Under this conception, perhaps most logically carried out in the universities of Nazi Germany, and specifically in their departments of *Rassenwissenschaft*, it became necessary to distinguish as many racial types as one would distinguish levels of development. But what would be the criteria by which one would determine the different levels of development? Neither the Hegelian nor the Marxist ones would do. Instead, anthropological notions were used: first, physical anthropology to distinguish human beings on the basis of physical features (ranging from apparent ones to invisible ones, such as blood types), and then culture, which was reinterpreted in nationalistic terms so that it served to distinguish not only societies (as it commonly does among anthropologists) but also levels of development among them by reference to one ideal type of culture, which, without any bashful ethnocentrism, was affirmed to be the Germanic one.

Against these versions of history, and their specific mode of conceptualizing change and difference, there have arisen some notable expressions of dissent — though, in all fairness, the bulk of historians, especially Anglo-American ones, have continued to work in their more specialized fields (diplomatic history, intellectual history, military history, ecclesiastical history, etc.) without paying much attention to these more theoretical issues of historiography, preferring a form of theoretical agnosticism to the pitfalls of these certitudes. Such a characterization is unfair to a number of historical endeavors, especially in social, economic, and cultural history, no doubt, but in its very exaggeration it seeks to draw attention to the fact that the conception of change and difference that is presently dominant, even in these areas, is that of the Hegelian-Marxist type and that the generally perceived alternative has been a fundamentally racist one. The chief dissenters have been the French schools of historians of the *Annales* persuasion or those known as historians of mentalities.

The former, gathered around the publication that has served as a useful label for their movement, have abandoned the forms of history that were mostly attentive to the narration of those events that impressed themselves upon the consciousness of the individuals who lived through them or that relied upon the memoirs of great personages, or even those who were concerned with the fate of nations. These are the very areas in which the inquiry into the *why* has been the most intense and yet least assured of the validity of its results. The Annalists are concerned with change and difference, but they believe that these result from a vast myriad of small-scale occurrences and developments, many of a highly technical nature, that generally escape the attention of those who live through them. There are no decisive events here, but an infinitesimal movement whose orientation can only be detected over the "long haul" (*la longue durée*). The historian does not tell a narrative because the actual movement of the action tends to be banal and the determination of the dramatis personae in the plot nearly impossible. The descriptive mode is favored, and the reader is presented with tableaux or *fresques*, forms of the representation characterized by stasis, hence the malaise that many readers feel in relation to this form of historiography: it seems to have lost history somewhere along the way. Change and difference are not abandoned, to be sure, but they are relegated to a dimension that is hardly explored, or rather in which they are hardly detectable.

The structure of this essay may be read as a narrative itself, one that has withheld until now the historian of mentalities — it is after all a foreword to a work that, in all fairness, can be described as belonging to this category — to allow that person to make a heroic entrance and dispose of the problems that have been erected as so many straw men to be triumphantly knocked down. That may make for better narrative and its concomitant pleasures than for cognition, for the historian of mentalities, far from striking a heroic figure, may perhaps more accurately be seen as embodying some of the predicaments of historical discourse.

The very term *mentalities* — a not altogether felicitous rendition of the French *mentalités* (chiefly in the plural) — is, in many ways, a fuzzy notion. Its use in a land in which reference to the mind as a locus of cognitive operations is decried as the most used up of philosophical ideologemes is, in itself, curious. But even more significant is the relationship of the term to the two other dominant schools of French historiography: the Annalist and the Marxist. With respect to the first, the historians of mentalities seem to represent a form of attention that is almost explicitly rejected from view by the practitioners of that school. It deals with how people live, think, and (to use the term that distinguishes the school) form mental representations of their own living conditions. One could almost say that the historian of mentalities seeks to endow the Annalist representation of material life and social organization with its mental counterpart. But to say this is to run into some difficulty with respect to the distinction of the historian of mentalities from the Marxist, for such a way of describing the project of the historian of mentalities is conceived of in the Marxist framework as the study of ideology. This has led some to suspect that the historian of mentalities is really a Marxist student of ideologies who no longer acknowledges his or her Marxism, or, more precisely has abandoned all features and tenets of Marxism save the one that constitutes the field of inquiry, which is then renamed for the convenience of distinction. Such a conclusion is not entirely wrong, inasmuch as it recognizes — or at least permits an acknowledgment of — the difficult predicament of some historians who have wanted to make use of the intellectual heritage of Marxism without having to find themselves obliged to defend policies pursued in the name of Marxism. The term *mentalité* has been useful in this regard. But one should be aware of the fact that its content has not been a stable one.

As with similar endeavors, one may think of precursors. Huizinga's classic *The Waning of the Middle Ages* is frequently pointed to as perhaps the oldest example of this sort of approach, although one ought to recognize its continuity with the philological approaches of a Vossler, for example. But, in any case, it is generally with the publication in the sixties of the works of Robert Mandrou on popular culture and on sorcery,[4] and those of Georges Duby on various aspects of the Middle Ages,[5] that the *histoire des mentalités* is felt to have come into its own. The term *mentalité* is used then without being defined except very vaguely: Mandrou equates it with *Weltanschauungen*, for example. But it is clear that the early forms of this historical approach were concerned with areas that could be described as cultural history or even history of ideas. Later developments were to take it into the areas of lived experience and everyday reality and to attempt accounts of attitudes, behaviors, and unconscious as well as conscious collective representations. Here one need recall only the work of Philippe Ariès or Michel Vovelle.[6] With a Carlo Ginzburg,[7] it becomes obvious that one is no longer concerned with the decision making of elites or even the mind-set of these elites but with the mental universe of individuals generally neglected by other forms of history since they were felt not to have contributed in any way to the "victorious march of mankind." These are the people whose sole historical accomplishment seems to have been that they lived. Until now, they have been without history. Some of the French historians, notably Emmanuel LeRoy Ladurie, have been determined to integrate them within history, though most of these studies do treat them in isolation. In this respect, José Antonio Maravall, about whom more below, represents an advanced stage since he seeks to describe the complex interplays between mentalities, institutions, aggregate interests, and the exercise of power.

Historians of mentalities, in other words, do not believe that principles of explanation in historical development are to be found in psychic phenomena. In this they differ from psychohistorians. Rather, trained as most of them have been in a social history attentive to the quantifiable aspects of social structure and interaction, they have begun to ask themselves what are the mediations, the dialectical relationships, between these "objective" features of reality and how people live them, how they account for them to themselves. In other words, they are concerned with how people live their historicity, not as a set of momentous decisions but as the framework of lived experience.

What is interesting about this is that the historical pursuit is no longer the exclusive appanage of the professional historian. The historian is but the specialist who seeks to make explicit the nature of lived historical experience as all of us, and at all times, of necessity do, though mostly unconsciously and certainly not in categories that history has generally acknowledged as its own. This kind of historical activity is not that distant from the fiction making that was, and continues to be, the concern of the student of letters, a fiction making that has no fewer cognitive goals and ambitions than the disciplined activity of the historian. Here questions of *why* and *how* intertwine in an attempt to weave a representation of something that we do not directly and immediately apprehend but that we experience: what for lack of a better term we can only call the changing face of history. The historian is the specialized wielder of a discourse who seeks to give us a figural representation of that face. His or her mode is that of the prosopopoeia, the rhetorical figure that consists in giving a face to that which does not have one. Prosopopoeia is a difficult art: it does not seek to achieve closure or finality as narrative does; it does not labor under the rule of verisimilar adequacy as description does; it seeks to represent not that which is absent, but that whose presence is so intense that we can only feel it and not see it from a safe distance. It is a presence that we never doubt but of which we have no knowledge unless we represent it to ourselves. The historian seeks to give us this knowledge.

Any national history will encounter this prosopopoeic problem to the extent that it seeks to account for the lived historical experience of the people whose past it interrogates. But some national histories clearly thematize this problem: one readily thinks of Russian history and the problem of the Russian soul, Polish history and the question of Polish destiny, and perhaps, most cleary, Spanish history and the matter of Spanish character. The work of José Antonio Maravall inscribes itself within this latter tradition, though its author is quite conscious of the limitations that the tradition has imposed upon Spanish historical thought. It may be useful, in this regard, to review some of the features of that thought and how Spanish historiography has been affected by them. The distinctive character of Maravall's contribution will then become more readily apparent: Spanish specificity will not only be preserved but made apprehensible against a wider background that includes more global forms of historical understanding.

It does seem to be characteristic of Spanish historiography, and of the Spanish sense of history more generally, to think of Spain as a distinctive historical entity, one to which historical laws, as the German historians of the nineteenth century liked to call their generalizations, would not apply. It is beyond the scope of this foreword to inquire into the causes of such a belief, though there is little doubt that two factors played a predominant role: the *Reconquista*, which necessitated a very early emergence of a sense that Spain had a special historical mission; and the hegemony that Castile established over the varieties of social experiences that prevailed over the territory of the Iberian peninsula. With respect to the first, one can find already in Saint Isidore of Seville the notion of a messianic Spain — a notion that will progressively find itself embodied as a specific sort of ideology throughout Spanish history in the idea that the distinctive character of Spain, its face as it were, emerged in the struggle of the early Gothic kingdoms against the Moors. It is this very ideology that one finds reproduced from age to age, and it appears even in the works of otherwise acerbic critics such as Quevedo.[8] The second in effect rides piggy-back upon the first. Under the pen of its propagandists, Castile was depicted as the bearer of this messianic mission, and its progressive absorption of the other Spanish kingdoms[9] was no less than a necessary step in the realization of the broader mission, which was the divinely ordained task of the Spanish nation to establish a strong Catholic central government over the disparateness of the peninsula. One will readily recognize here the official ideology of the Franco era, which justified its repression of any desire for any sort of local autonomy by direct reference to this mission. But it is also a very powerful strand within Spanish historiography, as is evidenced from the work of Claudio Sánchez-Albornoz, one of the most widely published historians of the post-Civil War period.[10]

It is against this nationalistic and obviously simplistic view that one of the great Spanish historians of our century erected his own vision of Spanish history, a vision that precipitated a great debate in the fifties and sixties and that finds itself widely institutionalized in Hispanic studies in the United States: *The Structure of Spanish History* by Américo Castro.[11] Castro was not really a historian, but rather a *litteratus* who, from exile, sought to change the dominant view of Spanish history by focusing on what appeared to him to be the greatest distortion perpetrated by the holders of the messianic view, namely the nature of lived reality during the long centuries of the Reconquest. This period, after all, spans much more than half of the history of Spain, and it can be labeled as the *Reconquista* only from a particular retrospective view that seeks to present the varieties of phenomena that constituted the historical experience of medieval Spain as one monolithic movement. Castro attempted to show that, far from pitting the Goths against the Moors, this reality brought together in forms of productive tension — what he calls *convivencia* — the three confessional communities: the Jews, the Moslems, and the Christians. While Castro's argument meandered into questionable attempts to determine whether given figures of the Spanish past were of Jewish or Islamic origin — thus fueling much rather nasty polemic[12] — it challenged the idea of the inevitability of the historical fate of Spain and proposed an alternative vision of its past as a project for the future.

Castro's approach, concerned as it was with the correction of what appeared to him to be gross distortions, was inevitably more speculative than probative, however; it was particularly blind to the fact that the messianic ideology had become the vehicle of particular dynastic ambitions — the Castilian ones — and eventually of the centralist conception of the Spanish state. Castro's aim was reconciliatory rather than analytical and, as a result, it stands as a sort of countermyth to the myth that it opposed. It is clear that this is the sort of position that Maravall wanted to avoid for his work from the very outset. While he would eschew the nominalism of a Meinecke, he would have sufficient respect for the task of the historian as a producer of an important body of social knowledge to avoid the realm of mythmaking as a strategy of myth debunking. Having come into contact with Braudel, and by his own acknowledgment been influenced by his work, Maravall was nonetheless more drawn toward a more properly *mentalités* approach,[13] especially since the latter is not altogether alien to the Spanish historical consciousness.

The French or the British rarely ask themselves about the meaning of British or of French history, perhaps because both nations have lived through revolutions that have shown that such meaning as history may possess results from the activity of those who live it. Spain has not really known such a moment of historical consciousness, and, to the extent that it was beholden to the messianic vision of its historical mission, it was likely that any change in the fortunes of Spain would be interpreted as somehow representing a secular equivalent of the Fall. This seems to have happened in the period that follows what the Spaniards like to call their Golden Age (and to repeat itself in significant segments of the society after the formal collapse of the empire in 1898). Although contemporary historical research has raised serious questions about the validity of any decline in the age of Philip IV, the perception the Spaniards have had of this period is that it marks a regression with respect to their previous greatness and a retreat before their appointed mission. Such a Fall had to have causes, and these have been sought in the Spanish character. Thus, as early as the eighteenth century, the prosopopoeic problem was thematized in Spain as Spaniards sought to divine the meaning of their history. The interesting thing about this enterprise is that it led to the application of a viewpoint that bears some distant resemblance to the history of mentalities and that was an original use of anthropological perspective in history: what is known as *costumbrismo*. This movement, which flourished in the early nineteenth century, sought to explore the nature of the Spanish character by investigating the lived experience of contemporary Spaniards. Its significance lies in its agnosticism with respect to any divinely ordained mission for Spain and in the fact that it brought to the fore so many of the lasting themes and motifs of subsequent discussion of Spanish distinctiveness.

Maravall is, of course, no latter-day *costumbrista*, but he seeks to reinscribe this properly Spanish mode of interrogating history within a broader framework. Unlike Castro, he recognizes immediately the key role that the hegemonic aspirations of Castile have played in Spanish history, and he focuses on the instrument that was used for the realization of these aspirations: the state. This is no doubt a controversial point that is best left to the debates of competent historians, but it is apparent that Spain did achieve relatively early in the modern period a form of state power and organization that may well constitute the distinctive feature of its past. Maravall thus can show that Castro's mythical *convivencia*, to the extent that it had any reality at all, was the result of deliberately conducted state policies, as far as the period of the Catholic kings and its aftermath are concerned. But he does not limit himself to the kind of broader institutional history that an attention to the emergence of a more modern form of the state could result in; rather, his focus has been on the specific ways in which the emergence of this entity has radically changed the mentalities of the people who have lived this change.

José Antonio Maravall's *Culture of the Baroque* is, perhaps, the work that sums up best an intellectual journey that began several decades earlier with the publication of his doctoral thesis — *La teoria española del estado en el siglo XVII* (Madrid, 1944) — in which the author was to connect the baroque, for the first time, with the political circumstances of the absolutist monarchy and was to set out on a field of research that has continued to preoccupy him to this very day. Maravall's work on the modern state and social mentality has become his trademark as a historian. Some of the key assumptions of his most important book on that subject — *Estado moderno y mentalidad social*, 2 vols. (Madrid, 1972) — have since been incorporated in his studies on baroque culture and in more recent writings dealing with honor, power, and the elite in seventeenth-century Spain.[14] A central claim underlying these inquiries is that absolutist power, realizing Castilian hegemonic aspirations, began in the fifteenth century by controlling and disciplining the nobles; eventually, however, it turned into a defender of the nobility around 1600 as significant realignments took place in the body politic, especially as Castile brought within its sway areas in which other social groups had achieved significant power and autonomy. Similarly, many of the changes that take place toward the end of the 1500s are attributed to the social tensions experienced throughout most of the century as a result of widespread presumptions of social mobility (geographic, professional, and social). The political program of the baroque is, then, the formal answer of the monarchical-seignorial segments of society to the assaults ("real" and imagined) that are launched against the traditional estatist structure.[15]

Here Maravall finds himself involved in a polemic with Castro, who shunned reference to broader period concepts as part of his global strategy of rejection against the then predominant view of Spanish history. Castro wrote: "There is no such thing as a gothic, a renaissance, a baroque, or a neoclassicism that, from an unreal space, conditions the flow of history as the moon intervenes in the tides."[16] This negation of the baroque as a historical concept was to be reiterated in a letter to Maravall, which the latter reproduces graciously as an homage to Castro in his preface to the present work. In that correspondence, Castro referred to the baroque as an inoperative concept, arguing that it was not "an agent of change." He was also to intimate that, due to the particularity of Spain's past, it could not be understood on the same assumptions as the pasts of England, France, Italy, and Germany. Ironically, Castro had come to defend a form of Spanish uniqueness, whereas his life's effort had been to put into question the constitution of that form of uniqueness into a messianic version. Once again, though, his failure had been to attribute to an abstract entity — which is what he took the baroque to be — the operativity that Maravall was attempting to uncover through painstaking analysis. Castro had taken Maravall's use of the term *baroque* to be some sort of Hegelian concept, whereas Maravall was engaging in the prosopopoeic effort to understand what the culture of crisis of seventeenth-century Spain had been all about.

It may be useful to recall that the baroque was first introduced as a period concept in art history and that it became hopelessly vague when there were attempts to extend it beyond the boundaries of that field, notably toward literature. Maravall's merit lies precisely in the reaffirmation of the baroque as a period concept and not just the sort of vague style-denomination that it had become, thus giving it operative value both for the historian and for the student of literature. From the outset of his study, Maravall makes clear that he does not focus on the morphological aspects of baroque art (Wölfflin) or on the supposed connection between the baroque and the movement of religious reform known as the Counter-Reformation (Weisbach). Similarly, he does not propose to deal with, or differentiate between, rhetorical and conceptual versions of baroque literature (Warnke).[17]

For Maravall, the baroque is a historical concept belonging to, and therefore affecting, the sphere of social history. While allowing for "national" nuances, he argues, with abundant references — and along lines opposite to those of Castro — that its general traits are applicable not only to Spain but also to other countries of western Europe. He goes on to define the baroque as a culture provoked by a social crisis of major proportions, one that was felt in all of Europe and, perhaps, most intensely in Spain during the greater part of the seventeenth century.

With his accustomed precision, he makes clear that he does not speak with the voice of an economic historian, and he states that in no instance does his "interpretative construction exceed the limits of the social history of mentalities."[18] Thus when he speaks of the baroque as a culture crisis, he distinguishes between the social and economic dimensions of that crisis, arguing that whereas the latter is of an intermittent character, displaying alternating periods of growth and recession (as Spanish historians Gonzalo Anes and F. Ruiz Martín have shown), the former, which has to do with the reinscription of the entire social sphere under the new authority of the state, is clearly of *longue durée*.

The precision with which the baroque is used as a period concept also obtains with reference to his definition of culture, which is viewed as the weaving of values, aspirations, beliefs, myths, and ways of living and acting as they articulate themselves on the level of a mentality.[19] This anthropological definition of culture, with its clear *costumbrista* resonances, allows Maravall not to limit the notion of crisis to the realm of pure economic history, inserting it instead in a much broader set of considerations that encompass the changing character of culture, history, and social life. Similarly, he never forgets that the concept of crisis is essential to historical understanding, going to great lengths, especially in some of his later writings, to remind us of the attempts that have been made over time to theorize on this very subject. To back up his claims, he cites thinkers of such different orientation as Marx, F. Simiand (an economic historian), and Jacob Burckhardt, the historian of culture who also happened to be one of the first to take seriously the study of the baroque.[20]

For Maravall, then, it is the perception of crisis and instability found among the groups in power and among the individuals in the middle strata of society (*gente intermedia*) who identified with them that brings about the political program of the baroque around 1600. In Spain, it is a culture contrived and manipulated for the benefit of the monarchical-seignorial sectors of society for the purpose of facing up to a world in which changes had seemed to turn things upside down. In this sense, it is a culture of reaction against the mobility and change that, for much of the sixteenth century, had threatened to erode the "hierarchical construction of estates." [21] Maravall would argue that, ultimately, it is the perception of change that counts. For whether change is perceived as progress or as retraction, as liberation or as repression, it implies a degree of transformation in the system of social mentality that, in turn, brings with it the potential for a displacement of values, rank, and authority. It is precisely to meet these challenges that the baroque world of seventeenth-century Spain organizes its resources along lines that are either openly repressive or more subtly propagandistic. Thus, for example, in addition to the use of various agents and means of terror — particularly the Inquisition and the private armies of the nobles — or the state's attempt to mold the Church into an *instrumentum regni* directed toward the repression of individual consciences, there is the massive propaganda campaign staged by those who possessed the instruments of culture or by their surrogates. The idea was to captivate minds through the use of theater, sermons, emblematic literature, and so forth, and to cause admiration and suspense through these and other, more overt, displays of power: fireworks, fountains, fiestas. It is a culture directed especially toward the multitude of anonymous and, therefore, potentially disruptive individuals concentrated in the cities, with a message suggesting the desirability of integration within the confines of an estatist structure. [22]

The dimensions and reaches of baroque culture among the urban publics of the 1600s have been examined by Maravall in this and other works, including *Teatro y literatura en la sociedad barroca* (Madrid, 1972). These studies have had a significant impact in a number of areas, most especially on the study of the Spanish "national theater" — the comedia of the 1600s. Perhaps the best example of the use of the theater for political and social propaganda is the work of Lope de Vega, the great playwright of the establishment in the early 1600s. The stage productions of these plays were meant to give a new, undiscriminating public — *el vulgo* — what it supposedly wanted: lots of action, a variety of verses and other forms, and, above all, the dramatic structuring of concepts with which most spectators learned to identify. These concepts were the defense of the monarchy, the safeguard of honor as the raison d'être of individual and social life and the constant reaffirmation of love as universal justification. The large theatergoing public of the comedia thus possessed a code, a horizon or system of expectations that Lope and other playwrights of the time learned to accommodate and nurture. (An important exception is Cervantes, who in the early 1600s circumvents the public stage and addresses his plays directly to readers.)[23] One of the key characteristics of that mass, socially heterogeneous public was a large degree of homogeneity along ideological lines. That is, from the lowest social classes to merchants, artisans, bureaucrats, and others, the public that frequents the theater identifies with the values or paradigms of the nobility.

With reference to the use of the honor theme in the theater (and to a lesser extent in the novel, especially the picaresque), Maravall argues that it is presented as a mirror for effecting and ensuring the integration of certain groups, whereas for others it functions almost exclusively as an instrument of marginalization. Among the latter groups he specifically lists manual laborers and, to a lesser extent, converts from Judaism or Islam. This, of course, is in line with Maravall's contention that the baroque promoted an estatist society under a powerful state rather than a caste system.

We mention this issue not only because Maravall was to go back to it in a substantive way in his *Poder, honor y élites en el siglo XVII*, but also because here as well major differences oppose him to Américo Castro, given the wide currency that the latter's views enjoy in the United States, Maravall's theories are likely to prove controversial. In this context it is important to recall that for Maravall, the historian of social mentalities, the occurrence of a way of life founded on honor is not particular to Spain but is common to the estatist societies of western Europe. Against the absolute importance given to blood statutes by Castro and his disciples, Maravall would argue that these cannot be taken out of the orbit of an estatist structure. Let us note that the centrality of the honor theme to the very structure of traditional society is a topic that also interested Lucien Febvre, who announced but never published a study on the subject.[24]

Although it is outside of the scope of this foreword to review all of Maravall's writings — some thirty books and scores of articles that cover the span of the Middle Ages, the Renaissance, the baroque, the Enlightenment, and contemporary culture — no introduction would be complete without at least making mention of a few of his other important works, especially *el pensamiento de Velázquez* (Madrid, 1960), *El mundo social de la "Celestina"* (Madrid, 1963), *Antiguos y modernos* (Madrid, 1966), and the forthcoming *La Picaresca vista desde la historia social*. All of these studies have a common thread: they are written by a liberal historian of social mentalities who has struggled for forty years, not from exile but from within Spain, to give Spanish history a new face.

Translator's Introduction
The Translating Mechanism

That's the difference between writing and translating.
They've got to think up ideas. I don't. I can write my ass
off, but there's no plot to worry about, no characterization.
Painting by number.

Gregory Rabassa

I

In the presence of another introduction, one whose task is to focus on the issues,
a translator's introduction seems from the outset redundant and superfluous. But
in this instance, translating as a cultural activity is an implicit component in the
baroque project. After all, translating depends on the existence of national cultures, national languages, and the capacity to distinguish between them. And
while the baroque is, as Maravall documents, a phenomenon that all of western
Europe experiences, it represents the moment when European nations anchor
their respective national domains. In other words, what they have in common
derives from what keeps them apart. Despite translation being a *national* activity
whose possibility is historically linked to the baroque, the very activity of translating retains a similar disjuncture that is not entirely unrelated: a translation
both is and is not the original, both is and is not a "native" work.

Translation has often been reflected upon; one might go so far as to say that
it has become a topos (or perhaps figure) of latter-day criticism: it has offered
itself for discussion in terms of metaphor (i.e., *translatio*), difference and same-
ness, temporal anteriority and derivation, and in the sense of a "frustrated"
dialectic. As is readily acknowledged, however, these related modes of posing
the translating question hold to the realm of the conceptual and tend to resist
being historically inscribed. Although there is always the danger of merely
repeating the obligatory move of self-reflection for the benefit of the genre, it
is important to understand why one examines translation only to point out its
aporia. In fact, this aporia, disjuncture, or contradiction has come to constitute
what is significant about translation, and as such its status remains "undecidable."

But how does one articulate this undecidability? To those who maintain what we might loosely call a mimetic concept of originality, translating is the manual activity (which, by being mere "work," is actually conceived as passivity, as being devoid of ideas) of writing without being the writing itself. This is a curious formulation, of course, but its presuppositions are easily recognizable and very familiar in traditional thought. Nevertheless, the complications emerge to the extent that writing itself is also not "pure" activity (i.e., not an *original* one), for one does not write without reading or having read, without reacting to other discourses. Yet, even more confusing, reading is possibly the very activity that keeps translating from being no more than a passive endeavor. To put it succinctly, translating could only be a nondiscursive activity if the translator had only to find equivalents: that is, if he or she did not have to read.

Since it is by now obvious that I am not speaking of translation in a limited, empirical sense, it is equally obvious that translation conceived broadly, as reading, mediating, or perhaps understanding, permeates and constitutes the social sphere of human activity. Its all-pervasiveness helps to explain why one has inevitably interrogated the notion of human activity solely by means of protagonists; for example, as one individual vis-à-vis society, as proletariat vis-à-vis bourgeoisie, as writer versus tradition, as difference versus identity, past versus present, and so on. Needless to say, these are strategies that we all make use of, not because activity itself is ineffable, but because it does not lend itself to representation. Protagonists serve as the means of representation: They are the stuff of history. Yet the means of representation are no less historical than the discursive economy allowing for our activity. In the same way, one's translating activity cannot be reduced to finger movements on a mechanical keyboard.

Poco dura el Imperio que tiene su conservación en la guerra.
Saavedra Fajardo

II

At first glance, *Culture of the Baroque* contains nothing that could be designated as revolutionary; it is a serious book of traditional history. It rarely resorts to puns or word games to make a point, nor is its language systematic in the technical, scientific sense. In addition, Maravall's topic has a long history; it takes its place alongside all those works that have sought to describe the constitution of the modern state. What, then, could be more mechanical than translating a book of this sort?

Unfortunately, and contrary to its etymology, the state is not a static problem — I mean this literally. The relationship of a state to its subjects expresses the two poles separated by the tension of activity: the supposed stasis of the state and the social changes that knowing subjects can presumably effect. Activity therefore always figures into discussions of the state, whether or not they are historical, just as stateness is inevitably the figure of action but never identical with it. As with translation, modern theories of the state still run up against their aporia in trying to articulate state activity, whether "progressive" or "conservative." For example, how does the State "wither away"? To answer this question (or perhaps to find out if this question is worth asking) obviously requires an interrogation of the notion of activity. But, as Maravall's reading shows, to understand the notion of activity is to conceive it in relation to the state itself: for historical reasons they cannot be thought of separately.

While it may seem as though I've gotten off course, the problems in translating this work result not merely from ambiguities within the words themselves, but also from the conceptions of state and activity entailed by the work and the words that constitute it. Thus before delving into this work's specifics of translation, it would be useful to refer to other treatments of the necessary relationship between activity and the state. Gramsci, for example, as perhaps the most far-reaching theoretician of the state, is able to analyze its workings precisely because he thinks it from activity: although one does not generally formulate it in this way, thinking the state from the perspective of operativity is what Gramsci derives from Machiavelli. In defining the "modern prince," Gramsci attempts to describe the move from individual to collective activity (that is, from activity as introduced by Machiavelli to his own notion of it): "And a definition must be given of collective will, and of political will in general, in the modern sense: will as operative awareness [*coscienza operosa*] of historical necessity, as protagonist of a real and effective historical drama."[1] *Operative* in this sense includes the ability to achieve effects, and the protagonist cultivates a sort of self-consciousness that expresses an awareness of its own ability to act, of its own historical role. This poses an explicit contrast to Machiavelli's notion whereby it is the individual who possesses a reflective self-consciousness (to put it anachronistically) and not the collective.

Gramsci utilitized Machiavelli's image of the half-beast, half-human centaur to elaborate the concept of (state) hegemony; Machiavelli, however, glosses his own image, foregrounding its individualist bias: "A prince being thus obliged to know well how to act [*usare*] as a beast must imitate the fox and the lion . . . . But it is necessary to be able to disguise this character well, and to be a great feigner and dissembler [*simulatore e dissimulatore*]. . . . "[2] The shift taking place in this passage has rhetorical or operative implications in itself; here I can only note in passing that use of the centaur metaphor passes into a valorization of one of its elements (the beast), which in turn redeploys the opposition between beast and human, though this time within the beast itself. This rhetorical shift should alert us to the nature of the princely enterprise: it foregrounds the rhetorical as a key element of the discursive economy. This is of course also why Machiavelli's text depicts the activity of the prince-as-beast in confrontational terms: as an agonistic encounter in which the lion can frighten and the fox dissimulate. Obviously I am not using the word *rhetorical* exactly as literary criticism conceives of it today; instead, I am referring to rhetoric in its broader political significance, as in the writings of Cicero and Aristotle. In any case, Gramscian operativity (more or less exemplified in the quote above) offers a discernible contrast to the rhetorical notion. The dominance of the rhetorical mode in what I have, for lack of a better term, called the *discursive economy* does not merely result in an acting out in the present. Rather, one derives one's ability to act from becoming conscious of oneself as the protagonist of history: historical knowledge, knowledge of the past that leads to the present, presupposes a historical force, an agent, whether it be named the state, the Schlegelian *Volk*, or a given class (and it goes without saying that some protagonists have been preferable to others at different historical junctures), and one must attempt to appropriate or realize that agency. In fact, the distinction between individual and collective agency correlates with the distinction between the rhetorical and historical, although the overlap is not without its discontinuities. It is of course the establishment of the state and the capitalist economy that intervenes to guarantee the supremacy of the historical (along with various other techniques of "statification," not least of which is the development of printing). Although this broad characterization does not depend on it, what I am referring to as the *historical* emerged because of the inability of the rhetorical discursive economy to maintain the state's hegemony.

   The preceding detour and somewhat abridged opposition between Machiavelli and Gramsci helps articulate Maravall's greatest concern (in this work and in others): the modern state, a concept he will refer to in the pages that follow. Maravall is dealing specifically with the Spanish state (which, in Schlegel's conception, supplied the prototype for all the states of Europe) when it is being constituted, that is, during a transitional moment in the reorganization of the social sphere. In the terms sketched out above, baroque culture is that culture put into operation to effect the transition from a discursive economy based on rhetoric to one based on history. Baroque culture as such never dispenses with its rhetorical base, with the elements of persuasion that constitute it, but, as Maravall shows, the "mass" element of its logic demands a different kind of rhetoric: baroque culture does not operate solely by means of persuasion in the older rhetorical sense — swaying the listeners by means of the finesse of one's argumentation about an issue — but in the ideological sense — without the issue ever being mentioned.

I see Masscult . . . as a reciprocating engine, and who is to say, once it has been set in motion, whether the stroke or the counterstroke is responsible for its continued action.

Dwight Macdonald

III

Few would argue with the assertion that translation is a conceptual undertaking and not just the transference of words from one language to another. As an activity, translating is both theoretical and practical; it cannot be reduced to the telos of a completed translation, for it must also be read. And although *Culture of the Baroque* says absolutely nothing about translation, the book's recurring problematic is how to describe activity as *means*, as mediation. Maravall articulates a central element of the baroque: "What we might call a simple *static guidance controlling by presence* had to give way before a *dynamic guidance controlling by activity*" (p. 68). This "controlling guidance," this *dirigismo*, poses very specific problems for the translator, as the translators of Gramsci have noted: *dirigir* can mean ruling, directing, or guiding.[3] But more significant here is the shift from presence to mediation, from stasis to activity. The rulers must learn to master the resources viable in the realm of mediation because they cannot be everywhere at once; because the mass is in the early stages of constituting itself, there are many places for the rulers to be to guarantee the state of affairs. To a certain extent one could conceptualize Maravall's interpretation of the baroque as akin to Gramsci's in recognizing two separate but related state functions:

> The baroque monarchy made use of a large repertory of means [*medios*]
> to succeed in dominating the tension of adverse forces; this, along with
> the novelty of some of these means, revealed what was constitutive of
> baroque culture. It included aspects all the way from physical constraint,
> based on military force, which is the ultima ratio of political supremacy,
> to psychological expedients [*resortes*] that acted on consciousness and
> created within it a repressed psyche [*animo*] . . . ; in between were
> diverse resources [*recursos*] used in a surprising fashion, a use explicable
> only in terms of the psychological and moral assumptions of the baroque
> (p. 36).

Nevertheless, although the differences between the Maravallian and Gramscian conceptions are unbridgeable (though possibly less so if Gramsci is read through Althusser), Maravall's text also has a very different focus and the formulations of this passage stake out Maravall's area of concern: the new shape that the modern state must give to — or assume because of — the realm of mediation. Moreover, this passage succinctly introduces the dilemma posed in the activity of translating this book. Any dictionary will verify that *medios, resortes,* and *recursos* are to a certain extent equivalent: they all mean *means*. They are not technical terms, and I have translated them in various (although predictable) ways. *Medios* and *recursos* represent more or less traditional issues for the translator. *Medios* are of course that which is operative in the constituted sphere of mediation; in other words, *medios* emerge as the cultural complement of the congregation of the urban mass, of the dissemination of printed matter, and so forth, all of which *Culture of the Baroque* describes at great length. In this sense, *medios* are not just means to an end but also *media*, i.e., mass media: "In sum, the baroque is nothing but a complex of cultural media [*medios*] of a very diverse sort . . ." (p. 58). In Spanish, however, it is all of these things at the same time, whereas in English we have to make a choice; as translators say, the context has served as the basis for selection. *Recursos* represents a similar case, although it is somewhat more localized — *this* as means for *that*; it has been translated by *means* or *resources*, depending on the instance. It is in *resortes* that all of these aspects come to bear, for *resortes* does not merely describe but also articulates the way in which the mechanism operates. To distinguish *resorte* but also to signal its similarity, I have in many instances rendered it with *expedient*; but in the Spanish text, use of *resorte* consistently represents a specific intervention that might be designated as ideological (see, for example, p. 46). Thus, although the words are used interchangeably (with certain evident limitations), it is in *resortes* that the text addresses the question of agency, the mediations provoking an expenditure of activity; *resorte* serves the text to describe the triggering effect that produces action and, therefore, inaction.

As I hinted earlier, translating *resorte* entails much more than an empirical analysis of how to render it in English; translating itself, as a reading, as a conceptual operation, relies upon a triggering of a *resorte*. And while it remains to be seen whether the triggering — the activating — can be described, it is beyond doubt that the agency itself pertains to a nonrepresentational order. Actions can clearly be narrated, but, as we are aware today, narration as the possibility of further narration has never been problematic: in fact, there are always too many narratives, and an infinite number of stories can recount the "same" action. The legitimating role played by narratives, by histories, and the logic of activity would seem to demand that to displace a master narrative one pose another narrative against it, one recuperate the excluded, one perform an activity that is somehow "revolutionary," if only on the discursive plane. Yet Maravall's text, and the translating problems it poses, reminds the reader that activity is itself historical, which is not the same thing as saying that it displays its changes correlative to the changes that have taken place and are recounted in the narrative of Western development. In *Culture of the Baroque*, an attempt is made to articulate the mechanism of agency prior to the moment when an action must be thought of as the effect of an agent.

In a world where grammar reigns, subjects perform actions; but if the subject is not all-knowing, the subject could just as well be being performed. In what is quickly becoming traditional history, the state is the subject of ideology (as both promoting and deriving benefit from it); yet describing the function of ideology is not without its pitfalls. "To channel and unify the individuals' modes of behavior, one must penetrate the internal mechanism of their motivations [*el interno mecanismo de los resortes que los mueven*]" (p. 59). This passage foregrounds the ambivalence of *resortes*: are they the motivations of individuals or are they what serves to motivate individuals? Is the internal mechanism within consciousness, the mechanism of thinking, or is it merely the way the expedient works? In a certain sense, it seems parallel to a statement like "I feel moved": one can never be sure who — or what — the agent is, or whether it is a subject or an object. The text itself describes it as the ambivalence of movement, of moving: "Thus the baroque attempted to guide human beings who were grouped together in masses, acting upon their will, psychologically motivating [*moviendo con resortes psicológicos*] them by means of a technique of attraction that, as such, effectively exhibited a mass character" (pp. 77-78). One might question the reference to the baroque as an agent (a procedure followed throughout the book), but it does not affect the description of the *resorte*: the will [*la voluntad*] is both subject and object, it is acted upon in order to act, or (to put it another way) it acts by means of having been acted upon. This complexity becomes even greater, for ideology cannot be described in simply teleological terms, in the familiar sense of "instrumental reason": "The baroque again proposed that [moving] . . . was the end to be attained: to set the will on its course, appealing to the expedients that unleash it [*a los resortes que la disparan*], which are not purely intellectual" (p. 77). Reaching the end through an intervention is in fact an unleashing that brings nothing to a close; accomplishing the goal of controlling the mass means relinquishing the possibility of ever achieving the end of total control. That is the danger to stability in all mass-based societies; it is perhaps not merely ironic that *disparar* (what I have rendered as *unleash*) also describes the firing of a gun.

Admittedly, if agency is nonrepresentational its description must necessarily be paradoxical; nevertheless, since agency is at the same time not ineffable, it does permit of articulation — which has historical implications. *Resorte*, of course, has a much broader semantic field than I have intimated; mechanically speaking, it refers to a spring that coils and stretches, that operates on the basis of this tension. The eighteenth-century *Encyclopédie*, the most extensive attempt to portray humankind on the basis of mechanics, gives a very succinct definition of the workings of a *ressort*: it is used to "react upon a [machine] part and make it move by the effort it makes to become slack" [*pour réagir sur une piece & la faire mouvoir par l'effort qu'il fait pour se détendre*].[4] One can immediately see the problem in describing this action: the act that "moves" the part is already a reaction; the movement that the spring is to prompt stems from the energy it expends in trying to remove itself to its "earlier" position. Since the late eighteenth century (in the words of the *Petit Robert*), *reacting upon* means "acting upon the agent, the cause of the action that is experienced, by opposing it" [*réagir sur l'agent, la cause de l'action qu'on subit, en s'y opposant*]. It is as if the spring served as the model for all oppositional activity, including the posing of political hegemony and counterhegemony. Yet the cause is always at the same time a result. One might be convinced, then, that the aporia has once again been reached, the paradox pointed out, that by denying an origin we have finally come to the selfsame limits of contemporary criticism.

But Maravall's book aims at sketching the mediating activity in sociohistorical terms, which does not mean it dispenses with the contradiction; it does, however, reinscribe it in such a way that it no longer maintains its center of gravity in a philosophical critique. As I alluded to above, statehood, activity, and massness are all interrelated. In fact, the state's existence depends on a capacity to move the mass: "It was not a matter of ultimately obtaining the public's intellectual adherence so much as *moving* it; therefore, this state of suspension was used to serve as the expedient [*resorte*] to launch a more firmly sustained movement. And that was the question: to move" (p. 220). It is not by chance that the cultural productions of our ultramassified society of the twentieth century rely heavily on the technique of suspense, an aspect not lost on Maravall.[5] Of course, suspense, a state of suspension, cannot be reduced to a mere anticipatory moment in a detective story or in any other story, for that matter ("Will the separated protagonists once again find one another?" etc.) although that is certainly not excluded. Specifically in narrative terms, it is the mechanism whereby plot propels itself, which is undoubtedly why Maravall discusses it in conjunction with Aristotle's *Poetics*:

> The idea [in putting into practice the Aristotelian concept of "wonder"] was rather that of a psychological effect that for a few instants brings the forces of contemplation or admiration to a halt so as to let them act more vigorously when they are afterwards released. . . .
>
> All these effects were achieved with studied means [*recursos*], by manipulating motivations [*resortes*] within the human being that were acted on to arrive at this transitory situation of suspense (p. 216).

Although it does not explicitly pertain to the translation problem that set us on our course, one might recall that in the *Poetics* Aristotle's *wonder* (*to thaumaston*) comes up not simply alongside his categorizing of plot but is also charcterized as inhabiting the tension between randomness or chance (i.e., a narrative structured episodically) and a more developmental narrative where actions occur consequentially [1452a]. The wondrous action must not follow from the previous action in a preconceived way or it will not be wondrous, yet it must — afterwards — *be seen to follow from it.* (It has long been recognized that the epic, as a contingent stringing together of episodes, represents a discursive mode that belongs to a social organization that is very different from a state society; in fact, this has been thematized as the distinction between an oral discursive economy and a written one.)

In putting forth the device of wonder as based on causality, the *Poetics* is not too subtly championing one notion of activity over another. In other words, the text does not simply pit contingency against causality, for wonder itself comes about on the basis of a relative contingency, so to speak. On the contrary, an activity that would be wholly contingent, dependent on chance or unforeseeable factors, does not easily lend itself to a narrative of development, for activity conceived in this way displays no beginning, no ending, only *reacting*: it is not anchored in an essence that would negate the temporal instability of reaction.[6] And it is surely not happenstance — at least in sociohistorical terms — that the texts of Aristotle also establish a by now well-worn distinction between substance and accident; nor is it any less surprising that these Aristotelian notions — of essence, substance (later, the subject), and of the narrations that trace causal, developmental change without endangering the (supposed) underlying essence — would be retrieved and redeployed during the baroque. The state as we know it depends on such notions.

Although it can only be alluded to briefly here, the reference to Aristotle shows that activity is inscribed within a configuration that includes discursive hegemonies and their intertwining with the construction and maintenance of the space of the social. In Maravall's text, *resorte* is the figure of this configuration as it pertains to the social space of mass culture and the constitutive state. Nevertheless, it would be a limiting reading to equate Maravall's mass culture with other theories of mass culture that conceptualize it simply as devalued vis-à-vis "high" culture (one immediately thinks of Greenberg, Macdonald, Lowenthal, Horkheimer, Marcuse, and Adorno, among others). Seventeenth-century mass culture is prior to the moment when the distinction between high and low culture becomes institutionalized through the workings of a specific historical narrative — literary history (in the Schlegelian sense of *geistliche Geschichte*) and the social institutions that disseminate it even as they draw their legitimation from it. What Maravall calls "mass culture" diverts and divests the activity of individuals at the same time as they are being socially constituted as the locus of "free" agency, or agency that is not yet provided for in the social logic. The *resorte* will mediate that localization of agency whereby individuals achieve their selfness.

A "crisis of authority" is spoken of: this is precisely the crisis of hegemony, or the general crisis of the State.

Gramsci

IV

The contemporary "crisis of authority," crisis of meaning, or crisis of the subject are all different inflections of the crisis taking place in the political-discursive economy. But, ironically, while activity seldom (if ever) assumes its place in the series of crises, they cannot be thought of apart from it. For example, in his essay "The Cultural Logic of Capital," Fredric Jameson attempts to grasp the nature of the "crisis": "This shift in the dynamics of cultural pathology can be characterized as one in which the alienation of the subject is displaced by the fragmentation of the subject."[7] To make explicit the oblique reference to activity, *cultural pathology* relates to the cultural economy whereby a particular logic of affectivity (pathos) takes shape; a shift in that logic signifies a shift in the constitution of the subject. Whereas Maravall depicts the *cultural logic* that will lead to a centering of the subject, Jameson is articulating what he sees to be the moment when it becomes decentered, fragmented. In theoretical circles, particularly those concerned with (oppositional) political action, this fragmentation of the subject correlates explicitly with a crisis of activity, specifically the crisis of efforts to pose a counterhegemony. Moreover, if one could conceive of metaphor in some sense that would not be wholly discredited, one might say that the subject has — since the advent of the modern state correlative to the making of subjects — been a metaphor for the supposed ability to act (and, it must be added, to act *knowingly*).

Jameson's analysis of the "postmodern" (perhaps not entirely by coincidence) takes its point of departure from a reading of Van Gogh's shoes and from a reading of the way those shoes are commented upon in Heidegger's *Der Ursprung des Kunstwerkes*. Heidegger's text proves amenable to certain Marxist conceptions of history, for it undeniably describes — as it denounces — the reification of subject and object, of the mere present-at-hand. Although one might be sympathetic to Heidegger's constant reformulation of how the unalienated, inalienable Being [*Sein*] lapses into mere being [*Seiendes*], it must be recognized that he never succeeded in working out a fundamental ontology. Indeed, this failure may be bound up with the project itself: as every reader of Heidegger knows, the closest he gets to Being is in coming upon traces of its withdrawal. In "The Origin of the Work of Art," *aletheia*, the unconcealment of "truth," is the much belabored notion inscribing the act in which Being slips away to leave Dasein amidst a world of beings. The stage of this happening is the *Lichtung*, the clearing; but as Heidegger takes great care in pointing out, the stage where the event occurs does not precede the event's occurrence, that is, the moment when the stage is set up. Not unexpectedly, an embedded etymology links this happening to history: that happening [*Geschehen*] of truth "is historical [*geschichtlich*] in many ways." But what does this have to do with activity as it is thought of historically in a way that may not be simply evenmential? The text offers a single *historical* example (among other more formulaic ones) of this truth-event that articulates the opening of Dasein's world: "Truth comes about another way — in the act that founds a State" [Eine andere Weise, wie Wahrheit west, ist die staatgründende Tat].[8] As the happening of truth (in the sense of *aletheia*), the act that founds a state can never take place once and for all, can never cease being historical.

The mechanism whereby the state perpetuates itself is the question posed by Maravall's *Culture of the Baroque*, a question that must be read in translating *resorte*. In this text, *resorte* expresses the material operation of ideology, both ideology itself — the expedients to set one's activity in motion — and the mechanism triggering that activity. To put it differently, this text historically sketches the social construction of agency and reveals the significance of misreading agency as located in and springing from the subject. In fact, the loss or gain of the subject is not the issue but the issue's concealment: the state depends on the self-centered subject to the extent that the subject acts of its own volition the very moment that the possibility of subjective agency is denied. Nevertheless, this reformulation of the sociohistorical remains distinct from the Althusserian equation of ideology and subjectivity, for it shifts the focus from subject to agency, making the loss or gain of subjectivity a moot point. Although the sociocultural sphere holds open the space of the state, that sphere must be traversed, and the discursive economy constitutes itself as the realm where discourse is bartered. Isn't this itself already — or still — translating?

T.C.

Preface

Some thirty years ago I presented my doctoral thesis at the University of Madrid, thus beginning my life as a scholar. Since then, the problematic question of baroque culture has never ceased being the focus of my concern, in conjunction with whatever other matters I have worked on. From the perspective of many of its aspects, so complex and changeable, I have tried to define the essence of this culture in which seventeenth-century individuals found themselves immersed and with whose elements they had to constitute their own personal existence. If the relationship between personality and culture always determines the modes of being unfolding before the historian, perhaps in few epochs has culture had the force — a culture not easily accepted, but contested and subject to profound stress — that it had in the baroque. To study this is, at the outset, to be confronted with a society subjected to monarchical absolutism and shaken by desires for freedom: as a result, with a gesticulating, contorted, dramatic society, as much on the part of those who were integrated into the cultural system that was offered them as on the part of those who were liable to diverse forms of deviation of varying degrees of intensity.

My *Teoria española del Estado en el siglo XVII* appeared in 1944. Underlying it was an entire conception of the baroque, but the subject matter continued to present me with unanswered questions, as though daring me to develop this conception explicitly (on the other hand, it was a conception then full of gaps that only a long and patient investigation would fill in). From that moment, I believe that few days have gone by when I have not reflected on some point touching on the baroque and its adjacent areas, when I have not written some pages on the subject. Parts of my previous books have dealt with the history and political community, with the modern state and its society during the Renaissance and the baroque. I have also been able to take into account fifteen monographic studies (which I have been revising for a collection) that are dedicated to circumscribed aspects of the baroque. In these circumstances, I believe that I can offer some words that might help to clarify the image of the baroque epoch, which is muddled by nature, or perhaps to confuse it definitively.

In 1960, while speaking about the modern state at a Spanish cultural foundation in Rome, I finally ventured to present an interpretation of baroque culture within a general scheme. The term *general* here is significantly restricted, however, because in no instance, neither then nor now, does my interpretive construction exceed the limits of the social history of mentalities. I have been moving in this direction for some time, precisely since I initiated the studies that were sketched in that lecture for the first time. I continued to develop these studies during lectures at Spanish universities, at the Ecole des Hautes Etudes, at the University of Paris at the Sorbonne. At the Sorbonne, I was able to develop the ideas during an entire seminar in 1970-71. Finally, in 1972-73 I presented an advanced course in my department at the Universidad Complutense of Madrid. Throughout these explorations, while the general lines of my interpretation have remained unchanged, its systematic development and the materials used to support it have changed sufficiently to form a new whole.

This brief autobiographical narrative has no more than a modest objective: I am attempting only to avoid being accused of improvisation or impatience. In recent months, I have once again revised my work and have reached the final version that is offered here. Perhaps I should have waited and tried out many more versions, but I don't have the strength for it, nor can I turn my back on other questions that now concern me. Above all, I believe that I have attained a general understanding of baroque culture, which has been a compelling goal for me since I initiated my professional occupation in the field of historical research and into which I have been inquiring for so long.

During this time, I had the good fortune of counting on the inciting, suggestive resistance of a teacher with whom I have disagreed and whom I have admired above and beyond all our differences of opinion. I am referring to Américo Castro. Readers of the present book will understand from its first pages that my interpretation rests on the fact that the Spanish baroque was but a phenomenon inscribed in a series of diverse manifestations of the European baroque, every one of them different from the others; yet all can be subsumed under the single and general historical category of *baroque culture*. Although the differences (not only in Spain but in other countries) may have been greater in some moments, or, put more rigorously, in some historical periods than in others (thus the example, to its own advantage, of England), there was always a common basic structure, a general picture that encompassed the culture of western Europe, with more or less vigorous brush strokes that distinguished one section from another. From this point of view, my thesis about culture — the culture of the Middle Ages, of the sixteenth century (what may be called the height of the Renaissance), of the kaleidoscopic century of the baroque, and of the eighteenth-century Enlightenment, so seductive in Spain — is that in the history of Spain all of its cultures can be studied parallel to those of the other western European countries. Their problems have much in common, as do their solutions, although on occasion the differences on this level may be greater and more dramatic.

Don Américo, however, would not hear mention of a Spanish baroque. When he published his study *Como veo ahora el Quijote*, Américo, in sending me a copy with an affectionate dedication, accompanied it with a brief letter that I would like to reproduce here in part because of the allusion it contains to the perspective on the baroque that I had advanced in previous works, one of which I had sent him days before:

My dear Maravall:

I am very grateful to you for having sent me this lexicographical analysis of the term *estadista*, so full of life and contemporary spirit — perhaps that spirit would be as fluent in *arbitrariness* as in anti-machiavellianism.

. . . I liked your study very much, and because of this I read it, despite my work load and afflictions. I have a lot of respect for those who have good intentions and are very learned: this makes for some friendly disagreement. It does not seem to me that *baroque* could be an agent or mover of history; it would be valid for architectonic constructions, built somehow in a series; but what was truly active in collective life and thought was the State that contained the propelling forces of each particular history during their existence (in the seventeenth century the differences cannot be bridged between England, France, Spain, Italy and Germany; they lack a common denominator endowed with a dimension capable of being written into history).

In no way does this observation affect the considerable value of your article and the interest with which it has been read by your friend, who sends you a very cordial embrace,

Américo Castro

From a long conversation, don Américo was acquainted with the principal points of the baroque interpretation that I was elaborating. By including here his opinion on the subject, in the book I announced to him and that he can no longer know, I would like to present my disagreeing response as an homage to him. To disagree with and esteem someone is a mutually enriching activity that the Spaniard rarely practices. Although I am very much at odds with many theses and opinions that have gained currency in my circles, I sincerely believe that practicing such a twofold activity constitutes one of the most exquisite joys, both morally and intellectually.

Yet I would like to add something that is important for me and — up to a certain point and in abstraction from my personal circumstances — for the readers of this book of history. Some readers may have become scandalized upon reading in this work's subtitle the words "Analysis of a Historical Structure." And if the word *analysis* can have aroused some surprise on being discovered in this context — in relation with the developments that follow — certainly the term *structure* will have provoked outright objections in referring to the book's method and content. How can a book present itself as a structural study when one does not encounter in it the "formalistic" aspects of the respectable — and rightly so — structuralism that, for better or for worse, is so widely cultivated nowadays? I am saying that the book is a study of a structure and not a structural study, which is not exactly the same. But I believe, moreover, that I am obligated to offer the reader an explanation for my use of the word *structure*. Nor can I avoid giving this response a certain autobiographical tone. The scientific issue entailed in the use of this widely discussed concept remains inextricably bound up with an issue of a personal nature.

In 1958 I published a book that I didn't dare entitle more than *Teoría del saber histórico*. In it I attempted only to throw a little light on the works of historical research that had begun to engage me about twenty years before and that so many other scholars were deservedly working on (there is no need to explain that I use the word *research* in the sense of scientific interpretation and not of a mere search for documents). In my opinion, the logical schema of historical knowledge had to change, drawing its inspiration in part, though still far removed, from the notable and awesome changes taking place in the logical process of conceptualization of the natural sciences. A history immersed in the pure knowledge of individual, absolutely singular, unrepeatable facts (or, to put it another way, of simple data), which means, consequently, a history given over to an insuperable nominalism, had to be confronted with a history — made up of data, of course (the more numerous and genuine the better) — that was not satisfied only with data and did not pause in its work until it was capable of presenting itself as a knowledge of complexes. *Historical complexes* were, for me, the object of historical knowledge. It was even possible to say that the historical fact is always a complex. The "complexes" are not things that are there, strictly conceived, in the naked reality of physical things. They are mental constructs that the historian assembles and in which the multiple and interdependent relations linking some data with others find their meaning. At that time I wrote:

To know a historical reality, to grasp its meaning, is to make intelligible the relation between the parts and the whole, in those complexes that constitute the object of history.

* * *

This presupposes that coming to know facts never gives us absolutely objective facts, but processes of observation in which, first, the facts end up being greatly altered and, second, more rests upon such facts than we find in pure facts (or data): that is, an interpretive theory.

But the theory that the historian constructs, applying his or her observation to a field that the theory itself previously constituted, is the mental image of a complex or is simply the complex whose parts have been related to one another through the observer's interpretation. In my 1958 book this is what I called *structure*; the concept served as a substitution for such similar terms as *series, formations, laws*, and *ideal types*, which other researchers had previously tried out, although, in my opinion, they were unsatisfactory for the historian. "Historical facts are not things; their reality vis-à-vis history as a science is their position in a process of relations. The formulation of this position has the value of a law and can be considered as a law when it gives us the position of all and each one of the facts in relation with all the others." Let me clarify that *all* here makes reference, as the book explains, to all the facts selected by the historian, to the extent that he or she has drawn them from a mass of facts that cannot in itself be grasped. Formulations of this type are not those corresponding to the classical concept of law; formulations arrived at in this way are different, more complex, and do not repeat themselves. For these reasons, at that time I used the term *structure*. "Historical structure is for us the figure — or mental construction — in which we are shown a complex of facts endowed with an internal articulation wherein the intricate network of relations taking place between such facts is systematized and acquires meaning." But the intricate network of relations cannot take place without the intervening observation of the historian. The French Revolution is not a single fact, nor is it thousands of facts, if in them we fail to become aware of the nexus relating them to one another in a structural complex. On the other hand, "whenever a complex is offered to us as a totality distinct from the succession of its data, we are in the presence of a structure."[1]

Twenty years after having used the concept of structure as the basis for my conception of historical work, and more than fifteen years after publishing the work where this conception is advanced, I consider myself fully authorized to utilize it in designating an interpretive construction that faithfully adapts itself to those theoretical assumptions. Before 1958, few used the word *structure* to designate concepts, more or less related, in the realm of theory in the humanities and social sciences (it was, of course, used in mathematics and chemistry). In linguistic and anthropological research it appeared early but its diffusion was slow, though isolated references can be found. If from the innovative study about "Les structures élémentaires de la parenté" (1948) to the resonant conversations of Lévi-Strauss himself on French radio in 1959, one can say that the word came to be popularized, it was only after 1960 that this terms expanded into a true neologism (in a sense far removed from the meaning that it was given in Marxist thought). It was somewhat later that *structuralism* came to be spoken of and that the names of the structuralists that are today in circulation appeared.

Rather than defending my originality, however, I am attempting to show that I have carried out research of a cummulative value that can serve as a support for the efforts of colleagues.

Before ending this preface, I need to confess something. In my work as a historian I proceed by observing the data that I have assembled, testing one or several hypotheses about them, and only afterwards do I notice whether the tone of the resulting interpretation is favorable or adverse, pessimistic or optimistic. I believe that I have never corrected an opinion with the purpose of turning around the tone of the appraisal. Like the eminent historian Sánchez-Albornoz — a teacher in Spanish institutional history to whom we owe so much — I believe in the slow but continuous transformation of the historical reality of peoples, although I think (as did he) about the far-reaching effect — sometimes over hundreds of years — of factors that he liked to call *historical constants*. The presence of such factors explains why, if we compare different historical periods in the life of a people, although they cannot always be reduced to mere repetitious examples, they are likely to present elements in common. Undoubtedly, one could underscore similarities between the events described in this book and what we are witnessing today, although we would be inadmissibly ingenuous to assume that the diagnoses of these situations are interchangeable. Nevertheless, in similar assumptions we can encounter the presence of negative influences that can effect the repetition (however differentiated may be the complexes in which they appear) of consequences of immobility, of petrification, of fossilized structures whose preservation works to maintain unjust inequalities. Then one can understand the obligation of the historian to contain his or her personal appraisals, precisely so that the play of those appraisals can be taken into account as objectively as possible by those whose task is to shape the present.

After all is said and done, what most properly belongs to history is to guarantee that the course of a people can truly be changed, that these transitions within a people's sphere be eased for them, that is, that ultimately there be opened a clear path toward the possibility of a people's governing and forming themselves under their own power.

J.A.M.

Culture of the Baroque

Introduction
Baroque Culture as a Concept of Epoch

Among the different approaches valid for arriving at an interpretation of baroque culture — whose results, precisely because of its diversity, will always be incomplete — I have focused my inquiry on the meaning and range of the characteristics making up this culture, so that its nexus, with its social relations, will stand out from those relations on which it depends and to whose slow transformation it, in turn, contributes. Perhaps this point of view will give us a broader and more systematic panorama, but we also must accept an accompanying limitation: the baroque is no longer a concept of style that can be repeated and that is assumed to have been repeated in many phases of human history; it has come to be, in frank contradiction with baroque as a style, a mere concept of epoch. My examination presents the baroque as a delimited epoch in the history of certain European countries whose historical situation maintained, at a specific moment, a close relation, whatever the differences between them. By way of derivation, the culture of a baroque epoch can manifest itself (and has become manifest) in the American countries indirectly affected by the European cultural conditions of that time.

But my approach certainly does not define the baroque as a European epoch situated between two perfectly defined dates. Historical epochs are not snipped away and isolated from one another by the dividing line of one year or one date; rather, by means of the arbitrary intervention of the human mind contemplating them, they are separated from one another along a broad zone of dates throughout which they mature and afterwards disappear, being transformed into others, passing their inheritance on to others in a way that it cannot be refused. The baroque, then, runs approximately from 1600 (without discarding the possibility that certain advanced phenomena of baroque significance appeared some years previously, in the later times of Michelangelesque Mannerism and, in Spain, with the construction of the Escorial) to 1670-80 (a time of economic change and the first echoes of modern science in Spain; cultural, political, and economic Colbertism in France; the unimpeded emergence of the Industrial Revolution in England). One may discover baroque manifestations counting among the most outlandish and extreme until well into the eighteenth century, but the sense of the epoch is different. In Spain, the years of Philip III's reign (1598-1621) encompass the period of transformation; those of Philip IV (1621-65) the period of its peak; and those of Charles II, at least in the first two decades, the final phase of decadence and degeneration, until a time of restoration toward a new epoch begins before the end of the century.[1]

The baroque, then, is a historical concept. It encompasses, approximately, the first three quarters of the seventeenth century, having its center of greater intensity and fuller significance between 1605 and 1650. If this zone of dates refers specifically to Spanish history, it is also valid (with slight adjustments) for other European countries. In Italy, however, with such names as Botero and Tasso, its beginning could be set earlier, at least in some aspects of art, politics, and literature.

I do not, therefore, use the term *baroque* to designate morphological or stylistic concepts, repeatable in culture, that are chronologically and geographically disparate. One may certainly establish certain relations between external, purely formal elements of the baroque in seventeenth-century Europe and elements present in very different historical epochs in unrelated cultural areas. A culture always has borrowings and legacies from previous and distant cultures. Let us recall the considerable and curious harvest of iconographic terms that Southeast Asia contributed to the European Middle Ages, as some of Baltrusaitis' ingenious studies have revealed.[2] But these antecedents and influences do not define a culture. They tell us, at most, that a culture of a given period is open to exotic currents that are geographically mobile. Examples include the introduction of the cupola in pre-Roman Catalan art[3] or the title *basileus* that was used for some Asturian or British kings.[4] Perhaps we are required, in characterizing a culture, to point out the dependence on a distant tradition (as with Mozarabic art, which has a Visigothic base with Islamic elements;[5] or the Brahmanic metaphors that until the eighteenth century were used to express the European estatist conception of society).[6] But these cases do not represent intracultural kinship so much as isolated contributions that are integrated into different complexes. Neither the mere coincidence in the utilization of separate elements nor the repetition of formal elements whose connection occurs in very different systems can serve as a basis for defining cultures spanning centuries and geographic regions of very diverse characteristics. These morphological correlations, established in abstraction from many other aspects that one needs in order to define a cultural moment, say little or nothing to the historian. The seeking out and formulation of such morphologies are no more than a play of wit that ordinarily becomes limited to a pleasant arbitrariness. Nevertheless, in recognizing these correlations through space and time we are able to ground some generalizations whose application in other fields of knowledge is indisputable.

But we situate ourselves in the realm of social history, which is first and foremost *history*: its object is not to limit what is conceived in consideration of its observable data, so that their observation — and every possible resulting induction — is maintained only on the superficial level of aspects recurring throughout distinct phases of the human past. Rather, its purpose is to attain the most systematic knowledge possible about each of the periods it submits to study, without discarding the possibility that they will afterward be compared with great precision. Its orientation is to supplement concretely the best knowledge of each epoch, not to establish abstract generalizations, and its method takes into account the greatest quantity and most varied data obtainable from what an epoch might offer and then interprets them in the complex in which they are integrated. These data include some that reveal similarities or congruences with other epochs. All this effort is not directed toward discovering baroque periods all the way from ancient Egypt to present America, but to completing the panorama of connections between facts of a multiple nature that may lead us to a better knowledge of what the baroque was as a unique period of European culture during the seventeenth century.

In the following pages I will refer to phenomena from various fields, but I have no expectation of running across similarities or morphological kinships that from outside bring the facts together, nor across manifestations of a style that from within inspires economic, political, religious, artistic, or literary phenomena. Yet I believe that one can speak of a baroque at a given time, in any field of human endeavor. In 1944, I noted in my book about Spanish political thought in the seventeenth century that I could just as well have substituted the phrase "in the epoch of the baroque."[7] Because such an expression would have still been unusual at that time, I decided not to use it in the book's title. Some years later, in 1953, a specialist in the history of painting, who was speaking about the baroque as the epoch concept of the seventeenth century, expressed the need for a study on baroque political thought.[8] By this time, my book had already been written and would soon be published in French, with a preface by Mesnard wherein he stressed the basic formulation that the work was advancing. Some German authors have spoken, in another realm, of *baroque theology*, an expression — untenable today — that was easy to elaborate because the appearance and development of baroque culture were for a long time closely related to its religious element.[9] Today it has even become common to speak about baroque science, the baroque's art of war, baroque economy, baroque politics, and so forth. Clearly in this one must proceed carefully. There can be a certain correspondence among external or formal characteristics occurring in one field or another. Undoubtedly certain aspects of the epoch's architecture or pictorial depiction can be (by way of example) especially apt for containing a reference to the majestic condition of the baroque's absolute kings. But, contrary to the arbitrary connection between cupola and monarchy proposed by Eugenio d'Ors,[10] Mousnier led me to observe that there is no seventeenth-century royal palace with a cupola crowning it at its center. I don't know whether it would be possible to establish similarities between navigation technology and Gongora's *Soledades* or between Quevedo's *Sueños* and the economy of fleece. I am sure that attempts of this type would be entertaining to read, but I fear that they do little to add to our historical knowledge of the epoch.

My thesis is that all these fields of culture coincide as factors of a historical situation and have repercussions in it, some more than others. In their transformation, proper to the situation of each time, they come to be what they are by the combined and reciprocal action of all the other factors. That is to say, it is not that baroque painting, baroque economy, and the baroque art of war have similarities among themselves (or, at least, their similarity is not what counts, without discarding the possibility that some formal comparison might emerge). Instead, given that they develop in the same situation, as a result of the same conditions, responding to the same vital necessities, undergoing an undeniable modifying influence on the part of the other factors, each factor thus ends up being altered, dependent on the epoch as a complex to which all the observed changes must be referred. In these terms, it is possible to attribute determining characteristics of the epoch — in this case, its baroque character — to theology, painting, the warring arts, physics, economy, politics, and so on. It is in this way that the crisis economy, monetary upheavals, credit insecurity, economic wars, and (along with this) the strengthening of seignorial agrarian landholdings and the growing impoverishment of the masses foster a feeling of being threatened and of instability in one's personal and social life, a feeling that is held in control by the imposing forces of repression that underlie the dramatic gesticulation of the baroque human being and permit us the use of such a name.

So the baroque is a concept of epoch that in principle extends to all the manifestations making up this epoch's culture.[11] The new concept of epoch came to be identified by means of art in Italian culture; Burckhardt noticed that, after the Renaissance period and continuing for a specific number of years, the works he contemplated in Rome had, in their deformations and corruptions of previous models, characteristics appearing to belong to a time that was somehow different. Around 1887, in the churches he was studying, Gurlitt, a historian of Roman architecture, observed forms of Renaissance classicism that were lacking in order. At first glance these forms differed among themselves, certainly, but they were dislocated by the same whirlwind of a disordered expression, and all of its products could also be framed between specific dates. Thus resulted the first observations about the baroque, and the vacillating estimations regarding it emerged already in reference to a more or less defined epoch: the epoch following the classicist Renaissance. Wölfflin ventured to extend the new category to the more extensive area of literature. When the characteristics pointed out in this series of works were broadened to other fields, the concept of epoch defining this new post-Renaissance culture was already prepared and, with it, its extension to the diverse sectors of a culture and to the group of countries where it had spread.

As interest in the baroque continued to grow and research on it became more productive, the estimation of its works changed in turn and its interpretation became more complicated and better adapted. The investigative work and the positive valorization of the baroque stage in European culture had its starting point in Germany, from there passing rapidly to Italy, then Spain and England, and finally to France. There the weight of tradition, specifically of classicism — considered only a few years ago to be incompatible with the baroque — made comprehension of the baroque more difficult, at least until recent times (always with some exceptions that must stand as precedents, such as M. Raymond). At present, however, some of the most suggestive works proceed from French scholars. The change in the historical formulation of baroque interpretation can be illustrated with one of its most extreme expressions, taken from the sociohistorian Lewis Mumford, for whom the Renaissance comes to be the initial phase of a new epoch that reaches its fullest meaning in the baroque. According to his thesis, we can characterize the Renaissance, with all its purity of precepts, as the first manifestation of the subsequent baroque.[12] It is worthwhile to underscore this definitive recognition of a conditioning link between both periods and the appraisal of a highly positive value that one must attribute to the baroque in European culture.

Certainly, I do not refer here to subjective personal appraisals regarding the works of artists, politicians, thinkers, or writers of the baroque epoch, which would be similar to attributing them with qualities of good or bad taste according to the preferences of each historian. In the eighteenth century, when the word *baroque* first emerged to qualify specific products of the creative activity of poets, dramatists, and the plastic arts, it was already tinted with a pejorative meaning. Inversely, in other circumstances — such as in Spain during the second quarter of this century — a heated enthusiasm arose around the gongorine movement for baroque creations. Here we have to dispense with such appraisals. Appealing to personal taste disrupts the perception of a cultural phenomenon; although its study takes into account appraisals of such a nature, we are ultimately liable for not seeing things with clarity. In a book that contains valid contributions but also serious limitations, V. L. Tapié, studying the baroque in comparison with classicism counterposes the permanent admiration produced (according to him) by a work of a classical character, such as Versailles, to the repulsion that contemporary good taste experiences before a baroque production.[13] But during the very years when Tapié was writing, the young reseacher J.G. Simpson considered Versailles to be saturated with baroqueness, despite its classicist details, and simultaneously tells us that its lack of restraint and proportion makes us lose ourselves there: "the grandeur turns into megalomania."[14]

The participation of scholars from different countries in baroque studies has enriched and helped give a more precise direction to its interpretation. Although the Germans (Wölfflin, Riegl, Weisbach) insisted (more the first than the last) on formal aspects, they already brought out the connection with historical circumstances: the counterreformist renewal of the Church, the strengthening of papal authority, the expansion of the Society of Jesus — all of which led ultimately to the systematic positing of the baroque as the "art of the Counter-Reformation." This interpretation, which was so influential for several years, gave maximum emphasis to the role of Italy, above all in art, and compensated by reserving for Germany the greater part of the literary baroque. Because of the recognition of Italy's predominant role, it was possible better to appreciate something that we have pointed out: the nexus between classicism and the baroque, whose affirmation led H. Hatzfeld to say that "wherever the problem of the baroque emerges, the existence of Classicism remains implicit."[15] Hatzfeld observed that keeping the Greco-Latin ideal and accepting Aristotle's *Poetics* go together at the baroque's origin (let us recall the role that Robortello's Aristotelian poetics played in Lope). The panorama that Hatzfeld outlined regarding the evolution of the baroque movement is of interest:

> With inevitable differences from generation to generation and with more or less ability, the theorizing Italy, Spain, which experimented with the Italian forms, and France, which, in slow maturation, came to its creations with a fully theoretical consciousness, harmonized their particular national literary and linguistic traditions in a baroque style. This is the same as saying that certain forms of the Italian Renaissance had become common to all of Europe, thanks to the mediation and modifying activity of Spain, and paradoxically culminated in French classicism.[16]

In granting the Mediterranean and Latin countries such a preponderant role in the appearance and development of baroque culture, we cannot forget the significance of such central-European figures as Comenius, whose work as a pedagogue and moralist is decisive in any attempt to define the baroque, nor, on the other hand, English literature and the art and thought of the Low Countries. From this new perspective, the baroque, while in force in Europe, covered more ground than it did in those already outmoded explanations that presented it as a complex of literary or pseudoartistic aberrations saturated with the bad taste that counterreformist Catholicism had cultivated in countries subject to Rome. At the same time, the period was accompanied by a complexity of resources and results that made it one of those most in need of study in order to understand the history of modern Europe. In any case, it can no longer be seen as a consequence following from a single factor, nor even from the varied consequences it provoked on the cultural plane; instead, it became manifest in connection with an extremely varied repertory of factors that together determined the moment's historical situation and imbued all its manifestations with those interdependent and related characteristics that permit us to speak, in a general sense, of the culture of the baroque.

The transformations of sensibility that in recent times came to be tied to new social conditions — whose first phase of maximum critical tension was reached in the 1920s — awakened a new interest in certain productions of Spanish culture. Until then, under pressure of a pedagogical classicism, many of these productions had been cast aside; the recently awakening interest has resulted in the incorporation of the rich area of seventeenth-century Spain into the study of the European baroque. The rediscovery of El Greco, the growing admiration for Velázquez, Zurbarán, and Ribera, the appreciation of the theater, of the picaresque novel and even of the more trivial lyric poetry, and, finally, of economic and political thought have prepared the way for a more developed study of the Spanish baroque. Admittedly, the rise of Spanish baroque studies was favored by the tendency, vigorously followed in the diffusion of seventeenth-century studies, to link baroque creations with Tridentine Catholicism, civil monarchy, pontifical absolutism, and Jesuit instruction, factors that were widely developed in Spain. Even in Tapié's book on the baroque, which dealt with France, Italy, central Europe, and Brazil, there was no mention made of Spain, although the fact would have proven unjustifiable from any point of view even at the time when the work was published. Francastel advanced the harsh objection that for this simple reason the work represented an improper development of the theme:

> Tapié takes the Italian origin of the baroque as an absolute given; personally I believe that the baroque is not born in Italy but as a consequence of the forceful penetration of certain religious forms that arrived from Spain and also, undoubtedly, through the penetration of certain modalities of a taste that, without being Spanish, perhaps was linked to the social order imposed by Hispanicization.[17]

Previously, S. Sitwell had maintained that one must study Spanish examples to find the characteristics that define the baroque with greater clarity and a more general validity; hence the advantage of also making use of the Portuguese and Spanish-American examples that are related to them.[18] This author as well as another English author, Watkin,[19] in accentuating the Hispanic factor in the baroque, link it to a dependency upon Catholic and Hispanic religiosity. What is certain is that the Spanish component in the baroque has tended to be more and more amplified. For reasons similar to those of the English writers I have cited, Weisbach also utilized Spanish data to a great extent in making the baroque an art of the Counter-Reformation. But perhaps no one has taken this position to as much of an extreme as H. Hatzfeld: for him, the baroque is linked to far-removed and constant ingredients of the Spanish genius — certain aspects could already be discovered in Hispano-Latin writers (Lucan, Seneca, Pruden-tius); the forms of religiosity that make the Spanish spirit unique (in St. John of the Cross, St. Ignatius) had a strong influence on its development; and, finally, one must take into account the presence of certain elements occurring in the Hispanic tradition (i.e., Islamic and North African elements). According to Hatzfeld, since the second half of the sixteenth century, Spain — penetrated with Italian culture in the sixteenth century, saturated with Italianism, present in Italy and influential there to a great degree — provoked an alteration in the cir-cumstances in which the Italian Renaissance was developing and compelled writers and artists to seek new forms that led to the baroque. In the formation of the baroque it would be impossible to deny the circumstances of Hispanicization in Rome, Naples, and indirectly at other points on the Italian peninsula. Spain, which contributed so effectively to the breakdown and removal of the Renaissance order, rapidly assimilated the incipient baroque forms of Italy, carried them to maturity, and diffused them into France, Flanders, Italy itself, and also into the Protestant milieu of England and Germany.[20] Counterreform, absolutism, and baroque went together, betokened by their Spanish base, and even the baroque art produced in Protestant countries was found to have a relation to the Hispanic influence — a thesis that others had already stated without playing down (contrary to what Hatzfeld does) the creative value of the Protestant baroque.[21]

Baroque culture thus extended to the most varied manifestations of social life and human works, although different manifestations predominated in different places; the geographic zone to which this culture extended — without making distinction between original and derived production — encompassed all western European countries, from where it is exported to the American colonies or had repercussions in eastern Europe. Finally, given the multiplicity of human re-sources participating in it, no less than the extremely varied attributes of the groups where it developed, the baroque depended upon similar or connected circumstances of a historical situation and not on other factors — for example, on its popular characteristics or on the particular causes of an ethnic group.

On the other hand, after the valid criticism of A. Castro and others, it is today impossible to take seriously the reference to similarities of style in Latin writers of peninsular origin, the attempt to find Hispanic characteristics "from their most remote origins" (as it was postulated by M. Pelayo), or the belief of finding echoes of Lucan or Seneca in Spanish writers when they are deemed of high quality. The thesis is no more tenable that aims to recognize Islamic components, in an attempt to show a Hispanic predisposition toward the baroque; the same arguments militate against this as against the former, although not all of the many who have spoken about the subject — arbitrarily to a certain degree — are disposed to recognize it. Besides, in what North African or Islamic country has the baroque taken place, if this concept is endowed with a meaning somewhat more consistent than a certain tendency to decorative outlandishness that is so common to so many peoples in so many epochs and civilizations, and which plays a secondary role in the historical structure of the baroque?[22]

There remains the question of appealing to the Spanish character itself, which in this case refers to religious attitudes and more particularly to mystical ones. Frequently — and this is what Hatzfeld does — the baroque is combined with mysticism and both are linked to the Spanish character and spirituality. In Spain, however, mysticism was an imported form of religiousness that arrived from Flanders and Germany before passing, in turn, to Germany and France — leaving aside at each moment the case of Italy. Spanish mysticism was a shortlived and delimited phenomenon, and nothing remained of it in the seventeenth century when, inversely, French and above all German mysticism were thriving magnificently. There did exist forms of magical thought that cannot be merely equated with mysticism; on the other hand, they could be found in all of Europe in this same epoch. Finally, the aspects characterizing mysticism, at least as it occurred in Spain (with St. Teresa and St. John of the Cross) were straightforwardly different from those of the baroque; they were rather anti-Baroque, without being divorced from the common ground of scholastic philosophy that was present in both.[23] Of course, I am not including St. Ignatius here as a mystic. The Ignatian mentality was disseminated and came to fruition in almost all European countries. To discuss the correspondences of Ignatian mentality with baroque propositions — which occurred more in his followers than in St. Ignatius — we have to appreciate the results of the coinciding dependency with respect to the same historical situation.

The reader of the voluminous collection of *Cartas de jesuitas* — which spanned the lengthy Baroque — encounters abundant materials that reveal the mentality of the time. I shall make use of some of them in the following chapters. But although there were baroque writers who proved susceptible to Jesuit culture (Tirso de Molina, Salas Barbadillo, Díaz Rengifo, etc.), another body of opinion disagreed with what they were proposing as a new mode of acting and feeling. Barrionuevo tells us that for many it was an error to admit such writers in any republic at all.[24] In several of the first group of the *Cartas* (those dated from January to July, 1634), there is talk of numerous writings from diverse sources against the Society: one of them (February 23) says that "it was raining papers against the Society." But we know that the king, in a harsh decision, gave the order to gather up the papers and condemn their authors, and he charged the Spanish Inquisition with carrying out the order.[25] These references continue to be valuable as an index: not everything remained in line with the Jesuits in the mentality of their contemporaries.

The baroque epoch was, certainly, a time of the faithful (which is not very significantly Jesuit, either, though it may not be entirely estranged), but of a faith that not only retained but reinforced its kinship with magical forms, which were frequently inclined toward superstitious manifestations — Volpe, Buisson, Granjel, and Caro Baroja have studied them in Italy, France, Spain, and elsewhere. The baroque mind was familiar with exalted and irrational forms of religious, political and even physical beliefs, and to a certain extent baroque culture displayed itself in support of these feelings. This doesn't have anything to do with Spanish mysticism directly: not Spanish, because it was a phenomenon taking place extensively and vigorously everywhere; and not mysticism, because its ground of belief was saturated with the current of rationalization that sustained scholasticism. The Church, the monarchy, and other privileged groups that had to draw to themselves sectors of opinion exerted all possible pressure to strengthen these extrarational aspects so they could make use of them. This process had also taken place in other epochs, but in the seventeenth century both within and outside of Spain the question had become much more difficult. And that greater difficulty is explained by the quantitative increase in the population affected, by the individualist energies that had become more intense, by a comparatively richer information disseminated in the media of the city, and by the very complexity of the media available. It no longer sufficed to sculpt an exemplary "history" in the capital of a column, to paint it on stained glass, or to recount it with the innocuous simplicity of a hagiographic legend.[26] For the new time in which the European societies were living, one had to find the most adequate — we might even say the most rational — mode for utilizing every extrarational resource, and one had to possess the technology for its most efficient application.

But the preceding leaves much unsaid. Although religious life and the Church played a decisive role in the formation and development of the baroque — religion occupied a central position for Catholics and Protestants in the seventeenth century and was incorporated by political interests — the manifestations of that culture did not always or everywhere correspond with those of religious life, nor did the problems it poses for our knowledge of it derive from a religious spirit. In the entire Spanish baroque, the greatest weight must perhaps be attributed to the monarchy and the composite of monarchical-seignorial interests that it enveloped. When E. Mâle tried to link the art of the late sixteenth and early seventeenth centuries to counterreformist influences (already pointed out by Dejob),[27] he scarcely mentioned Velázquez, and even this was in reference to the apocryphal portrait of St. Teresa.

The baroque, as an epoch of interesting contrasts and perhaps many times one of bad taste (individualism and traditionalism, inquisitive authority and unsteadying freedom, mysticism and sensualism, theology and superstition, war and commerce, geometry and capriciousness), was not the result of multisecular influences on a country whose character they shaped, nor did it result from influences that irradiated from one country that was supposedly endowed with such characteristics upon others related to it. Baroque culture emerged not from influences or character but from the historical situation. Consequently, whoever was connected with the historical situation participated in that culture, although in each case it varied according to the social position of the individuals in question. The baroque depended, then, on a certain state of society by virtue of which, and because of its breadth, all the societies of western Europe exhibited connected aspects. Within this framework personal and singular influences can be studied, such as those of Tintoretto or Veronese in Spain, of Bernini in France, of Botero or Suárez in the western monarchies. But what explains the characteristics of baroque culture is the condition of the societies in the general and particular circumstances as present in seventeenth-century European countries; within those circumstances, we must take into account the relation of religious and political power with the mass of subjects. Therefore, rather than a question of religion, the baroque was a question of the Church, and especially the Catholic Church because of its status as an absolute monarchical power. It is not any less connected with the other monarchies and inevitably with nearby republics that were related to countries of monarchical absolutism, such as Venice or the Low Countries.

When I speak of the baroque, I do so always in general terms; the national connotation that is present in this work serves only to introduce the nuances that vary the panoramic view when the vantage point shifts, although without losing sight of the whole. Saying *Spanish baroque* is equivalent to saying *European baroque* seen from Spain. Nowadays, it is possible and perhaps even appropriate to speak of the baroque in one country, while securing the theme within a general context. This geographic and historical consideration is parallel to another of a cultural type. The baroque cannot be abstracted as a period of art, nor even as a period of the history of ideas. It affected and belonged to the total ambit of social history, and every study of the subject matter, although legitimately becoming specialized, must unfold by projecting itself into the entire sphere of culture.

I intend this interpretation of the baroque, which will surely be debated, to be recognized nonetheless as applicable to those European countries in which that culture developed. The materials largely come from Spanish sources, and here I try to relate them to one another, placing them in the perspective of the history of Spain. But I take into account, when possible, diverse data from other countries, especially those most closely related with Spanish history. P. Vilar has written that "the drama of 1600 moves beyond the Spanish ambit and announces that seventeenth century, a severe one for Europe, which is today recognized as the time of a general crisis of society."[28] Later I shall return to this concept of "general crisis." The formation and development of baroque culture must be referred to that crisis, which offers a basis for explaining how it affects the whole of Europe. If only because of its peculiar situation and, consequently, the gravity of the characteristics of this crisis, Spain's part in the history of the baroque and its weight in relation to other countries is manifestly considerable. Therefore I believe that it is important to situate ourselves along the perspective of Spanish history. In few occasions has Spain's participation in European life played a role as decisive as in the seventeenth century. Its role was negative — using this word conventionally and, in this case, in a nonpejorative sense — because of the particular seriousness that this century's economic and social crisis reached in Spain, and its role was positive — using this word not in its affirmative sense — because of the efficacy with which baroque expedients [*resortes*] were manipulated, with the early techniques of mass social operation in the ambit of the Spanish monarchy, in achieving the social and political effects of a conservative character.

I recognize, however, that mass society cannot be spoken of in rigorously socioeconomic terms except within the framework of industrial society. Even at the end of the seventeenth century, nowhere — not even in France after Colbert — is there scarcely a statistical change from the previous phase (except for the initial takeoff of England). In Spain there is not even this, despite the pathetic recommendations of Sancho de Moncada, Martínez de Mata, and Alvarez de Ossorio; economically, this previous stage, corresponding to the conditions that prepare for the takeoff (in Rostow's terms, which are easily comprehensible today) can barely begin to be recognized during the century. The frequent use of the words *manufacture* and *factory* in an industrial sense and not merely traditionally would be a weak indication of what we are saying.[29] Soon we will have to emphasize this point from another perspective. Nevertheless, I have no doubts about applying the expression *mass society*. Why? The historian has to be aware that between traditional society and mass society, with its increase in population, there is an intermediate position in which society no longer exhibits the signs of its traditional period and offers others that will make possible the later concentration of manual labor and the modern world's division of labor. Perhaps few things have changed economically, above all in the order of the modes of production; socially, however, changes of greater import can be discerned, changes that may have their origin in the early economic transformations but that far exceed them. It is a society of spreading anonymity. The bonds of neighborhood, kinship, and friendship don't disappear, but they grow pale and are frequently lacking between those living nearby in the same locality (this is one of the most distinctly reflected phenomena in the picaresque novel). To a great extent, relations exhibit the character of a contract: in terms of houses (rent), workday (salary), clothes (buying and selling), and so forth; and to a considerable degree displacements of population occur (it suffices to think about the growth of cities and the rural exodus, which means that a considerable part of the population does not live and die in their place of birth).[30]

In such a way there appear social connections that are not interindividual, that are not between people known to one another. This alters the modes of behavior:

a mass of people who know themselves to be unknown to one another behaves in a different way than a group of individuals who know they can be easily identified. Hence socially this is already a mass society, and at its core it produces that depersonalization that turns humankind into a totality of manual laborers within a mechanical and anonymous system of production.

I: The Conflictive Nature of Baroque Society

Chapter 1
Social Tensions and
the Consciousness of Crisis

Economic and social crises are not always coincident phenomena, much less reducible to a single category, even though they are ordinarily produced in a reciprocal relation of dependency. Even when they overlap, the respective developmental curves of social and economic crises do not match in their risings and fallings, although the repercussions between them are beyond question. Perhaps a parallelism along the entire extension of both phenomena has never occurred (because of the logic of their respective mechanisms), no matter how closely they approximate one another. Most economists (except those of very specific orientations) consider economic crises to be a consequence of the market's objective laws or to be derived from immediate or mediate structures, and they are thus accustomed to ignoring the implications in the social milieu originating from such crises.

According to my thesis the baroque was a culture covering approximately the seventeenth century and consisting in the response given by active groups within a society that had entered into a severe crisis in association with critical economic fluctuations. Within certain chronological limits, the economic upheavals have been studied and are well known. Now, for the past several years, the associated social disturbances arising everywhere have begun to be studied. But it is not simply a matter of intermittent or isolated phenomena, of popular unrest, nor of the apparent explosions whereby they became manifest; it is rather that the baroque century was a long period of a profound social crisis, whose very existence allows us to comprehend that century's specific characteristics.

Bear in mind that the seventeenth century marks the beginning of the conscious-

19

ness (less clear at its outset than three centuries later) that there are periods in the life of a society in which difficulties emerge in the structure and development of collective life, thereby causing things not to proceed well. These periods, then, of differing duration, lead to the realization that society is not working in the normal fashion: relations between groups and persons become complicated, which is unfavorable in principle; driven by this very feeling that things have changed, alterations come about in what persons want, hope for, and do. The result is conflict, or rather, a generalized situation that we can designate as *conflictive*. Everybody knows that in seventeenth-century Spain the monarch was faced with asphyxiating difficulties of public finance, but the crisis went beyond the upheavals in prices that arose on a daily basis. Martínez de Mata, an intellectual who clearly saw the monarchy's critical situation, pointed out the distressing course of state finance, but he was not unaware that there was a general background of crisis constituted by "the other conflicts to be found in these Kingdoms."[1] This plural noun, and his insistent reference to the unrest of groups and individuals, makes us realize to what extent Martínez de Mata comprehended the conflictive nature of his time.

We shall abstain from idealizing some past time that offered a contrast to this somber aspect that the baroque begins to exhibit. The peasant in Andalusia, the weaver in Segovia, employees of the merchants in Burgos, even the merchants themselves and many others (and their counterparts in other countries) — would probably not have found themselves to be much better off in an earlier time. What is certain is that after the appearance of the type we have come to call the *modern individual*, there also began to develop in the individual the capacity to understand that things were not going well, principally in terms of the economy but in other branches of collective life as well; more important, this modern individual began to wonder whether things could be better. This consciousness of unrest and uneasiness was accentuated in those moments when serious upheavals in the social sphere became manifest, upheavals that stemmed largely from the intervention of these same individuals and their new forms of behavior, from the pressure that they — with new aspirations, ideals, and beliefs, and established in a new complex of economic relations — exercised on the social environment.

The word *crisis* had appeared some time before in the realm of medicine, and its derivative — the adjective *critic* (sometimes made into a noun: thus one spoke of the character of the critic) — began to be used in the early seventeenth century; but the word did not remotely signify the disturbing social states I have been referring to. Nevertheless, although the word may have been lacking, there was no lack of conscious awareness of the abnormal, unfavorable and especially agitated moments of social existence that I will call *crisis*. Therefore, people [*gentes*] were directly concerned with those disruptions of the common and established mode — or, at least, what they assumed to be such — whereby things take place in the life of society, and they set about discussing the adverse factors that may have unleashed such consequences. Furthermore, they went on to reflect — and therein resides what is most characteristic of those who are already "modern" — how and with what remedy such ills could be eliminated or eased. Hence, the immense literature of remedies or *arbitrios* that was written.

Therefore, in addition to economic and social disturbances that prevailed, individuals acquired relative consciousness of the phases of crisis that they were undergoing. They also showed a difference in their attitude — which can be underscored in the Renaissance and medieval Christian heritage — toward the events they were witnessing: an attitude not limited to passivity, but postulating an intervention. The model for this mode of behavior came from the example of physicians and surgeons, which explains the preference for metaphors taken from the language of medicine; it also explains why the same economic and political writers — some of whom were physicians — frequently alluded to the curative techniques of medicine, implying that similar disciplines could be applied to the sickness of a society. It was a time of tireless inquiry into the crisis phenomena that were experienced, a time of writing repeatedly about them, about the way to put the monarchy's dealings on firmer ground. The attempt was made to find a remedy for the numerous insufficiencies in society's health because the writers believed that responsibility for saving society from this critical situation rested in human hands. These seventeenth-century politicans and historians, who gave themselves over to studying the ways in which disturbing and abnormal circumstances came about (above all because of their enthusiasm for Tacitism), contributed to the revelation that the course of human affairs is sometimes unfavorable; but they maintained that it was possible to intervene, although positive results could not be guaranteed.

From the fifteenth to the seventeenth centuries, when precapitalist conditions began to take form, the first economic crises of a conjunctive type emerged; they were shorter and, in general, more abrupt in their beginning and end. Although these crises might have been unintelligible, they were perceived as such, and it was also possible to consider that the disappearances of their most ostensible effects could be achieved by manipulating factors that might cause the conjuncture's inversion. Therefore, when an improvement was experienced, it was because the crisis in question had been overcome — that is, the human remedies put into play had in some way operated favorably. Given that in the sixteenth century various cases of inversion of value were effected and that certain favorable results from such experiences lasted until the end of the century, it assuredly built up confidence in the reforming capacity of human work. It was accompanied by a transformation of the notion of human praise, according to the old topos of the *dignitas hominis*, raising to a high degree regard for the individual capable of producing effects [*hombre operativo*], of correcting or creating a new economic or natural reality. If we add that there was also the widespread impression — concretely in Spain — that after the country's anxiety-ridden situation — followed by the politics of the Catholic Kings, certain measures in the government of the emperor Charles, and even (at determinate moments) some interventions during the reign of Philip II — the anxiety was viewed as receding, being replaced by the inverse expectation, it becomes comprehensible that in the Renaissance epoch there came about an attitude of confidence in the human capacity to reform reality. This attitude can be well defined by the title of one of the works it inspired: *Nueva filosofía de la naturaleza del hombre*, a work containing a "Discourse about things that improve this world and its republics." The author, Miguel Sabuco, was a physician.[2]

But if human intervention can heal, it can also worsen a situation. Inept manipulation by those in government can divert and hamper recovery from a crisis; it can even cause a further crisis. Although those who were conscious of social and economic crises in the seventeenth century expected the rulers to have a capacity to overcome them, they could also attribute to rulers the sad results of a turn for the worse leading to the point of collapse. An anonymous writing addressed to Philip IV around 1621, which was probably inspired or written by Cellorigo, captured this state of mind in every aspect: "The negligence of those who rule is without a doubt the author of misfortune and the door through which enter all the ills and injuries in the republic, and in my mind no republic suffers greater misfortune than ours because we live with neither suspicion nor fear of catastrophe, trusting in a lackadaisical confidence." Therefore, knowing that the difficulties exist, that human things are subjected to the risk of reversals, but not being unaware that those unfavorable aspects can be overcome if one remains attentive to them, it must be recognized that Spain's situation is grave and sad, for that is easily the case if "one wants to cover up and cure the dangers with appearances of sweetness and words of confidence," when "the dangers are evident and have a remedy."[3]

It required time to note this state of affairs and paint such a dark picture, as so many seventeenth-century writers did. If social crises last longer than strictly economic ones — to the extent that it is possible to seperate them — the social crisis that was so threateningly present in the last decades of the sixteenth century, and perhaps more forcefully in Spain than anywhere else, was to last long enough to permit the consolidation of a series of responses that would be systematized under the interpretation of what we are calling baroque culture.

But because historians, until recently, concentrated on the minutia of the event, which they improperly called a "historical fact," their versions turned out to be of narrow scope; longer periods, such as the War of Independence, the Restoration, or the Dictatorship, could only be encompassed by the successive addition of some anecdotal incidents to others. Economists first became accustomed to working with more complicated and longer time periods, with managing notions of "processes" and "complexes," phenomena that are waves of a broader radius.

Now social historians are obligated to exceed the measures of time customarily used even by the very specialists in economic cycles and periods. They realize that periods of social crisis are frequently longer, and therefore that the interpretive structures in need of construction must be of greater breadth and more complicated if one is to consider true and complete *complexes* that are endowed with historical meaning.

The economists are entirely correct, when even a Marxist like Liublinskaia (since the Marxists were perhaps the first and the most likely to take longer spans of time into consideration) fragments the seventeenth century into various periods of boom and bust.[4] Perhaps there is no economic crisis encompassing the entire seventeenth century, or even the greater part of it in uninterrupted continuity. But I am venturing to speak of a crisis of seventeenth-century society that extended throughout and went beyond the limits of the century. Even in those places and during those years when the economic crisis receded, the unfavorable aspects of the social crisis were not overcome. If in this the economic factors proved decisive, there were other factors that made the misfortune more acute and that prolonged it, factors that cannot be forgotten in speaking of the seventeenth-century crisis. In those countries that suffered the crisis more profoundly and for a longer time, its characteristics were more indelible.

In recent years economists have spoken of a marginal tendency toward consumerism, whereby — although incomes might suffer a recession for some time — a rate of consumption equal to the previous rate continues to be maintained without showing any effect from the restraints placed on earnings. It is as if there were a certain time lag in adapting to the new circumstances. Thus the waves in social crises have a much greater amplitude, in part because that rhythm of adaptation to the new phase is much slower. Economic historians can delimit positive phases well into the seventeenth century, but that has little import for the general development of a social crisis. In the face of the circumstances of such a crisis, those retaining power and those who offer their support assume attitudes that are abandoned only belatedly, although decades afterward the situation may have come to be very different. The modes of exercising freedom and the structures of repression continue to be maintained. Because this interplay of freedom and repression affects culture at its very roots, social crises are processes that profoundly alter the social state of a people; furthermore, they are creators of a new culture. One of these cultures was that of the baroque, which emerged from the critical circumstances in which the European peoples found themselves; these crises derived from economic causes that changed several times throughout the century, usually unfavorably, and also from a series of "novelties" (as described in the language of the epoch) that were put forward by technology, science, philosophical thought, morality, and religion. Nor can one discount that this economy was bound up with ideological motivations whose actions and reactions in the face of the structural transformations — which at least in part happened in the seventeenth century — obligate the historian to speak of a new epoch.

The repercussions that an economic crisis produces in a social milieu are of a broader radius and continue to exist even though an improvement in the country's economic conjuncture has been produced. Social crises often show an autonomous continuity, and we can observe that their upheavals continue at length when the economic crisis that probably acted to set them in motion has either already ceased or has passed through intermittent phases of a positive or negative type. Thus the critical social situation of the seventeenth century was prolonged throughout almost an entire century from its beginnings in the last years of the preceding one, regardless of the moments of relative expansion that may have been occurring in the production process. The wave of social crisis that conditioned the development of the baroque was more prolonged and continuous than the economic crisis upon which it to such a great extent depended.

But this dependence fails to explain the baroque entirely; the complex phenomena of violent contrast and contortion that characterize the baroque would not have derived solely from such dependence. Another aspect must be taken into account: the immediate experience of those individuals living at the end of the sixteenth century, a complex experience that the Renaissance societies had known according to a very different tendency; this experience was specifically the case, within Spain, of Castilian society. I have dealt elsewhere with the expansive image of society that had spread throughout diverse social groups in seventeenth-century Spain and with the projection of that image onto the conception of a history turned toward what was to come — that is, onto a future-oriented view of human events.[5] When a situation in which one eventually expected the favorable became its contrary, when, instead of being able to count on the continuation of an upward movement, individuals were faced with the specter of the monarchy's ruin and collapse, of society's misery and laxity, of unemployment and hunger, the shock had to be sufficiently great to threaten many things. It called for the erecting of solid bulwarks in support of the traditional order, or at least of that part of the traditional order indispensable for maintaining the self-interest of those groups that continued to hold the power in their hands. Within this sphere, which was parallel to the sphere of reflection about economic problems (certainly not with an intensity comparable to today's reflections, but very much superior to that of any other epoch preceding it), people firmly believed that the adversity being suffered had human causes — causes, therefore, that could and should be corrected and that, from the outset, should be proclaimed. Gonzales de Cellorigo thought that human wisdom and prudence — autonomous, natural, secondary causes — allowed "the republics to be maintained in their well-ordered states and knowledge [*ciencia*] in politics to prevent their collapse"; in a similar way, physicians found the means to change the course of diseases and to cure them, despite the strength of astral influences.[6] Rulers could operate in the same way. There were those who did not shrink from saying: "Many times the ministers' insolence irritates men to do what they don't need to do" — that is, they provoke upheavals in a political system. On 12 September 1654, Barrionuevo made a remark to that effect with respect to one of the most serious conflicts of the baroque monarchy: the insurrection and war in Catalonia. There was an inexhaustible literature whose aim was to correct and put into order the system of social and political relations; in Spain, as in many other European countries, this literature numbers into the hundreds of volumes. To such an extent, we can consider what Juan Alfonso de Lancina wrote as material devoted to human operativity — whether it proved successful or was in error; in 1687 he alluded with melancholy to the construction of a political society, specifically the seventeenth-century Spanish monarchy (which, he maintained, some men attempted to raise up but never learned how to get off the ground): "I well know of a monarchy that could have towered over the world, had its plan not been erroneously sketched."[7] Furthermore, perhaps the most complete verification of this point is the example of Sancho de Moncada, who came up with the idea of organizing an entire university school for the study of politics so that the rulers of his time might not fall prey to committing so many errors because of irredeemable ignorance.[8] This view underlay the curious and interesting preoccupation of writing and teaching about politics, a preoccupation shared by seigniors, bureaucrats, and even simple citizens. It documents an attitude full of modern sentiment and born of a serious consciousness of a crisis situation; as such, it must be considered a valuable datum for understanding the epoch.

We are discussing social crisis with a view toward specific aspects[9] that can be verified. (1) In seventeenth-century societies we recognize an alteration in values and in their congruent modes of behavior, which attained a broadly observable level — honor, communal love (which was in the process of being converted from vassal fealty into patriotism), wealth, inheritance, poverty. (2) If every society assumed an active or resigned acceptance — we would not quite call it *consent* — of such values and modes of conduct,[10] the fact that they were put into question entailed alterations, of unequal intensity, in the processes whereby individuals were integrated when they possessed those modes of conduct to such an unequal degree. The role of such processes was to maintain the stability of the society in question, and already in many cases this role was not being fulfilled (in terms of one who may be destitute, devoid of class, sick — think about what the social transformation of the hospital means in this respect). (3) The effects of unrest and of more or less declared nonconformity became evident in relation to the social localization of individuals or groups, which provoked in them a sensation of oppression and anguish (recall the energetic explosion of zeal for "self-gain" [*medro*], for moving up in estate position, for becoming a noble, which was ridiculed by so many literary works in France,

Italy, Spain, and other countries). (4) Interrelations linking individuals to one another were transformed, relations that now seemed more burdensome to those enduring them, which was how they were viewed in the minds of the epoch's nonconformists (salaried workers, with even the seigniors' servants considering themselves bound only by their salary; those working in the marketplace; rural elements displaced to the city; women in families that had become rich bourgeois, etc.). (5) There is proof regarding the formation within society of certain new groups or groups resulting from modifications in already recognized groups (foreigners, merchants, rich farmers, city officials),[11] whose social roles underwent disturbances in all of Europe and perhaps even more in seventeenth-century Spain (even though the bourgeois groups didn't fulfill their role as "bourgeoisie," the nobles stopped fulfilling their role of "nobility"). (6) Critiques appeared to denounce the profound unrest, and they provoked, with a greater or lesser index of frequency, cases of deviant conduct and of tensions between some groups and others, which, if they attained a sufficient degree of intensity, broke out in revolts and seditions. We shall discuss these below.

In sum, despite the slight upward and downward turns, undulations in space and time, we are faced with an extensive and profound social crisis in Spain from the last years of Philip II's reign to the end of that of Charles II; it paralleled crises that were less acute in other European countries: in France, Germany, and Italy, and in England until the Revolution assured the triumph of those factors changing the structure of the country. That shared crisis of the seventeenth century cannot be identified with a new phenomenon derived from the general conflagration of the Thirty Years' War because it began a long time before, affected spheres not threatened by the war, was more serious in countries that did not suffer direct damages from the fire and troops of battle, and its process of reestablishment did not follow the line of recuperation of war losses.[12] The crisis of the seventeenth century cannot be understood in Spain without bearing in mind the broad European framework in which it unfolded, although in Spain its effects would turn out to be irredeemable for centuries. Nor is that crisis understood by referring only to economic difficulties (however serious they were) or to military destruction (the Iberian Peninsula saw less fighting than anywhere in Europe). It was the spectacular and problematic breakdown of a society within which forces driving it toward change struggled with other, more powerful forces whose object was preservation. Wherever the resistance to these changes was greater, although in no instance could things remain as they were, the elements of the new society were not permitted to develop and all the factors of immobility become privileged. In such cases, including in Spain, the effects of the crisis lasted longer and had a negative import.

The crisis of complex manifestations that left a broad imprint on the face of the epoch. Lucien Febvre has directed his observation toward this last aspect, focusing especially on the semblance of individuals, from the moment when the

Renaissance was "liquidated."[13] (I believe, however, that a historical experience is never liquidated, and I thus prefer to stay with the concept of "historical change.")

Many negative events struck the consciousness that the course of the previous epoch had awakened: the economic recession and poverty imposed at the end of the sixteenth century; the disorderliness and unrest created by repeated conflicts between states; the moral confusion deriving from the preceding epoch of expansion; and the unjustifiable conduct of the Church and the critiques it promoted, giving rise either to laxity or to pathological attitudes of exacerbated intolerance.

Today many historians — including Koenigsberger[14] and me[15] — do not hesitate to apply the modern concept of revolution to the upheavals taking place in Europe since the sixteenth century, when so many of these agitations began their process. The agitations that exploded in the seventeenth century across a broad geographic area must even more rightly be characterized in this way. The work of Porshnev,[16] R. Mousnier,[17] A Domínguez Ortiz,[18] J.H. Elliott, and others[19] takes this approach. The threatening picture that was manifest all over Europe in that century is today well known, and no less so in Spain, where if some still refuse to recognize that state of nonconformism — with its revolutionary basis *avant la lettre* — Elliott's studies and the consequences for a sociohistorical view of the Spanish baroque are very instructive. My own studies have outlined the tendencies that were adverse to the official order of the seventeenth-century Spanish monarchy.[20] Elliott observes that the word *revolution* itself began to take on a modern meaning.[21] In Castilian usage one can verify a similar semantic displacement.[22]

This interpretation serves to explain the mobilization of an extensive social operation whose aim was to contain those forces of dispersion that threatened to disrupt the traditional order. To such an end, the absolute monarchy was latched onto as an efficient instrument; first mobilized to discipline the course of development taking place in the Renaissance, it was applied in the new circumstances of crisis toward subduing the different elements that could be raised up against the prevailing order. Thus the absolute monarchy was converted into the foundation or, rather, into the keystone of the social system: in the absolutist regime of the baroque, the monarchy capped off a complex of restored seignorial interests, supporting itself on the predominance of land ownership that became the base of the system.

The contemporary enhancement of the nobility's social role — using *nobility* to mean individuals of an upper and privileged estate position (nobility of lineage, priests, elevated bureaucrats, the rich who had numerous servants at their disposal), although it was the hereditary nobility who set the guidelines as to social behavior — was linked in a reciprocal relation to the process of revalorization and concentration of agricultural land ownership, which became manifest in the very years of the economic crisis.[23] This could not mean merely a return to a feudal society of nobiliary predominance, inasmuch as the nobles themselves had in many aspects become more like the rich landholders. Above the level of the nobility, there was now the undebatable superiority of the monarchy — to this corresponded the effectiveness of a juridical-political notion that the baroque foregrounds, that of "sovereignty"[24] — and the unavoidable presence of other social layers. At issue were classes that could give rise to the threat of dissolution; to avoid this, there was no remedy other than trying to control them, in some way incorporating such layers toward the order's preservation, obliging them to defend it, moving them to increase their taxes, integrating them to the greatest possible extent into a system that we must for the most part consider new for this very reason. It was a question of the monarchical-seignorial pyramid, with a protonational base, which we are calling baroque society.[25]

In speaking of the baroque, so many have noticed a return to aristocratism or authority, to the aristocratic structure of bonds of dependency and to the order of privileged powers, which took place in opposition to concepts of the Renaissance as democratic and communal (though, on the other hand, this latter is no less debatable in terms of its time period). But by itself this observation tells us little and leads only to confusion, for in the Renaissance century the firm bases of the absolute monarchy, with its repressive regime of popular freedom, had not fully shown themselves; nor is baroque aristocratism reducible to a mere renewal of the feudal stage, nor even of a belated chivalric one. Although in the seventeenth century values of chivalric culture continued to exist and have been maintained even until now, this is not exactly the kind of society maintained by baroque culture. In the same way that monarchical absolutism cannot be confused with the arbitrary patrimonialism of the feudal reign (the English rightly speak of the *New Monarchy*), neither do chivalric and baroque cultures overlap one another. The economic upheavals (at first positive, later negative); the consequent changes in the structure of estates, however relative they might have been; the crisis of individualism that all realms were acquainted with in the seventeenth century; and the expansive character of culture in general (consider what printing represents), along with a participation of public opinion in new terms: all this gave rise to what, in reference to the baroque (since it comes after a broad Renaissance experience), can only relatively and figuratively be referred to as medievalism.

However, our affirmation that this anachronistic reaction was produced in connection with new economic and social data is in no way opposed to our recognition that this "baroquing" reaction was a drag on the development of the society in which it occurred, a serious obstacle to greater economic growth. Beyond the immediate economic reasons, the tendency to invest in land — which the rich and powerful of the city undeniably practiced before, though it was more pronounced in the seventeenth century — was also a product of tradition that continued in mental existence and that assured the maintenance of the nobiliary and military principle as the inspiring doctrine of an estate society, since "a bond is elaborated between the existing social order and a system of ideas seeking to give it rational justification."[26] The possession of land thus came to assume an extraeconomic value and to combine its rule with the system of social stratification, contradicting even broader interests. "In this way the hierarchy of lands would be preserved as the source of social esteem and social prestige, although it would turn out to be detrimental to national interests. In such a way the fundamental principle of a society would come to dominate even economic activities." In France, although the nobility with its habits of luxury siphoned off an important part of the revenue from possible productive investment, aggravating an economic crisis that has been pointed out many times, it nonetheless demands an even greater number of honorific positions reserved for it in public offices, with their pecuniary benefits. At the same time it clamored for the maintenance of external signs to differentiate between individuals of different estates in clothing and other ways;[27] it sought to augment its territorial dominions and, rather than entering into manufacturing or commercial enterprises, reinforced the prohibition (*derogeance*) of these pursuits as being incompatible with nobility privileges.[28] A seventeenth-century law allowed for the compatibility of nobility and commercialism, but very few entered into the system; in some cases, they made use of intermediary agents. In Spain, these same facts became much more rigorously manifest. The circumstances of French and Italian life were similar to those so often attributed, and rightly so, to Spanish society;[29] perhaps the Spanish difference was limited to the clergy's widespread and closed participation as a privileged group, to the system's most severe application, and to the unquestionable support that, after Domínguez Ortiz's studies, we know the monarchy to have lent to it — in some instances making use of the Inquisition itself.

Products as characteristically baroque as the theater of Lope or of Corneille reflected this state of things, not so much anecdotally (although some references of this type can be obtained)[30] as structurally. In a previous work, I have repeatedly dealt with Lope from this perspective.[31] Recall that N. Salomon, to study the social bases of Lopesque comedy, found it necessary to analyze economic phenomena in relation to the land and its seignorial tradition as they came to bear on the Castilian countryside at the end of the sixteenth century. Regarding Corneille, Bénichou has applied the description "feudal" to his inspiration as a dramatist because "the epoch of Corneille is precisely, in modern times, the one in which the old moral themes of the aristocracy have been revived with greater intensity." Corneille's work, contemporary to la Fronde, would comprise "a long and drawn-out shudder, undoubtedly the last, of feudal sensibility"; Bénichou's entire interpretation is based on making Corneille's work the expression of nobiliary morality — so rigorously, in fact, that we think it would perhaps be difficult to attempt its strict application to any Spanish writer of the epoch.[32]

Despite the similarity to events in other western European countries, the Spanish social situation revealed a much more rigid structure that froze the possibilities of growth occurring in baroque culture itself. Without a doubt, there was in the baroque a tendency toward immobility or, at least, toward directing the progressive forces that the Renaissance had set underway. But in the struggle between the two tendencies, the expansive forces to be contained were of such energy that, sooner or later — in England and France, respectively — they ended up winning the war. Shakespeare or Ben Jonson did not represent a culture that would make the Industrial Revolution impossible. Racine or Molière might have contributed to preparing minds for the renewing phase of Colbertism. But the theater of Lope or of Calderón could not escape the conditions in which it was produced and which their works reflected — though they were no less modern because of it. Nevertheless, they could not move toward a definitively modern world, breaking the immobility of the social structure from which their works drew support. Despite everything, it is only when the work of Descartes and Galileo entered the peninsula, and with them modern science, that one discovers some innovations in thought; notwithstanding the noble polemic represented by the eighteenth-century Enlightenment, these innovations will still not succeed in triumphing.

After the changes brought by the Renaissance, the baroque, particularly in Spain, fostered a readaptation to the social circumstances; with regard to that experience we can now ask ourselves the question that Rostow posed in relation to the phase of conditions prior to the stage of the "takeoff": was there in seventeenth-century Spain a minority capable of taking advantage of transformations underway since the preceding century and directing them toward a future development? Was there a minority strong enough to displace the anachronistic group of traditional landowners and, furthermore, of seignorial landholders in the old or a new mold based on privilege, a group possessing vast territories? Would it then be realistic to expect that a new group, with a new conception of society and of the objectives of civil life, would arrive at significant participation in power or obtain the sure help of the autocrat who retained it?[33] At most, individuals were capable of petty, self-centered greed and egoism, abandoning the public good: "All are seeking to escape, while the monarchy is falling," Barrionuevo observed to his readers.[34] Undoubtedly, such a group was not found with enough consistency. The appraisal of the situation present in the epoch's consciousness cannot be less favorable from this point of view. From the outset, it translated into criticism of what we would call the "administration," which was in the hands of distinguished individuals. In an interesting and significant passage, Pérez del Barrio lamented that the traditionally privileged class did not have the preparation and necessary drive even for the management of their own interests.[35] Much less could it be counted on for the administration of public affairs, whether one was speaking of the Castilian or Catalan nobility.[36] When some of its members reached a clear consciousness of the country's situation, or when individuals of other groups less prominent on the social scale tried to make their protests heard (there are traces of their attempting to participate in power), the results were completely negative.

When the praise of *mediocritas* is heard in so many Spanish and non-Spanish writers of the seventeenth century, one immediately becomes aware that it echoes the writings of Seneca, but one should also consider whether, in that epoch, the praise corresponded to a desire to endorse the formation and elevation of the middle class — or, better, the "intermediate" class — that had a larger part in the interplay of society and politics. Offering words of praise, Pérez de Herrera wanted to see the country integrated principally with "a sufficient and honorable moderation and mediocrity, for that is what common happiness consists in."[37] Using a more modern expression, Saavedra Fajardo also tells us that "the only republic that will endure for a long time will be one that consists of median segments, and not very unequal among themselves. The excess of riches in some citizens caused the ruin of the Florentine Republic and is today the cause of the restlessness of Genoa."[38] Perhaps it was Lope de Deza who sketched the most complete panorama of this intermediate class.[39] Such a program regarding the structure of society was also found in Montesquieu, who, from a clearly conservative perspective wanted to see a society of the middle aristocracy and farmers strengthened. Such would be the image of the French pre-revolution or the revolution of the nobility in 1788.[40] But if in France that program in part succeeded in its purposes at the end of the eighteenth century, the same thing did not happen in seventeenth-century Spain. Numerically it may have come to constitute a large group in the cities, but it fell under the power and influence of the absolute monarchy — which that intermediate class would be the first to dispute — and its powerful allies. Although at the time we are studying there were some cultural aspects that could be attributed to its influence (the vogue, for example, of the love-story novel), neither politically nor sociologically did it represent a great force in Spain. The intermediate class did not serve to limit and trivialize the nobiliary ideals; rather, it favored them with an epic heroism and gave them that aspect of being ideals appropriate for the public in general, as they were regarded during the baroque.

The Spanish baroque, under the insuperable domination of the monarchy, was ruled by the unadapted class of the traditional nobility, a class that was not equal to the times, even though the times made it change in more than one aspect; a class altered in its habits and conventions by a greater zeal for accumulating riches than for achieving profits; a class of people (Pérez de Herrera would say) swept along by their great expenses, who feel "an extremely ardent desire for property, and they do not hesitate in borrowing to get it";[41] a class, in sum, that was largely incapable of seeking wealth by properly economic means according to the modern mercantile economy. On the other hand, it was a class that, in defense of its privileges, was capable of blocking the way of those who would have been able to open other channels for society had they been assisted by power they did not have. The closest the nobility came to economic activity, with no conception at all of the problems, was in imposing rent increases and in other related practices. In addition, the wealthy members of other groups who entered individually into the nobility [*hidalguía*] indirectly accentuated and expanded these characteristics, thereby preventing this directing, reforming group that Rostow calls for from ever constituting itself; this group didn't appear in Spain until the eighteenth century, and even then with few results. Domínguez Ortiz, who has studied the problem we are raising here (although from other perspectives), came to conclusions allowing us to continue along our line of interpretation:

> The role of the nobility in local life was relevant, with no relation to its numbers, and had more splendor in the cities of the southern half of Spain, where its small number was compensated for by the abundance of wealth and titles; by means of the cities the nobility dominated in the Cortes and in this way it assured itself a discreet influence in the government of the state. In the rural areas, the greater facility for the wealthy elements of the general state to accede to the nobility in one way or another, eased the tensions. And this is how a situation was being elaborated in which the essential distinction was not between the nobles and the populace, but between landholders and day laborers.[42]

In the seventeenth century the privileged estates, who put advantageous practices in effect, were accompanied by the outside elements that had been incorporated into them and had, with the strength of their money, augmented the strength of the group; such practices included occupying positions in municipal administration and making use of such positions to administer in their favor the division of the quotas of *servicios* and other taxes and to place the greatest burden on the modest taxpayer. By this same route, in the utilization of the peoples' goods, it was assured that the powerful would receive the articles of greater quality, through more or less fraudulent or threatening means. At times, in exploiting their possibilities, they arrived at practices that, despite the minor importance in terms of volume, nonetheless had a very clear meaning: the Sala de los Alcaldes de Casa y Corte de Madrid told Philip IV (in 1621?) that the seigniors and potentates had an overstock of provisions in their homes, which allowed them to sell delicacies, capons, chickens, rabbits, veal, and wine without license, without paying taxes and at abusive prices, going beyond the limits of justice.[43] (There is no doubt that, even in its insignificant aspects, the myth of the economic disinterest of the seventeenth-century Spanish nobility is pure fiction; it is only that the interest, more or less concealed, had to follow in so many cases an unhealthy course.) But on a greater scale and with more serious consequences, when the occasion arose, the rich of every class adopted modes of activity that were more harmful for the majority; for example, monopolistic manipulation of the price of cereals, causing its rise or decline according to what the small producer had to sell at harvest time or had to buy at the end of the agricultural season. They caused the downfall of those who had no means to resist, and they bought in favorable circumstances the properties of those who were ruined. Secular and ecclesiastical domains were extended (these latter, in addition, under the appearance of the free will and testament) at the expense of communal lands or personal property. And when the weak saw themselves ruined, the purchase of their lands was realized at ridiculous prices. If it is possible to speak of a first phase of *mortmain disentailment*, with the sale of fallow lands in towns and villages, Philip IV's anonymous informant also made it known that the rich were the ones who bought such properties and rent them later to the poor at much higher prices, depriving the towns [*pueblos*] of them.[44] The texts of Caxa de Leruela, Francisco Santos, Fernández Navarrete, Lope de Deza, Martín de Cellorigo, Pérez del Barrio, and others describe in a black tone this iniquitous mode of procedure of the oligarchic groups: first, within the limits of the towns,[45] then within the limits of the state, they had the councillors — positions monopolized by the municipal oligarchies — elected as representatives in the cortes of the towns and cities. All this had as a consequence the ruin of the small landowners and sharecroppers, their abandonment of the countryside, the continuous entrance into the city of a mass of needy people,[46] the formation of groups inclined toward subversion, and, finally, the vigilance to contain the possible explosions that these new conditions of urban growth were producing.[47] Thus, the increment on a social level of the power of the seigniors and of their newly ascended fellow travelers explains many aspects of baroque culture that would not make sense or would have been something very different if it had not been for the dismal poverty of the social conditions or this threatening displacement to the cities.

One item of information cannot be more telling: the royal support for the economic well-being of the powerful, even going against the opinion of the Cortes (or, at least, of the Cortes' most intelligent representatives). Such is the case with the disproportionate protection the crown gave to the *Mesta* (association of animal breeders), which was simply protection for migrating livestock. New privileges granted in 1633 excluded stationary livestock, over the protests of Caxa Leruela and others, who saw in small-scale raising of livestock the wealth of the countryside and of the country as a whole.[48] Official protection was clearly directed toward the privileged groups, the owners of large flocks (the nobles, the church, some nouveaux riches) — those who constituted the founding strength of the monarchical-aristocratic, authoritarian government over against the democratic or popular influences that could arise from an economy of small flocks maintained in conjunction with agriculture. On occasion, baroque theater also supported the official policy of the intimate correlation of nobiliary and monarchical power. The spaces reserved in the major university colleges for the sons of the more prominent estate corresponded to the same tendency, during a phase of state formation when a system of bureaucratic selection was being constituted.[49] If the entire baroque was an epoch of "nobiliary reaction" (the expression is from Domínguez Ortiz),[50] in its last decades the phenomenon became accentuated. When seen from within, the situation is explained and defended as a mechanism whose logical functioning was beyond all arbitrariness. In effect, in accordance with its program of adhering to the network of the epoch's monarchical-seignorial interest and of its self-exaltation, in the midst of so many favors, dignities, titles, aids, ecclesiastical offices, benefices, and prebends of all sorts that the Spanish monarchy constantly bestowed, Almansa y Mendoza — panegyrist of the system, who filled page after page of his *Cartas* with nothing more than a stating of French concessions — transparently explained the meaning of the system: "As the true practical reason of state is to make sure the vassals accrue benefits so that they have no desire to change their lord or their fortune, in distributive justice one must take great care that benefiting the nobility is the most obligatory bond." Such, then, was the reason and meaning of the system: to privilege those who were most prominent with every kind of advantage so that they could maintain order together. Almansa maintained that "nothing proves more constitutive of their [i.e., an empire's] duration than lavishness."[51]

The bourgeoisie's loss of strength and dissolution in the first half of the seventeenth century stemmed less from its own crisis, less from a retraction of its role, than from an intentional strengthening of the nobility's power; to garner assistance, the nobility enlisted the rich in its cause and the other ascendant groups were restrained. Rather than speak of a genuine "betrayal of the bourgeoisie" (a phrase that has become famous), in this case one would have to speak of a defeat of the bourgeoisie, which in Spain abandoned the contest very quickly because it had lost in advance. According to Domínguez Ortiz,

> in the quantitative aspect it appears probable (although statistics are lacking) that the number of those in the privileged ranks increased; on the one hand, because their higher level of existence constituted a relative defense against the abnormal death rate; on the other hand, because of the incessant pressure that the most fortunate of the lower classes exerted to climb the social ladder . . . Although the increase within the privileged classes was great in absolute terms, their relative growth was greater, since the poorer classes diminished in number . . .; [but] if the numerical increase of those in the privileged ranks increased the degree to which the common estate was held in check, the common estate's deterioration in turn made the upper classes' situation more precarious.[52]

This social panorama explains the development of a culture in the terms we have been using to describe it: some upper, prominent groups try to maintain and increase their privileges and wealth, which they consider to be threatened by crisis (apart from the nonconformity that the crisis provokes in turn); these groups count on an aggregate of social power and political means to achieve their ends, and, below, an estate of common people is overcome by the scourges of the plagues, poverty, hunger, and war; because of its social origins, this common estate cannot be limited to the base resignation of those peoples from the very lowest social levels, and, as a consequence, they repeatedly demonstrate attitudes of protest ("Wherever you go there is a stretch of bad road," a sentence that Barrionuevo repeated again and again; he also originates the exclamation: "Poor Spain, out of luck!").[53] To quiet such demonstrations of restlessness, those in power, thinking that the means [*resortes*] of physical repression may not be enough, see themselves obligated to help and make use of those who can furnish them with effective cultural expedients. Predominant in this culture, congruently, are the elements of attraction, persuasion, and compromise with the system, constituting an attempt to incorporate within the system's defensive integration that common mass that is much more numerous than the privileged groups, despite their increase, and that can threaten their order.

Such results, contrary to what has generally been assumed, belonged essentially to sovereign authority's parameters of conduct in baroque society: a strengthening of seignorial interests and powers as a platform that underlay the absolute monarchy, guarantor in its turn of this seignorial network. To strengthen the system, the seignorial network was assimilated into the seventeenth-century ideals of the nobility and of the prominent estate. Even the Church included in its code of "Christian" social morality those modes of conduct, precipitated out from aristocratic interests, that probably formed the least Christian framework of the Church of Rome throughout its entire history.[54] The ideals in the Count-Duke's Spain were no different from those of Richelieu's France, with the contempt of each toward the bourgeoisie that preserved itself as such, with their constitutive harassment of the common people.[55] In this way, we comprehend the following description of the most popular baroque poet among the Spanish public: "Lope's most agreeable and familiar dramatic subject is showing us how humankind's natural instincts behave in the realm of providential and social bonds and dependencies, barriers and echelons."[56] The description also applies to everyone else; all of baroque art, from Lope's comedy to the novel of Mateo Alemán, to Zurbarán's paintings of saints, becomes a drama of the estates, the gesticulating submission of the individual to the confines of the social order. The same thematics underlie arguments that on the surface seem indifferent to the question, and in works of a very different nature — by Villamediana, Quevedo, Gracián, and others.[57]

The characteristics we have just articulated were not imposed in the face of static circumstances in which nothing had altered secularly, but rather sought victory vis-à-vis opposing forces unleashed by sixteenth-century expansion;

therefore, they confronted a conflictive situation. To understand the seventeenth-century crisis, one must necessarily take notice of the manifestly opposing situation of the preceding century: baroque culture is inexplicable without taking into account a basic situation of crisis and conflict. The culture constituted itself under the pressure of the forces of contention, which dominated but did not annihilate the liberating forces of individual existence. Those energies of individualism that were once again to be submitted to the estate mold, thus preserving the traditional structure of society, occasionally appeared despite a powerful, vicelike social order that subdued and reorganized them; precisely for that reason, they became manifest in a manner that was constrained and somewhat deformed by accommodation to the social space that authority delegated to them — much like human figures that the medieval sculptor presents in a contorted shape so that they could fit in the architectonic space of the tympanum or of the capital in a Romanesque church. A gesticulating culture, one of dramatic expression, was produced whenever a situation of conflict arose between the energies of the individual and the ambit containing it. Vossler observed with respect to Lope that if people had been less oppressed, his characters would have been less developed.[58]

The baroque monarchy made use of a large repertory of means [*medios*] to succeed in dominating the tension of adverse forces; this, along with the novelty of some of these means, revealed what was constitutive of baroque culture. It included aspects all the way from physical constraint, based on military force, which is the ultima ratio of political supremacy, to psychological expedients [*resortes*] that acted on consciousness and created within it a repressed psyche (I shall deal with these aspects more extensively below). In between were diverse resources used in a surprising fashion, a use explicable only in terms of the psychological and moral assumptions of the baroque. For example, because sacriligious acts had been carried out in Madrid at various times and, on one occasion, twice on the same day and in different places of worship, repressive and purgative measures were taken that consisted of suppressing the *comedias* for eight days and imposing sexual abstention: "There were no public women." Almansa y Mendoza gives an account of this in his *Cartas*.[59]

The expressive character of that basic conflictiveness affecting the human being's social position was common to all the products of baroque culture, especially in Spain where the two antagonistic extremes acquired a considerable potency. The seventeenth-century Spaniard's horizontal nobility — that is, in terms of geography and profession — had been at a high level (because of the population movements in the peninsula, the colonization of America, and the European undertakings), the vertical mobility, to a lesser degree, had also been appreciable (although only as an effect of the preceding). Individuals thus saw themselves driven from their allotted positions only to come up against the rigid boundaries constituting those positions. Elsewhere I have spoken of the erosion and even the profound alteration undergone by the estatist social order. But this society reacted by trying to conserve its structure; although in the struggle it lost some of its most characteristically integrating elements, it imposed its victory throughout the seventeenth century with a reactionary power, unfortunately, that had no parallel in Europe.

Although the seventeenth-century crisis had economic motivations to which we must attribute a determining role, it also had human aspects that lent an especially dramatic cast to the manifestations expressing that crisis and constituting Spain's baroque culture. In their own time, some of the writers concerned with economic matters and reflecting about the painful conditions of the people they were contemplating also indicated the human side of the problem. Today, these writers are of increasing interest to us, and their meditations on the functioning of the economic factors that set the crisis in motion still constitute a valuable work. Their interpretations are better in helping us to comprehend the faults in the mechanism of the Spanish economy than many of the explanations offered later. But along with defects in the manufacturing, mercantile and monetary expedients, they also considered the human element as simultaneously cause and effect of the crisis they witnessed. For centuries afterward, only the heroic side of our sixteenth-century history was revealed — whether in the theaters of war in Flanders, Germany, or Italy, or in the scenarios of Lope's *comedia*, which were dedicated to the exaltation of the topical values of seignorial society. Even during that time, however, a writer as acute and independent in his appraisals as Martín G. de Cellorigo saw that the ills did not come from war but from "our own weakness."[60]

With a more biting expression, Sancho de Moncada, a teacher at Toledo and a priest and writer on the economy, whom the Inquisition did not view in a politically favorable light — the Inquisition was a political organ — went even further: Spain found itself in grave danger because "all the people [are] so indulging and effeminate."[61] This may seem strange today, but it was reiterated at the time. Some decades later, Pellicer de Tovar pointed to indulgence and effeminacy as the causes of the country's distressing situation.[62] Although we know that preachers tend toward exaggeration, in a 1635 sermon Fra Francisco de León, prior of Guadalupe, pronounced some words along those same lines that would serve to verify where the basic source of ills was sought: we see, spoke the severe prior, "men converted into women, from soldiers into effeminates, covered with hair falling over the ear, trailing locks in back, and frizzed up in front, and who knows if they aren't made up and dressed up in things resembling what women wear."[63] Pellicer's *Avisos*, besides citing crimes of illicit sexual relations, pointed out cases of homosexuality that were no less common among the laity than the clergy.[64] The proposals of tribunals and councils requesting the renovation of adornments and uniforms that were worn ordinarily attributed the reason to their luxury and effeminacy.[65] Unquestionably, this oft-repeated accusation, just as the lewd seventeenth-century literature about which so little is known, is often nothing more than a rhetorical ploy. Nevertheless, it helps us to verify how the seventeenth-century crisis had transformed the image of Spaniards from that of the preceding century; in showing that it affected the human basis of society, it revealed a generalized condition of moral laxity. As for Suárez de Figueroa, always concerned by the situation of the time he was contemplating, he spoke of the useless male adolescents at the court, of the affected and made-up females, of the "current little sissies": "the vanity of songs and dances entertains the effeminate and makes them waste their time in embellishing their faces, curling their hair, raising the pitch of their voice, in feminine caresses and affectation, and in making themselves equal to women in the delicateness of their bodies."[66] Evidence like this doesn't have a direct validity, but it tells us about the extent of sensuality in the seventeenth century, the zeal for pleasure, laxity, and even about the obvious reaction against the severity of another epoch's manly customs; *tenebrismo* and *macabrismo* rest on this foundation and therefore are derived tastes, just like the shabbiness of a pretended poverty in today's consumer society. If to this one adds the contemporary consciousness of the uncontainable and well-supported public and private immorality, Barrionuevo's saying becomes explicable: "There is a lot to clean if one would really sweep." This undercurrent of laxity explains many aspects that were projected into the farthest reaches of baroque culture.[67]

The conclusion we draw from all these facts, and from countless other facts taken from other fields, is that seventeenth-century Spaniards, in distinction to those of the Renaissance epoch, were shaken by a grave crisis in their integration process (after 1600, current opinion universally recognized that there was no way to stop the collapse of the Hispanic monarchy as the regime of group coexistence and that all that could be done was to shore it up provisionally). That crisis translated into a state of disquiet — which, in many cases, could be characterized as anguished — and, therefore, a state of instability. They themselves had a consciousness of irremediable "decadence" before the eighteenth-century enlighteners formed that idea of the preceding century. Such concerns were expressed in the considerations from the Consejo Real to Philip III (1 February 1619), speaking to him of "the miserable state in which your vassals are found," and in the severe warning in the same document that "it is not unlikely that they live discontented, afflicted and disconsolate."[68] They are repeated in dozens of writings from individuals or from high organizations, not just to Philip III but even more so to Philip IV; in the latter, ordinarily so insensitive, this evoked a sincere moment of anxiety when he confessed that he was aware of the distressing situation that supported his reign: "Today we are all on the verge of being lost."[69] The baroque's thematic repertory corresponded to this intimate state of consciousness — let us bear in mind what the themes of fortune, chance, change, fleetingness, decay, and ruins represented in seventeenth-century art.

A similar situation occurred in all spheres of society. The conflict was so visible in the urban milieu that I fail to understand why Tapié wants to limit it in its structural circumstances to the peasant world. It is undeniable that, in the latter, "society is at that time more hierarchized and, to a certain extent, more stable. Men of the land are more resigned to their subjection, and even accept the religion of their overseer, and expect protection and aid from him; in their harsher misery they are inclined to rebelling with violent and blind outbursts that, on the other hand, are quickly put down by the regular army."[70] The conflictive situation was a normal ingredient of the baroque; it didn't have the occasional character that these quoted words seem to indicate, and the opposition was more manifest in the city than in the country — although attacks of violence were out of the ordinary in both places. This situation would be more strongly, more severely established in Catholic countries; but it also occurred among Protestants with an intensity sufficient to give a tint to the panorama of the epoch.

In my opinion, Tapié's well-meaning thesis cannot be sustained; according to it, the baroque would arise from the enjoyment and pleasure the rural peoples derived from seeing the luxury and wealth that the grandees displayed with such exuberant ostentation because, to a certain extent, in contemplating the wealth and luxury they could participate in them. Something else became manifest in the violent revolts alluded to by Tapié and in the bitter flavor accompanying so many baroque creations, which exemplified their protest circumstances. If we read H. Hauser's book on the epoch,[71] which deals with the ostentatious and apparently well-accepted French monarchy, we find that under Richelieu's government the traditional aspects in the structure of power and society were in many cases not only maintained by force but that the subjection imposed on the people and the harsh repression of their protests — here *the people* also comprehends the group of bourgeois — revealed the presence of conflict and the effort to contain it. "Punishing was always the reason of state," wrote G. de Bocángel;[72] but its raison d'être was never made a basic principle as it was in the seventeenth century.

Recent studies have elucidated a much more conflictive image of the sixteenth century, and even more so of the seventeenth, although the tendencies of opposition and the protests that exploded remained suffocated beneath the weight of absolutism and its social system. The opposition movements were more numerous and frequent, and the resulting manifestations of violence were harsher. One curious and significant observation is that Braudel, in the second edition of his magnum opus that is so often cited here, places greater stress on the multiplying and hardening social struggles.[73] After Villalar, the stances of opposition did not disappear in Castile, nor in other peninsular regions less directly affected by that political defeat of the cities; such opposition sometimes came to armed violence, but more frequently it remained at the level of public protest (as in the Cortes de Madrid of 1588-93, 1618, etc.); at other times it was limited to severe critiques of the policies carried out by the government of Madrid, whether in placards and other printed media or in conversations. In a letter to the archbishop of Toledo (16 February 1580), Rivadeneyra commented that "all the estates are bitter, displeased and perturbed vis-à-vis His Majesty...," so the king "is not as well loved as he used to be." He added that people didn't want to fight in the war against Portugal, "seeming to many that what would be won in Portugal is an increase for H. M. and his Royal Crown and not for the properties and honors of those who are to fight." [74] If here the concern was about Philip II, late in his reign, I have at another time indicated a text of Matías de Novoa in which Philip IV was the object of criticism. [75]

In confirmation of what others were already saying, Barrionuevo informs us that papers frequently appeared cursing the government and criticizing and even ridiculing the king. We are never told that they promoted an agonistic public reaction. They were placed on some church walls, in plazas, on corners, even on the palace. In all public places could be seen painted placards — "amusing," commented the author — that critically attacked the king and his ministers. [76] One painter and his helper were arrested for circulating lampoons or painted hand-bills — they were recognized as his because of the painting, just as in other cases they were recognized by the writing — that "were very acute, biting, and painted and colored all over." [77] Could this be seen as the origin of the current liking for critical posters? "In Galicia," Barrionuevo also tells us, "it is said that many different placards, like here, have been put in various places and with the same complaints, and if no remedy is found for them, they say that Portugal is not too far away." The protest in this case was tied to a serious threat of secessionism.

We have testimonies whose authors cite discussions carried on between persons they presumed to be more or less familiar with governmental matters and who were esteemed because of their studies, wealth, or hereditary rank; but other genuine disputes were limited, on occasion, to simple persons who were interested nonetheless in public matters. The lawyer Alonso de Cabrera informed Philip IV (20 June 1623) about the complaint of the widow of Hernando Vásquez, who, for having handed the previous king a memorial "regarding things touching on the government of these realms, at which Duke of Lerma took offense," was incarcerated "and in prison was violently killed within fifteen days" (the informant bade caution that the judgment not bring down the wrath of whoever was then cardinal). [78] Pellicer offered information about the imprisonment of one person who often visited and accompanied seigniors of the upper levels: "the cause was speaking ill of the king and government"; he added that the judicial authority intended to give the man the garrote, but he hoped that the outcome would be banishment. [79] Whatever suppositions can be made today, the Jesuits declared that the imprisonment of Quevedo owed to "something he said or wrote against the government."[80] Pellicer also said that Quevedo was arrested very quietly and that all of his furniture and papers were sequestered, for speaking ill of the monarchy, the government, or (according to others) for spying.[81] Some days later he reported that according to rumor Quevedo was beheaded although it was not confirmed.[82] Pellicer also related the case of a farmer who was suddenly put before the king to protest about the way the government was going.[83] The Jesuits, in one of their letters, also cited such an occurrence: Set before the king, the farmer shouted: "They are deceiving the king, this monarchy is nearing its end, and whoever fails to save it will burn in the flames of hell."[84] Nevertheless, Pellicer tells us that the king prohibited the authoritative teacher Agustín de Castro, S.J., from delving into certain political matters from the pulpit.[85] Similarly, Barrionuevo wrote about a preacher who, before the king, spoke crudely from the pulpit about the monarchy's misgovernment; on ending his diatribe he exclaimed that they could go ahead and arrest him and cut his head off if they wanted, but he was only doing his duty by speaking in such terms.[86] We don't know what happened with these people, but the newspapers contain items similar to this one by Pellicer: "Sentences were issued against those who take part in memorials for and against the seignior Count-Duke" — sentences of heavy fines and banishments.[87] We are acquainted with a curious case that tells us how far the possibility of conflict had extended: Almansa recounted a plot or strike within the palace itself, saying that "just yesterday there was no one to carry dinner up to the king, and the count ordered all the chamber assistants arrested." The *Noticias de Madrid (1621-1627)* tell us that the event it took place on 26 August 1624.[88]

These cases corroborate the impression we draw from literary sources. Ruiz Martín recorded the backlash of a violent political discussion that ended up in blows between the workers in a textile workshop in Segovia during 1625-30. Suárez de Figueroa rejected the "moral philosophy that, naked and hungry, reforms the world from a secure perch, reports on mores and discovers defects in everything."[89] Some writers of the epoch warned of the danger involved from the monarchy's immobilist and ultraconservative point of view; sometimes they revealed an outright sympathy for those who backed the established order, or they commented adversely on the whimsical recommendations put forth in such instances, or they merely alluded, as if it were an everyday occurrence, to the fact that ordinarily in the public promenade "there is talk of politics." Reflecting the social mores surrounding him, Céspedes has one of his characters say that all of us "young gentlemen and promenaders of the neighborhood [get together] in the doorways or on the benches in our parish, from where we customarily limit the power of the Turk, the activities of the Hungarian, the status of Italy, and voice our censures, governing the world with our opinions''; the same author tells about some travelers who happened to be going his way: ''we politicians began to govern the world, its states and forces, comparing some, and highly praising or reproving others."[90] This concern for politics, which in the sixteenth century had been inherent in the conversations and writings of high bureaucrats, scholars, gentlemen, people of the court, and prominent persons,[91] had become generalized, democratized, had come to be a common pastime. People spoke publicly and, considering themselves capable of doing so, critiqued the administration of those in control. Francisco Santos tells us that in the public plaza, anyone spoke up "to discuss the shortage of basic foodstuffs" so that each had his own chance at abusing authority.[92] A curious text, recently discovered in the Vienna state archives and composed of four folios, bears the following title: *Dialogue between four people coming at the same time in the boat from San Lucar de Barrameda to Seville, during the time when the coming of His Majesty to Andalusia had been disclosed*; it bears no date and may have originated sometime after 1620. The document reveals the degree to which political talk had achieved popular currency and the extent to which the Andalusians remained unaffected or openly opposed to royal politics in Philip IV's reign. Of the four interlocutors, one does nothing more than criticize the "afflictions" characterizing the king's situation; another considers it impossible "even to stave off the many turmoils and losses forced upon him [the king] by necessity"; referring to the Spanish, and without a doubt the allusion is to those who are governing, the criticism is put forth that "every day they make very significant errors diminishing the public weal and the Royal Treasury" because they don't know — or don't want to know — "how to allocate the revenue for what is owed." One person comments caustically: "No one does anything for the common weal, all seek nothing but their own interest; this war at home hurts us more than the enemies of the crown."[93] There is no doubt that baroque Seville did not await the king's arrival with fervor.

Public opinion thus assumed a new role, and a coincidence of opinions could form into a dangerous stream and could even inspire a threatening movement of protest.[94] These movements of opinion were important for the monarchy: R. O. Lindsay and J. Neu have collected and published seven thousand pamphlets that circulated in France between the mid-sixteenth and mid-seventeenth centuries, and the total figure of those that appeared is incomparably greater.[95] We don't have data from Spain, but in the study published by L. Rosales on the success of political satire during this epoch, a great abundance of materials comes to light.[96] In print and in voice, "everybody complains and everybody is right," commented Barrionuevo, who might be called a gazetteer of the opposition; he advised his readers that of "the many tragedies I am telling about here," so many incredible notices about governmental measures without purpose or reason, he is writing "about what is seen every day."[97] Yet more than thirty years before, did not Páez de Valenzuela write to Philip IV himself in similar terms? The kingdom was plagued by so many misfortunes "and every one of its members groans, the kingdom being formed as it is, of those who are solitary and individual, and these so weak and worn-out that they cannot hold up their heads."[98] Still, at this point we must cite an unusual item coming from Barrionuevo; while it is not verifiable, it at least reveals the extent to which adverse criticism surrounded the monarchy everywhere. On one occasion in Rome, the monetary necessities threatening the monarchy were made known in an effort to obtain economic concessions from the clergy; those negotiating on the part of the monarchy had to endure being given the answer that "the best option [the king] has is to change governments."[99] Given such universal grumbling and criticism, a Jesuit in one of his letters commented that, among the many vices and evils of the court, one must mention that "congregations are formed to grumble about the government." He accuses their members — in a shoddy and base attack, common in the political arena — of living an evil life: "in their house the gambler's industriousness performed miracles."[100] Another one of these letters requested banishment from the court for the "*noveleros*," the nonconforming and alarmist commentators of political events.[101] And Gayangos cited in his edition of such letters a passage from another *Noticias de Madrid*, an anonymous work that recounted about 1638 that some common people and some persons with titles had been effectively banished "because of gamblers who, getting together in the gaming houses, grumble about the present government and its most principal ministers, for no reason at all."[102] Years later, Barrionuevo reported that "the Royal Council has ordered the authorities to arrest all those speaking ill of the government."[103] Around that time the preachers had made their criticisms from the pulpit more severe, which put pressure on His Majesty. Some advised him to banish them, but the king answered that he didn't dare. In a particularly curious case, Barrionuevo tells on 24 April 1658 that "it is said that Fra Nicolás Bautista has been ordered not to preach so straightforwardly to the king nor to be rash about speaking truths in the pulpit; instead he will be granted an audience at any time so he may speak them in secret — anything else is to give rise to the people's feelings and promote sedition."[104] Sedition: here is the specter whose conjuring is already evoking fear in Europe. But bear in mind that, within the assumptions of baroque society, those words of straightforward and severe criticism were not, properly speaking, directed to the king but were a confrontation and dialogue with public opinion, whose presence could no longer be disguised. Villari observed that in Naples, which in the seventeenth century had a much greater geographical scope, the critiques frequently didn't allude to an occasional "bad government" but instead implied "that the political system is being placed in question."[105]

The attitude of the governments of the absolute monarchy, and their repressive politics, must necessarily be referred to this broad background of discussion, dissent, and possible public protest; until the mid-seventeenth century in Protestant countries and until much later in Catholic ones, this repression included religion as a subject where dissent would be dangerous. In Spain, because of the silence imposed centuries ago on manifestations of religious dissidence, it has gradually become customary for historians to assume the nonexistence of such dissidence, except for exceptions like the already distant Usoz, or some of our contemporaries such as M. Bataillon, E. Asensio, and A. Selke. Nonetheless, many instances such as the following existed: people unhappy and irritated about the failed wedding of the Prince of Wales and a Spanish infanta "tried to throw the blame on the theologians" — a curious indication that a good segment of public opinion was not in agreement with the religious policies being followed.[106] Interesting in this context is Jerónimo Gracián's work, known but scarcely studied in this aspect, with its violence against the "atheists."[107] In baroque Madrid, explosions of an exacerbated antireligious position — certainly explicable from a psychological point of view and interesting to study — were witnessed: explosions caused by the harsh and eye-glazing discipline that dominated everywhere and in even the most unexpected moments of one's life. The *Noticias de Madrid*, from 1621 to 1627, related instances of genuine psychological explosion against public acts of worship that were confirmed by Almansa's *Cartas*.[108] Another striking example of this problematic undercurrent has remained concealed beneath the crammed shelves of official historiography; the example is extremely revealing of the dissidence present in both the social and religious spheres and of its political significance in contributing to the formation of the absolutist system. We know that in 1633 the king delegated Fra Hortensio F. de Paravicino to preach the funeral oration for the infanta Margarita de Austria, who died as a nun in the Descalzas Reales. Paravicino, in vociferously expressing what he regarded as an indisputable fact, referred to the appearance of public posters against the Christian religion affixed "on the corners and doors of Madrid's buildings." About these, Paravicino made the following comment: if it is certain that someone has put up "a placard or lampoon of the type that the ill-contented commoners put up against the rulers in one century or another," it is an act that, since it contains the "danger of offering a vicious example," deserves and "demands punishment, blood, and to be exposed to the final degree"; it is fitting to ask ourselves what "posters against the Law," "placards against God," "lampoons against Christ" will not deserve, here in the Catholic court, before the eyes of the prince himself. And Paravicino added, speaking entirely in contemporary terms and referring to the public: "Recall when it seemed strange to hear me make so many accusations against atheism and look to see if you have abundant signs of it, if not the guilt itself."[109] Some sources of the epoch spoke of the "atheists of Madrid," and one of Tirso de Molina's characters, as if drawing upon the feeling of certain people, said: "There is no God to bother about me, / Everything else is delirium . . . / Living and dying, there is nothing more."[110]

In remarking the misfortunes and calamities that came upon the Spanish monarchy, Barrionuevo commented: "We are the ones who don't know how to live in the world," and he lamented "this great negligence of ours and the weakness of our existence."[111] It was an internal state of disarray, of discord. Its tensions affected the relation between nobles and commoners, rich and poor, old and new Christians, believers and nonbelievers, foreigners and subjects proper, men and women, central government and peripheral townships, and so on. Everywhere there were mutinies, riots, and rebellions of great violence: in the peninsular towns of Bilbao, Toledo,[112] and Navarre ("the noise of revolution in Navarre is so great . . ." commented the Jesuits);[113] and, again, in Toledo, in events that another Jesuit related by saying, "The other day there was a large riot in Toledo. A great number of common people, such as weavers and others, assembled together, saying they wanted to kill those governing the city because there was no bread to be found." It seems like a tableau from the nineteenth century: undoubtedly a crisis of necessities, but in these disturbances they were not burning the baker's house or attacking the farmer, or at least it was not limited to that — they wanted to kill the rulers.[114] Barrionuevo tells us that in Palma (Andalusia) the people revolted and killed the crown judge; in Málaga the mayor [*corregidor*] had to flee; in Palencia and León there were severe disturbances and upheavals; in Lorca and other places more or less in Andalusia, 1,500 men revolted and took up arms; in Rioja they killed two judges and many ministers;[115] in Belmonte the people mutinied against a company of soldiers.[116]

Taxes, necessities, and shortages were the resounding motives, just as they were in the first half of the nineteenth century. Thus can we understand a news item Pellicer offers sometime during those years: the king decreed the declaration and registration of all offensive and defensive arms possessed by natives and foreigners.[117] And outside of the peninsula, just as much was happening: in Brussels, where under the leadership of an apothecary a high magistrate met his death; in Naples, with the people "so unrestrained in their opposition to the nobility"; in Bari, where those hoarding bread were beheaded.[118] Yet the most serious insurrections were those originating not in conspiracies or assassinations [*golpes de mano*] but in popular disturbances that continued to increase and become more damaging.[119] The separatist uprisings (Naples, Catalonia, Flanders, Portugal) and similar conspiracies (Aragon, Andalusia, etc.) occurred in this way.[120] An odd character who exemplified his epoch, Alonso Enríquez de Guzmán referred at one point in his work to the upheavals that a certain Captain Machín caused in the kingdom of Valencia: ". . . the disturbances and mutinies and revolts in the kingdom of Valencia, where so many virgins were corrupted, and nuns violated and widows dishonored and altars robbed and many other hideous deeds," to which must be added what he also said about the revolts in Mallorca: "huge and enormous excesses were done, such as carving up boys in the butcher shop as if they were mutton, and others placing them on the ground as targets for shooting the crossbow and other similar things."[121]

Other tensions were not lacking: the inhuman consequences of the purity of blood statute, which has been studied by Sicroff;[122] xenophobic manifestations that were feared by the rulers;[123] the first nonconformist feminine voices.[124] Prostitution and gambling were also on the increase as an antisocial expression, and, participating in a protest they didn't even try to formulate, well-to-do and noble youths ran away to be swallowed up in a vagabond existence [*en medios de picaresca*], such as the tuna fishing of Cádiz,[125] or they appeared with long hair on the city streets, and were condemned by some critics and moralists.[126] Through Pellicer we learn of a student revolt that was a violent protest: "In the same way there has been in Salamanca a nasty student revolution against a judge who arrived from the Chancery and whom they tried to hang and burned the court papers."[127] Furthermore, through Barrionuevo we find out about a no less violent school incident that aids us in understanding the basis of irritation and discord taking place on the most diverse levels and in the most diverse environments. Children at schools where they learned reading and writing fought among themselves, and when the authorities came to arrest them, the boys armed themselves and let loose selectively on the agents. The authorities returned afterward to arrest the teacher, considering him the instigator, but the boys beat them back with slingshots.[128] Clearly the most violent tendencies were present in the opposition between nobles and common people, between rich and poor, which on the whole are parallel divisions to the point that in the Cortes, and in the pages of some writers, there was talk of the hate some groups had for others.[129]

To respond to this multiple and complex fervor of discord and protest (in circumstances where the means of opposition had become more subtle, the cities had grown demographically, and the population participating in the manifestations against oppression had increased to a threatening degree), the absolute monarchy saw itself faced with two necessities: strengthen the physical means of repression and look for means to penetrate the consciousnesses and achieve psychological control — means that, favoring the process of integration and combating dissent and violence, would assure its superiority over the whole. One manifestation of baroque culture was, without a doubt, the military system of citadels well furnished with artillery, capable of putting down an uprising within urban centers (the diffusion of the use of the citadel is a baroque achievement); yet another was this entire complex of social, artistic, and ideological expedients that were cultivated specifically to maintain authority psychologically over the wills of those who might, as it was feared, be led to take up an opposing position. The baroque monarchy, with its structured group of seigniors, bureaucrats, and soldiers, and with its group — more informal but not less efficient — of poets, playwrights, and painters, put into play both possibilities.

It practiced them both even in extreme cases when it seemed that all social bonds had broken down; nevertheless, beneath the apparent contradictions, certain factors remained that could be played in favor of integration and could even serve to impose it, morally or physically, on the others.

From this point of view, for example, one can broach the very baroque theme of banditry. This extreme form of antisocial protest and deviant conduct grew at an alarming rate in the seventeenth-century crisis, and it provided baroque theater (Lope, Mira de Amescua, Vélez de Guevara, Calderón, etc.) with abundant subjects. If the adverse economic conditions at the end of the sixteenth century, which were accentuated in the following century, brought to all of Europe an alarming increase in misery, vagabondage, and banditry, as Braudel has insistently maintained,[130] such consequences were well marked in the Spain of Philip III and Philip IV, giving rise to what has been called the banditry of the baroque, important in Catalonia and in other regions.[131] At the end of the sixteenth century, when one begins to speak of the baroque one must not forget those groups of picaros, workhands, and beggars who inundated the cities, nor those bands of vagabonds, false pilgrims, and bandits who wandered along the paths of Europe. Let us not forget to mention the role that the theater gave to female banditry (Lope, Mira de Amescua, Vélez de Guevara). Those masses of the needy, deviant and full of animosity, emerged from the wars, epidemics, oppression by the powerful, and from the unemployment made obligatory by the economic crisis. In the seventeenth century they were found everywhere: France, Germany, and Flanders are familiar with them. Villari speaks of instances of priest banditry so widespread that the Church was obliged to leave priests in the hands of secular jurisdiction.[132] In Spain we have evidence of bandits going through Valladolid, Valencia, Murcia, and La Mancha.[133] Barrionuevo assures us that in Old Castile "all paths are full of thieves, particularly on the way to Andalusia," with groups of men on horseback forming gangs of thirty of forty individuals. One friar who had a falling out with his superiors escaped to Sierra Morena and headed a troop of bandits (this was a good plot for one of Mira de Amescua's comedies).[134]

Banditry constituted a shadowy area in seventeenth-century culture that must not be overlooked; the baroque's cultural techniques themselves, as we shall see, were designed for use in relationship to it. Braudel, who was perhaps the first to highlight the phenomenon of banditry in the history of the sixteenth and seventeenth centuries, related it with forms of social marginalization endemic to the Mediterranean. Thus might one explain the great upsurge in Catalan banditry; P. Vilar assigned it prenationalist and romantic traits, which seem to us a little premature. Reglà, dealing with the same theme, considers that "banditry, as a social phenomenon aggravated by the economic crisis and very frequently related with political events in extenso, constitutes an extremely important factor in baroque Catalonia and has visible effects on the internal relations of the Hispanic monarchy, and even on the international relations of the European West."[135] Reglà later insisted on the phenomenon's ideological, political, social, economic, and geographic causes,[136] allowing us to comprehend its connection with the general historical circumstances of the epoch.[137]

I do not intend to assert that baroque culture emerged to integrate bandits or extreme cases of deviation. Nevertheless, there was no lack of attempts, undoubtedly calculated to show the system's broad validity by carrying it to marginal cases. An entire series of dramatic works demonstrated how the integrating force of social values operated even upon the bandit — social values such as those maintained by baroque culture through its religious aspects, as in *La devoción de la Cruz* (Calderón), monarchical aspects, as in *La serrana de la Vera* (Vélez de Guevara), or nobiliary aspects (which to a certain extent were fused with the others) such as those we are led to see in *El catalán Serralonga*, which Coello, Rojas and Vélez de Guevara wrote in collaboration. In this drama, the authors make a famous character into a noble and present him as bound to traditional social morality; along with the ossified nobiliary principle of "I am who I am" or the honor of the sword,[138] he holds to the irresistible *timor Domini* fomented by the Catholic church (no more than by Protestantism), with respect for the royal charisma and its representatives. The bandit Serralonga, with his gang, catches sight of people arriving on the path. They are transporting money to the king and, upon realizing who they are, he orders his second in command to let them pass, ". . . que al nombre del Rey / Que el Sol tocar no se atreve / Este respeto se debe / Por natural común ley" [By universal law of nature, this respect is owed to the name of the king, whom the sun does not dare touch].[139] In this fashion, not even the extreme (i.e., criminal) "deviation" of the bandit escapes integration into baroque society, fulfilling in a certain way his role in it; he does not break down the values on which society is based, but rather recognizes them as fully prevailing. He becomes a typical manifestation of the relation between seigniors and bandits that characterizes traditional society, inasmuch as we consider it an inconsistent fantasy to interpret it as anticipatory of romantic nationalism.

The proceedings of the Cortes acquaint us (although in this respect they have not been adequately studied) with the names of lawyers who, during the years when the baroque was being forged, protested severely against the politics of the government. In addition, Pedro de Valencia wrote to the royal confessor about the "athropophagy" that the king and those who had power subjected the towns to, and he accused the preceding confessor of concealing an analogous writing that he had previously submitted.[140] Sancho de Moncada informs us of the existence of a current of opinion that was complaining around the same time about the prohibitive measures suffocating the Spanish. Martínez de Mata organized groups of beggars to pass wailing through the streets — which the Inquisition prohibited — and cited the criticism that Damián de Olivares, the Toledo merchants, and other businessmen directed toward the socioeconomic policy followed by the government.[141] All these critical observations show that Spaniards were kept at the margin of active participation in determining the lines of the country's policy; by comparison, in England the butcher's opinions were already being consulted in deciding a question regarding the provisioning of meats.[142]

Since the end of the sixteenth century, the Spanish lamented the prohibitions, persecutions, and accusations that towns had to undergo. Shortly after beginning his reign, Philip IV drew up — or had drawn up — a program of government (a very significant document because of the modernity of its formulation); on 28 October 1622, he sent it as a royal letter or message to those cities having a vote in the Cortes. In it, he referred, with outright indignation at such wretched events, to the fact that some had put together, without any basis or authority, registry books of lineages and families (which were called "green books") and that someone need merely make reference to what others had seen in those pages to start up disputes, lawsuits, or calumies. The king prohibited the making of such registers and announced that penalties would be imposed on violators — something that was never put into practice, since the inquisitorial denunciations were carried on separately.[143]

People — including writers — also lamented the privileges of the powerful and the difficulties, which extended even to starvation, of those not among the elite; the state of exploitation and submission in which the monarchy's subjects were held, although they were supporting a crushing burden; the inequality that the plague made manifest in its most pathetic forms; and the ills of war and unruliness of the undisciplined troops. This latter complaint brings up an interesting issue. As we have seen in the case of France, Spanish society was rigorously based on the estatist principle whereby the nobles monopolize military action; but when war broke out the nobles not only refused to answer the king's summons[144] but in fact cast this burden upon those who were already suffering so successively from the levying of taxes (since these latter, in compensation, were held to be officially exempt from military service). The upshot was that the hardening of the structure of privileges in the baroque freed the nobility even of practically their sole obligation, which was military service; in violation of the very bases of the traditional system, it was cast on the shoulders of those responsible for bearing the brunt of fiscal contribution. When the king summoned the nobles to accompany him on a maneuver against insurgents, the people recognized that the nobles were ill-disposed to go to war, and there were comments — as one Jesuit alluded in a private letter[145] — that the king would soon resign himself to receiving two or three hundred escudos from each one. From a similar source we know that the nobles excused themselves from entering into battle, and since they availed themselves of the excuse that they were without the necessary funds to finance the expedition's expenses, the king ordered them to abandon the court and go to their rural lands — there they could cut back their expenses and save money, so that the next time they would find themselves with the funds to fulfill their obligations.[146] These threats were not carried out, and the nobility slipped out from under its military duties. This understandably produced a bitter protest, which Gutiérrez de los Ríos attested to in the name of the anonymous people: "The poor should not go to war alone, as has been done until now; the obligation of the rich to go to war is greater."[147]

The objection was not an isolated instance, which emphasizes its currency in the public opinion of the epoch. The novelist María de Zayas commented that to fight in the war in earlier times "it was not necessary to take men by force or in chains, as it is now, to the unhappiness and misfortune of our Catholic King."[148] Barrionuevo mentioned that the drafting of people was decreed, "but there is no man to be seen by the squint of one's eye"; given the country's situation and the behavior of the upper groups, there is no money, there are no people, "nor is anyone going to serve by virtue of love or one's own willpower, but only by means of force which accomplishes nothing." On receiving the news that some captains had left Madrid to raise people, he commented: "I don't know where they are; few are left and those are very cowed."[149] A political and economic writer, with a blatantly critical character, showed his indignation for the fact that while the nobles were the ones obligated to bear arms, "against all the laws of these kingdoms, they constantly use force to carry the poor day laborers to the armies." That was written by Álvarez Ossorio,[150] and his words make it understood that it was not a question of widespread aversion to war (a feeling that was far from being the case in the seventeenth century) but the forced imposition on the people at large — an imposition the absolute monarchy seized as part and parcel of a system of measures to favor the seigniors[151] (a system that, on this point and others, Cánovas del Castillo would still staunchly defend).

The subject of revolts and sedition became a necessary element in the literature of the first half of the seventeenth century; an entire technique of repression was developed, remotely echoing Machiavelli, but having nothing to do with Machiavellianism. Now it was not a question of the "prince" as an individual dominator but of a subversive attitude casting its shadow over the entire state: "Those who are seditious," Luis de Mur wrote, "transgress against those who deserve their respect and against the state, upsetting its tranquility and disrupting the axes of stability."[152] Therefore, Saavedra Fajardo, who did not feel to content with Spanish policy and who did not hesitate in speaking out for popular participation (which in one passage he called "freedom"), was opposed to formulating this as the establishment of a republican government. The Tacitists — very representative of the baroque as writers of political literature — repeated the references to problems of this type to the extent that someone in the epoch accused tacitism of attracting those who sought "to plan attacks and uprisings against their princes."[153] And in the seventeenth-century crisis there was no lack of individuals in Spain who, confronted with the threatening state of affairs emerging at a moment's notice, demanded a more severe repression (something not unknown to us today): many presumably intelligent individuals said that to remedy the situation there would have to be harsh punishments. In a report denouncing Martínez de Mata, an irascible and brutal "twenty-four" of Seville made a statement that well reveals the state of mind of a certain irresolutely conservative social sector that was caught in the middle of the epoch's restlessness. This person, Martín de Ulloa, referred to the agitations promoted by M. de Mata, some of his friends and followers, and other individuals, thereby putting the cities "in danger of turmoils." Ulloa added: "This is a word that when I hear it pronounced in public by someone who is impudent, although it may be in passing or dealing with events of another order, I would like to pull out his tongue and string him up."[154] Many let themselves be carried away with the passion and necessities or the fears they are experiencing. But then there were also comments (as there are today) like: "When a remedy is requested of everyone, no one has to be punished."[155]

Faced with such a serious, threatening situation (remember that at the height of the baroque the first beheading of a king took place in England, and a minister was beheaded in Spain),[156] the monarchy and its instruments of physical repression responded by encouraging the means of social integration, putting into play a series of technical resources designed to win over adherents, thereby constituting baroque culture. I emphasize what I have advanced above, because for me this is the key to the question.

Two objections have been made to the points I have just outlined. First, the role here given to dissent against the sociopolitical regime of absolutism has been contested; on the contrary, it has been argued that the people accepted with their own free will the values of the traditional system of integration, as would be proven by the small number of repressive agents at the absolute monarch's disposal. This observation turns out to be completely indefensible: even without making recourse to the strategic location of "citadels" capable of dominating a city militarily,[157] to exceptional intervention by the royal armies (mentioned by Tapié in the text previously cited), there was frequent repressive intervention by seignorial troops (which still existed in the seventeenth century) allied with the king. From accounts of the epoch, we know that in every sort of town of a certain level, whenever the people showed the least activity, the nobles and caballeros with their retinues rushed into the street to subdue them. The seigniors, said Castillo de Bobadilla, "keep things within their proper boundaries [policía], in proper order and harmony."[158] In addition, absolutism in Spain relied on a means for the exercise of power to find its way into consciousness that closely approximated totalitarianism. I am alluding to the activity of the Inquisition, whose courts punished the attacks and even the simple improprieties against the established social system. This is how Pellicer can tell us that the Inquisition ordered the confiscation of the writing against the Count-Duke entitled *Nican-*

dro[159] and also sequestered and ordered the expurgation of a sentence hostile to the whole of Spanish nobility from Ferrer de Valdecebro's *Gobierno General, moral y político hallado en las aves más generosas y nobles.*[160]

These facets of absolutism can be related to a personal and curious observation by Augustín de Rojas: in praising Seville, he confessed that two things about it astonished him above all others, one of which was the jail, "with such an infinity of prisoners there for such strange crimes."[161] Some years before, Cristóbal de Chaves, a lawyer from Seville, also marveled at the size of this jail, in which the prisoners "were generally more than eighteen hundred in number, not counting those in the jails of Audiencia, Hermandad, Arzobispal and Contratación."[162] Similar comments were made about Madrid, leading one to think that it was a phenomenon linked to large cities with a crowded population and corroborating the extensive urban character we have attributed to the baroque. Moreover, it necessarily manifested an aspect of seventeenth-century Spanish society under the baroque monarchy. In Madrid, Barrionuevo related, they arrested so many thieves that "they don't fit into the jails standing up, and one person cannot be told from another; [so many thieves] that necessity finds no other occupation on hand." That is already revealing of the social and economic circumstances of the Spain of the Hapsburgs; but there is more. "The women's prison is so crammed full that they no longer fit standing up" filled with women arrested for leading a life of ill repute and various other things (let us not fail to stress the undifferentiated variety that was mentioned). This had been the case for some time. Barrionuevo's references were from the years 1654 and 1656, but already in a document of (approximately) 1621 the Sala de Alcaldes de Casa y Corte had said to Philip IV: "the Court jail is very closed in and there is often some contagious disease, because of the many people and the little interest in cleaning; and the Council has purchased the houses next to the jail which consist of the entire block, and the building of a jail has been ordered; the plans are done, and because of a lack of money it is not being built."[163] But Barrionuevo informs us (just as he completed his reference to the origin of those who would populate such an inhospitable place by force) that in Madrid, on the Calle de las Premonstratenses or Calle del Almirante, at the entrance to the little plaza of Santo Domingo, "they are purposefully constructing a jail very quickly, one able to hold as many people as daily fall into the rat trap"[164] (he refers specifically to the Inquisition). Perhaps the pressures deriving from the abundant penitentiary population in Spanish society under the Austrians (and the damaging problem it could cause in anyone susceptible to them) prompted the early appearance in Spain of a book describing itself as about "the matter of the jail," that is, on its moral and material problems. The lawyer Tomás Cerdán de Tallada effectively dealt with these problems in a work entitled *Visita de la cárcel*, written before these last documents I have cited; therefore, it was written in the initial years when the situation of the epoch we are studying was already being articulated in one of its more somber aspects.[165]

The second objection is directed against that interpretation that, like ours, refers the culture characteristic of the seventeenth-century regimes, what we call the baroque, to the situation of those very regimes that made it necessary for them to rely on resources that would create a mental state favorable to the prevailing system. In this view, the baroque appeared in connection with the interests of the state and of its prince, in support of the social organization culminating in the sovereign. In contradiction to this thesis, it has been insisted that the baroque was a provincial art that was more or less spontaneous, without organization, and produced in places removed from the capital of the state — from Paris, in this case, thereby running counter to its rationalist and centralizing policy.[166] We shall soon discuss the presence or absence of rationalism in the baroque or in the absolute monarchy; but let us say right now that speaking of centralism is completely inappropriate, at least until the last years of the seventeenth century, when the baroque had already ended: consequently, it would scarcely be possible to invoke the baroque as opposed to centralization. This same monarchy, however, which was far from exhibiting the characteristics of rationalization and centralization attributed to it — characteristics that, to the extent that they were possessed, were not opposed to being used in a baroque sense in any case — assembled this great campaign of guidance and integration in which baroque artists, politicians, and writers collaborated. Undoubtedly there existed a relationship between the baroque and social crisis. We are faced — not only in Spain, but in all of Europe — with an epoch that, in all spheres of collective life, saw itself dragged along by irrational forces, by appeals to violence, the multiplying of crimes, moral laxity, and hallucinating forms of devotion. All these aspects resulted from the situation of pathos wherein the underlying social crisis was exteriorized and expressed in manifestations of the epoch's general mentality.

The social crisis and (with some auspicious intervals) the economic crisis (that is, a complex of social agitations encompassing the period from before 1590 to after 1660, approximately) helped to create the psychological climate from which the baroque emerged and nourished itself, inspiring its development into the most varied areas of culture.[167]

II: The Social Characteristics of Baroque Culture

Chapter 2
A Guided Culture

Although the conditions present in Europe in all areas of peoples' lives, from politics to economics, art or religion, must be related to the intensely conflictive nature of the epoch's social situation, they gave rise to a culture specific to the epoch that we have been calling baroque culture. We shall see that it offers us the basic lines of a view of society and of the human being that orient the behavior of individuals living in it (if not in each case, at least with a high number of people). But, given the image of society and of human existence that the consciousnesses of a specific time hold to be valid, and the mode of putting it into practice for the manipulation, guidance, and governing of groups and individuals, it is inevitable that the means utilized — whether created anew or taken from tradition and reelaborated — have to be adjusted to the delimiting circumstances and to the intended objectives of having a shaping effect on human beings. These means differ from one historical situation to another; those used in the period we are here studying constitute the complex of baroque culture.

Confronting the baroque today, we can to a certain degree see it as something similar to what some books of sociology call *behaviorism*: seeking to bring together "that which the individual himself experiences, and which can only be stated in terms of his experiences, with the experience which belongs to everyone." According to that, in studying baroque culture we do not expect to obtain results of the type premeditated by the scientist when, for example, he or she applies electrical shocks to the nerves of a frog. It is not a question of finding reactions to stimuli, but rather of preparing responses to questions that are posed. Neither is it a matter of wanting to make manifest individual consciousnesses, but of discovering the responsive behaviors that, in principle, individuals hold in common. This assumes then a social psychology, taking its point of departure from the prior consideration that an individual's behavior can be known and guided inasmuch as the individual forms part of a group.[1]

In this way, then, and within the indicated limits, the culture of the baroque is an instrument to achieve effects (i.e., the product of a conception such as we have just articulated) whose object is to act upon human beings. Human beings are the object of a determinate conception (to which the culture must be conditioned) that is designed to ensure that they behave, among themselves and with respect to the society of which they are a part and the power that controls it, in such a manner that the societies' capacity for self-preservation is maintained and enhanced according to the way they appear structured under the political primacies in force at the moment. In sum, the baroque is nothing but a complex of cultural media [*medios*] of a very diverse sort that are assembled and articulated to work adequately with human beings, such as they and their groups are understood in the epoch whose limits we marked off, so as to succeed practically in directing them and keeping them integrated in the social system.

In the previous chapter I said that individuals felt capable of intervening in the mechanism of the economy and of altering it. As a consequence, individuals — or at least certain more evolved groups — addressed the rulers, requesting changes distinct from what had been supported in the past and different benefits. This observation of Rostow[2] is valid in the area of policy, which provoked so much criticism. The sixteenth century was a utopian epoch par excellence. But afterward, in the seventeenth century, although it diminished its drive toward reform and novelty, the epoch nonetheless didn't lose its confidence in the transforming force of human activity. By means of that confidence the seventeenth century sought to keep the transforming force in hand, to study and perfect it, and to forestall its disruptive (today we would say *revolutionary*) use. Instead of taking a more conservative attitude, it accentuated (if possible) the desire to guide the multiple aspects of human coexistence: a strongly guided economy in the service of an imperialism aspiring to glory; a literature at bottom committed to upholding order and authority, although at times it was not in agreement with both; a science, perhaps dangerous, but contained in the hands of prudent scholars; a religion rich in heterogeneous types of believers, assembled in harmony by the Church that had again come to dominate the jumble of its multitudes who have been seduced and nourished with novelties and foods of a rare and provocative taste.[3] After the broad experience with which the Renaissance ended, these and other aspects will constitute the diverse field of the guided control [*dirigismo*] of human beings.

In effect, what we have just seen — the program of acting upon human beings collectively — closely corresponds to what at the time was called *politics*. Politics occupied a big place in seventeenth-century culture. To a certain extent, what the theologian or the artist did corresponded to a political proposal, strategically if not in terms of its content. Individual conduct itself was considered subject to the categories of political conduct, as was attested to, for example, by applying concepts like "reason of state" or "statist" to private life.[4] Acquaintance with the stratagems used by and against the individual constituted a theme necessarily attracting the attention of everyone to the extent that they were concerned about guiding an individual in some way and overcoming the individual's reserve vis-à-vis others — for the individual was well versed and cautious. Salas Barbadillo defined the attitude of those who proceeded in that way: "Curious spies of human hearts and minds . . . are wandering students, their university is all the world, their bookstore so abundant that for them any man is a book, every action a chapter, the least movement of their face a voluminous discourse."[5]

To channel and unify the individuals' modes of behavior, one must penetrate the internal mechanism of their motivations [*los resortes que los mueven*]. While they were architects of baroque literature, the theoreticians of conceptism were not properly moral philosophers but rather moral preceptists who sought to apply their thought to mores and, furthermore, to psychological techniques of morality designed to shape behavior. This being the case, however superficial their writings, underneath there was constant preoccupation with a "program."[6] Thus Racine, in commenting on some passages from Aristotle's *Poetics*, put particular emphasis on the importance of the study of mores: "Mores, or character, are found in all sorts of circumstances";[7] but they are different and mask their face to someone who doesn't know how to overcome their secrets.

Therefore one has to do whatever possible to come into the knowledge of this dynamic and aggressive human being. One must find out what the human being is in order to make use of the most adequate expedients [*resortes*] against him or her. If in the seventeenth century, an epoch when modern science was in its first phase of definitive constitution, all knowledge had the objective of dominating the zone of reality to which it referred, this applied no less rigorously to the science of the human being. If, in general, with the words of F. Bacon, "scientia est potentia"; if, in a phrase from Descartes, knowing is the attempt to become "masters and possessors of nature," let us say that with knowledge of the human being one is trying to enter into possession of history and society. To a certain extent, a well-known formulation found in M. Weber's famous study about religion and capitalism underscores the pragmatic character of the baroque, which could be compared to what Weber called "the utilitarian adaptation to the world, the work of Jesuit probabilism" (on the other hand, it would remain very far from the ethical and religious spirit of capitalism).[8] Obviously neither of the two things was identical, nor could either simply be referred to attitudes of scientific rationalism. But they were related in time, in the historical situation that was manifest in the interest they held in common: to become acquainted with the object one was trying to manipulate and in this way to reach, technically, the goals one pragmatically expected to attain. Although writing at a time immediately beyond the period we have marked off, La Bruyère wrote in his chapter "De l'homme" as if he were giving a summary of baroque experience on this subject, so characteristic of the epoch's spirit: "Know exactly what you can expect from men in general and from each one in particular, and then plunge into the commerce of the world."[9]

That knowledge of the human being, directed toward what we are calling operative ends, had to be situated on two levels that are subsequent to those indicated by La Bruyère. First, one had to begin with knowledge of oneself, an affirmation that seemed to correspond to a traditional Socratism (such as was present in medieval Christianity)[10] but that now acquired an efficient and tactical character, according to which one did not go in search of an ultimate truth but rather of tactical rules permitting whoever obtained them to adapt to the circumstances of reality in which he or she moved. Because one might be interested in remaking oneself, and because it was impossible to overlook the urgent need to make oneself in order to attain better results in one's life, knowledge of the human being began with a knowledge of oneself,[11] as the gateway to knowing everyone else — to start "to know, knowing oneself," said Gracián.[12] Knowing oneself to become one's own master, which led to domination of the surrounding world: Calderón affirmed that this was the greatest manifestation of power (*Darlo todo y no dar nada*), and that was said in a positive sense. And he added (*La gran Cenobia*): "A small world am I, and in this I establish / that in being lord of myself, I am of the world." In *Cinna*, a line from Corneille articulates this same correlation: "I am master of myself as of the universe."

Access to the second level takes us to the knowledge of other human beings, coming to a practical knowledge about the internal motivations [*resortes*] of others' behavior; in whatever situation we might find ourselves we can predict their conduct, adjust accordingly our handling of the data, and secure the results we are pursuing. Knowing oneself and knowing others is dynamically knowing the possibilities of conduct in their tactical unfolding. "Knowing how to live is today the true knowing," counseled Gracián, which is equal to postulating knowledge not as contemplation of a substantial being (that is, not as the ultimate knowing of the essential form of being or of a thing) but rather as a practical knowing, valid inasmuch as a living subject makes use of it. For Gracián and baroque individuals in general, to live was living on guard among everyone else, which leads us to understand that this baroque and Gracianesque "knowing" boiled down to a maneuvering development adapted to existence: "Method is essential for knowing and for being able to live."[13] Because of this, Gracián personifies the individual possessing a "negotiating" type of knowledge, a subject with a technologized behavior who is the representative par excellence of the species of "the human being who knows how to operate."[14]

If the apparently traditional theme of Socratism underwent a profound alteration, the primitive Pauline sense in which Erasmus and Erasmists spoke of the "interior human being" was also transformed into something else: the mechanical aspect of human psychology that first appeared with scientific trappings in Huarte de San Juan became common currency among baroque writers. In their pages they included outright declarations — we have no reason to consider them insincere — of spiritualism, while nonetheless their reflections of a practical nature on the mode of human behavior were imbued with a forthright mechanicism.

This concern for knowledge, domination, and manipulation of human conduct led to an identification between them and mores, between behavior and morality. That implies a pragmatism that in the end turns into a greater or lesser (but only superficial) mechanization of the mode of human behavior. This, in turn, becomes the key problem of baroque mentality. Poetry's moral end, as articulated by the writers of the epoch, became a practical system, according to Carballo, to "reform, emend and correct human mores."[15] "These moderns have to keep being persuaded that to imitate the ancients they should fill their writings with moral sententiae, bringing into view that praiseworthy attempt to teach the art of living wisely."[16] But it is beyond all doubt that these moderns were aware of such a doctrine and practiced it to the point of satiation, not only in drama, poetry, and the novel, not only in every kind of writing, but also in the entire wide range of art; they were bent on adapting morality to the situation and on utilizing all the possibilities of morality to its benefit. Therefore F. Pacheco could think that most praiseworthy in a painter were the "ingenious moralities" giving color to his work.[17] Painting, poetry, the novel, and, above all, drama lent all their resources to such an end. Whatever may have been the evolution of Spanish seventeenth-century comedy — even if it be divided into five phases, according to Ch. V. Aubrun's proposal (a periodization in turn criticized by N. Salomon) — it is certain that all phases coincided, as even Aubrun has maintained, in presenting themselves as "adaptations of ethics to the social occasion."[18] In K. Borinski's already classic work, the discussion of Gracián is based on presenting him as a preceptist of behavior who was concerned with establishing a behavior model for the elite.[19] But Gracián was not writing a "mirror" where the individual of an established social group was to be reflected, that is, the courtier; rather, he inverted this position, supposing that acceptance of his model was what allowed someone to turn into the new type of the elite. That assumed, apart from a reduction to a mode of democratization of the type, its reduction to a pragmatic pattern. Frequently Gracián gave the pure and simple name of "human being" to the exemplary person formed with the knowledge he provided. "Human existence doesn't exist without the human being who knows"[20] — that is, whoever knows the maxims Gracián formulates for him. Every baroque writer put behavior as the central problem and, to attract others to the system of relations held to be fundamental for society, proclaimed that in following such a system one attained the "outcome" or success and happiness. "Our happiness depends somewhat on fortune, and still more on our behavior," maintained Méré.[21] On the other hand, just as baroque writers believed that their scrutinizing provided the means of facing and overcoming or avoiding fate, the accomplishment that we can call *human life* depends most effectively on behavior.

Baroque culture was a pragmatism with a more or less inductive base and regulated by prudence. "Everything falls under human prudence," wrote Liñán;[22] Calderón recommended: "Have prudence, Cenobia, for that is the world" (*La Gran Cenobia*). And Suárez de Figueroa made prudence equal to reason, practically the sum of virtues.[23] This exaltation of prudence as presiding over human works was found not only in moralists like Gracián or in politicians like Saavedra Fajardo, Lancina, and many others,[24] but even in preceptists of art like, among others, Jusepe Martínez,[25] a writer on painting. Italian moralists and politicians present the same aspect — Strada, Zuccolo, Settala, Accetto, Malvezzi, and others.[26] Of course, prudence was also a central concept in seventeenth-century French writers and philosophers; the fullest pragmatic formulation is found in La Rochefoucauld, in his Maxim 182: "Vices enter into the makeup of virtues, just as poisons in the makeup of medicines. Prudence unites thems, tempers them, and makes use of them against the ills of life."[27]

The predominant role of prudence corresponded to the common point of view of people in the baroque. This was probably what gave the baroque the appearance that, beneath its sometimes hallucinating excesses and exaggerations, it was a culture whose disorder somehow made sense, was regulated and under control. One could even maintain that not only in the most cultivated sectors, but also on the lowest levels of cultural formation, the baroque represented a discipline and organization greater than in preceding periods. Let us recall the observation made by Tapié that with the baroque one observes a more conscious attitude, precisely in the sphere of religious life: if against the calamities suffered in the countryside (plagues, widespread disease, droughts, floods, etc.) recourse was made to the intercession of sanctified persons, the saints represented in the Church's statues or painted altarpieces (just as at other times recourse was still made to the remedies of sorcery), there is no doubt that the worship of agrarian saints and thaumaturges was characterized more by reason than the obscure practices carried out by a sorcerer.[28]

Although it may not often be visible beneath the baroque's outrageous manifestations, the appeal to prudence obviously brought about an ordering that, nonetheless, could not be formulated by a mathematical reasoning, even if it was a matter of a studied and tactical adequation of means to ends.

This explains the tactical prudentialism that predominated in baroque individuals: the substitution of a criterion of morality by another moralistic one that was brought to bear at every step. That presupposed at least a relative mechanization in the use of the human being's internal motivations [*resortes*], which occurred even in the realm of religion, as was manifest in G. Fessard's study of Loyola's

Spiritual Exercises.[29] It was a question of arriving at a method with a high degree of operative rationalization (Gracián's "method for knowing how and being able to live"), which implied admitting that human behavior can be blind or can be inspired in nonrational values, but it had a structure with an internal order whose rules could be formulated by the reason of whoever contemplated it. In an interesting and little-known study, Joaquín Costa said that Gracián's maxims seemed to be written for a society of artificial individuals:[30] in effect, they articulated modes of conduct for individuals considered as "artifices," according to the way they were seen from the baroque perspective of the technique of prudence. Let us not forget that the Scholastics debated whether prudence was an "art," that is, a technique, or a "virtue." The Machiavellians and the Tacitists accentuated this first aspect even more. And we cannot ignore the strong impression that both camps had on the baroque epoch. The virtue of doing something good was of less interest than the art of doing something well.

We are speaking of the baroque and rationalism because whoever was planning how to act effectively upon human beings began by thinking that they represented a blind force, but also that whoever knew that force would be able to channel it rationally — just as the impetuous flow of a river is tamed by the canal bed that is mathematically calculated by the engineer.[31] The Solomonic column was turned into geometry, as the illustrations of the epoch's architectural books reveal; they were more rigorously illustrated than ever before. Fessard tried to construct the geometric schema of the Ignatian *Exercises.*[32] For some time it has been said that, in the background of the world Calderón presented to us, there lay a legal system whose schema was similar to that of science.[33] Treatises on fencing were a typical baroque product; they presented the study of this art geometrically, and those who cultivated it during the epoch were called *anglers* to distinguish them from those who practiced the traditional method.[34]

It is absurd to deny the baroque a bourgeois character simply because it failed to exhibit a complete process of rationalization. "The rise of the bourgeoisie will have a rational character favoring severe rules that are inspired in ancient models: one will recognize this as incompatible with the fantasies and excesses of the baroque," maintained Tapié.[35] But even leaving aside what of ancient inspiration was rigorously practiced in the baroque, and, at the same time, what there was of orgiastic excess in the ancients (which the modern bourgeois have often sought out), the bourgeois were passionately given over to a taste for grand ceremonies, an extrarational admiration for the sublime, and an attraction toward chance that disrupted all rational order. This is one of the errors deriving from a historiography based on the method of "ideal types": to end up affirming, as did Mannheim, that the nature of the bourgeoisie's historical activity is that "it doesn't recognize limits to the process of rationalization."[36] This could not even be said of the eighteenth-century bourgeois who cried on hearing Haydn, much less of those of the seventeenth century, when the force of extrarational, magical elements continued to be great on their minds (L. Febvre convincingly showed this some time ago). In producing effects [*operar*], the seventeenth-century bourgeois utilized fragments of rationalized processes; they made use of instruments with a high degree of rationalization that were linked to others of a radically opposing nature.

Accustomed to our rational view, we easily believe that the new scientific discoveries contributed to discrediting the notions in the Bible, but that wasn't the case.

> Ever since 1618 at least there had been talk of the dissolution of society,
> or of the world; and the undefined sense of gloom of which we are constantly
> aware in those years was justified sometimes by new interpretations of
> Scripture, sometimes by new phenomena in the skies. With the discovery
> of new stars, and particularly with the new comet of 1618, science seemed
> to support the prophets of disaster. . . . It is an interesting but undeniable
> fact that the most advanced scientists of the early sixteenth century included
> also the most learned and literal students of biblical mathematics; and in
> their hands science and religion converged to pinpoint, between 1640 and
> 1660, the dissolution of society, the end of the world.[37]

Of course we will never come to see a mathematization of the relations of human existence alongside the technification acquired by morality, politics and economy, the theater, poetry, and art in the baroque. We don't intend to consider as part of the baroque the *Ethics* of Spinoza, "secundum ordinem geometricum demostrata," nor W. Petty's *Political Arithmetick*, for no other reason than the fact that these works went far beyond the conceptual schemas of the baroque. Nevertheless, within this framework Álvarez Ossorio could write: "Mathematics comprehends all sciences: it should be taught with particular care in all the universities and principal places so it might serve to defend the kingdoms and enrich them with all kinds of works and arts."[38] In view of this and similar statements in the seventeenth century, one might say that the mind of the epoch had come to believe in the ultimate mathematic structure of human work. But let us not overemphasize it. It is a question of simple conjectures.

Nevertheless, contrary to our reducing the scope of this illusion to mathematize the human "matter" in the baroque, we must affirm the tendency toward attaining a technical manipulation of human conduct; to a certain extent such manipulation permitted some of the results to be predicted. A science of the human being will always have an inexact character because it is a knowledge of contingent realities, but — as Álamos de Barrientos maintained — in departing from this assumption it must be admitted that most of the time one will be on the mark, and one will be mistaken less often; for this reason we can say that in general this human science is valid.[39] It was a matter of a statistical knowledge serving as the foundation for this "engineering of the human" that came to be baroque culture.

The technification of political behavior in the prince — an eminent manifestation of what we have been describing, but essentially the same in many other aspects — was not expressed in a mathematical formula but in symbols. These symbols may have been of very remote origin, but from Machiavelli to the individuals of the baroque they underwent a process that divorced them from their magical references, turning them into a conceptually formalized language. Symbols like the serpent and the dove, the fox and the lion, now played that role.[40]

Medicine was the closest model used to express a possible system of knowledge regarding human things of the baroque type; it also had to do with human beings. A great advance toward scientific constitution took place in the field of medicine, despite the continued existence of a traditional symbolism. Many writers in the seventeenth century, including Descartes, believed in drawing upon medicine for ways to govern human conduct. In 1634, Gallego de la Serna maintained that there was no way to enter into a knowledge of morality "sine cognitione artis medicae."[41]

Besides the direct, though partial, assistance represented by medical knowledge, it was the structure of this knowledge that led some to hope that it might serve as a model for obtaining knowledge about human beings in line with baroque aspirations. Such was the reason, inversely, why so many doctors believed themselves capable of speaking about politics, morality, and the economy. Cellorigo used the example of what doctors had accomplished to prove that there could be a science of politics. Sancho de Moncada wrote: "As there are certain principles and infallible rules showing one how to remedy the diseases of bodies and souls . . . there are infallible remedies to cure the ills assaulting the kingdoms as a whole."[42]

In relation to the previous aspects of knowing the human being, there were two interrelated phenomena (suggested to us by something A. Chastel has indicated): on the one hand, the epoch's macabre iconography was influenced by the development and diffusion, in printed works, of anatomic knowledge and the interest in scrutinizing the composition of the human body by examining the skeleton or the alterations undergone by the cadaver; on the other hand, those funeral representations were inspired by the zeal in making a studied penetration into the structure of existence, to whose essence inexorably belonged the final step of death.[43] From Rembrandt to Poussin, from Alonso Cano to Valdés Leal, the examples are numerous: one can consider the image of the human cadaver as a baroque theme, an image occasioned by the representation of the death of Christ, whose body appeared dramatically humanized, without the glorifying elements that were still present in El Greco. The experience of death and the lifeless corpse was the material utilized to enter into the experience of life and of the living human being.

For a knowledge of the human being, in the sense of an empirical knowing based on observation and directed toward a practical, operative end, one takes into account three spheres. First there was the face and the human exterior in general, which in the baroque century prompted the great development of studies of physiognomy: "que la muestra del pecho es el semblante" [one's countenance is proof of one's courage], Calderón said in *De un castigo tres venganzas* (recall what this meant in the many followers of Furió Ceriol's political proposals, or what it represented in the painting of Ribera or Rembrandt). Second, there was the internal movement of psychical life, giving rise to the widespread study of impulses, passions, affections, and so on, along with interest in psychology and specifically in the cultivation of one of its branches, the "treatise on the passions" (from Descartes and Spinoza to the politicians who trivialized the subject, as we can see in Saavedra Fajardo; in 1641, the Jesuit Sénault published in Paris a treatise whose title expressed the study's final aim: *De l'usage des passions*). The connection between the two aspects was affirmed on the physical level of medicine. Cellorigo tells us about a physician for whom "the perfection of his art consisted in examining the good or bad disposition of the individual, by means of the movements of soul and body, that is, each one enjoys a state of health to the degree one lives in accordance with what is natural and moral."[44] The relation when seen from the opposite point of view had to be no less certain, and baroque writers and artists had complete faith in it.

Finally, a third aspect: the external conduct of human beings, whose continuous successivity gives rise to historical events and of which history (about which so much was written in the baroque) offers us an inexhaustible reservoir of materials for observation. From these materials science seeks its data as a base for formulating its pronouncements, whose scope goes far beyond the particular case it departs from (such was the historical-scientific schema of Hobbes, which underlay more or less confusedly all seventeenth-century writers). The discovery of differential psychology, as it was basically consolidated in the work of Huarte de San Juan, spread belief in the diversity of characteristics of individuals and peoples, from which were derived the inevitable variety of mores and modes of conduct (recall what Huarte's psychology meant in Carballo's poetics, and the examples were repeated in similar terms). This supporting proof of Huarte had broad repercussions in political thought, beginning at a time still within the Renaissance (with Furió Ceriol) until the final years of the baroque[45] (with Lancina): "Mores go hand in hand with the nature of the place, with various countries producing various natures of human beings. It is customary to have different mores in one and the same nation, according to the variety of the climates." Words similar to these, from Suárez de Figueroa,[46] were repeated with greater currency in the seventeenth century. The idea that this psychological particularization of peoples and individuals was necessary created consciousness of a no less necessary adequation in politicians, moralists, artists, and writers, inasmuch as they attempted to act upon a mass and consequently had to subject themselves to the qualities or "genius" of each group. Seen this way, we better understand the interest awakened during the baroque in the study of psychological differences and in history and biography, wherein the particularities characterizing peoples and individuals were molded.

History and that part of psychology depicting the characteristics of individuals and peoples were probably the subject matter most read by the politician, writer, or artist of the baroque. They give us knowledge of human beings, and with their results we can establish the rules to guide them. "These deceptions and political arts cannot be known without knowledge of the human being's nature, a knowledge precisely necessary for whoever governs to know how to rule and guard against that human being."[47] Here we can understand *govern* in the broader sense, as each activity of guiding human groups in some sphere of their collective existence.

Nevertheless, during all times, in all societies, it has been a question of guiding or governing individuals — not only politically, but in the multiple manifestations of existence. Ultimately every pedagogical concern corresponds to the intention of guiding the human being, making him or her see things in a certain way so as to proceed in the required direction. To teach the individual is for the most part to guide, and the greater the effort to make a society stable — perhaps because the crisis situation obligates it to expend a greater effort — the more certain is this statement.

But antiquity and the Middle Ages had such a firm and immovable faith in what was considered to be established truth — although in each case it was no more than a way of seeing socialized by tradition — that this belief in perennial truth came to lay the foundation for two other truths, no less firm and stable: truth is of itself accessible to humankind; and the persuasive force of its evidence is such that it need only be shown to the human being for it to be followed. Thus classical-medieval culture rested on an intellectualism, as complete as it is ingenuous, according to which humankind ruled itself by truth; therefore, what must be done is to give oneself over to it in its own terms, knowing that once known its dominion is assured.[48] The humanism of the first Renaissance decades would be the last episode of this long Socratic tradition.

But since the middle of the sixteenth century, and more emphatically in the seventeenth, the criticism and opposition derived from the initial dynamism of Renaissance society came to be accompanied by doubt and insecurity (within the limits described by L. Febvre).[49] All experience of social and geographic mobility — however limited it might be — accumulated by the individuals of the Renaissance had been sufficient to make them understand that in the general crisis situation taking place in Europe during those two centuries, it was not possible to think about the omnipotence of truth (or what the dominant groups in the culture considered as such). It could not be expected that furnishing the masses of individuals with some intellectual notions about morality, religion, politics would guarantee, by the weight of presumed truth, that they would faithfully follow them. From the outset, ensuring that kind of reception was less than impossible. In *La pícara Justina* we read this lively observation, which tells us much about the popular state of mind: "There is no one attracted to reading a book or a story of a saint."[50] There was need, then, to make use of other means.

What we might call a simple *static guidance controlling by presence* had to give way before a *dynamic guidance controlling by activity*. In the French baroque, Jean de la Taille expressed it in these words: one must proceed "by moving and wondrously pricking the affections of each one."[51] In the pages that follow I will insist on that central point.

One must be rigorously in possession of a knowledge of truths about the world and existence, and this knowledge must be dispensed to individuals if one is to shape them — baroque minds continued firmly in that belief. But it was not enough to reveal it to them: they had to be induced, moved and attracted toward the objectives that society proclaimd.[52] Individuals had to be guided, of course, but now this resulted in a more complicated operation because they had to be guided in a way that was technically adequate (according to the estimations of the seventeenth-century moralist or politician); nor could they be guided toward some desired end without taking into account the responses that might be expected from the public opinion previously constituted among those who were guided.[53] Thus one comprehends the displacement in the direction of the pedagogical efforts proposed by Comenius: "Never undertake to teach someone without having awakened the student's pleasure beforehand."[54] Yet in a certain way, and only after manifesting the necessity of relying on particular data of the subject (individual or people) who was on the receiving end of a guiding action (whether didactic or political), the writers and artists of the baroque considered it possible to establish a general system of expedients [*resortes*] to be manipulated in such a guiding endeavor.

In a certain way, the baroque anticipated — in its own terms — the first conception of a behaviorism inasmuch as it was trying to gain possession of a technique of conduct based on intervention in the psychological motivations [*resortes*] that affect conduct: we can trace the movements of the human being by watching the interplay of its components. La Rochefoucauld thought that "the human being believes it is leading itself [*se conduire*], when in reality it is being led."[55] Here let us connect with a new reference to methodical rationalism, according to which one begins with the assumption that it is possible to dominate and rule a mass of individuals if we know the elements of their nature. Along this route, it is possible to take control of human motivations and apply them toward leading [*conducir*] other human beings, impelling them along the lines of a belief, or better of an ideology and the modes of conduct it translates into (and in correspondence with the system of social interests inspiring it). When E. M. Wilson maintained, in terms of Calderón's Segismundo, that the formulation of his play takes its point of departure from the norms of moral conduct coming from the empirical game of life,[56] this is probably a common trait in all baroque mentality: this is how, knowing and intervening in this game, one can act upon others' conduct.

Baroque writers, in accordance with the way the rationalist thinkers of their time formulated it, tended to conceive of human beings by reducing them to their simple elements. They presented them (to continue the metaphor) in the mode of a tabula rasa, but in relation to which one would have to begin by relying upon the very nature of the tabula (here this mode differs from the pure Aristotelian tradition). The theme was formulated this way in Malebranche's *Conversations chrestiennes* and in the figure of Andrenio in Gracián's *Criticón*. The character of Grimmelshausen's *Simplicissimus* was presented in this way, and such was the basic assumption of Saavedra Fajardo's educational and moral doctrine: the human being, said the latter, is born with "the tabulas of the understanding wiped clean [*rasas*]"; the doctrine can be efficiently imprinted upon them, but to achieve this "it is necessary to observe and be attentive to what constitutes the tabulas' nature" and adapt oneself to these data to shape the human being, correcting him or her with reason and with art. Primarily with the authority of Cicero but also of Aristotle and Seneca (all were explicitly cited by Grimmelshausen and Saavedra), these writers tended to place all the weight on or to give the principal role to the elemental basis of nature, or at least to attribute to it the greatest force in the human being's formation. The baroque writer came up with a subtle combination in order to accept the image of the elemental human being while at the same time strengthening the guiding force of education. If a Renaissance du Bellay judged it unquestionable that "what is natural can more easily do without teaching than teaching can do without what is natural,"[57] the baroque writer preferred to stress inversely the shaping efficacy of the power of culture or of cultivation vis-à-vis the human being. Barrionuevo wrote that "teaching and mores can do everything," and for him the conception had certain mechanistic roots because, in making such an affirmation, one explains and lets it be understood that a monkey could be taught gestures proper to the human being.[58] A preceptist like Carballo discussed the theme, exalting the possibilities of education.[59] Saavedra Fajardo said that education constituted a second essence, and "the essence of teaching [*doctrina*] is no less important than the essence of nature," so that "teaching [*enseñanza*] betters the good and makes good the bad."[60] With that, baroque writers departed from the simplicity of the elementary data of the human being and saw them become diversified into a multiplicity of characteristics that — influenced by the Vives and Huarte de San Juan tradition — they strove to reduce to types. Keeping the nature of these types in view (at least this is what was intended), they applied the shaping and reforming efficacy possessed by education, placing the work of culture above everything else. The more and more generalized use of the word "culture," whose meaning evolved to approximate the current meaning, signified the role it was recognized as having.[61]

Thus education gained a decisive importance as a way to propagate — or, rather, to socialize — the segregated culture of baroque society. "The children's teacher is one of the most positive of things that have any importance whatsoever," according to Francisco Santos.[62] School begins to be seen as a workshop of social integration.

In the seventeenth century, this socially integrating activity coursing through all its channels was very important, even decisive. We must take our point of departure from the basic fact of this activity of those in power, of the dominant groups: an activity consisting of working on public opinion, controlling it, shaping it, and keeping it in line with their views during the diverse manifestations of crisis that threatened their position. In one eloquent example, at a time well into the critical phase (on 19 February 1641), Pellicer tells a piece of news that reveals the mode in which the organs of power operated in reality (which accords with what we have here been advancing): "The seignior presiding over Castile assembled the prelates of religion last week for each of the preachers to be advised of their obedience and take care in their sermons of this Lent to temper their words so that they do not offend the matters of government, so as to keep the distressed people from becoming disconsolate about everything."[63]

In the epoch's conflictive situation, amid the struggle being carried out in such diverse realms, all in solidarity with one another, the adherence of groups of individuals played an important role and their conduct turned out to be of serious consequence when they found themselves together in an urban setting. One cannot underrate the adherence of individuals to a religion, a political belief, a government, or to one of the factions and opinions confronting them. On the level of urban development reached in the seventeenth century, this adherence to one or another of the opposing forces presupposed an opinion that was translated into an ideological line. Those acting in defense and for the empowering of one of the parties in contention were forced to attract the masses toward the ideology sustaining it. There were various ideological currents, of Catholics, Protestants, and other religious groups; there were those of the French monarchy, the Spanish monarchy, and others, there were also those of the privileged and underprivileged groups, of the rich and the poor, of centralists and federalists [foralistas], and so on. Argan was right when he affirmed that adherence to a determinate position involves an *ideological choice*, and since this choice entails consequences regarding the play of opposing forces, each party attempts to attract ideologically the greatest possible number of adherents. Because "*ideological persuasion* can determine the shifting of the masses and compromise the equilibrium of political forces, such persuasion, whether religious or political, becomes an essential mode of the exercise of authority."[64]

Thus, if in the Renaissance there was a "subsidized" poetry, now there would be a "commissioned" poetry. All those in power recognized the utility of poets and made use of them: poets acted upon public opinion, making and unmaking it. Since the end of the sixteenth century, there existed an apologetic poetry and a polemic poetry in the service of authority. Literature should include the watchwords of power, should give expression to a "single doctrine, controlled and guided by power."[65] Among hundreds of examples is Francisco de Rioja, who as a political polemicist and author of a book, *Aristarco*, replied against the *Proclamación católica* that had been published in Catalonia during the uprising.[66]

One must also refer to the appearance of some early journalists who practiced an art of information in the service of the baroque order and even in some cases of the rulers guiding it. Such was the case in Spain of an Andrés Almansa y Mendoza, who wrote some *Cartas*, a form frequently taken by the newspaper genre in the seventeenth century, to publicize the interests of the monarchy under Philip IV and to exalt the personage of the Count-Duke. His work was a defense of royalty, of nobility, of religion, and of the social system based on these three pillars. These *Cartas* offer us a favorable view, with no fissure whatsoever, of the state of the monarchy, without failing to present readers with a sublimation of all the values on which the system was based, from the piety that sought to become public to the wealth that turned into ostentation: "The happiness in the government of this fortunate monarchy proceeds in glory; the reign of our seignior Philip IV the king is for Spain a golden century, such happy beginnings promising such prosperous ends"; "this century for Spain is glorious."[67] The significance of this attitude does not become clear if we do not compare it with the attitude of genuine journalists of "opposition," such as Barrionuevo, who was capable of breaking out in the apostrophe we have already cited: "Poor Spain so out of luck!" This reveals the conflictive force of such materials and the suspicion with which authority viewed them even when they manifested themselves in its favor, an aspect that must be taken into account in understanding the formation of baroque culture — the authoritarianism that shaped it and the closed, conservative character that came to immobilize it in many of its manifestations, with everything subjected to its dominating efficacy.[68]

The guiding control [*dirigismo*] of the baroque inevitably led to an authoritarianism, inasmuch as it was inspired by the interests of a system of authority. "Baroque culture" — affirmed A. Hauser — "becomes more and more an authoritarian court culture,"[69] an affirmation we can accept if the word *court* has the value it had during the epoch, which was very different from the Renaissance meaning. During the baroque it was defined as a social and administrative center manifesting a sovereign authority. This authoritarianism was none other than that of monarchical absolutism. What characterized that seventeenth-century absolutist order was the dissemination of the principle of absolute power throughout the entire social body, integrating all the manifestations of authority, strengthening them, and (by means of such manifestations) being present in many spheres of social life and to a certain extent inspiring them. L. Lowenthal maintained that social culture was constituted to keep people occupied and in a state of self-forgetfulness or obedience to foreign directives; when they freed themselves from their busyness, it was recommended that they relax in games and diversions.[70] In conformity with this last observation let me add that in the seventeenth century — and in this the "enlighteners" of the eighteenth century differed very little — there was the attempt, in principle and beyond, to control the moments of leisure and all those moments in which a public or a group of individuals could be placed in contact with a work, or better with a human creation, and feel in experiencing it a call to freedom. The art and literature of the baroque, which frequently declared themselves on the side of the artist's and writer's freedom or of freedom in the tastes of the public where the work was to be received, nonetheless came under the influence or even under the mandate of the rulers, who granted subsidies, guided appeal toward a certain taste, or (should the case arise) prohibited certain works. They were subjected to the control of the ecclesiastical authorities as to orthodoxy or simply as to apologetic norms, an intervention legitimated after the renewal of the discipline imposed by the Council of Trent.[71] Directly related with these imposed tribunals of authority were the academies — which were partly made up by seigniors and, above all, by their secretaries and other employees or servants. Academies proliferated in the seventeenth century, notably in Madrid, Seville, and Valencia; if they appeared to be informal gatherings, they nonetheless had a strong influence on arts and letters.[72] Richelieu's initiative to bring the organization of the academies into the state mechanism was no more than the culmination of a process already at work, whereby poetry and art were being linked to power.[73]

All the multiplicity of controls that governed in the baroque were centralized in the monarchy. This was the keystone of the system.[74] Bodini rightly saw that under the image of the "sun," identified with the absolute monarch, *La vida es sueño* was a work dedicated to the exaltation of the monarchy.[75] But this excess of power accompanying monarchical absolutism produced great disturbances wherever, as in Spain, it succeeded in either absorbing or eliminating every factor of resistance by means of alliance with the nobles, subjection of the bourgeois, suppression of the intermediate "corpora," and the mental and economic annihilation of the lower groups. On the one hand, a largely successful attempt was made to penetrate into the innermost interiority of the conscious-nesses, according to the formulation of A. López de Vega: the sovereignty of those who rule "has been extended to want to subordinate also our understandings and to persuade us that we should obey and serve not only with the members of our body but also with our reason, giving to all their decisions the same credit as to the decisions of God, and frequently in contradiction with these latter and with the natural laws on which they are based."[76] In this way, the internal sources of thought and of the personal capacity of creation became blinded. But there was more. Power, beyond measure and without order, insurmountably constrained social existence. The proposal that the royal physician Pérez de Herrera so heatedly defended is not, of course, to be taken as a faithful reference to an existing institution, but we can consider it an adequate reflection of the state of mind hovering over Spanish society: he proposed that in towns, villages, and neighborhoods some censors or representatives be established to secretly investigate everyone's manner of living, their dealings that were possibly illicit or a bad example, so that they would be punished — in this way "all may live with suspicion and fear and with the utmost caution, no one having the certainty that one's behavior and living will not be found out." That this regime of "fear" and "uncertainty" was bound up with the interests of the dominant classes is revealed by the fact that Pérez de Herrera proposed that in the cities these positions be given to gentlemen and other persons "of virtue, quality and property."[77] In this way the nobility and the rich became agents of the system of control that culminated in the Catholic monarchy. In fact, without coming to such a distressing extreme, something similar did in fact occur with the privileged individuals' monopoly of governmental positions in municipal administration and the state.[78]

But now let us foreground the other side making up this character of guided culture as exhibited by the baroque. In a certain way we can consider this other side as marking the occurrence of its positive aspect. Although the baroque had an accentuated and, furthermore, disproportionate authoritarian character, this is not what constituted its specificity but rather the nuances with which that authoritarianism manifested itself in relation to the epoch's circumstances. We have said that the purely material means of control based on physical repression did not suffice. It was not a question merely of imposing silence but also of enticing. Amidst the harsh conflicts of the epoch, rather than destroying the reserves of combative energy, it was necessary to subdue and channel them, inclining them definitively and radically toward their own defense and preservation. On the other hand, if the system of the imposition of authority was now harsher than in the preceding regimes, the resistance could be more broadly based and stronger — resistance stimulated by the awakening of individual energies at the beginning of modernity.

Although in the command-subordination relation it has never been possible, as Simmel maintained,[79] to reduce subordination to a purely passive value, in the historical situation of the baroque whoever exercised a form of command (as sociologically defined) was obligated to rely on the active incorporation of those given to obeying or being guided. More than in any previous historical moment, in the seventeenth-century crisis, regardless of the specific relation of authority — from a playwright's authority to that of the prince — its shaping effect required a degree of acceptance and incorporation of the public. Now it was a question of guiding, promoting adherence by means that extracted it on the level of the individual.

Therefore, in baroque authoritarianism, in relation with its guidance objectives and given the active role corresponding to some extent to the receptive party, the way of thinking of this latter must be taken into account. Sovereign power arose in the seventeenth century with characteristics known since the beginning of time, one being that an absolute power maintains itself over the shifting ground of opinion. From there proceeds the value of persuasion and the means that promote it. Let us refer once again to Argan. Those who guide possess a consciousness of the necessity to persuade; to this corresponds an attitude on the part of the public in which they allow themselves to be persuaded. This is not a question that is formulated merely in the realm of art, but in all those areas where opinions can be formed in support of the strength of ruling [*dirigentes*] groups and, above them, of the sovereign power. Using an Italian formulation, Argan says that people are interested in "farsi persuadere" [becoming persuaded]. Rather than letting themselves be persuaded, therefore, it is a matter of making themselves persuaded, which seems to offer a more active nuance. That is, they possess a cultivated predisposition to be persuaded. Thus Argan explained that in the baroque the influence of Aristotle's *Rhetoric* took precedence over the *Politics*, precisely because the former is an art of persuasion:

> Art is no more than a technique, a method, a type of communication or relation; and more precisely, it is a technique of persuasion that should take into account not only its own possibilities and means, but also the dispositions of the public it addresses. The theory of the passions, put forth in the second book of the *Rhetoric*, thereby comes to be an element in the conception of art as communication and persuasion.[80]

This formulation is valid for the whole field of culture that is, to such a great extent, constructed with the technique of rhetoric. This may perhaps be the most characteristic aspect of seventeenth-century culture, essentially the origin giving rise to so many of the resources appealed to.

On all levels and in all areas, the baroque epoch was a period of polemics: "nowadays persuading is much more important than demonstrating." If, along these lines, art becomes a technique of persuasion going from above to below, in the same direction as the imposition of authority or executive order, we must nuance this observation: first, in extending verification of this trait, in its twofold sense of persuasion and authority, to all the manifestations of culture; and, second, in pointing out that a difference exists, nonetheless, between mandate and persuasion; with persuasion demanding a greater participation on the side of the guided, requiring that he or she be taken into account and thus be given an active role. Did Suárez, in his theology, not speak of "active obedience" in defining the position of the created being with respect to its creator? A similar idea could be applied to the general manner in which the seventeenth century considered the position of the subject in the order of power.[81] One could by way of analogy also speak about an active public participation in support of the guiding actions of baroque culture. In this sense, one must sociologically and historically interpret the role of public taste that Lope acknowledged in the theater[82] and no less in the novel.[83]

Baroque culture thus sets itself the task of moving its addressee. We are here touching upon a new and final aspect of its guiding control. One of the means that proved effective in reaching this objective — which can very well be exemplified in art, but also in other areas — consisted in introducing or implying and, to a certain extent, making the spectators themselves participants in the work, which succeeded in making the spectators almost its accomplices. Such was the result obtained by presenting a spectator with an open work that could come about in various ways: a character in a painting addresses whoever contemplates it with an invitation to become incorporated into the scene; or, with the technique of the unfinished scene that seems to be continued in the foreground, the spectator becomes involved with it; or perhaps involvement comes about by turning the spectator into a coauther, making use of the artifice by means of which the work changes along with the viewer's perspective.[84] But obviously the individual confronted by the seventeenth century must be moved from within. According to López Pinciano, art seeks "to move and amaze."[85] Distinct from the serenity sought by the Renaissance, the baroque set out to stir and impress, directly and immediately, by effectively intervening in the motivation [*resortes*] of the passions. Wölfflin already observed this, recalling that many baroque artists manifested neuroses — Bernini, Borromini (we might add, among others, Alonso Cano).[86] Along with its contemporary, Descartes, baroque thought considered that human judgments are based "on passions by means of which the will lets itself be convinced and seduced beforehand."[87]

This thesis was repeated an infinite number of times, giving the idea of amazement an internal, dynamic character. Human beings must be moved by acting with calculation upon the extrarational workings of their affective forces. "Man sees by the eyes of his affection," wrote M. Régnier.[88] In a literary work, Suárez de Figueroa valued "the acute efficacy in representing the affections."[89] A Jesuit wrote a letter from Aragón to a Dr. Gaspar Martín, speaking to him about the life and virtues of Dr. Francisco García de la Sierra, a native of Cercedilla and a great preacher. He praised the fact that "in his sermons he did not worry about pleasing the ear, but about piercing the heart . . . He availed himself of animated and effective reasons."[90] The efficacy in affecting, in awakening and moving the affections, was the great motive of the baroque. Let us not assume this was only for reasons of style; underlying them were social motivations that showed themselves to be related in all categories. We know of a concrete example that reveals an entire program of activity in this sense: Barrionuevo recounts that during the War of Catalonia it was requested of the preachers that they, from the pulpit and with animated and scathing nuances, attribute the atrocities being committed to the French occupying the Principate, "all with the effect of moving the psyches of the soldiers toward going to serve the king." In 1654 a similar expedient was already somewhat worn out, and the gazetteer added: "and everybody was lending a deaf ear."[91] The scant success of such a propaganda campaign does not stop us from recognizing that it existed and, furthermore, that it was organized by what we have been indicating as the baroque's authoritarian activity. In reformulating the significance of Racinian tragedy, which some critics have undertaken in recent years, E. Vinaver commented that everything shows how Racine, aside from the Aristotelian rules of dramatic composition, was interested in nothing more than a dramatic theory based on emotion, the poetic spectacle of human fragility — analogous to the dynamic excitement recommended by the words cited from his contemporary, Jean de la Taille.[92]

The epoch's preceptists emphasized the problem of *moving* to such an extent that, although their pages were full of humanist and Latin tradition, this is an aspect wherein we encounter a specifically baroque doctrine. The baroque moralist who studied the passions with such interest, and the politician and others who rely upon effecting the crowd's movements, did not attempt to suppress the passions nor even stoically to silence them; rather, they tried to make use of their force. The Jesuit Senault — following Montaigne — maintained that "those who want to remove the passions from the soul remove all its movements and render it useless and without power." He noted — thereby making manifest the root of the problem — that "there is no passion in our soul that cannot be usefully manipulated."[93] One must accept the presence of irrational forces in human beings (their affective movements), become acquainted with them, dominate their workings, and apply them properly by channeling their energy toward the intended ends. One must operate with human beings as one operates with the elements of nature, which are only governable by making use of their own forces. Recalling a recent experience of this last type, Bocángel wrote: "Que no hicieron los cielos la violencia / tan absoluta (y más si la arma el viento) / que no la venza al fin quien la obedece" [The heavens did not make violence so absolute (and more so if the wind is behind it) that whoever obeys it will not overcome in the end].

Two significant texts make the ground of the question obvious. F. Pacheco advised that "the painter seek to have his figures move psyches, some figures disturbing them, others making them happy, others inclining them to piety, others to disdain, according to the quality of the stories. And if he fails in that, may he realize that he has done nothing."[94] The other text is from V. Carducho, a writer of treatises on painting and a great fan of Lope, in praise of whom he wrote these words: "Note, observe and pay attention to how well he paints, how well he imitates, with how much affect and force his painting moves the souls of those who listen . . . provoking tears from the hardest of hearts."[95]

Gracián was different from others (such as López Pinciano) because he realized the change undergone by the concept of amazement, traditional among the Aristotelians; thus he observed that it is not *amazement* that is to be strived for, but *enthusiasm [afición]*;[96] "conquering the understanding means little if the will is not also won over."[97] "The greatest happiness in the world does not consist in ruling over worlds, but over wills," said Francisco de Portugal, taking the theme to an obvious degree of trivialization.[98] Later, like a faraway echo, Palomino said in recording the experience of this epoch that the objective was "to enthuse the will."[99] To move human beings, not convincing through demonstration, but affecting them so that their will is unleashed: this was the question. Only in this way does one succeed in drawing the individual, inciting his or her adherence to a determined attitude, and only in this way is one able to keep the individual in solidarity with it. For the baroque mind, this was the sole option that succeeded in attracting a mass whose opinion must be taken into account and imposing upon it, channeling its force in the desired direction.

It is not enough to say that the baroque remained faithful to the thematic, according to the Horatian and Aristotelian tradition, of *delectare-docere*, merging the two parts into a single tendency.[100] The knot of the question is ignored if one forgets the third aspect that includes and profoundly alters the intellectualist nature of *docere*: that of *moving*. The baroque again proposed that this latter — at least in its decisive role — was the end to be attained: to set the will on its course, appealing to the expedients that unleash it, which are not purely intellectual.[101] When Díaz Rengifo asked himself what poetry is good for, he came up with this response: "for teaching and moving";[102] when the second of these two terms is stressed, it transforms the meaning of the first and "baroquifies" it.

The baroque *will* is obviously not one of an unconditional freedom, gratuitously endowed with a total power to subjugate passions and instincts in the way that traditional moral thought saw it; it was a will capable of dealing with extrarational, perturbing, blind factors to arrive at a programmed result and ultimately to impose its domination by all means. It will be said that this signifies Jesuitism, which is undeniable. Although both the baroque and Jesuitism coincided in being formulated in a similar fashion, one can nevertheless not make the first dependent on the second; let it suffice to affirm that the Jesuits became a pure expression of baroque mentality, which, notwithstanding, was present with no less force in other spheres. We cannot, however, brush aside the fact of the diffusion of Suarezismo and the predominant role of the will derived from its doctrine. It is well known that the Jesuits diffused the study of Suárez in France, Germany, and elsewhere. This fact attests to the mental state of the epoch in the aspect here under consideration.

Thus the baroque attempted to guide human beings who were grouped together in masses, acting upon their will, psychologically motivating [*moviendo con resortes*] them by means of a technique of attraction that, as such, effectively exhibited a mass character. From there emerged the very function of prudence — the predominance of which we have dealt with above. With prudence, said Juan de Salazar, "psyches and wills are attracted and captured."[103] It was practiced in this way by everyone from the architect and painter to the politician and moralist. In the middle of this scale, and in relation to a sphere that is of great interest to us because it represents a very important area in the application of baroque culture, Suárez de Figueroa tells us that it is "in the government where prudence is more concerned with wills than with understandings."[104]

Chapter 3
A Mass Culture

With regard to the seventeenth-century crisis, it is not immediately obvious that the dominant class (in the broadest sense of the term) was attempting to arrive at a faithful reestablishment of the model of knightly society, conducting itself according to prototypes of a medievalizing seignorialism. From the outset, the seigniors made no effort to retain their military functions. Far from having their influence and prestige hinge on the monopoly of bearing arms, they looked for other reasons to regain their privileges. In a few cases, they reestablished their economic situation by improving administration, in others either by raising rents, employing coercive means for being given the best lands in the division of communal property, or succeeding in making part of their patrimony lands to which they had only juridical right, thus giving them an economic content. As a rule, then, they tried to increase their patrimony, frequently making recourse to obtaining new royal gifts as the most secure means. Therefore the powers of the privileged groups, which had declined but little, were gaining in strength; at the end of the seventeenth century they were stronger than a century before. Certainly the pyramid of social stratificaton was maintained, although it was partly ordered according to other criteria, which in itself did not mean that it would not be strongly eroded in the long term.

Thus we are, to some extent, faced with a new society, whatever may be the restored traditional element present in it. Consciousness of that newness is found in innumerable writings from the epoch, which did not specifically criticize the individuals of one or another group who were not fulfilling their obligations so much as the shift that these groups had undergone in terms of the whole. In part that corresponded to the fact that society was presenting other characteristics, was finding itself to be of a different makeup. Without taking this change into account, without noting everything that had become new, it is impossible to understand the baroque phenomenon. A new society — even though we can only speak of it in relative terms — needs a new culture to give shape to the new modes of behavior and the new ideological bases that must occur within it: a new culture is manipulated as an instrument of integration — such is the fate of every cultural system — in the new state of things. With this culture, those who propagate it hope to dominate better the tensions threatening society from within, although they may never come to be eliminated. This is the point of view from which we must consider what we are calling baroque culture, a culture developed to bring under control not only religious disquiet (as has so often been said), but all the insecurity produced as a consequence of the long period of changes that the western European societies had been undergoing for centuries.

Baroque culture emerged from an epoch that had known a noticeable increase in population. This demographic imbalance, even at its highest points in the sixteenth century, stayed within the limits of a population movement that, although favorable, did not go beyond the same growth rates of traditional society — even if at some point it was on the verge of doing so. When this growth gave way and the tendency reversed itself, a consciousness of the masses of population being very numerous remained until much later (it is humorous what the town of Ocaña said in response to the 1578 questionnaire: "It is understood that there have never been as many [inhabitants] as at present, but one thing may be more noteworthy than others: this settlement must be one of the towns most full of people in the world, because we have seen many [people] who have traveled far and wide become amazed with regard to this particular").[1] But above all there remained, for a long time, the belief that the people in the world abounded in greater numbers than ever and that the consumption of goods was much greater.

The memory of a demographic boom in the preceding period, which was considered over and had to be reestablished in order to come out of the crisis that its disappearance engendered, turned almost all seventeenth-century writers on economic matters into "populationists" (i.e., advocates of the idea that societies with a great population mass are richer and more powerful). As González de Cellorigo maintained, "The greatest wealth of the realm is many people";[2] or Sancho de Moncada, who wrote an entire discourse on "Population and the Increase in Number of the Spanish Nation";[3] or Álvarez Ossorio, according to whom "the multitude of vassals enriches the monarchies."[4] The abundance of individuals constituted a stimulus for production. It was noted early on that an entire series of political, economic, and social phenomena were related to one another, and everyone in the baroque believed with satisfaction that they were going to find themselves living in societies that in a short period of time would be overflowing with people and, consequently, with property, power, and prestige.[5]

Before the beginning of the baroque century, everybody in Spain knew that serious losses of population were taking place in the country. Cellorigo considered that of all the ills afflicting the monarchy — wars, famines, plagues, mass death, negligence — the greatest was "the lack of people that here has been making itself known for some years."[6] The seriousness of the matter was recognized in official documents of Philip III and Philip IV,[7] and Pedro de Valencia applied a rudimentary statistical criterion to determine or, rather, to calculate what this loss was.[8] There were debates about the causes of the phenomenon, which some blithely attributed to wars and emigration, whereas others, reaching a more profound level in their analysis, looked internally and deemed them to be a consequence of certain aspects of the social structure or of the government's economic policies. All wished for great masses of population. Of course this does not imply that they anticipated mass phenomena, nor, in the event that the country became abundantly populated, that such phenomena would occur. To a certain extent, it was a precondition that would be at the origin of the new phenomena. When a burgeoning population was desired or obtained, formulations of a mass type were already being made.

Yet the two things did not coincide. If we take note of the years when it occurred, this is shown by the well-known decline in the population index in Spain. Phenomena of a mass type would appear precisely at the conjunctural moment when the demographic development took a downward turn. But already that aspiration to overcome such a negative situation would remain to a certain extent as an echo of the tendency to formulate the aspects of state and social existence — i.e., military, alimentary, urban aspects, even (as we shall soon see) those referring to school curriculum and study[9] — on a gigantic mass scale. The original cause of mass forms was the populationist tendencies, which were held in common by all seventeenth-century Spanish and non-Spanish writers, and not at all the effective attainment of an abundant population in a given country (France, for example), although they were nonetheless necessarily bound up with one another beforehand. When the seventeenth-century state — the early modern State — wanted to count on a large population, although it didn't always achieve it, this owed to the fact that it was already a political form with mass culture characteristics.

In the seventeenth century, however, the population became relatively more concentrated in certain areas even as it declined in absolute terms. The demographic alterations, accompanied by changes in the interrelations among groups — changes in mores, beliefs, and modes of living — signified a profound transformation of culture, apart from the structural changes studied by economic historians. In his famous study of kitsch, Greenburg wrote:

The peasants who settled in the cities as proletariat and petty bourgeoisie learned to read and write for the sake of efficiency, but they did not win the leisure and comfort necessary for the enjoyment of the city's traditional culture. Losing, nevertheless, their taste for the folk culture whose background was the countryside, and discovering a new capacity for boredom at the same time, the new urban masses set up a pressure on society to provide them with a kind of culture fit for their own consumption. To fill the demand of the new market a new commodity was devised: ersatz culture, kitsch . . .[10]

It was a culture — an art, a literature, distractions and social games — produced by the requirements of a new situation of society and translated into the new relations between the market and the position of the consumer population in it that had at its disposal certain commercialized products. (Clearly, no matter how far back we antedate the fact that the exodus of rural multitudes to the city led to new forms of popular culture, the examples offered us by the cultural commerce of kitsch in this incipient moment could never be the same as those that social researchers are concerned with today. But this difference cannot prove an obstacle since, in terms of the baroque, we are not speaking about the process of social massification implied by kitsch: at that time there would have been no radio or widely circulated newspapers that the public could make use of; they didn't exist in 1830, much less in 1700, yet this concept has been applied to the sociocultural situation of both time periods. I shall try to show that its beginning — always emphasizing that it is a question of incipient forms — can already be discovered in the baroque.)

In the seventeenth century, the peasant population's invasion of the cities was already taking place to a considerable degree, and this is why the early manifestations of kitsch have to be set in this century. Until now these subproducts of high culture have not been studied; at most, an art or literary textbook has, in bringing each epoch to a close, dedicated a small chapter to authors of lesser quality. Now a great interest has arisen in the study of those levels of socialized culture, but since it has emerged specifically in researchers from countries that in the last thirty years have known a more spectacular level of development, along with an invasion of the means of mass communication and a fabulous increment in the mass consumers of standardized cultural products, the phenomenon has tended to be seen as a novelty, as something that had never before occurred. That is understandable because the circumstances of industrial development of the last decades have also never been known before. In addition, those specialists who are today studying the phenomenon throughout the countries where they live (the United States, Germany, etc.), have not been inclined to see more than direct economic reasons in the theme that has so recently become an object of study. The great manufacturing firms, applying themselves to the realm of cultural production, would have given rise to kitsch for market reasons.

I am not convinced by either argument. The diversification of cultural levels — which have always existed — and the appearance of popular and mediocre culture in its specifically modern form, although developed to a greater or lesser degree, are phenomena that have to be antedated to the time of the social crisis constituting the beginning of modernity. Although, as D. Macdonald claimed, there is no good or bad Gothic painting[11] (to my understanding, it would be better to say that there is no painting whose good or bad quality is determined on social grounds), there is good and bad baroque painting and theater, and every sort of cultural manifestation — from architecture to the novel — is either good or bad because of the influence of social conditioning. In saying *bad* we are tying this unfavorable qualifier to the conditions giving rise to kitsch: a popular culture characterized by the establishment of types with a standardized repetition of genres representing a tendency toward social conservatism and corresponding to a manipulated consumption. We are establishing these characteristics by basing ourselves largely on those that P. F. Lazarsfeld and R. K. Merton attributed to modern-day kitsch.[12] Naturally, if the means of mass communication are of a different nature today than those we can consider as such in another epoch (there was no radio or television in the seventeenth century, but there were books, commercialized theatrical representations, painting in abundance, songs in vogue, posters, programs, lampoons, etc.); if it is easy to comprehend that such media, according to their nature and their possibilities of influencing, are always, both in the present and in the past, relatively dependent on the structure of property and on its forms of expression; and if that gives rise to the fact that even today, given the structural differences existing between one country and another, one cannot even speak of the Soviet Union and the United States having the same aspects of mass communication; then the aspects characterizing the possible kitsch products in the seventeenth century would have to be even more different than what was seen later. An accumulating population and a culture industry at its service is revealed by the fact that organized companies were provided with an apparatus for assembling scenarios, which was perhaps more or less primitive or complicated; that halls were constructed expressly for the comedia, so that its representation had become an occupation, and the acting occupation was put forth as a form of employment (let us recall the anonymous *loa* in praise of this job, which figures among those collected by Cotarelo), i.e., as an activity of economic production; that cartloads of books were sent from Lyon and other European cities in "absolute hordes," as Saavedra Fajardo hyberbolically described it.[13]

We have often discussed the seventeenth-century rural exodus to the cities, which is not to be confused with a necessary abandonment of the agrarian profession: the economic difficulties of the time thrust sizable groups of day laborers into urban milieus where they drastically changed their forms of life and their character. Diego de Colmenares described the arguing and quarrelsome habits that led toward confrontation and street disputes.[14] On the other hand, in smaller but still appreciable numbers, there was an increase in the number of merchants and in diverse types of professions; there was also an increase in the number of nobles and in their employees and servants who came to inhabit the city, passing through its streets and gathering at its meeting places. This growth implied the necessity of seeking in this urban milieu a cultural sustenance for all this jumbled-together population; most were content with works of a "middle" or "low" type, and in some cases creations of the highest cultural level were required, so that the urban growth of the baroque epoch ran parallel to the demand for cultural growth in all social layers.

The seventeenth-century cultural expansion probably had a positive side: individuals who learned to see, listen to, read, and assimilate works of great culture (Porreño's well-known reference to the popular reading of the *Quijote*, of Malón de Chaide, and of Montemayor's *Diana* is significant) arose from among those who were incorporated into the urban milieu, those who were close to personages already a part of the urban cultured group, and, besides those, from the many more who attended the university lecture halls — whose total capacity, with the creation of universities and professors' chairs in the Renaissance, had increased considerably. But that expansion also had a negative side: the numerous displaced population lost its connection with its traditional milieu where what I will call popular culture [*cultura popular*] was being secularly preserved and renewed, cut its contacts with Church and family members, with people of other professions, perhaps with certain institutions, and even with persons of prestige that in the rural ambient could be related to as neighbors and friends. This situation made necessary a culture to replace what was lost, a culture derived as a subproduct of high culture: kitsch. This cannot be taken as a dissemination of limited amounts of cultured knowledge, of small doses of high culture transmitted more or less crudely to other layers. No: even then it was a question of producing a popular culture [*cultura vulgar*] for the urban masses, probably — this could be studied today with computers — according to a level corresponding to that of the middle classes, which knew how to read and practiced this cultural activity more assiduously because they had enough leisure time to dedicate themselves to reading and similar activities. (Although in the novel and theater — and if we take note of its iconographic elements, also in painting — cultured elements appear that seem to correspond to a "high" formation, in general they are products that would be equivalent to what one sociologist has called *midcult*; in many cases — ribald ballads, farces and other kinds of theatrical representations — one must accept that it is a question of pure and simple *masscult*.)[15] In any case we are encountering manifestations of kitsch, to which belongs the greater part of seventeenth-century theatrical and, especially, novelistic production. The thousands of comedies published for the epoch's consumption cannot signify anything else.

Will this aid in explaining, on sociohistorical grounds, why in studying the baroque we must study or at least take into account the presence of bad taste, of the ugly, of the work of low style? In previous epochs we might be able to dispense with this component; in the baroque, that would be impossible. Until a short time ago, every so-called baroque style was identified with a style of bad taste. But it was simply that, for a series of social reasons, kitsch emerged, and then even work of high quality was produced simultaneously and in competition with works of those other levels of culture for the common people [vulgo]. Sometimes the same author was responsible for works of more than one level — let us recall Lope and Calderón. But to the extent that it was necessary to produce more culture because there was more consumption, there was also a greater lack of individuals to produce that culture. This resulted in the phenomenal increase, which can be measured statistically, of writers and artists who in the seventeenth century appeared everywhere; among them, as a new element, one would have to include the popular [adocenados] writers and artists who were enjoyed by the public of a mediocre level. As the kitsch of our time, the popular [vulgo] baroque was not a counterculture of a popular [popular] tradition (it could not be farther from it), nor properly speaking a substitute for culture; however, this expression can be used in market terms, keeping in mind its consumption possibilities. It was rather a culture of low quality that might become a pseudoculture or a pseudoart. It might even be called a bad culture, but always sufficiently similar to high culture for it to be designated with the same word: they fulfilled, ultimately, the same or similar function because they responded to a demand of the same nature.[16]

But how does the mass character of baroque culture come about, and how is it explained? Although at different degrees of evolution, the dominant social and economic forms — which were directly dependent on sixteenth-century demographic growth that continued in the cities in the seventeenth century, even if by then the population factor was arrested or being reversed — have by some been characterized as mass production. In the epoch itself, the printing industry came to be considered as such. Since the middle of the sixteenth century, the books produced by printing were said to be so numerous and inexpensive that no one, no matter how tight one's budget, found it necessary to do without any book one might want. Mechanical printing was capable of providing the market with great quantities of books: "Because of this, books, which used to be rare and high-priced, have become more commonly available and affordable," according to one appraisal that we can easily verify.[17] Relying on this and other devices, which could achieve an inexpensive and mass production and were capable of reaching a large public (specifically in the area of cultural dissemination), the baroque can be presented as a phenomenon of kitsch. The seventeenth century experienced an expansion that lay the groundwork: printing was judged as an industry of culture that worked for a great quantity of consumers.

Although only in its incipient stages, painting also exhibited the first hint of a tendency that would later consolidate itself along the same lines. Every production of this type sought to pay attention to demand, of course, but did not subordinate itself directly and individually to previous orders; instead, to a certain extent, it prepared and shaped the demand. Such would come to be the case for Giorgione and Titian, who worked for the market and not for prior individual requests.[18] It has been said that Rubens applied "methods of industrial manufacture to the organization of artistic work" and that in Amberg a great number of painting and engraving masters — more numerous than those employed in certain food industries — followed similar methods: all that proclaims a mode of production of the manufacturing type.[19] Something similar could be maintained about Alonso Cano, Murillo, and others. Some painting treatises of the epoch, and especially Francisco Pacheco's,[20] are for the most part instruction books for serial production. These are closely linked aspects of the economy, the culture, and seventeenth-century society. As a typical case of a system of prefabrication that proposed — and practically imposed, at least to a certain extent — models of premade products, the baroque city was acquainted with shops selling ready-made clothing. In one of his novels, Lope introduced a gentleman who, upon arriving in Madrid, "buys his servants gallant clothes from that miraculous street where so many are clothed without taking measurements."[21]

Not all European societies reached the same level of development; regardless, the baroque was formed and matured alongside the development of labor in shops of the manufacturing type — as an example, Max Weber cited a Velázquez painting, *Las hilanderas*. Of course, much time would pass before manufacturing production reached an appreciable level, except in England (in Spain, one would even observe a retrogression). Nevertheless, that the epoch's mentality appraised industrial activity in a different way was revealed by the fact that the terms *factory* and *manufacturing* became widespread to designate, in Spanish, the epoch's means of industrial production, as can be verified in the lexicon of the economists — Sancho de Moncada, Martínez de Mata, and others. Naturally, there was no factory organization of production, and the fact that those two words and the word *workshop* were used without differentiation informs us of the incipient level of the changes.[22] On the other hand, let us observe that there is taking place today a mass production and consumption of science fiction in countries that are not fully participating in the development of contemporary science, despite which we are discovering that the mentality corresponding to this diffused, hybrid genre is being communicated and absorbed. In a similar way, the seventeenth century contemplated the development of a mentality and modes of life having a mass character, along with the development of manufacturing, even where industry scarcely reached such a level. But, in addition, given that this initial mass character had a general projection, it can clearly be considered prior to its more full-blown appearance in the economic realm and independently from economic determinations, although always in relation with conditions operating upon the economy itself.

It has been said that the Industrial Revolution produced the masses. It uprooted people from agrarian communities and crowded them into the cities growing up around the factories.[23] The Industrial Revolution, however, is not something that suddenly appeared and immediately transformed things. Many alterations that were underway since the Renaissance reached an appreciable level in the seventeenth century and underwent a greater expansion in the eighteenth. When the large factory superseded the manufacturing workshop, kitsch art and culture encountered two conditions that until then had not been present: a "standardized industrial production" for a "prototypical consumer." Since mass society developed in historical complexes taking place successively and over long periods of time, I believe that the first appearances of mass society came about in the seventeenth century in a manner correlative not to serial production (as this concept is used in the regimen of the large factory) but to production based on short-term repetition, such as takes place in manufacturing. When these conditions of production occurred in the realm of culture — the book, the engraving, etc. — they were brought to bear on the fact that work was being done for a "public" already having an impersonal character, at least within the possibilities of the time. In this way, the masterworks of the baroque epoch were in all areas accompanied by masses of low and mediocre works, by *midcult* and *masscult* works that motivated kitsch's popular inspiration. Factory and industrial production had not reached the same level in all countries, but all the baroque countries were acquainted with manufacturing and consumed manufactured products; consequently, kitsch appeared in all of them as a necessary companion to baroque culture. But regarding the change in the modes of production, the appearance of kitsch above all depended on social causes (behind which, in turn, there could be economic factors) rather than on a direct economic motivation; in this case, it was a question of the concentration of population masses (partly of a nonproductive character) in urban centers.

If baroque culture was bound up with a restored seignorial society having an agrarian base, this interpretation does not contradict its having been a direct manifestation of the manufacturing epoch, or rather, stemming from the development of the consumption of manufactured products. The economic conditions emerging from this fact must be taken into account — although the manufactured products may have been manufactured outside of the country (as often happened in Spain), arriving through legal importation or smuggling. But the great changes of the time depended largely on the social conditions of the great European monarchies. Let us not speak, then, about industrial production in series as something fully developed, but rather about the early mass phase of an early modern society that assembled an abundant population or perhaps a population incorporated and made present as never before. Nourishing and managing this population demanded mass means that had never been used until then and entailed new proposals for governing society.

Undoubtedly the level of manufacturing for the public at large required a series of economic and material conditions that, even in the nineteenth century, only some European countries had succeeded in attaining: a great concentration of manual labor, special buildings where machinery and workers could be brought together, a high degree of development of the division of labor, an elevated rate of capitalist investment, technical inventions, commercialization practices, and expansive consumer markets. None of this was present in the seventeenth century (except for a serious beginning in England), but the first glimpses of the later development were appearing everywhere. It was certainly not a question of a powerful, dominant class going about excluding the broad masses from superior cultural and aesthetic enjoyment. Although not everybody (nor even most individuals or the majority of any social group) could participate in this cultural enjoyment, precisely because of the inferior social conditions of poverty and subjection, it would never have occurred to the dominant social group to use the products of popular culture so that in consuming them the public at large would stay at a low level of development. That could not happen until it began to be realized that there existed an accumulation of human beings who were acting as a mass, as a public, and that correlatively there were appropriate means of production available to increase the manufacturing rates of items — furniture or paintings, comedies, novels or church images — destined for such a public, so that they could be shaped in a predetermined way. Thus before the economic conditions extensively imposed the kitsch cultural industry, political and social conditions were already encountering new possibilities for group interests, possibilities consisting in making use of the incipient manifestations of what we might at the least call *cultural manufacturing*, which was capable of producing in quantities greater than those necessary for maintaining a critical, creative, and original culture (because here quantity fundamentally enters into account).[24]

The problem, then, concerned the way to form an opinion that the masses would receive or that would be suitable for mass reception. Kitsch in the baroque correlated to what there was of the technique of manipulation: the same thing, therefore, that made it a "guided culture."

In relation to mass culture, the problem has always been formulated as to whether the public is given what it desires or whether one succeeds in making it desire what is offered. There is no doubt that the public is conditioned by the offer confronting it and that everything hinges on that offer being presented in such a way that certain feelings are provoked to which the public seems to respond. Whoever undertakes the production of kitsch culture is directly interested in that process and has placed himself or herself in the service of the interests served by that culture. Opinions are manipulated in the service of determinate interests. Since the scholars who have studied the social phenomenon of popular culture in our time belong to the larger countries their research has focused on the printing firms of greatest circulation, the largest department stores, and the biggest organizations of radio and television; as a consequence, it has been easy for them to discover, behind all these complexes, commercial interests on a grand scale. When in the seventeenth century, however, the first productions appeared that were oriented toward a "public" proper (or, more rigorously, to a public sociologically defined as such) kitsch was used as the effective expedient to shape types, form mentalities, and group masses together ideologically. Thus there were individuals whose opinions were extrarationally based, in the service of the epoch's economic, political, and social organization — in the interests of the monarchy and the seignorial group. To applaud Lope in his *Fuenteovejuna* was to be on the side of the monarchy with its vassals, freemen, and plebs. To applaud Quevedo was the same, although there could arise cases of disagreement among those who formed the ruling group; the same goes for deriving enjoyment from Góngora, Villamediana, and Arquijo. In none of these cases — in those I have cited and many others — were the works praised because something in the text, on the canvas, or in the scenario proposed adherence to the system; rather it is because they helped to prepare the mentality that was to serve as its base.

The seventeenth-century culture industry — the thousands of paintings and sonnets and theatrical works, but also clothing, lampoons and placards, ways and occasions to converse, stroll, be entertained — anchored its manipulation in the centers where taste was imposed. Was it happenstance that there were centers — and even disputes about them (recall the preceptist Carballo and many others) — where it was established that one had to form whatever taste proved acceptable, centers that were always coextensive with those upon whom power acted? Of course this doesn't mean that rejections of what was proposed did not frequently occur: one must keep in mind the conflictive nature of the seventeenth century. And undoubtedly the many creations conceived by Spanish baroque writers and artists — creations that highly cultured individuals took pleasure in — produced no less often a full and direct aesthetic enjoyment on a level above conflict and disagreement.

Macdonald observed that for political and not commercial reasons masscult in the Soviet Union is imposed from above and aims more toward propaganda and pedagogy than entertainment. Even without knowing the Russian world from within, whoever has observed the masses of visitors passing through the rooms of the Tretyakov Museum in Moscow will understand this distinction. Similarly, the seventeenth-century absolute monarchies first showed the necessity of attracting and moving the masses in their opinions; there already existed many different incipient and incomparably small mass groups, and their adherence was decisive in the epoch's conflicts and more so in its wars. These same monarchies comprehended that they had to use cultural resources that allowed for influencing not the differences between individuals but "the reflections that one individual shares with any other." Thus the predilection for using techniques — or perhaps simply procedures — of reproduction; all kitsch technology, from printing to television, tends in itself and from its first moment toward repetitive production.[25] Applying it to contemporary times, Giesz wrote: "Kitsch and mass psychology have the same structure. Today's producers of kitsch are not naive thinkers but astute mass psychologists, that is, persons who undoubtedly possess a consciousness of kitsch, who even go so far as to investigate systematically the techniques to produce the specific lived experiences of kitsch."[26] Today this is beyond question. Did Richelieu and the Count-Duke conceive of it in this way? Did Lope and Molière know about it? Undoubtedly so. If we take into account the infinite storehouse of notions about individuals' mass reactions that can be found among the disorderly pages of the Tacitists, we become convinced that many were trying to disseminate a type of culture — without failing to cultivate works of a higher level — based on reiteration, sentimentalism, easy passions that valorize the self, subordination to a recipe book of known solutions, and literary poverty. Furthermore (and perhaps this helps to explain why it is so difficult to discover what the baroque was, specifically in terms of the greatness of its cultural works), there is scarcely a baroque work of high quality — from Bernini's *Santa Teresa* to Poussin's *Pastoral*, to Calderón's *La vida es sueño* — that escapes being touched by kitsch elements. Everything that belongs to the baroque emerges from the necessities of manipulating opinions and feelings on a broad public scale.

As the sixteenth century advanced, those concerned with religion showed themselves to be more interested in the problems of its preservation or dissemination among the popular masses than in anything else. Those in charge of affirming and consolidating the monarchical governments or, in general, the princes of each country relied more on the necessity of their reception among the peoples and the problems deriving therefrom. Those who wrote, painted, sculpted, and instructed seemed to act before more numerous publics, so that the problem of acceptance or rejection by one or another single individual disappeared, and in its place was posed the complex problematic of mass adherence or rejection.

But the public's incorporation into society and the formation of communal or public opinion did not mean that those masses of population individually obeyed uniform criteria. Precisely the shaping techniques used to make the baroque secure reveal the intention of forming unanimous opinions in favor of one or another position, but concretely it turned out to be in favor of the ruling minority of society governing by virtue of its traditional power. Let us recall that as the baroque was on its way out, La Bruyère, seemingly recording an aspect of the baroque inheritance, defined the automaton: "The automaton is a fool, he is a machine, a jack-in-the-box [*ressort*]; the counterweight takes him away, makes him move, makes him turn, always in the same direction and with the same regularity; he is uniform . . . What appears least in him is his soul; it does not act, does not perform, it rests."[27] In its final results, the baroque engendered a certain measure of automatism as a product of the "culture industry" we have already mentioned. But then, as at any other time, the masses did not eliminate disagreement among themselves, and their activity merged and was even unified above the differences. Therein resided the tension that in baroque society, no less than in any modern society, characterized the vacillating discord, opposition, and struggle. In a report to Philip IV about Hurtado de Alcocer's *Discursos* (22 July 1621), López de Madera observed that among people there are individuals who are always wanting to introduce new things, whereas others want to stop everything to interrogate and criticize it; some agree only with the freest imagination, others consider everything impractical that "comes from the diversity of human ingenuity, some being inclined to invent and others to doubt and dissent."[28]

During the baroque's stage of uneasy concern, of violent tensions, this old topos of the incalculable variety of opinions was forcefully and lively expressed in Saavedra Fajardo; moreover, in grasping this fact he came to formulate the first theory about the ideological conditionings of the milieu: Saavedra brought to the fore

> such disagreeing opinions and ways of thinking as there are in men, each one differently understanding things in which we find the same incertitude and variation, because if they are placed here or there they change their colors and forms, either because of the distance, the nearness, or because no thing is perfectly simple, or because of the natural mixtures and varieties that are offered between the senses and sensible things, so that we cannot affirm that they are, but only say that they seem to be, forming an opinion and not knowledge [*ciencia*].[29]

But precisely because of their multiform, changeable, and shifting character, the established disagreements and dissents proved an obstacle to arriving at a positive, univocal course; yet they facilitated a momentary fusion, as by way of irruption, in whatever might be the negative action. In terms of mass psychology (according to Freud), the individual reveals that "his ability to affect becomes extraordinarily intensified, while his intellectual activity is markedly reduced . . . "[30] In such circumstances the diversity of opinions proves ineffective and even comes to be a resource for their annihilation, while all the affective expedients become strengthened.

We still have to formulate an interesting aspect acquired by the restoring or conservative tendency of the baroque, precisely because the period already exhibited those characteristics of massified behavior. It was a society that underwent a seignorial restoration, which, in principle, does not mesh well with the mass character we are attributing to it. Nevertheless, that is an evident manifestation of the conditions of novelty: we are faced with a society whose traditional elements were encouraged, but also one in new circumstances. The Church, the monarchy, and the seignorial preeminence were not simply imposed, as in feudal society — for this reason, the unqualified use of the word *feudalism* to refer to these times is lamentably antihistorical. Now, in fact, the restored tradition was debated or, at least, put into question. That tradition felt the need for acceptance by the masses and made use of means to address them. Baroque culture, in all of its aspects, required a way to approach the popular masses; thus, without taking away from the variety offered by the resources, those manipulating them always attempted to spread them beyond the circle of the aristocratic minority — whatever may have been the principle of selection — to "get to the motivations [*resortes*] of popular emotion."[31] Tapié, following what M. Raymond and others have said, foregrounds the tendency of the baroque to address the masses so as to bring them together and integrate them, prompting their admiration by means of pomp and splendor.[32]

"Popular" and "mass" are not equivalent concepts, but whatever may be the nuances differentiating them, what interests us here is what they have in common. The "bold" painter (*a lo 'valiente'* as he was then described), or the cruel preacher, or the king dressed in his regalia — the first in decorating a church, the second in declaiming a sermon, the third in displaying his majesty — counted on the fact that the expedient [*resorte*] they mobilized would set loose a statistically equivalent reaction in the individuals of the multitude. In the seventeenth century, we are viewing an early phase in meaning displacement in the concept of a *people* [*pueblo*]; now it was equivalent to a crowd or a sum of indistinct, nondifferentiated individuals, to an anonymous mass, a meaning that in the texts of the time was more than once represented by the word *vulgo* (i.e., the common people). In the seventeenth century the *vulgo* was always present, whether one was speaking about literature, dealing with theatrical representations, or commenting on the war, economic difficulties, or politics. "The common people is a body of many heads that is content with nothing," Cellorigo said.[33] The volumes of the *Cartas de jesuitas* probably do not mention a protagonist more often; we may hear very bitter sentences against them, but that constitutes no more than a recognition of their force.[34] The *avisos* of the epoch also frequently refer to them, saying that they are abusive and feared, and advising that they be pacified and calmed.[35]

In the excessive and distorted cultisms of the epoch (and not only in poetry), it was not a question of the author yielding to the elite group or to those who were truly learned, but to those who, because of their frequent contact with the upper groups, had come to hold certain notions or simple learned references and liked displaying their knowledge. The factor of the "common people" was everywhere in baroque society. "Góngora's language mixes the illustrious and the common . . . . this alloy between the literary and the common breaks with the Renaissance tradition and complicates Gongoran language." This penetrating observation by L. Rosales regarding the most striking example can be applied to all baroque products.[36] Since the end of the sixteenth century, it was also manifest in the social forms of piety as spectacle. It happened in such a way (as in other areas) that a new taste appeared, as L. Febvre has observed, for the collective, for anonymity: a taste for "the slow shuffling of feet by those in the ranks of the entourage" so that these processions could be seen from every direction.[37] At this moment, contrary to what Febvre so quickly assumed, there is no reason to conceive of these manifestations as an instance of the Hispanicization of western Europe; in Spain they would remain as an externally imposed form and as "common" expedients of religion.

"The common people reason as common people ultimately, like plebs," noted Pellicer. It was not that they reasoned well or ill, in truth or in error; it was something else, a question of their form of thinking in itself — it was plebeian, not elite, it belonged to everyone else and consequently was appropriate for the concentrations of people when they occurred.[38] Nevertheless, the attitude of the baroque writer had been qualified as against the common people [*antivulgo*]. Mopurgo-Tagliabue was thinking of this when he wrote that the baroque writer "incites an impulse toward the new, the unique, the difficult, as a system of privileged conventions."[39] However, he failed to note that in proceeding in such a manner one is seeking to distinguish oneself from those without privileges. The theme is more complex than it appears. What is sought? A scholar of the theme, A. Collard, tells us that in invoking the word *culto* — a word that develops so much from Herrera to Góngora — Herrera "translated his ideal of an aristocratic idealism, his disdain for the ignorance of the common people, a true antithesis of the *culto* [learned] understood in this way. It is clear that to be a learned poet is equivalent to being a polished, erudite poet and, we should say, an exclusivist one, for minorities."[40]

But it does not suffice to stop there. These minorities were new, alien to any hereditary system; they distinguished themselves precisely by acquiring a good that was at the reach of all if the decision was made to enter on the free course of study. They were not a group apart; they were those who had come to be the few among the many. Their presence demanded the base of the common people, hence the word *culto* would come to be an object of satire and irony in being applied to those with less instruction — that is, it drifted toward a form of kitsch. Today we can see an extreme case that is similar in the problem of the culture of crossword puzzles, which are cultivated by those without learning [*los no cultos*] or, rather, by the consumers of what D. Macdonald calls *midcult* (nor can we fail to see it in masscult). Thus in the seventeenth century the diatribe against the common people became aggravated precisely in those works destined for widespread (within that epoch's proportions) consumption and written by individuals in the service of a public with such characteristics. In *La gran Cenobia*, one of his works directed toward the middle level, Calderón spoke of the "novelesque common people." María de Zayas spoke of "commoner novel-mongering," when what she herself did was write novels of "commoner," i.e., popular culture. Apart from the overworked example of Lope, who confessed to speaking in the common idiom to impose his kitsch products, let us recall the example of Agustín de Rojas in the prologue to *El entretenido*,[41] which contains the harshest diatribe against the commoner public, in a book that can only be written for them.

A passage from López Pinciano prompts us to further reflection: "Notice that the princes and grand seigniors speak with gravity and the utmost simplicity; and notice that lesser people are so witty in their conceits and sayings that in their biting wit they pierce one's skin, pierce one's eardrum."[42] That was certainly one way to arrive at "distinguishing," to make the qualities of this group stand out in distinction. The mass without distinction here appears as participating in literary values. Therefore it is very fitting that the characters of the picaresque novel are admirers of "conceits." Also in 1617, when the baroque was in full bloom, Suárez de Figueroa said that the literary works that mainly manifested artifice and wit — two values that Gracián has taught us to be baroque at its best — were appropriately only about and for common persons, which the author made equivalent to persons from the city.[43] These persons in turn in their social conduct made up the anonymous sum of the urban mass. In the rural milieu, the massification phenomenon proper did not take place.

In all of seventeenth-century Europe, demographic growth came to a standstill or the population declined — and in Spain this recession was manifestly serious; but the large cities generally increased in population, both those that were already consistently acting as the state capital and those that increasingly play an important role as a market or artesan center of a given region. They were in fact the site where the first symptoms of proletarization took place.[44] They were also where the professional activity of the popular groups was represented in art; in their occupations, revolts, and fiestas a multiplicity of behavioral modes occurred, making evident that the baroque explicitly relied on the presence of these groups. Therefore, and without detracting from the fact that baroque culture was mounted as a response to the phenomenon, an attempt was also made to deal with it by another means: to relieve the large city's overcrowding, to cut off this process of massification. As the reaction behind it was inspired in forms of traditional agrarian society, whose restoration was at stake — at least to whatever extent possible, although it was more and more realized to be less viable — the proposed solution, with its evident simplicity, was to reestablish the populations in the countryside.

On 1 February 1619, the Royal Council told Philip III that to empty out the court he should mandate that people return to their lands; the council observed that although the court, as the homeland they held in common, was beneficial, it followed that each one's land of origin must not be any less beneficial. But the council prudently warned that to achieve such ends one must begin with the rich and powerful and not with the common and low-class people. The poor were present at court not because of its amenities but they were drawn there by the presence of those who are to maintain them: it would be wickedness to throw out the miserable people "to some place where they will have no work nor any way to earn something to eat." The council realized that a countryside without seigniors was not a society like the one they imagined restoring. With the rich and the seigniors established in their villages, the farmers would see their products consumed, the lands would be populated, there would be work and prosperity. "Although the Court, the Chanceries and Universities are always glowing with people because money comes from outside and is spent there, if spent in each one's native place, the villages would be more glowing, more populated, and more at ease, and the Court more calmed." (The Royal Council repeated this advice on 4 March 1621; on 23 May 1621 the Junta de Reformación under Philip IV gave him the same advice in very broad terms; the junta repeated it again on 23 August of the same year.)

At the beginning of his reign (28 October 1622), Philip IV's letter to the cities having a vote in the Cortes admitted the advantage of having the grandees and those with titles return to their villages, with the poor and working common people following. To achieve this he announced that indirect measures would be taken to encourage them to abandon the court and to establish themselves in the small settlements in the countryside. These measures were decreed in the *Capítulos de reformación* of Philip IV (10 February 1623), where certain benefits were instituted along with other favorable measures that might indirectly lead the grandees, seigniors, and those with titles who possessed villas with vassals to establish themselves there and personally administer them, at the same time that restrictions were placed on immigration to the large urban centers (Madrid, Seville, Granada). The interest in dissolving the anonymous world concentrated there was already clearly observable in this letter from Philip IV to the cities: "the increase in this Court's population and the many people congregating here, are in every way held to be great disadvantages because in the court there is an excess of danger in leisure, waste in government, and expense in maintaining the living arrangements, since the circumstances and obligations are greater." Measures were announced to overcome these difficulties; but the matter already stood out most prominently, with no pretense, in the *Capítulos de reformación*: it explicitly stated that measures were taken to preserve the court's good government and avoid the overflow of people "so that the court has no more than the necessary people and the congregating of so many is avoided and everybody knows who everybody else is, what they are doing, the reason for their presence and how long they have been present, thereby avoiding all the confusion until now."[45] In fact, however, nothing could arrest the tide of urban concentration, for pleasure was found even in the common people's immense anonymity. Jáuregui called it: "This mundane common people, without number / and different in their inclinations."[46]

We can now offer some support that will allow us to comprehend how baroque culture made use of media that were tailor-made for the masses and the mass effects that were problematically put into operation. For example, the cultivation and widespread interest in the biographical genre is significant. In today's literary world, we know that biographies serve as educating models, based on the figures they present — exemplary or at least suggestive figures, whether positively or negatively; they are used as devices to introduce or preserve, on a mass scale, a general human type or certain behavioral values whose socialization is sought. Lowenthal has studied biographies used to such an end in contemporary North American magazines.[47] By looking at contemporary publishers' catalogues, we can see that publishers who produce for a large public issue many books of this type. The baroque epoch coincidentally discovered the value of biographies as a vehicle of political and moral education (or, rather, of political and moral "shaping") when this latter, whose object is social integration, was directed to a number of people who, compared with previous epochs, could be taken as a multitude of insuperable anonymity. In any case, the dissemination of the genre and its quality reveal tastes belonging to groups of such circumstances. Let us recall the large number of political biographies written by a representative baroque author, Juan Pablo Mártir Rizo,[48] who, well aware that the genre was widely consumed by his contemporary public, also translated some biographies from a French baroque writer, Pierre Mathieu. Seventeenth-century Tacitists and moralists seldom failed to write works of this type, which also found considerable dissemination in the theater.

Few things have such an eloquent mass character as the Spanish comedia. Perhaps because of this it advanced certain traits that are comparable to products of the present time. R. Menéndez Pidal maintained years ago that Lope's works could be qualified as "cinedramas";[49] with analogous criteria, A. Hauser has said that the dramatic creations of Shakespeare have their own continuation in the cinema.[50] Rousset, who has made such fine morphological analyses of baroque works, has compared the production of comedias in that epoch to the current production of films.[51] For N. Salomon, the Spanish baroque comedia, in the greatest phase of its unfolding, developed in social and economic conditions that were uniquely similar to those of contemporary cinematographic production.[52] Without our making a study of the structure of baroque dramatic literature, these references are sufficient for us to accept the relationship of the comedia to forms of art obviously belonging to an epoch with a mass characterization.

It is symptomatic that a writer of novels and, moreover, of some picaresque novels, Salas Barbadillo, hit upon the significance of the Lopesque revolution: what it offered were new precepts that Lope had "better based on reason and adapted to taste."[53] The precepts that were to be followed changed because the addressee of the work changed and the means of the former had to be adapted to the latter. And who was this addressee? The followers of the same school give us the answer. Guillén de Castro tells us that of the comedias in Spain, "their object is striving / to make an entire people hear them, / giving the scholar and the ill-bred / something to laugh and cry about."[54] But perhaps nobody would formulate it as did Ricardo del Turia: "Those who write do so with the object of satisfying the taste of those they write for"; well, the Spanish writers were engaged in "satisfying the many" and they must be praised for that, since instead of always following the same pattern — which would be appropriate for a conservative mentality, for persons based on the high privilege of the traditional estates — they were obligated to "follow new guidelines and precepts every fifteen days." A curious and revealing anecdote tells us the same thing: Lope used to attend the representations of comedias, both his own and others, focusing on the passages evoking the greatest applause from the public so as to keep them in mind when he wrote.[55] Recording the experience of the Spanish comedia, Bances Candamo said that the theater was not for enjoying in solitude nor for superior minds "but to be recited to the people." Its multitudinous character, where the addressee was anonymous, came to be understood — such had been its function in the decades he was examining — when it made manifest this significant social fact: "What worker, no matter how low, does not for mere pennies constitute its judge and lawyer at the same time?"[56] From this multitudinous, nameless, and ownerless circumstance that derived simply from having purchased a ticket — a cheap one that anyone could afford[57] — one obtained the right to become the theater's collective addressee, a very relevant manifestation of baroque culture.

Let us also take note of the indisputable fact regarding the baroque artists' and writers' utilization of symbolist and allegorical procedures that went beyond the boundaries of learned production and occurred in urban fiestas, religious ceremonies, and political spectacles. This technique, utilized as a psychological means to impress people directly and dynamically, was no less characteristic of periods of mass mobilization of opinion. Below we will focus on this question from another angle: its status as a visual medium; but now let us pause to make explicit the significance of referring to public opinion, in terms of the seventeenth century and baroque society.

When, several years ago, I wrote my first book on this epoch, I already called attention to the theme of public opinion.[58] The importance the political writers attributed to it, the warnings directed to the rulers regarding its force, its variability, and the means of channeling and dominating it were all worthy of note. Saavedra Fajardo went so far as to maintain that it was the sole basis for holding on to power.[59] Political writers, as well as moralists and costumbristas insisted on its almost invincible influence (above all, those writers influenced by the current of Tacitism and of a belated Machiavellianism). In the political sphere but also in the entire realm of social existence, it was declared to possess an operative effect that could not be ignored. "Opinion holds the key to reputation," Lope put it.[60] Ruiz de Alarcón deemed it an inexorable law: according to him, given the compelling character with which it imposed itself, it was no less inexorable to submit to opinion, to the point that not even the most powerful were exempt from being subject to it.[61] "Opinion moves the world," wrote Juan Alfonso de Lancina,[62] and Hobbes attested that the world was governed by opinion.[63] For his part, Pascal declared acceptance of the thesis he found explicit in the title of an Italian book — *Dell'opinione regina del mondo:* "Thus opinion is the queen of the world."[64]

Almansa y Mendoza, one of the writers who in the first quarter of the seventeenth century became an instrument for producing opinion, recounted to his readers that the king had sent a projected pragmatic sanction, with many resolutions provided for reforming the kingdom, to many seigniors, in each city and at the head of each faction, so they could study it and make propositions regarding the material. Almansa exaggerated the scope of the consultation, but that in itself informs us of the gesture represented by taking public opinion into consideration. Contrary to what a formal assembly of the Cortes would have entailed, thus without appealing to the approval of the "kingdom," inquiring into their wishes, and, therefore, without in any way diminishing his absolutism, Philip IV nonetheless informally made a broad concession to the opinion of the country.[65]

Not without serious grounds in the sociohistorical circumstances of their time, Richelieu and Mazarin and even Louis XIII were interested in early manifestations of newspaper printing: they protected the *Gazette* of T. Renaudot and included in it their own writings or writings drawing direct inspiration from them, demonstrating the interest that authority has in controlling an instrument addressing and dedicated to the public, a mode of access to anonymous opinion that has been utilized ever since.[66] In Spain the first development of printing and the pressure of the state on it also take place at this time.[67] On the occasion of events such as those taking place in the War of Catalonia, Francisco M. de Melo realized that "letters and reports" were used to influence psyches, on the part of all parties.[68] José M. Jover called attention to the great quantity of newspaper and fly-by-night printed matter that were launched during certain phases of the Thirty Years' War to intervene in a passing public opinion.[69] Such a procedure began earlier and still continued later; realizing that seventeenth-century printing had a greater dissemination than might be believed, we understand what a force it had in itself on a restless society. The writings of the epoch referred to the eagerness with which people awaited the appearance of these papers or volumes of news (allusions exist in Lope); in addition, there were references from Andrés de Almansa y Mendoza himself, one of the authors of the earliest genre, about the zeal with which people wanted to be informed: "It is always good to find out something new,"[70] he commented. There was a market for news, and the printers sought it and used their money to print and disseminate it. "News is merchandise," it has been said, and if this began being the truth of merchants and perhaps rulers in the seventeenth century, we should think about who bought the papers and booklets, who participated in its reading by listening to it being read, and who received the reverberations of the news: three circles, each one wider than the preceding one, which added together formed a considerable mass in the cities of the time. Varela collected curious data about reprintings of Madrid's *Gazeta Nueva* in Seville, Saragossa, Valencia, Málaga, and Mexico.[71] The editors of Almansa's *Cartas* collected, as an appendix, bibliographical notices of more than a hundred *relaciones* of events and similar writings of an informative nature from the few years spanning the time of the so-called *Cartas* (from 1621 to 1626). In the following decades their number soared. The infante Juan José of Austria — during the second half of the century the most uneasy figure in the Madrid political milieu — utilized these instruments of occasional printed matter on a grand scale in his genuine "campaigns" of opinion, which were already noted as such by the duke of Maura. In any case, we still know little about what affected Spain and about the public authorities' intervening in the publication of the *relaciones, avisos,* and *gacetas* (aside from what was pertinent to censure), for the origins of printing continue to be very little studied. There has been scarcely any investigation concerning the collaboration of the rulers with the newspapers. Even so, the partial study of E. Varela Hervías has led to the discovery of two interesting references to Philip IV's direct interventions, personally making emendations in some texts published in the *Gazeta Nueva*. In Varela's study we find that the editor of this publication, Francisco Fabro Bremundan, moved in the circles of some of the highest personages (and we would expect that he was on the receiving end of certain ideas and probably something more). Those papers — booklets or simply loose leaves or handbills with news — often referred to religious events and gave rise to constant intervention by the Inquisition, which, when it acted to condemn and punish, was sometimes supported and applauded by other publications.[72]

In this new appeal to public opinion, it was not a question of giving access to the people's judgments and estimations, which would accord with the natural good discernment that was attributed to them in traditional society. In medieval society, popular judgment was considered to be a natural element, with a healthy and original character and endowed with elemental virtues, a trustworthy and sure support for the inherited secular order in society: it manifested a reasonableness in which testimony expressed itself by the natural pathways of divine reason, a reason that ordered humankind's commonly held life by means of the same innately reasonable nature. Popular judgment was the spontaneous channel of moral reason. Such is the meaning of the aphorism "vox populi, vox Dei." But when after the sixteenth century these words appeared more and more rarely and instead phrases with an opposite meaning were repeated over and over, it arose from the fact that in place of the traditional, medieval image of the people, there now appeared the image of the common populace as an anonymous mass whose way of thinking did not translate exactly into a natural order of reasonableness. This formulation reflected an inherited opposition, one from the medieval and Aristotelian tradition; only now, in the early modern centuries, its meaning was altered. In effect, the traditional moralists had distinguished between reason and opinion, recognizing in the first the ordered and constant transcription of truth and in the second a disordered, whimsical, and unstable way of thinking that was ordinarily liable to error. In *La Celestina*, Fernando de Rojas had his characters attribute to the common people the trait of being awash in opinion, contrary to the truths of reason.[73] But baroque writers contemplated the experience of the invincible force evident in mass ways of thinking. They were even aware of the revolutionary energy instilled in some cases, and the disquiet that always proved disruptive vis-à-vis the established state of things: the people, wrote a Jesuit, "are always perturbed in their very nature."[74] The figure of the agitator of opinion had its origin in the Tacitists.[75] They explained that it was thought impossible to oppose them head on, just as one could not go against the current of a flooding river (the image of the "current of opinion" would appear at once). Opinion, which was perhaps fickle yet overwhelming, was the mass way of thinking. "The people have a booming voice, with a sentence and decree that is terrible and frightening," notes Céspedes.[76] It could not be contained: "The popular voice runs with great freedom," as it was said in *Guzmán de Alfarache*.[77] These writers who affirmed the force of opinion in the world never asked themselves — at least during this early stage — about its justice, truth, or rationality; they only noted that it must be taken into account and that means adequate to its nature must be used to guide and dominate it.

We saw how culture has grown on all levels since the incipient moments of modernity, although in later times its growth has been more accentuated. There was evidently a great surge in the seventeenth century, as there has been an incomparably greater one in more recent times. But this growth was not equal, nor did it follow an arithmetic ratio, in the three levels that sociologists — some of them cited in the preceding pages — have come to distinguish: refined culture, midcult, and masscult. The two latter expanded considerably, and especially the third. I venture to maintain that this was linked to a (specifically modern) phenomenon: since the seventeenth century, the upper groups paid more attention to the opinion of the lower groups. They did not hold them in a higher esteem intellectually — nor was there reason it should have been otherwise. But we know that the lower groups became accustomed to seeing, hearing, being informed, and forming criteria about many subjects that had been completely foreign to them, giving rise to a public opinion that constantly became broader and expressed itself more forcefully. Before this, says Shils (although he would postpone the fact until a relatively recent time, I would antedate it to the seventeenth century), "the cultural life of the consumers of a mediocre and brutal culture was relatively silent, unseen by the intellectuals. The immense advances in audibility and visibility of the the lower levels of culture is one of the most noticeable traits of mass society. This is, in turn, intensified by another trait of mass society, i.e. the enhanced mutual awareness of different sectors of the society."[78] It is precisely these phenomena, obviously to a lesser degree of development than later, that we have attempted to indicate in the seventeeth century.

The opinions of the multitude of common people were presented — by those dealing with it at that time — in terms of a concept that underwent an important alteration during the baroque: taste. The anonymous mass of people act according to their taste, whether they are applauding a theatrical play or exalting the figure of a personage. Taste is an opinion that, distinct from judgment, does not derive from a mental elaboration; it is rather a valorizing inclination that arrives by extrarational means. R. Klein has studied and distinquished the concepts of *giudizio* [judgment] and *gusto* [taste] in the Renaissance and has pointed out the change in the latter term during the baroque. But Klein limited his study to an individual plane; accordingly, taste comes to be the criterion of valorization with which a person intuitively and immediately ascertains the value of the contemplated object, whether by his or her spontaneous and natural exquisite qualities or because of the excellent sedimentation that is internalized through the cultivation of sensibility and intelligence. Thus, according to Klein's study, taste rapidly acquires a normative character that is revealed in the frequent expression of "good taste."[79] The cultivated, learned individual is said to have taste, which implies that this individual accepts an entire system of norms that, although not possessed by rational means, are adhered to on deeper levels. In this way there occurs an approximation between taste and judgment that keeps both on a level of upper-class values.[80]

But in addition to this, the baroque knew another meaning of the word "taste" in which it was not referred to the solitary individual, nor was it characterized as making a choice; on the extrarational side, it was stressed to the point that it turned out to be incompatible with the very idea of qualitative norms.[81] In this sense, taste was the disordered, irrational, confused criterion of value (which was free only to the extent that it was such) with which the unlearned common people establish their preferences; that is, not the individuals that singularly made up the people and whose personal quality didn't enter in, but the popular mass as a whole that let themselves get carried away by their passions, without reason, without a mentally elaborated and objective norm. In both senses, the concept of taste projected into the sphere of morality and subsequently into that of politics.[82] This led to the efforts of the ruling groups to impose themselves on the plane of mass taste. Lope — exuding privileged culture — eagerly served the flighty taste of the common people, which means that he was eagerly trying to control it. In this light one must see the presence of the *public* that the Lopists counted on for their comedias;[83] the *multitude* that was involved in as many rebellions as occurred in the epoch, and whose image was outlined by the Tacitist politicians; the *common people*, whose esteem elevated or humiliated, and whom Gracián and so many others who cultivated morality tried to influence by writing an infinite number of maxims; the *mass*, whose force, in any case, was terrible and had to be channeled; or, finally, the *people* [*pueblo*], who, far from being innocent, unanimous, and offering a noteworthy resistance to any moral recommendation, were a blind force that had to be contained with an ailing apparatus. Prudence, wrote friar Juan de Salazar, uses "loving deceptions with the people, beneficial and useful to teach them and obligate them to do what they should."[84]

The seventeenth century was an epoch of masses, undoubtedly the first in modern history, and the baroque was the first culture to make use of expedients to produce mass effects. This is attested to by the character of the theater, in its texts and scenario procedures; by the mechanized and external piety of post-Tridentine religion; by the politics of attraction and repression that the states began to use; by innovations in the warring arts. Might not printing, which since the mid-sixteenth century became the fundamental instrument of culture, also be considered the first known example of anything close to mass communication?

I have taken into account several characterisitics in making use of the concept of mass in these pages. First is the heterogeneity of the components of the mass in regard to their estate of origin or with respect to any other criterion of social group formation: individuals act outside the limits of the traditional group to which they in each case belong, and they are united in functional and impersonal forms of behavior extending beyond differences in profession, age, wealth, and beliefs. Some have said that within the open-air comedia theater, one could be without class distinction, "democratically"; but this adverb is out of place: it was not a democratic effect; it was a mass effect. Second, there takes place a situation of anonymity that, on the one hand, stems from this estrangement from one's personal background where one is more or less known and, on the other hand, from the great number of juxtaposed existences where it is possible for an individual to be inserted into a mass milieu without being able to take into account the singular circumstances of each one. Third, one's inclusion in the mass is always partial, in terms of time and of the totality of the individual, who can continue being and appearing as a fundamental and irreplaceable singularity in other activities of existence. Fourth (and contrary to what some passages from Le Bon and other sociologists seem to say), although the mass does not presuppose physical proximity, its individuals can find themselves personally isolated from each other, united only in the identity of their response and in the shaping factors acting upon them. Let us recall the examples of the Church and of the army that

Freud cited as mass formations. Protonational bonds that linked members of baroque societies also had a mass aspect. Its individuals, unknown to each other and spread over a broad territory, felt united by an emotional inclination toward the community and toward their prince, who was presented by ad hoc propaganda as the example of those values which had socialized within the group.

In the city of the baroque century, those characteristics began to emerge in close relation to the conditions of its peculiar urban ambit. Now we are going to deal with this new aspect that is typical of baroque culture.

Chapter 4
An Urban Culture

"If we ventured to give a formula, we would say that the Renaissance was an urban civilization whose creative centers represented small zones of activity; the baroque, on the contrary, was a product of imperial mass civilizations, of Rome and Spain."[1] These words from Braudel confirm the thesis I put forward in the previous chapter. But although in the baroque the initiative and direction of culture passed from the city to the state,[2] this does not mean that the city, with its own specific characteristics, was not the setting for baroque culture. In its physiognomy and social structure and in the role it played, the fifteenth-century city had nothing to do with the great urban centers of the seventeenth century. The new culture of the epoch cannot be understood without taking into account the social phenomena deriving from the cities' peculiar circumstances. We could introduce the following distinction: if the culture of the fifteenth and sixteenth centuries was more city oriented (and a certain degree of municipal freedom and of personal relationship among the inhabitants is linked to this concept), the baroque was more properly urban — putting in this word a nuance of anonymous and administrative life.

During the stage of the baroque, its rulers and the individuals of the dominant classes in general were not seigniors who lived in the countryside, and although efforts were made to staunch the flow of absenteeism, it only became greater: the rich lived in the city, and the bureaucrats administered from there and became rich. At the same time, although there was peasant unrest that exploded everywhere into occasional revolts, in the seventeenth century it was the urban populations that proved disturbing to those in power, and the politics of control was usually directed toward them, which even translated into topographical changes in the baroque city. This city was also where the historical monuments were erected: the creations of painters, architects, and sculptors were concentrated in Rome, Vienna, Prague, Paris, Madrid, Seville, and Valencia, along with many others. The voluminous quantity of literature in the seventeenth century was produced and consumed in those baroque urban centers. This very literature reflected the indisputable predominance of the urban ambiance: almost all of Pérez de Montalbán's series of novels have Spanish cities as the setting for their plots;[3] the geography of twenty of María de Zayas' novels encompasses perhaps all the important cities of the Hispanic world.[4] Céspedes incorporated the city into the novelesque story in such a way that the story ordinarily includes, as an integral element of its development, an elegy of the city where the narrative happens[5] (apart from the many times when cities are mentioned in the body of his longer novels).[6] Each picaresque novel is necessarily linked to one city or another. This reference to the geography of the city that is contemplated in the baroque has an apparent sociohistorical significance. From the outset, we are made to see that its protagonists live in the cities and move from one city to another; the action happens there; the great fiestas animating the seventeenth century take place in their ambit, with such a contrast of light and shadow. The drama of baroque culture is a characteristically urban drama.

   In establishing, like so many others, a connection between baroque and society, Tapié presented the baroque as a rural culture that was dominated by a peasant mentality under the effect of an agrarian economy, so that the new cultural forms would not have penetrated the countries with a more developed commercial economy. The apogee of the monarchy, the fortified hierarchization of society, the strengthening of land ownership, the reconstitution of the great seignorial domains, and the worsening of the peasant's situation were the basic facts of the epoch, and they denoted "a predominantly agrarian society that is seignorial and noble on top, but peasant in the immense majority of its components."[7] Tapié cited a curious case: the dissemination of the cult of St. Isidro, who was canonized in 1622, with the cult soon extending from Castile to Tirol, Italy, Brittany, and Poitou. From that he deduced the fact of the predominance of agrarian society, which was evident, along with the widespread preservation of the customs of peasant life. But the sociopolitical aspects that this predominance entailed — from the administrative predominance of bureaucratized monarchies for the most part, to the land ownership revalorization that was produced by urban investments or the urbanization of seignorial customs in daily life, even though in some cases those with power returned to the countryside — were characteristic urban manifestations. (Is it by chance that this Isidro the Farmer belonged to the ambit of Madrid life and was honored when the greatness of the capital city was at its summit?)

   Tapié's point of view offers a version that is dubious at best: according to it, the baroque spread throughout the countryside because the peasants, in poverty and perhaps starving, were given the chance to contemplate the abundance and magnificence of the palaces and churches. Despite seeing them only from outside, they could experience all this as if it were their own and thus could participate in the wealth. In the church where they could freely enter or in the palace whose image they were able to envision, their miserable and hard life was thereby given access to the enjoyment of the rich and the marvelous. For these reasons, Tapié assumed that the peasants were gratified with the baroque instead of rejecting it as too luxurious or ostentatious. The bourgeoisie, on the other hand, only felt itself attracted to the extent that it enjoyed the cruelty and the spectacle, without ever choosing to cultivate it. The royalty and nobility, inasmuch as they were seigniors of the countryside, were strongly interested in the baroque. Ultimately the baroque "became widespread in the agricultural milieus."[8]

Against such an explanation, we cannot but think about the large and resplendent churches of the seventeenth century that were generally not found in the countryside, as were the rich Cluniac monasteries or even the great Cistercian monuments, but in the middle of populated and expansive cities. This is the ambit of the sumptuous Jesuit churches, and we know of no other more representative of the baroque. But, in addition, we ask ourselves how many peasants would have entered into the interior of the palaces, whose surrounding rural ambience (in the very few cases where it actually existed) was extremely artificial.

In a later work, Tapié retained his reference to the peasant base of baroque society, alluding to the restoration of seignorial powers and pointing out the economic boom in the countryside where the seigniors' properties were located, but he added that one must take into account the commercial wealth of the maritime cities where a zeal for ostentation developed, given impetus by the lavishness of the rich bourgeoisie. Contrary to his previous articulation of a determining and almost exclusive bond between baroque and agrarian economy, he now admitted not an incompatibility but, instead, a congruence between baroque and bourgeoisie.[9] Certainly, there are numerous baroque retables preserved in small localities, immersed in rural environments. These are found in Spain, as everyone knows who has gone through little Anadalusian, Castilian, and Aragonese towns. They are found in France, according to what we now have at our disposal of the rich inventory and the rigorous study published about those in the northwest region of the country.[10] But this very study makes us realize that it is a question of belated works that depended on prior patterns coming from more active urban centers, from where they would have been disseminated to the rural milieu.[11] I believe that in Spain one would come to the same conclusion.[12]

Francastel, who in so many points was opposed to Tapié's thesis, nonetheless came to agree about linking the appearance and development of the baroque to an agrarian milieu. His words can thus lead to confusion about its urban character:

the baroque triumphed wherever a feudal and agrarian type of society was maintained, wherever a traditional order dominated by Church people reigned without objection.[13] However — leaving aside the unqualified use of the term *feudal* as an anachronism that leads to error, and the fact that one cannot say that the rule of the traditional order was imposed without objection — when we become aware of the strong social tensions on which the baroque was based and from which this new culture was born, we think one should be more precise: the society where this culture occurred should be more properly designated as "of an agrarian economy" rather than "of an agrarian type," since the cultural guidelines that were imposed in conformity with its predominant groups were markedly transformed by a process of urbanization.

The foregoing analysis, which is based on authors who, although they polemicize among themselves, agree on key points, shows us that important transformations have occurred in the panorama of the question, with alterations in the role delegated to the social groups and to all sorts of factors that have an effect on the theme. After forty years of study (and based on my own research, which, although it draws support from Spanish sources, seeks to keep in mind those from other countries), I have come to the following formulation: the baroque was produced and developed in an epoch when demographic movements already obligated one to distinguish between rural milieu and agrarian society. At that time the culture of the city emerged, dependent on the conditions within which urbanization continued to spread; those conditions even had an effect on the nearby zones of peasants that had relations with the city. The city culture remained bound, like urban society itself, to a base of a prevailing agrarian economy in which, notwithstanding, a considerable level of monetary and mercantile relations had been attained, leading to consequent mobility. The first results of this mobility must serve as the point of departure for understanding the cultural and social facts that the new epoch offers us.

As a theoretician of "social change" has said with respect to the preindustrial societies of an agrarian base, and with a certain degree of amplitude in mercantile operations, "the city is the principal source of innovations for such communities and holds the political, religious, and economic reins."[14] This can be confirmed in the seventeenth century, and in this way we can comprehend the complex phenomenon of the baroque being an urban culture, the product of a city that lived in close connection with the country, and upon which it exercised a strong influence.

In the historical phase of the seventeenth century, production took place in the country; from there came all the food products and the greater part of the artisanal industry. Notwithstanding, the city drained almost all of the revenue because, once it was transformed into money — at least to a considerable degree — the city absorbed it in the form of taxes (sometimes still paid in kind) with which bureaucrats, military men, court servants, the free professions, and others were paid; or it received it in exchange for ecclesiastical, laical, or seignorial rights and for other duties administered outside of the rural milieu. The produced wealth was concentrated to a great degree within the urban ambit. That drainage of money accumulated in the area of the city and disappeared from the village, making its commerce difficult at the same time that a reduced self-sufficiency made a greater volume of commercial transactions necessary. Simultaneously with this general European phenomenon,[15] when an appreciable number of small towns responded to the question asked by the royal administration about what they were most in need of (in the *Relaciones topográficas de los pueblos de España* ordered by Philip II and with data corresponding to the moment immediately preceding the epoch we are studying), they said money for commerce.[16] The affirmation made about the boom of the cities is valid not only in sixteenth-century but also in seventeenth-century Europe (apart from the case of England): it did not come from industrial growth but from their commercial expansion into the surrounding area and from their domination of the countryside, whose supply and demand relationship the urban areas controlled to a great extent. If peasants continued to think about producing to meet their needs, under an archaic ideal of autarchic unity, it is certain that the responses contained in the *Relaciones* show that they were ceasing to think in this way.[17] From there came the social influence of the city over the country, which gave rise to the dissemination in the latter of modes of dress and other aspects of culture. Let us recall the acute observation made by Lope de Deza: the zeal to imitate the city dwellers ruins the farmers, the country people, "principally those in the areas surrounding the cities and big towns"; and once they go to the city they never want to leave it, despite whatever difficulties they find.[18] The shifting of economic power to the city — the rich living there even though their wealth was agrarian based — explains the city dwellers' continuous buying of lands, above all in the areas near the most important centers, one of the phenomena most seriously influencing the structural disturbances of the epoch.

Many factors accentuated this process, which began in the later medieval centuries; in the seventeenth century, it reached a new level. Let us consider the unfavorable structural circumstances taking place in Spain — and no less in that part of Europe that had an equivalent baroque experience. There was an accumulation of property in the hands of the seigniors, lay persons, and priests. Support for this was drawn from a wide-ranging order of jurisdictional, administrative, and fiscal privileges that, contrary to what it had been claiming, the monarchy had not combated nor attempted to limit. If we add to this the injurious social consequences of the disturbances provoked by the monarchy's monetary and public spending policies, which resulted in misery and starvation, we can recognize the circumstances that so harshly cut short the production development already underway, annihilated work productivity, ruined artisans, small landholders, and day laborers, and gave an even greater impetus to the concentration of the ownership of lands and livestock — accentuating the separation between landholders and those without land and worsening the situation of the latter. All this in itself did not inevitably lead to an uncontainable tendency toward reversing the predominance of the country in favor of the city. But in the European historical situation of the late Middle Ages, the escape from such an unfavorable configuration of circumstances would lead to a displacement of the center of gravity to the urban nuclei. The consequence was to prompt a rural exodus and a growing absenteeism that underlay the characteristic demographic transformations of the epoch. Since the end of the fourteenth century, Europe was acquainted with the phenomenon of the abandonment of populated towns and the appearance of the ghost towns, which were so frequently and dramatically referred to, two centuries later, in Spanish economic and political writings.[19]

The effort to return rich, city-based landholders to their rural properties must be viewed as a consequence of this development. Political reasons led to the search for this regress from above: to avoid the presence of distinguished persons around whom the discontented masses could rally. And there were socioeconomic reasons on which all the others depended. In the recommendation of 2 September 1609, the Council of Castile, in hopes of improving production in the countryside, introducing discipline among the peasant groups, reintegrating the privileged groups into the sentiment of their traditional duties (which would constitute such firm support for the situation), and relieving the city's threatening congestion, proposed that measures be taken for the seigniors to return to live on their lands. With them closer to the villages, the peasants would perceive themselves better supported and the farms better administrated; the products of the land would be more abundantly consumed, and thus money would circulate better and the taxpaying producers could have more income at their disposal to pay sales taxes, *tercias*, or other imposed levies.[20] The Council of Castile was probably inspired by two motives: a political one, to put distance between the court and those seigniors whose attitude of discontent and criticism was becoming more and more dangerous; and a socioeconomic one, to strengthen social discipline in an effort to increase falling production. Measures from the epoch of Philip IV continued to affirm the necessity of relieving Madrid's congestion.

In the seventeenth century, the Mediterranean and western Europe greatly increased their demands for cereals from the Baltic countries, forcing them to seek an increase in production. In Russia, this demand led to the concentration of great masses of serfs under the domination of rich landowners in the countryside, which presupposed submission of the peasantry, reduction of the importance of the intermediate groups, and a diminishing internal market, with the consequent ill nourishment of the lower classes. Ultimately, it resulted in a strengthening of the feudal regime, similar in some of its effects to what occurred in parts of Andalusia. In this recommendation by the Council of Castile, underlying an apparent economic motivation one observes an entire policy that was directed toward the strengthening of the seignorial social order; such a policy proved an obstacle to structural changes because the urban establishment of the powerful groups threatened to disrupt that social structure.

Despite everything, including some of those isolated examples in Andalusia (which certainly did not contribute to pacifying the opposition tendencies), it was not possible in the whole of the country to create a situation similar to that of the northern Slavic countries. I don't know whether the recognition of the development of individualist energies in the Renaissance had any part to play; probably the economic factors were not the same, and all the cultural and religious motivations mitigated against a solution based on force, which was what fostered servitude in Russia. The crisis continued being harsh, its negative consequences of a greater and greater scope. But an element of vigorous individual life or, if one prefers, of freedom proved an obstacle to the subduing of energies that were present in the seventeenth-century crisis. Those in power, obsessed by order, did what they could: the absolute monarchy put its expedients into play, and the councils obediently proposed measures of severe control. But some lucid minds comprehended what was going to take place in this serious city-country tension. Sancho de Moncada, for example, had no confidence in direct means for cutting the excess of population in the court, and he rejected the idea that people should be forced to leave:

> First, because it is an impossible means, for all will defend their staying, as they have done many other times, and when they leave today they will return tomorrow, whenever enforcement is not so rigorous. Second, because to force somebody to live in a place against his will is the same as putting him in prison. Third, because how can one force persons to live where they will die of starvation and where there is nowhere they can earn enough to eat? Fourth, because the means are violent and thus do not last long; therefore, the only sure way is for their own advantage to lead them to their lands.[21]

But now I must emphasize a point that frequently leads to confusion: rural exodus was not equivalent to agrarian exodus, nor did the predominance of the city, in the realm of culture, deny the existence of an agrarian economy; nor did forms of mentality linked to this latter become eliminated, but rather they were integrated in the early phases of a process of urbanization. At the end of the sixteenth and first half of the seventeenth century, the total population was diminished in all of Europe and very pointedly in Spain. But that diminution either did not affect the urban population or affected it to a lesser degree than in the country; in many instances, the portion lost by the cities — for example, in the plagues that proved more the scourge of urban population centers — was offset by immigration coming from the country. In Spain, the century's four plagues reduced the population of Castile by approximately one-fourth; but frequently the cities recuperated and even increased their level of population at the expense of the country, although on other occasions they remained below the figures of the second half of the sixteenth century.

These declines in the urban population turn out to be more dramatic if one considers that a good part of the poverty-stricken rural population had gone to take refuge in the city. In that century there was a concentration of the Castilian rural population, produced, on the one hand, by the tax burden, which was making life in the villages and towns more and more difficult; on the other hand, by the concentration of property. The creation of new seignorial domains also contributed; the seigniors were interested in depopulating their small towns so as to take over their communal lands. Owing to this varied set of causes central Spain was covered with ghost towns; some disappeared completely, others became private farms in which the old church played the role of the chapel.[22]

In any case, then, regardless of the set of factors, the city took on a greater importance despite the fact that in absolute terms the population of many cities was diminished and that as a whole there was a demographic decline. One would even have to add that the majority of the cities participating actively in the development of baroque culture saw an increase in population, although all around there was a dramatic recession.

The phenomenon that Braudel observed in the meridional area of the European continent became more acute in the seventeenth century: in the middle of human deserts, the growth of urban nuclei gave the population centers an oasis character. In the Mediterranean, the cities were true oases that frequently appear in the middle of broad expanses of desert, a fact that travelers pointed out with respect to Spain but that was common to the geography of the region.[23]

In the judgment of Domínguez Ortiz, that redistribution, based on rural exodus and urban concentration, explained the peculiar structure of the Castilian and Andalusian countryside, with settlements of several thousand inhabitants separated by tens of kilometers of unpopulated zones.[24] The Royal Council pointed out to Philip III — in an important recommendation on 1 February 1619 — the distressing situation of the realm's small peasant towns: "The houses collapse and no one rebuilds them again, the lands lie fallow, the residents flee, never to return, and leave the fields deserted and, what is worse, the churches abandoned."[25] This problem obsessed all those writing on questions of government in Spain, and even nowadays some have interpreted it as a univocal manifestation of depopulation, in the way that the seventeenth-century critics understood it. But in many cases it was no more than the result of a displacement that led a rural group to abandon its old dwellings — in years of penury, on occasions of an epidemic, or fleeing a tyrannical seignior — and transfer to the cities. Indeed, depopulation was a well-known phenomenon in the Spanish seventeenth century.

The houses of many towns collapsed, along with those of some cities; nonetheless, in others new ones emerged or the suburb began to appear. What is certain is that while some cities at the end of the sixteenth century had diminished in size, such as Valladolid, Medina del Campo, or Córdoba, the majority of the Castilian cities were growing, and they preserved this increase in the repeated demographic crises of the seventeenth century. In some cases, such as Madrid and Seville, the increase was spectacular.[26] Contemporary writers, such as Sancho de Moncada, Benito de Peñalosa and Lope de Deza, were fully conscious of this phenomenon.[27]

From the fifteenth century forward, the countries of the Mediterranean area in particular continued to be areas of an agrarian economy (until the different times when their industrial revolution took place, if it did at all); but this agrarian economy remained pressured and even guided by the urban centers, whose provisioning, in one aspect, continued to be the principal mercantile activity of the region where they were located, and whose system of culture ruled the surrounding social life.[28] Contrary to the tradition of the self-sufficient and autarchic country, the literature gives us the picture of a country life that depended on purchases from the city: a young woman in one of Tirso's novels tells us, as if it were the customary thing, that those living with her in the country went to the city "for the things necessary for our comfort."[29] Even when, as in the case of the Spanish seventeenth century, the cities decreased and in some cases came to exhibit an air of decay (about which Domínguez Ortiz has collected some data),[30] its superiority over the countryside was so firmly established that it lost nothing of its preponderant position.

The type of domestic and bourgeois life that became widespread in the seventeenth century was related to this predominance. Thus we find scenes that seem to be drawn from a nineteenth-century comedy by Bretón de los Herreros: one of Suárez de Figueroa's characters "praised each night's home entertainment, the amusement offered by novels and other reading in front of the stove."[31] The transformation and boom of novels, which were characteristic of the baroque, were bound up with social conditions giving novels a content representative of family occasions where they were read in a domestic circle. In this circle, intermezzos and similar productions were put on, some entitled, like one of Francisco de Avellaneda's intermezzos, *Las noches de invierno*. Middle-class entertainments and gatherings typical of this time were organized,[32] and the reading market was filled with volumes that correspond to the character of seventeenth-century urban society.[33]

In speaking about the preponderance that the cities exercised over the surrounding rural areas, I am not attempting to affirm some type of paradigmatic role that was effectively projected, thereby disseminating certain urban modes of behavior. But it cannot be doubted that, in one aspect, the cities played the role of stimulant with respect to the surrounding territory's economic state and its social life in general, including fashion; they had a greater or lesser effect depending on the case, a fact that to some extent has to do with the demands they made on the neighboring areas. Above all, the cities were a center of attraction for immigrants from the country, for diverse reasons. Occupations increased in the cities, a new development that was insistently pointed out, despite the general crisis in employment. Lope de Deza observed that it used to be sufficient for a single artisan to practice an occupation of a narrow focus (i.e., a painter, a gilder, a wood carver) in an entire province; now that was no longer the case "with the artisans having multiplied hand in hand with the spending and demand for their arts."[34] A greater population than ever before had assembled in the city, one that had marginally retained the inclination toward spending as in other epochs, always to a greater degree in the urban rather the rural milieu; in any case, in the seventeenth century those who had money to spend chose to go to the city, as did those who had nothing to eat. The Royal Council informed Philip III (1 September 1619) that people abandoned their lands and villages and "here [at the court] they all move in next to each other, buying houses and again making them very expensive."[35] If this trend led to an increase in the city population, it undoubtedly did not compare with the increase provoked by the throngs of those who were unemployed, starving, and in need, hanging on to the coattails of the rich as they were entering their new urban homes. The urban populace increased considerably because of this attraction, as the economists, counselors, and ministers recognized (and they were already identifying it as a cause of the countryside's depopulation).

Although this double phenomenon had been underway since the fourteenth century, it became intensified during the seventeenth-century crisis, whose difficulties in so many cases encouraged the peasant population to abandon their land and be incorporated into the urban milieu; although they might not find a cure there, they could at least find a passing and occasional palliative for their hunger and misery. The presence of these people coming from diverse places worried the Royal Council with regard to Philip III, because it supposed that "they must hold us in contempt and loathing."[36] By means of these displacements — just as by means of the groups of workers and traveling salesmen who daily went from nearby villages to the cities and the city residents who now and then left to work on their farms, to supply themselves with goods or simply in search of the country pleasures that were already being desired — urban life had an undoubted influence on the rural world. Consider the meaning of the gatherings and festivals held in seventeenth-century Spain on the occasion of the two annual sessions of the Mesta, celebrated in the towns of the provinces of Madrid, Segovia or Soria in September, or of Extremadura in March and April. At these festivals, representations of comedias and other urban fiestas took place in which cattle and sheep herdsmen were together with lawyers, clerks, functionaries, even with the president of the Council of Castile and his following.[37]

As at all times when a transition is taking place toward a greater degree of concentration of urban life, certain texts from the entire baroque epoch paradoxically display an apparent rejection of the city. One can already find in Seneca an assertion of a similar phenomenon;[38] one observes this in the fifteenth and sixteenth centuries, as was evidenced by the taste for certain rustic values. At the end of the sixteenth century, the fact became clearer and acquired a certain forcefulness. I have in mind passages from texts by Argensola, the one condemning "the vain rich and powerful city dwellers" — once again wealth, even if it were agrarian, continued to refer to the urban world; the other praising the life of the village for its virtuous sobriety, in sentences that reveal (in anticipation of the sentimental agrarianism of the eighteenth century) a sentiment at one with bourgeois intimacy: "Room in the lodging / is confined; but, thank God, ours, / though humble, has comfort."[39] Let us not forget Enríquez Gómez's songs in praise of retired village life, valorizing its simplicity, its calm and repose, its virtuous poverty.[40] Coinciding with this, we know that there were seigniors and rich cattle dealers and landholders who established themselves in small towns. There were assuredly economic reasons for this (concern about improving the administration of their own interests), the same that inspired the councils and juntas to recommend measures for the return to the countryside of seigniors and people of the upper level; but sometimes they were also instances of psychological weariness provoked by urban life itself.

The ideal of an agricultural and aristocratic society, which ran from Philip III's councillors to Montesquieu, inspired — as a compensating sublimation — this taste for nature that was precisely the counterpoint of those people seeing themselves so strongly urbanized. Thus came about certain anticipations of an interesting Rousseauist cast.[41] These anticipations were very visible in Saavedra Fajardo, who went so far as to make an inflamed defense of child rearing only by the children's mothers because the contrary contradicted the laws of nature.[42] But in any case, although the presence of the rural myth is no more than evidence for what we have been saying, baroque people knew themselves to be well established in the city; they found advantages there that they were not inclined to renounce. As Gabriel del Corral tells us, they did not endure "a lack of anything beautiful and varied that a numerous population offers, because of the certain and displacing influx from the countryside."[43] It was in the midst of the city where culture esteemed by the baroque individual was produced, along with "the communication among learned individuals," as was the case (according to López de Vega) of Madrid, where people arrived from all provinces and nations.[44]

Although the baroque was an urban culture, it was above all a culture of the large city. Populous cities already existed in the Middle Ages, but now they attained an initiative and force in leading the country's economy and culture that were much greater than at any previous moment. The role of the large city is reflected in literature. Consider the part corresponding to Madrid and other large cities in Lope de Vega's theater.[45] Even though one who had not been successful in commanding the city's respect would make an embittered reference — recall Góngora condemning "those in Madrid throwing away their money" — what was remarkable was the way and the frequency with which the principal cities were praised in seventeenth-century texts. When, with the greater ease of traveling at the end of the Middle Ages, the cities were repeatedly praised — as Alfonso de Palencia praised Barcelona, Florence, and others — what was made to stand out was their good administration, their liberal government; now they were praised for their demographic, economic, and urban magnitude: this was said of Madrid, Seville, and Paris. What excited the admiration of the starving displaced peasants who, abandoning their rural milieu, arrived in Madrid? It was described in multiple passages from the theater, from novels, and especially from picaresque novels, which were so characteristic in this and many other points. But I have no intention of claiming that a novel gives us the real feelings of a villager who appears in it; rather, I believe that the novel translates the mode of viewing and valorizing things that prevailed at least in determinate groups of the society where this novel was produced. The author of *Teresa de Manzanares* tells us that "the grand scheme of the buildings and the many people of its streets proved amazing," and the protagonist comments at one moment: "How huge Madrid is."[46] There were those who thought that "it didn't make a lot of sense to leave Madrid, where everything was plentiful, to go to a village where everything was lacking"[47] (the idealization of the village in the Renaissance had shifted its meaning, and the myth of the natural had taken another turn).

Exactly what became intensified during this time was Madrid's accommodating, cosmopolitan, and crowded atmosphere. In recent times, Viñas Mey has called attention to the heterogeneous population in seventeenth-century Madrid, with its always greater diversity in terms of place of origin and profession, forming "a multiform and crowded whole, one that is restless and discordant."[48] But in the epoch itself, it was again and again acknowledged to be nothing short of amazing: "Babilonia of Spain, mother, marvel, garden, archive, school . . .," said María de Zayas.[49] Francisco Santos made the same reference: "that Babilonia of Spain" amazed him with "the royal elegance of its streets and houses" and "the majesty of its houses."[50] Salas Barbadillo called it the "common fatherland" — an epithet that had previously been given only to Rome: "common fatherland and universal mother of strangers."[51] Céspedes arrived at the same appraisal,[52] and Tirso developed the theme in a wide-ranging encomium that carried him to an outrageous etymology: "mother [*madre*] of all (as its name reveals), the sea [*mar*] that is peaceful for virtuous and becalmed spirits, although stormy for those who are restless and full of vice," Madrid amazed him with its "miraculous plazas, luxurious houses, streets, fountains, churches, magnificences, peaceful confusion and free vassalage."[53]

Let us focus on the image of another great center of the baroque: Seville. A character from the picaresque genre also declared that although "it seemed that the Court proved advantageous to everyone . . . he found in Seville a scent of the city, another *je ne sais quoi*, other magnificences. . . . Because there was a very great sum of wealth and very much underestimated. For there silver changed hands between people, like copper everywhere else."[54] Tomás Mercado had said of Seville: "it is the capital of merchants." Its economic power was exalted: "All this sand is monies," said Lope (*El arenal de Sevilla*), which was translated into its monumentality. Ruiz de Alarcón (*Ganar amigos*) was amazed by "its high buildings." Above all, it was praised for its incomparable excitement and for the diversity of its multitudinous population: the "universal plaza" where "such a diverse nation" comes ashore, commented Lope. "Seville, metropolis of Andalusia, populous city and one of the richest of Spain," in Castillo Solórzano's elegy,[55] was again and again admired for what the baroque mentality esteemed: the magnitude and cosmopolitanism of its urban life. "If everybody lives here, / if everybody has a place here," one can understand how Agustín de Rojas was so filled with surprise that he called it a "shelter for strangers," an "archive of diverse people."[56] Analogously, the anonymous author of *Estebanillo González* exalted it as "relief for all peoples [*naciones*],"[57] finding there a freedom of life that understandably attracted youth; this latter was what Céspedes emphasized.[58] Even in the critical moments of the seventeenth century, Seville would continue to be what Braudel has written in reference to its phase of splendor, when it presented itself as an exceptional and feverish "extreme" of development: "Seville is a mode of feeling, living, acting, playing . . ."[59]

In Toledo, another characteristically urban milieu,[60] a picaro tells us something similar about his forays: "Enthralled, I walked from one street to another, looking at the riches of the merchants, their grandiose shops,"[61] while another admires it because of "its eternal buildings."[62] Jerónimo Yáñez de Alcalá's same picaro states that at another moment he also thought that in Segovia, "because of its noble and abundant trade, he would find some facility in earning something to eat, for he had heard it said that it was the true mother of strangers, and that since it was so rich it offers shelter to everyone and receives them with open arms."[63] Again the city of Segovia, this time from the mouth of María de Zayas, received praise for being "so adorned with buildings . . . enriched by merchants."[64] Cellorigo, besides emphasizing the hugeness of its plaza and pointing out other positive things, admired in Valladolid "the new buildings that it has."[65] About Saragossa, someone pondered "the beauty of the streets and the expansiveness of its buildings."[66] The *loas* of Valencian dramatic writers advance equivalent judgments about their city. In a work containing observations similar to those already cited about Madrid and other urban centers, this comment was made about Paris: "Its grandiose population and that multitude of people, occupations, arts and modes of dress, so many different ones and in such great number, which is one of the great things of Europe, proved amazing."[67] And still further, Céspedes remembered about Malinas that "the houses are magnificent, the plazas are large, and the streets are wide."[68]

Sociologically, one of the most characteristic aspects of the baroque is confirmed by its urban status: ostentation as a law that ruled in the entire realm of culture. Ostentation was the law of the large city in a society whose order was based on privilege. There one could find the luxury and riches of modes of dress, the great number and opulence of banquets and dinners, the tremendous and magnificent buildings, the multitude of servants, and the riches of domestic furnishings ("in the Spanish court, where all the home furnishings are so expensive and rich," commented Almansa):[69] ultimately, everything that friar Benito de Peñalosa admired as the spectacle of a city.[70] In a society with great differences in stratification, the upper social stratum based itself on the power of having at its disposal a great mass of goods and people. In the rural milieu, because of the low density of population and its stable character, everybody was known to everybody else and a readily apparent display of possibilities was unnecessary to demonstrate that one belonged to the elite level; but in the anonymity of the large city, the law of ostentatious expenditure was imposed for one to attain this recognition. The Royal Council, in the document addressed to Philip III, emphasized the overwhelming law of ostentation that governed in the capital, stressing its negative side: in ostentation one lives "according to the laws of opinion, having forgotten the law of nature that is content with moderation, which is what illuminates and endures."[71] But the urban residents of the baroque were much more in favor of ostentatious illumination. This same ostentatious character of the baroque revealed its connection with the problems of a social order based on privilege, with its urban framework, and with the mass characteristics that this social manifestation exhibited.

But here we must also be more precise: not only the city, even the large city, conditioned the appearance of the baroque; instead, the baroque went hand in hand with the city, which had lost its municipal autonomy and become converted into an administrative nucleus, incorporated and governed from the point of view of the state. The baroque was an urban product within the ambit of extensive political concentrations that were constructed around monarchical power in European towns. Although Rome, with its painters and architects, attained the significance of becoming the "spectacle city" typical of the baroque,[72] we have to bear in mind that this took place within the limits of the ecclesiastical monarchy and as a reflection of its grandeur. It is unnecessary to speak about the decisive role of Madrid because everyone gave it a special prominence. But even Paris (which, from different positions, Huyghe and Francastel minimize) could be referred to:[73] despite its much noted rejection of Bernini, and disregarding the baroque elements of its architects (specifically at Versailles), we cannot fail to perceive its influence on the theater — not only on Hardy's theater, nor even Corneille's, but the theater of Racine himself, which still preserved a great number of baroque elements.[74]

The city's prominence is explained because the new function of the capital city corresponded to the political creation of the baroque monarchies.[75] The capital city, with its predominant role in the social, political, economic, and artistic order, was an indispensable element of this monarchy (which in his time Eugenio de Narbona requested that the prince locate "in a large city and in the middle of the realm").[76] Argan rightly gave the name of "Europe of the capitals" to baroque Europe of the first half of the seventeenth century.[77]

From the outset, that city-capital was a populous agglomeration, ordinarily the most populated of all the cities in the country and the city to show the most rapid growth of the epoch. An example would be Madrid, which, despite the declining situation in general, proceeded from about fifteen thousand inhabitants at the beginning of the sixteenth century to a tenfold increase by the second decade of the baroque century.[78] It is a phenomenon that the epoch was clearly aware of and that preocuppied and frightened it. At the beginning of the century, the Cortes protested this disproportionate increase and requested measures to contain it. Bartolomé Leonardo de Argensola wrote on the subject.[79] We are already acquainted with the liberal opinion of Sancho de Moncada, and others meditated on the disquieting fact.[80] In the meanwhile, groups that took the initiative in important aspects of the epoch's social life sought to accomplish this process of concentration: this was how it happened with those who were involved in businesses of finance.[81]

The expansion of the large city was a fact that prevailed in direct dependence on the complex of interests to which it corresponded. *La Dorotea* speaks of an imaginary character who can figure out how to devise a scheme so that "Madrid will be as large as Paris, combining it with Getafe."[82] In the laudatory literature about Madrid that was published in the seventeenth century, it was recognized that as a capital it was not as large as other European capitals; thus González Dávila maintained that, as the home of the court, Madrid had no excess, being for this reason a paragon of temperance and of other virtues; he gave the following data: it possessed 399 streets, fourteen plazas, and ten thousand houses.[83] Fifty years later, Nuñez de Castro asserted that in the interior of its houses there was nothing to equal it, although he did concede that on the exterior some cities might have greater ornament. He went on to say that, although it could not sustain itself from its own cultivation (abandonment of the medieval ideal of self-sufficiency), it made use of supplies from many places, possessing nourishment or food and drink in abundance; it had a great variety of fabrics and beautiful clothing, with prices that were not among the highest in Spain, and even though it offered fewer diversions than other capitals, the ones it had were more appealing, in addition to the significance of its cultivation of the comedia; it was not the city of greatest population, but it was the one most suitable for a large court; it possesses, he tells us, four hundred streets, sixteen plazas, and sixteen thousand houses, with more than sixty thousand inhabitants (this last is a completely fantastic figure).[84] This difference between ten thousand and sixteen thousand houses must be taken as a mere index — with no statistical value — of the advance that must have occurred in the matter of construction.

The baroque inhabitant of Madrid and the visitor of this time, however much they cultivated their imagination, knew that Paris was a much larger city. But even so there was a very broad margin to celebrate the growth of the capital. Perhaps because the theater carried out the extensive propaganda campaign in favor of the social system of the baroque monarchy, Lope (for example, in *La villana de Getafe*), Tirso de Molina (in *Los balcones de Madrid*), and others exalted the growth of the capital, praise that would not be interrupted even when the court abandoned it, undoubtedly because its leaving was only temporary. A letter of Pedro García de Ovalle gives us an eyewitness account of the boom taking place in the capital: "When your lordship returns you will not know Madrid, because of the things that are being built every day, buildings as much as parks."[85] Salas Barbadillo, for his part, made a comment whose coincidence with the preceding appraisal is significant: "I am infinitely beside myself, and rightly so, from seeing in Madrid so many new buildings and then seeing them immediately occupied; every year it gives birth to new streets and those that were only side streets yesterday are today main thoroughfares, and they are so fabulous that one chooses with ambivalence, for everything is equal."[86]

Notwithstanding, it was Céspedes who left us a writing with a curious, incomparable passage about how the expansion of the Hispanic monarchy's capital had come about. It is difficult to find, whatever may be its degree of hyperbole, a more straightforward assertion about how the epoch's consciousness appraised a process of what was judged to be a vertiginous urbanization dominating the surrounding countryside. With the recent transfer of the court to Madrid, said Céspedes,

> little by little it began growing and extending itself, almost arriving at the
> grandeur and splendor in which we now see it; as it grew all of its objects
> took on a new being because the far-removed fields on its outskirts were
> converted into attractive streets, its cultivated fields into large buildings,
> its small chapels into parish churches, its hermitages into convents and its
> common lands into plazas, common markets and places of exchange.[87]

Expansion, then, of the city-capital, as a patch of urbanization that rapidly expanded, absorbing the surrounding rural space — this greater expansion gave rise to what was admired in the cities of the baroque (once again coinciding with modern times): the heights of its buildings. As we have seen repeatedly in the cited texts, the buildings receiving comment were becoming taller and taller.

This was an aspect of the vertical growth of the seventeenth-century city that sociohistorian L. Mumford has related to the scarcity and greater costliness of urban space, which stemmed from the oppression it suffered because of the new fortifications and troop quarters that surrounded and dominated it.[88]

In that capital (and also in cities that, because of their importance, function as a capitals for a large region) appeared the social, economic, administrative, and political phenomena that, under the state regime of modern monarchies, found in those agglomerations a milieu adequate for their development: the formation of absolutism and its repressive military resources, the bureaucracy, the money-based economy, the concentration of property along with a new "privatistic" conception of it; the erosion of the traditional systems of social stratification and their initial substitution by a dichotomous image of the poor and the rich (this latter has been pointed out with special emphasis by F. Braudel), and the subversive tensions.

Within the large city and in connection with what we have just said, there was also the diffusion of a zone of anonymity that became more and more extensive; because of this, a serious loss of freedom took place in the administration and government of the city and in the life of its citizens, but the individuals, in finding themselves immersed in this anonymous milieu, gained a negative freedom or a freedom from controls, especially from those based on personal bonds.

The negative side, which has been greatly stressed, was an essential aspect of the freedom of the mass and urban anonymity in the seventeenth century. I have already indicated the increase in banditry in the seventeenth century; it played a significant role in the epoch, but it came from a direct and uninterrupted traditional source. What we now want to focus on is something different: the increase of crime in the ambit of the city, crime that was fomented and protected by the conditions the city offered, although public power raised up the most effective means of repression against criminal manifestations of a varied sort. Attestations such as the following are frequent in the *Cartas de jesuitas*: "Besides death from disease, we have violent deaths every day, which this year have been so numerous that such a thing has never been seen in Madrid";[89] and further on, "This year's violent deaths are numerous."[90] The *Noticias de Madrid (1621-1627)* more than once report about individuals killed by thieves.[91] Pellicer's *Avisos* are insistent and even terrifying with respect to these items: "A day does not dawn without someone being wounded or murdered, by thieves or soldiers; houses are broken into and young women and widows cry about assaults and robberies — this is how much confidence the soldiers have in the War Council"; or also: "Nowadays this place is bloody with robberies and murders. . . . Things are such that one can't even go out at night without being heavily armed or with a lot of company." He remains insistent: there are so many assaults "to such a degree that there is not even anything to eat because no provisions come to the Court out of fear of these excesses."[92]

Items of this sort are no less voluminous and serious in Barrionuevo's *Avisos*. Here we offer a selection: "One cannot live for the thieves who enter the houses in broad daylight to commit their robbery"; "Many priests have been made prisoner by thieves" — and then he goes on to name names, a reference that he repeats two years later in a similar fashion (bear in mind the coincidence with the ecclesiastical banditry that Villari indicated in Naples); "Thieves wander about like flies," he writes on another occasion, and in the same letter he repeats near the end that there are many nobles and priests among those imprisoned by thieves; the vicar of Madrid allowed the secular judges to arrest and prosecute the priests who were found implicated in robberies; he repeats that in Madrid one is robbed in broad daylight by "infinite thieves," "where at every step you can see a thousand murders." A very grim comment underscores the issue: "Since Christmas it has been said that more than 150 disgusting murders of men and women have happened, and no one has been punished."[93] The connection of underworld people and influential persons had been known for some time: sources from the epoch mentioned the favors received by thieves, criminals, and rebellious people, to the point that someone indicated that it was "the license for crime inherited from wealth."

The numerous, newly arrived, and complex population of Madrid — which was duplicated in all the capitals — constitutes a political question that was more than one of public order, although that was also seriously at issue:

> as a factor of disorder it is linked to the political questions and contentions
> that shook the kingdom and even to the problems of international order,
> for, as was logical, those undesirable elements placed themselves in the
> service of whoever would pay them; and when the seventeenth-century
> antagonisms and discussions emerged (opposition between those with
> influence, struggles among ministers and favorites), the contenders found
> in those elements an abundance of rebellious material to provoke public
> discontent and prompt mutinies, on the pretext of foodstuffs but in the
> service of their cause.[94]

Pellicer recounted the panic that spread through Madrid because of the rumor that this mob was going to attack the palace. (Already at this time the question of a lack of basic foods began to acquire the revolutionary charge that it kept until the Revolution of 1868.)

These references make us understand that it was not a question of a passing, circumstantial, sporadic phenomenon within the system: their number (which we could multiply), the variety of the writings they came from, the disparity in the character of the sources (from conformists and supporters of the government to nonconformists and writers even hostile to it, such as Barrionuevo), and finally the broad time period they encompassed (those collected here spanned twenty years) tell us otherwise. The phenomenon went hand in hand with the system, corresponded to the characteristics of the economic, social, and political structure of the seventeenth century (and it occurred, therefore, not only in Spain but in Paris, Rome, and other cities), which reveals that it is somehow related to the order that forged the culture of the baroque. We previously saw that tensions of a much broader scope were bound up with the formation of new cultural expedients that could dominate them; this relation — occurring within the large cities or capitals, along with the anonymous existence that was beginning to develop in them — also collaborated in the historical process whereby baroque culture evolved as an instrument for containing the consequences of disturbance that were an integral part of such a process.

But the phenomenon of demographic concentration — in view of the conditions of its occurrence in the seventeenth century, which only became more accentuated, given the characteristics it acquired — presented another consequence. This system of urban anonymity entailed a negative freedom. Along with relaxing the controls of juridical repression, which the epoch's political regime sought to reinforce (even if it had to use strongly reprehensible means), the social controls of coexistence were no less relaxed. In the preceding chapter we saw that one of the reasons for wanting to relieve the congestion of Madrid had to do with being able to know everyone's identity. In the large baroque city one was usually unknown: this provoked a certain laxity that led to crime, but it also left others of a more refined sensibility in the freedom, sometimes rich perhaps, but always difficult, of their own solitude.

Ultimately this freedom turned out to be the freedom to be alone. The physical agglomerate of people in the large city, causing an insuperable difficulty in individuals' getting to know one another and in relations with others, was accompanied by a distancing between persons that created around each one a sphere of isolation. The crowded multitudes of the city engendered solitude. One of the epoch's thinkers happened upon an understanding of this situation; Francis Bacon wrote: "Magna civitas, magna solitudo."[95] The greater the city, the greater the solitary life surrounding the individual.

Probably living this experience of the unbridgeable distance separating one from everyone else was what conditioned the development of the baroque theme of solitude. Aside from Montaigne's essay, this them was expressed in poems as well known in baroque literature as Góngora's *Las soledades* or Th. de Viau's *La solitude*; although they differ from one another, they nevertheless coincide in the topic on which they are based. The richness of the theme of solitude in seventeenth-century poetry can be verified in the study Vossler dedicated to it.[96] It went so far as to become a literary topos that also infiltrated the novel with the *Soledades* of Jerónimo Fernández de Mata (1639) or Cristóbal Lozano's

Soledades de la vida y desengaños del mundo (1652; 2nd edition, 1662).[97] In the greater part of these instances, and especially in the poems, they took their point of departure from the question's presence in the sociohistorical reality of the epoch and gave it a stoically inspired literary treatment. López de Vega made a formulation that bears out the situation: in the village, "it is impossible for a man to live there and exercise his own free will" because the intrusion of others oppresses him and the austerity of solitude evokes an irritated and malignant curiosity that surrounds him at all times, while at the court his greatest advantage is that "he is looked at neither kindly nor severely, as if he were not a very noticeable thing."[98] The author felt, then, the solitude of the large city and captured its favorable aspect: that negative freedom of feeling oneself to be alone whereby the individualism of the modern human being is affirmed.

From the outset, this situation of relative exemption from control had to be accompanied by a greater degree of moral laxity in the baroque city, owing as much to the simple fact of the numerical increase of people and the corresponding confusion in terms of their origin as to the consequential expansion of anonymity. It is easy to perceive the emergence of an inclination toward forms of "deviance" in the behavior occasioned by the social alterations. Pellicer's *Avisos*, and Barrionuevo's, being in a form adequate for the same anonymous public addressed by the news collections of the gazetteers, gave abundant information about the little edifying mores in Madrid — it is not necessary to make reference to the mores of Rome or Paris. The works of the theater presupposed an environment with characteristics of this sort — for example, in Lope's comedies such as *La viuda valenciana*, *Los melindres de Belisa*, *El anzuelo de Fenisa*, and *El acero de Madrid*; others could be cited from Tirso, Moreto, and from Calderón himself. Many of them could be placed under the title of a risqué French comedy that had made its debut years before: *Lorsque l'enfant paraît*. Some of the epoch's plays treated much more scandalous themes.[99] According to the panegyrists at the beginning of his reign, Philip IV, worried by the corruption of mores he witnessed going on around him, resolved to clean up the court. Almansa reported that "he has ordered some seigniors to leave the Court and live with their women, just as he ordered those who bring them"; elsewhere, "men and women leading a scandalous life are thrown out of Madrid," and at the beginning this attitude is so severe that "nobody dares to live scandalously."[100] Shortly thereafter, life in Madrid arrived at its lowest level of public and private morality. The *Sumario de las nuevas de la Corte* informs its readers about the reprimands the king gives to well-known persons, generally for having concubines; for similar reasons, he advises no less than an admiral: "Don't keep company with anyone who might prove a hindrance to your entering the Palace."[101] Just a short time later, a widespread laxity made itself felt all the way from the realm of sexual relations to administrative business. The issue prompted much polemic, repeated so often thereafter in very different circumstances, among people of a liberal cast or of reactionary sentiments, regarding the morally favorable or unfavorable aspects of the epoch. As an example of the bitter debate taking place around the question, we can cite (although they are from a little later) Galindo's accusing work[102] and the response, comprehensive for its time, of F. de Godoy.[103]

The effect of the more liberal manners engendered by the populous city cropped up in all spheres, among them the political sphere. In the mass milieu of the baroque cities, the increase in the possibilities of information and the rupture (partial at least) of traditional modes of thinking, which were the result of traveling, cosmopolitan trade, and the development of individualist energies, contributed to stimulate the forces of opinion. In referring to opinion we must immediately recognize the existence of differences — of criticisms adverse to tradition, to authority, to the establishment. Because they were favored by the concealing ambience of anonymity, they became accentuated and aggravated the manifestations of opposition, of revolt.

The city was, by antonomasia, the conflictive milieu of the seventeenth century, although the difficulties of provisions and of demographic surpluses reached the countryside. Despite the rapid expansion of the market, the sixteenth century had been able to meet the new demands, improving the nourishment of the populations; but at the end of the century, this fact was reversed and the alimentary situation worsened to the point where starvation, along with plague and death, decimated the countries of western Europe and destroyed people who were no longer able to make recourse to their own labor and who could hardly support themselves with their already scarce products. The lack of grain and its rising price — to a degree much greater than even its scarcity (a phenomenon that would later be called the king's law) — especially ravaged the cities. The problem of the lack of wheat, of the costliness and scarcity of foodstuffs, was most acutely observed not in the countryside but in the city. "When the curtain falls on the sixteenth century," commented Braudel, "let us not forget the dramatic character of the question of wheat in the Mediterranean. The cities, overwrought with misery, become threatened, whether it be the Rome of Clement VIII or the Naples of the Duke of Osuna. This is a crisis that is going to last. The revolt of Palermo in 1647, will it not be a consequence of the frightful scarcity of 1646?"[104] One could easily extend the list of cities that experienced bloody events brought about by the economic crisis, especially on the peninsula, with names as significant in the baroque as Seville, Lisbon, Cordoba, Madrid, Barcelona, and Valencia.

The violence that in the Middle Ages pitted some professional or family gangs against others no longer occurred in the baroque city; instead, movements of opposition and subversion that affected the social and political order began to be formed and more than once to get out of control. Although these tensions could quickly be reflected in the surrounding rural areas, they principally germinated in the cities. But above all in the countryside there occurred repeatedly during the seventeenth century violent upheavals that could be put down by armed troops, as happened more than once, without threatening the bases of the system. Today these upheavals have been extensively studied (one might recall the books by Porshnev and Mousnier).[105] It would be possible to add others: the Andalusian "disturbances," recently investigated by Domínguez Ortiz[106] and, as the century closes, the great peasant insurrection of Valencia.[107] But this was something different: a matter of outbursts without an organization, a program, or a future. It was in the cities where the subversive movements had to take hold in order to assume a character of prerevolutionary revolt and to threaten not specific persons but an entire system. "The fortune of the peasant insurrections is decided in the cities," Porshnev concluded.[108] The class of those in power, headed by the monarchy, needed to construct a regime based on their joint interests and capable of reacting with arms, of course, but much more profoundly through the creation of an entire repertory of means to act on the social behavior of individuals as group members; in other words, through the creation of an entire culture.

Inherent to the baroque city was the encircling placement of barracks that, like strong pincers, could subdue it. An abundance of beggars, vagabonds, picaros, con artists, and thieves assembled in the seventeenth-century city, a wide range of types from the extensive deviant subculture that belonged to the conditions of the baroque. Thus, correlatively, baroque culture emerged as a complex of resources to overcome the forces of deviance or of opposition present in the society of the epoch. If, as Barber has written, "in all past and present societies, those at the top of the system of social stratification tend to establish themselves in the metropolitan areas, where they will probably carry out the most highly valorized social functions,"[109] this clearly applied to the city of the seventeenth century: those in power lived in the city and from there promoted the development of a baroque culture in defense of their own interests; those down below were incorporated into the urban milieu, some because it favored their possibilities of protest, others because that was where the cultural resources [*resortes*] of the baroque presented them with means of integration.

In the baroque city, churches and palaces were constructed, fiestas were organized, and dazzling fireworks were displayed. The arches of triumph, the catafalques for funereal honors, the spectacular retinues: where could they be viewed, except in the city? In the city existed academies, contests were celebrated, handbills, lampoons, and leaflets circulated, which were written either for or against whoever was in power. Locales for the theater were constructed there (a great novelty at the time), and people went to stage representations that involved the most dynamic shaping activity of baroque culture. In these terms, the modern creation of baroque culture, an urban work because of its public, its ends, and its resources, was the instrument of the city's culture par excellence.

Chapter 5
A Conservative Culture

Every society presupposes that certain beliefs, aspirations, and behavioral guidelines can be established in common by means of the channels of socialization adequate to its circumstances; this socializing operation thereby performs an activity that mentally imprints and secures an image of society that is already in place. In this sense, the means of socialization that are directed toward a mass to make it participate in such a social image, have, in their integrating effect, a conservative character. The object is to disseminate and consolidate the image of society established in support of a system of interests, under the pretense of preserving order. The socialization factors used to have an effect on the masses are by their nature conservative.[1]

Since baroque culture unfolded as a complex of factors of this sort, its conservative character derived from its own operation. Besides pointing out conservatism as one of the characteristics of every type of mass and popular culture, Lazarsfeld and Merton have emphasized that, given the instruments and persons ordinarily involved in the organization of means of mass communication, in intervening they contribute to the maintenance of the established economic and social system.[2] It goes without saying that the force and the efficacy reached by today's media techniques of mass communication relate neither quantitatively nor, consequently, qualitatively to the distant approximations of seventeenth-century techniques of mass manipulation. But on its own terms, we cannot doubt the latter's mass character. The distant connection between the procedures of the baroque and those of today is sufficient to allow for the demonstration of the conservative nature on the part of one to reinforce such an affirmation on the part of the other.

Nevertheless, a concrete historical situation such as the one taking place at the beginning of the seventeenth century in Spain can offer an apparently paradoxical result, for this situation emerged as a consequence of the force with which the innovative zeal had irrupted and been considered in broad layers of the urban population.[3] It can happen that there is a need to rely on the attraction of the "new" precisely to effect the desired results, in line with conservative aims, in the mentality of the city's restless multitude. That is, use must be made of the force of novelty to consolidate an established system, which can lead in two directions: either diverting the impetus for the new toward spheres of collective life wherein innovation will not be dangerous for the future, or sanctioning the presentation of the inherited tradition under new aspects. All that occurs without failing to carry out an active campaign that is designed to eliminate the prestige of the innovative frame of mind, at least among those social sectors whose adherence is more significant.

Novelty, which in the seventeenth century did not stop eroding estate society, was nonetheless condemned in general terms and in itself. This does not mean, however, that it was not accepted, defended, and even exalted wherever it did not prove threatening and where the masses could derive satisfaction from it without endangering the order. In this realm, on the contrary, appeal to novelties was one of the most efficient expedients of baroque culture.

Novelty in social life was rejected. Thus emerged the tendency to attribute a taste for novelty to certain groups that in a given society — in this case, in the baroque — carried a negative connotation, a greater or lesser adverse quality (those who lacked knowledge, who were poor, youths, women, or foreign groups such as Indians or other peoples).[4] Lope repeatedly attributed that taste to the indistinguished mass, which he proclaimed everywhere: "The common people experience, / in their lowly condition, novelties."[5]

Novelty was change and thus disturbance, and, finally, a concatenation of upheavals. It was equal, then, to a threat against the established system, at least when it affected its fundamental aspects. This explains the illusion that, in compensation, would arise among the popular masses in the sad and crowded conditions of the seventeenth-century city; that is, the desire for change on the part of those who were unable to feel themselves jointly involved in a system from which they scarcely received any benefits. Inspired in this notion, the masses — in many cases, as we are today becoming more aware — tried, even by violence, to transform the system. It is understandable, then, that this would be an inclination that was watched and controlled by those interested in maintaining and preserving the prevailing order.

Elsewhere I have said that the word *preservation* [*conservación*] expressed the central question for the epoch's moralists and politicians.[6] The problem resided in the fact that "all newness is dangerous," a warning offered by Gabriel del Corral, a Spanish seventeenth-century writer in touch with his times.[7] The forces of competition, of opposition, are lying in wait everywhere, according to the understanding of the baroque individual, and one must "preserve oneself" in the face of an adverse attack; this is a valid formulation — so continues this way of thinking — in the sphere of the state, society, and the individual.[8] Fernández Navarrete turned the famous Council recommendation to Philip III (from 1 February 1619) into a subject worthy of fifty discourses, whose central theme was the work's own title: *Conservación de monarquías*, which was the problem of those with knowledge.[9] That same title was later (1648) repeated in friar Francisco Enríquez's work, which in the name of the conservative principle struck out against the ignorant plebs — another proof of the internal tension of the epoch's groups.

The unrest must have exhausted the hopes born in public consciousness in the sixteenth century regarding the destiny of the Spanish monarchy and society, specifically when those hopes were compared with experiences of the distressing situation that surrounded everyone. From the last years of that century, this situation was more pronounced within the Hispanic complex, becoming more and more acute as time went by; it was this unrest that led to the formation of the myth wherein the rise and fall of empires was a natural movement — a myth we frequently find formulated in seventeenth-century literature. To understand how widespread this theme was in political writers, let us recall some of the lesser known passages. López Bravo assures us that "empires and laws (although Plato and Morus have greater dreams) grow old like everything else; nature has determined that nothing endures or lasts forever: all things change with time."[10] In the prologue to his work addressed to Philip IV — the baroque king par excellence — the Tacitist Eugenio de Narbona, basing himself on the government of this same king, wrote: "Republics meet their end and are carried away (as are all natural things) by the stream of time and by change."[11] In the face of this, it was possible only to intervene — and one must intervene dynamically — to extend the span of time. Nothing else could be hoped for. Because of the instability of fortune — an insuperable natural condition — and because of the ineradicable margin of imprudence in human action, Suárez de Figueroa said, there is "no perpetual [political body], for after a broad span of time it decays no matter how good the organization applied by the prince."[12] The thesis reached even to the limits of the throne: councillors and ministers repeated it. In the document from 1 February 1619, the Royal Council warned Philip III: "Cities, kingdoms and monarchies pass away, just as men and all other created things." It is the thesis that all regimes of an alienating authoritarianism make recourse to when things begin to go sour, so as to be cleared of guilt in the face of public opinion, but it is also a bitter stimulant to provoke a king to action. "Kingdoms are changed by changing the mores,"[13] added the council, which left many possibilities in the ruling hand should the king decide to act. The sonorous verse of Calderón was responsible for propagating this version, in which an apologetic attitude with respect to failures that were impossible to hide, losses of every sort that had been happening for some time, was combined with the call to an ultimate possibility for a restoration movement in that baroque crisis: "But what steadfast state/does not decline, while another grows?" — implying a general theory of political decadence that can be attributed to the uncontainable march of happenstance. "In a quick and easy turnaround / the monarchies change / and the empires exchanged" (*La gran Cenobia*).

Therefore only a conservative attitude was possible, one that would attempt to keep things in their order, reducing to whatever extent possible the crumbling of the prevailing system by the threat of time. The problem of the Spanish monarchy, the Royal Council said to Philip III (4 May 1621), was the "preservation of everything," something that "one views as very much in danger and at risk."[14] At an early date, Cellorigo had conceived of the program contained in his *Memorial* with these words, which served as the work's subtitle: "effective restoration of the Republic of Spain." His notion was to try to preserve a monarchy that could collapse; for this reason, in the third part of his *Memorial*, he insisted on the idea that one must seek to grasp remedies that do not have the risk of making the disease worse, in the same way that doctors are content with palliatives that keep the sick person in his or her present state when the application of decisive remedies could threaten the patient's life. Sancho de Moncada, in view of what he was witnessing, realized that the problem was the "preservation of Spain": "To many the Spanish Monarchy seems eternal because of its greatness, but everywhere much is spoken about its danger." He warned that, nevertheless, "security" is not possible, inasmuch as in every instance "monarchies are as mortal as men, and the monarchy is many men and all are mortal."[15] If prudence was the baroque virtue par excellence, the sum of virtues for each and every politician and moralist of the epoch, and to their minds equal to reason itself, those who possessed it were the "preservation of the world," Suárez de Figueroa said.[16] By antonomasia, the effect of prudence was to preserve. In the ultimate baroque preceptist making use of this basic virtue — I am referring to Gracián — we find the principle underlying the formulation of the attitude we are trying to define: "Preserving is much more than conquering."[17] In one of the *Cartas de jesuitas* (from 13 October 1637) it was said: "The ultimate of glory and reputation consists in self-preservation."[18] "The principal occupation of the prince is preserving his states," according to one of Saavedra's maxims (*Empresa* LIX). Thus one must consider this "razón conservatriz" of the state, as someone called it, to be a general attitude.

This conservative attitude was a reaction by those groups that, despite everything, had maintained a significant level of predominance in response to the pressure of the changes that were initiated in what we might here allusively call

the "Renaissance epoch." The social transformations of the sixteenth and seventeeth centuries had disseminated a taste for the new in the urban population — particularly forcefully in Castile, which had contemplated such great novelties. But
decades later, before the end of the sixteenth century, we also find that a monarchical absolutism that informed the entire political order, was erected to close
the door on all political and social changes and to maintain energetically the
estatist framework of society. It had to be this way to the extent that "an essential
function of the stratification system in society is the *integrating* one."[19] With
the greatest rigor possible, that absolutism had to maintain the system of estates,
whose ordered stratification guaranteed the defense of traditionally organized
society. To accomplish that, giving it an actual effectiveness, it had to revi-
talize the table of values, with its levels of differentiation, whose prevalence
(i.e., whose acceptance by all those at the heart of society) could allow for the
social integration of the mass groups that must now be taken into account. The
primary goal was to maintain and strengthen the estate order itself, whose image
was a fundamental value in support of the system. A manifestation of what we
are saying can be found in the baroque interest in preserving, at least in principle,
the traditional thesis that the literary genres correspond to certain determinate
values and each of them to certain socially defined figures. An adequation was
maintained between a literary genre and the social condition of the figures presented in them: tragedy — the world of the heroic — was concerned with seigniors;
comedy — foreign to heroic values — dealt with common people, with urban
dwellers, one person said.[20] We shall later see what significance the appearance
of the tragicomedy had in Spanish theater and, by way of derivation, the French
theater.

Let us examine a curious aspect of social contraction that foregrounds the
nature of the epoch. In the phase of vertical social mobility that, to a certain
extent, corresponded to the sixteenth century, school studies had been a way of
access to the upper levels; without being present as a general movement, it was
recognizably a means for self-gain or of climbing the social ladder in a considerable number of individual cases. That induced many towns where the rulers were
capable of appraising such a phenomenon favorably to establish for their children
schools for teaching grammar and the humanities to prepare one either for the
university or for more prestigious and productive occupations. It was an interesting phenomenon in the Spanish Renaissance. In the baroque crisis, however, the
rulers wanted to close off, or at least make more difficult, this way of changing
one's social level: first, to avoid the unrest that could accompany an appreciable
number of promotions in the estate hierarchy; second, because when this way
was undertaken and one did not achieve the self-gain [*no se "medra"*] as expected,
a state of discontent and hostility was produced that, in the tense situation of
the seventeenth century, was to be avoided as much as possible. Therefore, for
the preservation of traditional society (closing, in effect, the escape hatches) and

for the maintenance of a spirit of conformity in the ambit of the towns, the Royal Council recommended to Philip III (1 February 1619) that grammar studies be suppressed in towns and small villages because their proximity made it easy for many workers to send their children and thus remove them from the occupations in which they were born and raised and to which they were destined. For this reason, the council held, the children could not derive any benefit from their studies, and the majority remained ignorant because (among other reasons) there were not good teachers for so many students. A similar petition was repeated in yet another writing, and in the *Capítulos de Reformación* (10 February 1623) Philip IV — to avoid the dissemination of these studies of poor quality from which no one ever left properly taught, "and thus many do not go on to higher studies and lose all the time they have spent on Latin, while if they had been employed in other occupations and jobs would have been more useful to the Republic and to themselves" — gave instructions that there could be no grammaar studies in specific towns, even if they were endowed with sufficient revenue.[21]

If, since the fifteenth and in the sixteenth century, study was a means for moving up the social strata; and if, despite everything, it would remain such no matter how many obstacles were put in the way, it took somebody involved in seventeenth-century social conditions to realize the foregone conclusion that study would also be utilized as a means of subjection and repression. The Seville lawyer Chaves, with whom we are already acquainted, when confronted with the abundant penal population that filled the jail of Seville and wanting to rid the city of this blemish, assumed that the majority of the prisoners were foreigners because in Seville "not only principal persons, but also the common and working people who have little wealth and property, raise their children with a tutor who lives in their home."[22] To submit their children to a discipline of study was not a means for them to elevate themselves but a way to separate them from the viewpoints that sowed the seeds of disorder; these were the viewpoints that authority tried to match with resources of violence or cultural shaping (the choice between the two was determined by the case at hand) that succeeded in overcoming resistence to integration. Only a writer fully immersed in the social conditions of the baroque epoch could think that making children study was principally an effective repressive solution. But let us return to the theme of the controls of ascendant social mobility, whose containment was recommended in the uneasy society of the seventeenth century.

One must endeavor, it was said, to have everyone continue in the position that an inherited and traditional order had assigned. One must limit the cases wherein an individual passed from one level to another; in absolute terms, such cases could not be eliminated in any society, but they could be made more difficult and limited if action were taken with regard to all the procedures and paths of ascension that were indiscriminately offered to groups of potentially large numbers of individuals.

Acceptance of the system of submitting to the difficulties of hierarchical change in society, according to the demands of the estatist order, were sublimated as a moral value of the highest esteem. "One will be all the more despicable, the more one becomes separated from one's estate and obligation, which nowadays is so little heeded," maintained Luque Fajardo,[23] and his words attempted to say that the sole way to merit high esteem was to abide by the duties of one's own and invariable estate. All the evils of insatiable greed arose from a lack of this ordering: Suárez de Figueroa thought that "all evils, it is certain, coincide in those who are neither content nor at ease in any estate or condition and whose end is constituted not by what they have but by what they intend to have."[24] It was thus frequently repeated that only he who remained in his place was happy, in accordance with a principle of integration characteristic of traditional society. "To measure oneself by one's own estate, being content with it, goes a long way toward putting one at ease," advised F. Santos, who — significantly — supported his thought in a popular proverb of archaic knowledge: "A cobbler I was supposed to be — back again to what suits me." In this way, with "everyone going to one's occupation, everything is at ease and in peace." And when a similar norm takes hold from within, being interiorized in each one's consciousness, the system reaches its maximum solidity and the fullness of its virtues: "Fortune gave me no more property than what I have mentioned, but with it I live at ease and with pleasure, I listen and I keep still: in this way I enjoy the world."[25] The theater, which was linked to propagating the monarchical-seignorial system, explained such theses better than anywhere else.[26] In this sense, Vossler was right in writing: "The leveling of differences is something absolutely foreign to the spirit of the Spanish stage. On the contrary, the bonding together of things, estates, feelings, and temporal and godly values is only imaginable on a very severe hierarchical scale."[27]

In this one is not only to see an echo of a previous condition that continued in the seventeenth century. The many who found themselves to some extent involved, even if critically, in preserving baroque culture maintained the force of the estatist schema; this does not refer only to the literati or to dramatic writers. Elsewhere I have emphasized this point regarding the preservation of the tripartite estatist order within the limits of the seventeenth century, while indicating that it was the necessary basis for germinating phenomena of decomposition and fragmentation, whose appearance can be observed.[28] Here is a clear attestation (and especially valuable because of its author) of the existence of this traditional ordering: Cellorigo spoke about the three orders, "the one of priests and the other two of nobles and plebs, which the Prince has to work with so that they do not become changed, disturbed, mixed up or equivalent, but that each one preserves its place, order, and harmony, so that the diverse voices will make a perfect consonance."[29]

This rigorous distribution had to be maintained in all spheres. The politicians had to keep it in mind in all the obligations and services that they demanded from individuals and in the rights and freedoms they granted them. For their part, the poets, like the painters, had to give persons their estatist "decorum" — that is, its ambience and manners — according to the social condition of the group they belonged to, "attributing the wise with wise sayings and deeds, the rustic with rustic words and deeds, the scholar deals with his school, the pastor with his flocks, the Prince with his government, the vassal with his family, the seignior orders and the slave obeys," avoiding those manifestations that "are improper to the person's estate" — this was how a typical baroque preceptist explained it.[30] But if this was so greatly emphasized, it was because a new force that was moving at the heart of society was pushing for a collapse of this construction. Cellorigo also warned against the tendency of the Spanish who try "to equal everybody in everything, perverting the natural order whereby it is certain and undeniable that some were born to serve and obey and others to order and govern" (surprised at his own words, perhaps, the author expressly rejected the Aristotelian thesis of natural servitude, apprehensive that he would be interpreted in such a way).[31] The Spanish seventeenth-century texts repeating such a thesis are very numerous; they attempted to contain the threatening break-down of a social order that these writers frequently criticized.

The measure reputed to be the principal one for containing the possible break-down of the social order on which the monarchy must base itself — an image that translated the epoch's experience of crisis — was perhaps the hereditary nature of people's occupations and their corresponding social levels. A writer dealing with the economic disarray and its associated social upheavals, Cristóbal Pérez de Herrera, asked that steps be taken "for many to be directed toward following their fathers' occupations."[32] Making use once again of the writings of Suárez de Figueroa, we find that he — offering us one of the earliest examples of a paradigmatic presentation of the Chinese, prior to the physiocratic myth of the eighteenth century — proposed the Chinese practice of obligating the sons to follow their fathers' occupations, which promoted enthusiasm for the guild and skill in the profession.[33] The zeal to immobilize the order led to the extremes, proper to a romanticism *avant la lettre*, of maintaining that Spain should preserve its national mode of dress and not admit the foreign mode, as Castillo Solórzano said.[34] Therefore, the way that was everywhere judged to be most effective in guaranteeing this order of society was to attribute the estatist determinations to lineage. At that time all of Europe still based itself on this principle, which in the Spanish baroque was again and again articulated as the constitutive principle of the social order. Nature operates through the blood of one's lineage and, behind nature, God. The hierarchized societies of baroque Europe were based on this scale.[35]

At the same time that a strengthening of the estatist order took place, we find an economy that again — as an indirect effect of the crisis and as a direct consequence of the princes' policies — became subject to the predominance of land ownership in the hands of old or new seigniors (the latter having turned toward a mentality influenced by nobiliary modes of behavior). That economy could create a very favorable atmosphere for a vigorous and organized reaction against social changes. There was an evident interaction between the structures of society to be safeguarded, the complex of myths and values that diverse media were used to disseminate, and the economic forms on whose survival the system was based. The estatist principle of these socioeconomic forms can be read in the words of Pérez de Herrera, which were repeated by so many writers, in one form or another: one must assure "what is appropriate in clothes, food and household to everybody according to his or her station."[36] The same thing was demanded by the French nobles gathered in the Assembly of Troyes in 1651, renewing previous petitions from 1614;[37] it was heard throughout Europe, drawing the outlines of a traditional world preserved even in England,[38] although there it would immediately begin to fade away.[39]

Notwithstanding, proceeding with a minimal historical rigor, can we simply stop there? With the setting up of all this defensive apparatus for preserving the traditional order, had not something else been attained other than immobilizing the situation and restoring those aspects that had undergone the greatest erosion during the Renaissance crisis? Do we really have to accept in its fullest sense the thesis that individuals at the end of the sixteenth century had to carry out a liquidation of the Renaissance (a thesis maintained by L. Febvre)?[40] Not at all. Conservative society carried within itself elements that would be incorporated into the incipient stages of modernity; its restoration had to be made by combining surviving aspects with new strokes. Therefore the baroque, on the one hand very medievalizing, was on the other hand even more modern than the previous century (Europe would go through a similar experience with romanticism, which the baroque anticipated in more than one aspect).

Speaking about the internal tensions of society in chapter 1, I pointed out the tendency toward the formation of an intermediary layer. Let us now return to touch on this theme from another angle. In the baroque there was an endeavor to consolidate this intermediary stage, thinking that it would lead to a consolidation of order; later, in the eighteenth century, Montesquieu and his followers (and, drawing inspiration from them, the entire group of the middle level and agrarian nobility) supported the thesis that an ideal of mediocrity had to be maintained as a way to assure the maintenance of conservative forces. It was already a thesis expressed by Pascal: "nothing but mediocrity is good . . . straying from the median is straying from humanity."[41] To have a middle term, there had to be two extremes; therefore, mediocrity preserved the differentiated order. Because of this, we can read in Cellorigo:

> There is nothing more pernicious than the excessive wealth of some and the extreme poverty of others, in which our republic is very out of

proportion, as much because of the many primogeniture endowments, which are made every day, as because of tributes of domain [*censos*] with which some grow larger and others lose. And although it would not be good to say that all have to be equal, it would not be unreasonable for these two extremes to be more in proportion; for everybody wanting to be equal is what has made them the most unruly and has left the republic most confused: from the lower to the middle and from the middle to the higher, everybody leaving their standards and order that they should keep according to the station of their properties, occupations and estate."[42]

The anonymous writing to Philip IV (perhaps from 1621) that we considered to have drawn its inspiration from Cellorigo made a case before the king for those in the middle group "who are the ones harassed on all sides and the *ones who sustain everybody*."[43] It was a commonly held opinion among writers and politicians.[44] If we recall what we previously read from Cellorigo against the tendency toward equalizing, we will understand to what extent the defense of *mediocritas* was grounded in it, as in all conservative thought. This was characteristic of all those offering a defense and apology for the median life.

What we have just said signifies, in its complexity, a new formulation with respect to preserving the social order and implies a certain change in this order itself, keeping the essential. Let us bear in mind the ideological relation that this doctrinal line had with the thinking of someone like Montesquieu, and which represented a compromise between the middle-level landholding nobility and the rich of a nonnoble origin. Viewing it in this way, one might possibly come to the conclusion that what ultimately changed in the absolute monarchy and in the seignorial agrarian economy at the beginning of the seventeenth century would turn out to be much more and, indeed, lead to more radical alterations than the transformations happening in the previous hundred years.

Elsewhere I have written extensively about the phenomena revealing the erosion of traditional society.[45] At this point I will merely add some data to allow us to verify the general significance of this erosion. We have seen the clear terms in which Pérez de Herrera abided by the traditional pattern. But something else was introduced inadvertently in his exposition. The traditionalist conception of the estates exhibited a tripartite division, always subject to the same schema: priests, warriors, and farmers. These three groups were identified with three parts of the body and ranged from the highest to the lowest according to a multisecular metaphor that was accepted as if it were a direct expression of the natural world.[46] Yet in attesting to the state of erosion undergone by this image of society in the minds of his time, Pérez de Herrera allows us to understand that the hierarchical estatist order had been transformed in such a way that the warriors were no longer the arms nor are the farmers the feet. With a scientism derived from his medical training and in an image the author reputed to be perfectly comprehensible for his readers, the farmers, ranchers, functionaries, and workers were the liver ("which by way of the veins sends sustenance to all") and the grandees, those with titles, gentlemen, and rich and noble persons were the stomach, since it — with its natural heat — is the place of digestion where the foods are transformed, forming the substance that doctors call chyle.[47] In the allegory now being proposed, we immediately observe that the warring function has disappeared, being replaced by the economic function: therefore there is no talk of warriors, but of the rich. In turn, the hierarchical distribution remains distorted. It is clear that neither the grounds nor the significance of the social divisions is the same.

Other writers offer us similar instances that reveal a lack of understanding of the tradition they were seeking to preserve: Salas Barbadillo in *El sagaz Estacio*, Enrique Gómez in *El siglo pitagórico*, and Jerónimo Yáñez in *El donado hablador* wanted to refer to the diversity of estates of social life; but instead of presenting them as a manifestation of a social ontology, as tradition deemed them to be, they converted them into products of certain psychological characteristics that were more or less linked to specific professions that, on the other hand, offered a great diversity. Although the literary genres of comedy and tragedy were attached, in the representation of figures, to their own estatist groups — because the values reflected by the genres had to refer to those groups — one of those proposing such a social differentiation of genres no longer understood why this must be the case and assumed the reason to be that if one proceeded in another way, the seigniors would raise an uproar in the theater locale and disastrous consequences could occur:[48] thus a merely pragmatic explanation.

From the point of view of the baroque mentality and in connection with the real situation that it reflected, the desire to preserve and strengthen a social order certainly implies that this order appeared to be profoundly altered in its grounding support, significance, and ends. The divisions of the levels were kept firm, but the traditional schema had been seriously altered and these divisions now took into account only differences on the scale from riches to poverty, which moved according to shifts along this line.[49]

To a certain extent, what was altered (for example, the relationship between sovereign and subject or the nexus between land and landowner) supported the conservative interest groups and maintained the established order. But even this established order underwent changes. For example, there was an alteration in the fiscal pressure of the state (which was of a conservative tendency). When the taxes were such as proceeded from the seignorial tradition, they were imposed only on commoners and were known as ordinary and extraordinary *servicios* [emergency direct taxes]; now, when it was a question of new forms of tribute of recent invention — *millones* [taxes on certain commodities], *donativos* ["voluntary" contributions], and incremented indirect taxes — they came to bear on nobles and commoners. This tendency toward tributary equality eroded the traditional concept of nobility. The sale of titles, nobility, and commissions accentuated the decay of the old society's values, giving a greater emphasis to economic values. The nobles' abandonment of the military function accentuated this process of decline;[50] simultaneously the appearance of arms that were technologically complex and expensive to acquire, along with the need to make use of them in considerable quantities, helped to advance the values of wealth. Although baroque literature — poetry and theater — seems to imply the contrary, it is undeniable that the values had changed to a great extent.

Undoubtedly a transformation in the conception of public tribute (the fact that we can speak of public tribute without too much impropriety is already a great novelty) does not suffice to explain Lope's theater, but without that circumstance it would have been different from what it was. In the traditional order, property as it was divided or within the pyramid of the seignorial order was an element in support of that order; now, inversely, the order was viewed (perhaps somewhat out of focus, which would not be corrected until the bourgeois revolution) as an element in support of property, and property was less and less a pyramidal superposition of rights in the hands of a titled elite, to be transformed into the absolute and sole right of an individual landholder. The exclusion system of bourgeois property appeared as the goal of the state before Locke expressed it in this way.[51] Let us refer once again to Suárez de Figueroa: the political society, which he called the "civil consortium," existed so that "men can preserve their property [*haciendas*]" under the protection of power; this was not only for public property to be protected, out of necessity and for common benefit, "but also so that each one's individual property is preserved."[52] Because of this, at a very early date and in the phase of early mercantilism, tendencies appeared in Spain that encouraged a broad margin of economic freedom in the agricultural sector (which contradicts the thesis of A. Hauser and others that is based on a somewhat simplistic view correlating mercantilism and baroque authoritarianism in all sectors). From my conflictive view of the baroque, in which I consider it a culture in tension, I maintain that it was an authoritarian culture but precisely one that was reorganized or reelaborated in new molds, bearing in mind the conflicts and possibilities posed by freedom, among them certain aspects of economic freedom. The recommendations of Philip III's baroque councillors were not contrary but complementary to the baroque's absolute monarchism (once again referring to the 1619 document): they recommended "that the farmers have no rate for selling the bread made from their harvested grains . . ., that they be given permission to freely sell in their baked bread whatever was of their harvest and from their own farm,"[53] a commercial freedom of grain and of its manufactured product 150 years before Campomanes was present on the political scene. But this had its own significance: it corresponded to an entire bourgeoislike transformation that was undermining the privileged estatist order even as there was talk of preserving it.

Naturally, the old forms of property continued to exist. Privileged property, of a seignorial, secular, or ecclesiastical character, occupied everywhere — and most seriously in Spain — a greater area than private or free property. But what was new was that private or free property began to be jolted in its immobility by the influence of the conception corresponding to civil property. Let us omit discussion of the appearance of the first measures of ecclesiastical disentailment, which were quantitatively not very important, although perhaps more so than they are ordinarily deemed to be.[54] But even when that property fell into the hands of nobles and ecclesiastical institutions, it was profoundly altered by the feeling of greed that inspires the rich (a characteristic of modern economic life pointed out by Ehrenberg, Sombart, and many others).[55] There were also alterations in its administration and in its use, without, however, associated forms of capitalist investment (or only very rarely).

The task of preservation cannot be accomplished without contaminating the tradition to a great extent. From the outset there was a need in the seventeenth century to increase considerably the number of those implicated and interested in the system, because its effective defense needed more financial, military, and psychological means; it needed to spend more, have more armed men at its disposal, to rely on more adherents. There was no remedy but to allow the individuals of new groups, the urban rich and the rich from the countryside (those "rich farmers" who play such a role in baroque theater)[56] to participate, in some way, in traditional society's order of privileges and values. Of course, there was no absolutely closed and stationary society where some changes did not have to be taken into account; but, besides this, in the case of the baroque — given that after the expansive experience of the Renaissance it was impossible to close the door on all innovation without being exposed to dangerous agitations — society was instilled with a tolerance for the introduction of the new in certain sectors. In those realms where it was not dangerous either politically or intellectually, the doors had to be left open for novelty, a great clamor had to be made around it to attract the people's attention, and such novelty had to be taken to extremes to satisfy the appetite for it. The irruption of outlandish elements in poetry, literature, and art compensated for the deprivation of novelty elsewhere. Thus the virtuosity of novelty, characteristic of the baroque in those areas where it did not possess a corrosive force, was explained by some direct social motivations.

A passage from Jerónimo de San José articulates the terms of the problem with great precision:

> Let us then, very felicitously, maintain firm and immobile the terms, utterances and words that Antiquity introduced in the matter of Religion, dogmas and doctrine, and that time has always successively observed and venerated, as well as the words and formulary phrases in the laws, decrees and forensic questions, and in every art and science; but in everything else

concerning style and current language one need not bind ingenuity and eloquence to the unpolished nature of ancient speech.[57]

To deny the introduction of new terms was to deny the appearance of the new things that were expressed with them, although in the seventeenth century neologism and invention went together. Therefore certain areas remained deprived of mobility: the area of religion, where dissent had taken root with such fire; of law, where modernity had undertaken the battle of the *ius novum*, which was dangerous to the preservation of the estatist order; of science, where the sphere of discovery and invention teemed with those restless "discursist and scientific" spirits whom Saavedra Fajardo draws our attention to; and of technology itself, which altered the relations of social and economic life, bolstering competition. What remained, ultimately, for the efforts of innovation? Artistic and poetic caprice.

Only in the latter areas could there be acknowledgment of that "freedom of ingenuity" exalted by Gracián.[58] Limited to this area, the work freely accomplished with respect to paradigms and norms became an object of esteem for the baroque critic. In speaking of one of the painters he admired — Navarrete el Mudo — Jusepe Martínez, the Saragossan painter who was a friend and admirer of Velázquez, praised above all "his free mode of painting."[59] Commentaries of this type could be multiplied, but we limit ourselves to recalling that novelty and freedom were the two values that Lope's *Arte nuevo* was inspired by and defended, despite what he wrote against novelty. Basing himself on French sources, which were ordinarily judged to place greater weight on norms, Rousset was able to write that the baroque "generally rejects rules to proclaim itself innovative and modernist."[60]

This innovation, which we could term an *anticlassicism* hostile to prevailing norms of exemplarity, characteristic of mass activity, was linked to the role of taste [*gusto*] that we indicated before, bringing it into focus from a different angle. This left the mass without an objective authority [*instancia*] to abide by and instead gave it over to the so-called "free taste," a subjectivism more apparent than effective. What happened in reality was that the mass was left defenseless vis-à-vis the shaping control exercised by those in power with their manipulated resources. A French writer, protesting against taste and characterizing it as a licentious influence, came to recognize its contradictory reign in terms that help us to understand the problem being raised here. In effect, Mathurin Régnier, in a brief poem whose title was furnished by the aphorism "Individual taste decides all," stressed the dissolution of firm and objective criteria that accompanied it: "and good and bad depend on the taste of men," with which "each one persists in his decision [*son party*] according to his own taste."[61] This was the consequence that was to be attained: by suppressing the objective paradigmatic authorities — which nevertheless were well known by the free citizens of the Renaissance communities — and replacing them with a license for outlandishness and caprice (recognized only where no possible danger was involved), the mass eagerly persisted in adhering to the faction it selected, believing that it acted of its own choice [*por gusto propio*]. Defense of this apparent optative freedom of choice [*opción*] took place again and again. Lope, once more the representative par excellence of baroque culture, this Lope who was so committed to preserving the interests of the absolute monarchy and its seignorial base, wrote in an outburst of anarchic freedom: "Put no limit to taste" (*Quien todo lo quiere*).

But Lope knew very well that this appeal to free taste was to leave the mass devoid of resistance in the face of the effective shaping activity of the expedients that baroque culture placed in the hands of the artist and, consequently, of the individuals in power for whom the artist worked. Perhaps until recent times, no culture other than the baroque had sought this apparent freedom and disorder, this normless subjectivism, and probably no other had deployed such an effective force of attraction and shaping. This shaping no longer took place in relation to a minimal number of select individuals, such as those affected in the Renaissance, but in relation to mass groups of urban concentrations. Without concerning himself with the historical reason for the phenomenon. Wölfflin was very much on the right path when he came to notice, perhaps deriving from his profound knowledge of so much material, that beneath its apparent freedom and lack of norms the baroque was subject to a strong principle of unity and subordination.[62] In imposing itself upon a great variety of singular elements, this predominance of the total unity of the composition corresponded, with its molding and limiting action, to a unity of domination inspiring the entire organization of baroque culture. Such was the basis of what in chapter 2 we called its guided character. Formally, the baroque did away with rules, but some rules continued to rule harshly in the background. Vigorous precepts were imposed on the themes, characters, destinies, and no less on the characters' feelings and modes of behavior, which was what counted; its demanding rules valorized morality, religion, and politics, which rose above the others. As Ph. Butler has said, despite their much boasted "freedoms," the artists had never been more closely watched in their production or subjected to external influences. Whatever the differences of country, temperament, or personal talent, in this respect the Europe of this epoch exhibited a noticeable unity in its artists.[63] What the artist did (and the moralist or political writer as well) was directed toward shaping the mentality of groups of people in numbers that until then had never been taken into account. If baroque poetry (which we could easily take as the representative genre, whether it was spiritual or obscene, realist or imaginary, absurdly pompous or limited to a simple popular expression) reveals a quest for the new, surprising, and unexpected, even when making use of traditional means reworked into such new effects or under forms and methods that may also have been new, it was always "profoundly conservative or, rather, reactionary."[64]

As an urban culture, the baroque took place in cities where, besides a multitude of "deviants," popular classes were being constituted, heterogeneously made up of day laborers, artisans, small proprietors, modest financiers, and individuals of certain professions — physicians, lawyers, and soldiers, in addition to the large number of friars. They all "opinionated," to the point that at one time, to contain the threat from a formed state of opinion by giving public satisfaction in some respect, the authorities punished a minister with the gallows (as in the case of Don Rodrigo Calderón); or to subdue it they mounted an efficient operation capable of disfiguring it on the conceptual plane and of cutting short its further dissemination (as in the case of the murder of the count of Villamediana).[65]

A more common solution, however, was to reinforce the repressive means of the state, hardening the activity of judges and other agents of justice. In Spain, the Inquisition offers a sad verification of this. Yet even with these measures for reinforcing the organs of punishment, the ruling powers had to respond — to some extent, in some way — to public opinion, and everything could not be reduced to the application of force without accountability. In chapter 1 we noted important cases of repression whose procedure went so far as to resemble lettres de cachet. But we now observe that this seventeenth-century absolute monarchy could be confronted with an opinion like that of the Jurors of Seville. Writing to Philip IV on 30 December 1621 (they were referring, then, more to what was done in the time of his father than to what was beginning to be done in his time), they requested that in crimes of murder and other serious offenses the accused be heard up to the second tribunal so as not to leave the defense of the right to life in a worse position than that of the right to property; in civil lawsuits, where the interest of property was judged, there were three tribunals, whereas there was only one in these other suits where life and honor — which were of greater importance — were submitted to judgment. Much as later bourgeois systems of authority, property enjoyed greater political and judicial guarantees than did persons. The Jurors of Seville added yet another vigorous protest: the fact that some were punished instead of others, the innocent instead of the guilty, was caused by "the harsh torture carried out by the judges, exceeding what is granted by law, telling the accused that they are convinced of their crimes so that the accused will sometimes confess to what they have not done, as has been seen in many cases wherein they have confessed crimes they have not done because of the severity of the torture." Without question, baroque society experienced a worsening of repression, and even within that society it was appraised as such.[66]

Both this hardening and the protest against it occurred in cities where citizens had lost their political rights and their initiative vis-à-vis the powers of the state. There they lived under a political crisis of reaction: on the one hand they were dominated administratively by functionaries acting for the absolute monarchy; on the other, they were subject socially to the influence of the seigniors who supported themselves with landholdings whose income yields had improved.

Over and over, baroque writers preached obedient submission to the laws, whatever these might be, reverence for the princes, although they be tyrants, and for the magistrates and upper levels; their expressions frequently surpassed the level of obedience offered in other epochs.[67] Formulas of a sugary Neoplatonism — which Lope used repeatedly (recall his *Pastores de Belén*) — prepared the psyche for such subordination.[68] We are encountering a regime where there was talk about the ''glory of obedience.''[69] Correlatively, baroque art arose from these conditions and developed so as to maintain them.[70] In this sense we can say that it was the art of the great monarchies — not that one can morphologically call the baroque a monarchical art (in the way Eugenio d'Ors has done), but because it emerged sociologically from the social conditions present in the regimes of monarchical absolutism and because its characteristics corresponded to the necessities deriving from the program of supporting such regimes.

In sermon literature, one can glean the program of encouraging the monarchy's charismatic quality (which in Spain had hardly been present before), now attempting to incorporate it, with its royal personages of flesh and bone, on the plane of supernatural existence. Paravicino, overlooking the dogma of the natural equality of human beings and even certain precise evangelical maxims, maintained that God particularly enjoys the worship and reverence rendered to a royal person, to the point that it seems "he brings the royal person near with a hidden bloodline of relation."[71] In different tones and with a grave admonition, when Ximénez de Embún, a Carmelite and cathedraticum of Saragossa, preached a sermon at the exequies of Queen Isabel (de Borbón), he insisted on referring all the events of the monarchy to a biblical collection of anecdotes, applying their symbolism. The basic schema could not be more vulgarly simple: the death of a queen, being the loss of a great treasure for the people, signified divine punishment for the people's sins. "Alas, Spain, Spain, a cluster of grapes in a beautiful season because of your fertility, your abundance, but today, if I turn my eyes on almost all of the estates, how few good and healthy grapes has this cluster, some are rotton in the filth of lasciviousness, others dry of all the juices of virtue, the rest green from idleness, every one cast out to ruin."[72] Francisco Xarque, dean of Albarracín, pronounced a sermon on the occasion of the birth of Philip IV's son. His contribution is an extreme attempt to present the monarchy as included in the divine order, applying the symbolism of the events narrated in the New and (more repeatedly) the Old Testament. "With a coarse brush, although with bright colors from both Testaments, I drew the subject of the Fiesta we are today celebrating, using little board." With this male birth after the death of a first son, the orator was attempting to present an event of direct divine providence regarding the monarchy, which in this way was saved by being given a successor — an event to which he attributed biblical characteristics. Such a sacralization of the monarchy's historical accounts came as support for the preservation of the political-ecclesiastical world in which the monarchy was included. With this male birth, God wanted to grant "to the House of Austria the stability of heaven; to the Catholic Monarchy the duration of the firmament; to the Kings the steadfastness of the two great bodies of light, for they are of the Church's Heavens; and to the Church the permanence of Paradise." [73] (What really happened was that this prince died shortly afterward and Xarque's prophesy was not fulfilled with a great deal of exactitude).

In affirming the existence of a connection between the baroque and the social crisis of Italy, Joyce G. Simpson has come to generalize the question in these terms: "The baroque is a glorification of the established powers. It is the art of authoritarian regimes . . . that dominates the awed spectator and carries him or her away so that one forgets to doubt and question." [74] The same author observed that in France the influence of the court made the artists most linked to it incline necessarily toward the baroque, and when criticism, headed by Boileau, postulated criteria of pure classicism, the artists working nearest to the world of the court and under the influence of its tastes and interests remained faithful to the baroque and its "freedom of ingenuity." [75]

Everywhere, the seventeenth-century theater reflected (although not necessarily in a direct way) the forms of life, the feelings, and the moral values of the code established in monarchical-nobiliary society — not those established on a real level, of course, but on the level of sublimation deemed effective for accomplishing the defense of this society in the midst of the tensions of the time. To submit oneself to these norms, which the playwright was to make a contribution toward disseminating, was considered the path of "reason," according to what we are told by the characters on stage; that reason was identified, should the case arise, with the monarch as the highest level of the system of seignorial privilege. One can make similar affirmations about all aspects of baroque culture, of which the art of the stage was perhaps the fullest manifestation. "A culture always grows protected by a social power, and the original sense of baroque art, above all in its most perceptive form, literature, is a particular sense of privilege," Mopurgo-Tagliabue has written. [76]

Like the theater, the other great art of the epoch, painting, strove no less to integrate the public that contemplated it into the system of values of the nobiliary society in whose service its activity unfolded. The works of Rubens or Van Dyck, the royal portraits of Tuscan painting, and paintings of French portraiture that in this respect culminated in Ph. de Champaigne or Rigaud were examples of this general attitude. A. Hauser observed that in Holland the collective portrait, which in the sixteenth century encompassed all the undifferentiatied members of any group, was now limited to official members. The case of Zurbarán is highly significant. On the canvas, he represented his saints below the image of Spanish ladies of the epoch, working with the symbolism of the aristocratic apparel whereby they appeared before the spectator and making use of the meaning of a socially privileged social rank corresponding to that mode of dress.

In this way (it has been said) he was alluding to the rank of the saints in the realm of the spiritual, but at the same time he was confirming the spiritual rank that the prevailing order intended for one to continue recognizing in the aristocracy.[77] In agreement with this interpretation, Tapié has asserted that the retables not only contained a doctrine, not only attracted one's imagination with their plastic elements, but, because of the elements' internal distribution and their placement in the church, they corresponded to a feeling, a propagation of hierarchy in the roles attributed to personages and beliefs.[78] In addition, I believe that those saints declared by the baroque (St. Teresa, St. Tomás de Villanueva, St. Luis Beltrán, St. Ignatius, St. Francisco Xavier, St. Isidro) were celebrated and extolled in support of a social system, for the glory and protection of the monarchy whose charisma they strengthened. The poems singing the praises of their canonizations were also taken advantage of for glorifying the monarchy and its order, which henceforth would have yet another guardian in heaven. One must also take into account a certain political literature of a glorifying sort that is very different from the abundant opposition literature that we have seen.[79]

Those efforts of restoration carried out by the baroque, which included, as a notion of maximum efficacy, the revamping of the agrarian economy and the apparent sublimation of rural life — recall the great number of comedies dealing with farmer thematics, which were written by someone as tied to the city as Lope — entailed the foregrounding of certain traditional manifestations in literature, writings about morality and politics, and art.[80] Even the mythology that continued to be used in the baroque frequently depended more on the medieval version than on the original classical version.[81] These holdovers from the past were, of course, not lacking in Spain, where the harvest of such instances would be very abundant; but neither were they lacking in other European countries, above all in those experiencing a flourishing baroque — Rome, Venice, France, and the Catholic Low Countries.[82] Let us recall — although only to correct the tendency to believe that any question dealing with Spain is different and that there is no reason to go outside of Spain to understand it — that A. Blunt has stressed the extent of the presence of medieval elements in Italy's mannerism and early baroque.[83] In the realm of literature, M. Raymond believed that in France, as in Germany and other countries of central and northern Europe, the baroque mode seemed to be inserted in the medieval tradition of the gothic, manifesting itself as a reelaboration of gothic forms.[84] In the realm of architecture Piovene has made similar affirmations with respect to Venice.[85] Thus the process of a medievalizing restoration was not lacking anywhere or in any sphere of the collective life of western European peoples, from art and literature to religion and the economy.[86] Although the holdovers were medieval elements that had not yet disappeared and that would persist for a long time before disappearing, in the seventeenth-century crisis they acquired a particular emphasis. The much discussed ''refeudalization'' had a European scope.[87]

This analysis leads us to the area of politics. Although the absolute state, with the relative newness of its sovereign power, was to a certain extent a modern creation, it was imposed upon a complex of inherited circumstances, upon the continued existence of traditional political forms. A recent scholar on the baroque in France has drawn attention to the reintroduction of the crusade ideal under the pretense of reconquering the Holy Land. This ideal was presented to Henry IV by an obscure dramatic writer, Billard, whereas the well-known poet Malherbe unfolded it before Louis XIII. And the image of the monarchy that the 1651 Assembly of the French nobility proposed to Mazarin and Louis XIV was the image of St. Louis's feudal monarchy.[88] Equivalent aspects in the Spanish monarchy are well known. But let us not forget that the privileged groups influencing the conservative policies did not occupy a merely traditional position, nor were their interests, ideals and beliefs simply the same ones as before (nor were those of other groups). In this way we can understand how, with such a conservative polity, one could nevertheless arrive at the transformations of the modern state. Simultaneously, the utilization of medievalizing elements did not restore knightly culture to its previous forms; rather, it constructed a baroque culture, which in so many points could be considered characteristically different from knightly culture.

In the seventeenth century, are we encountering a return to what Sombart called a traditionalist or empirical economy and its corresponding polity, both oriented toward preterit forms, past experiences, prototypes of tradition? Can the entire significance of baroque culture be defined in these terms? Can the baroque ultimately be reduced to a medievalizing conservatism? Undoubtedly not. Although the interests of the privileged groups were based on tradition, their interests were not consumed in it. They assumed aspirations, appraisals, and new modes of behavior. In their consciousness that they were operating in specific circumstances, they made use of means [*medios*] that in part — at least in their mode of application and in the immediate effects they are seeking — turned out to be new and necessarily led them to the limit representing a new epoch. The people of the baroque, finally, judged themselves and their epoch to be "modern."[89]

III: Elements of a Baroque World View

Chapter 6
The Image of the World and Human Being

In the first half of the seventeenth century, the social consciousness of crisis weighing upon human beings provoked a world view wherein the minds of the epoch felt overwhelmed by an innermost disorder. They were sad human beings, as Lucien Febvre once called them, who began to appear on European soil in the last few years of the sixteenth century and who continued to be found until well into the second half of the following century. It is probably inaccurate to say, as Highet did,[1] that the generation living right at the turn of the century contemplated the final spark of what had been the Renaissance; but it is certain that with this generation was disseminated a pessimism influenced by the calamities that would continue for several decades. Consider what the four great plagues meant in Spain. Some historians have calculated the losses in very high percentages: about one-fourth of the population. And in the Spain of this time, starvation and misery went hand in hand with the plague. The other European countries also experienced lamentable spectacles in their cities and countrysides, and even more when the losses from the Thirty Years' War punished such extensive areas so severely. In a letter of 30 July 1638, the Jesuits tell us that "the needs and hunger are so unprecedented that they go so far as to consume their neighbors," owing to the tragic effect of war. Everywhere a gloomy existence was remarked: lives were lost, properties ruined, farms and workshops destroyed or abandoned.

The seventeenth century was a tragic epoch: this assertion served Mopurgo-Tagliabue as a point of departure, although he continued to say that, notwithstanding, the baroque was tragic only to the extent that it documented this tragedy.[2]

Omitting discussion of this latter point for now, let us take into consideration here how the societies of the epoch were subjected to a series of violent tensions that disrupted the ordered view of things and of society itself; although it was left to some to attempt a restoration of this threatened order, the profound disturbances upsetting the environs must be taken into account. Mopurgo added: the baroque was an art of crisis but not an art from crisis; it expressed a mentality and not a consciousness (which led him to commit the mistake of maintaining that the baroque revealed a complacency and not an uneasiness). The baroque departed from a consciousness of disaster and suffering and expressed it: "The globe has not seen a more corrupt century," commented Céspedes; according to him, however, the reference was not to political ailments, reasons of state, errors by ministers, or accidental failures, but to the upheavals that Europe was undergoing and the moral disorder of its guilt, which explained the disasters being suffered.[3] A few decades of harsh suffering influenced the creation and diffusion of a spirit of disenchantment, of disillusionment; La Rochefoucauld alluded to this when he spoke of the melancholy that came upon him from without, inundating his spirit, in addition to the melancholy that arose for intimate reasons. In France of the mid-seventeenth century, *chagrin* was a very widespread sentiment; in 1661, as an expression of the state of mind lived by the baroque, La Mothe Le Vayer wrote a book on the subject.[4] R. Burton concerned himself with the *Anatomy of Melancholy* (1621), and sloth was a state of mind that Spanish letters repeatedly made manifest.

All of this helps us comprehend the diffusion of the *madness of the world* topos that was so much a part of the artistic and literary manifestations of the baroque. Without a doubt, since the changes provoked by modernity began, there have been minds thinking that the world and human beings were being assaulted by a great madness.[5] But in the seventeenth-century crisis, this view became widespread in the face of the abnormality — from the traditional point of view — of so many of the events taking place. "Madness is universal," declared M. Régnier.[6] Quevedo's criticism did not concern a perennial and natural condition of the world, as might be offered in a Bosch painting, but the condition that he was witnessing, "the deliriums of a world that today appears to be raving."[7] Similarly, Saavedra Fajardo denounced the "madnesses of Europe."[8] In the theater, the one who unveiled things as they showed themselves in their social and moral confusion was the "comedian," repeatedly presented as the figure of the madman: "What madman will surpass this madman?" pondered Lope about one of them (*Lo cierto por lo dudoso*).[9] We suspect that it was no less possible to refer to this aspect of the world view the repulsive practice of using buffoons; they were used more unrestrainedly in the Spanish court than anywhere else. Whatever may have been the echo that the use of buffoons still retained from a classical Latin antecedent (would it then be possible to maintain that it was an example of humanism?), as in the way we find it mentioned in

Seneca's dialogue *De constantia sapientis* (11.2-3), the seventeenth-century taste for buffoons stemmed from the perception that they were comic evidence for the world's disharmony and senselessness. Saavedra Fajardo (*Empresa LXXII*) tells us that madmen are held to be "mistakes of nature." This mode of paying attention to the "natural rarities" was derived from the Renaissance; but whereas the Renaissance individual had sought such "rarities" by investigating the exotic, the baroque already revealed its divergence. The theme was doubtless inscribed within the limits of the "madness of the world" topos and in the topos of remedies for a melancholy caused by madness — a melancholy so pronounced in the Spanish kings because of the disasters they constantly underwent.

Barrionuevo put this general consideration before his readers: "We are all madmen, each and every one of us." [10] But although Barrionuevo meditated on the issue in this way, it reflected the fundamental basis giving rise to this moral judgment: the monetary, economic and, ultimately, the social disorder that was disrupting everything around him. There was a general confusion affecting the world, but this idea translated a historical experience: "Everything is confusion; beating one's head against the walls, no one knows what to do or how to succeed at anything." But what was prompting this? "Everything is due to excessive prices." Inflation — here was the specter. Inflation was serious in all of Europe and beyond all measure in Spain; it was a phenomenon that circumstantially, in cases of blockades, plagues, or bad harvests, was already known; but never with such a long-lasting rise, much less with the sequence of permanent upheavals that it caused everywhere. Such was one of the profound causes of that mad confusion: "Everything is due to excessive prices," to which Barrionuevo could therefore add, "What is happening is madness no less than what in the matter of money is seen every day." [11] If to this one adds the unfortunate events that were reported daily and that Pellicer included in his *Avisos*, his comments, made at an opportune moment, are comprehensible: "One cannot imagine these events to be accompanied by any more novelty worthy of notice, by any more confusion." [12] When baroque individuals spoke of the "mad world," this topos translated into an entire series of concrete experiences. At times the ruinous disorder suffered was such that one could see people, as in Andalusia, Barrionuevo tells us, "who walk through the streets as if madmen and spellbound, looking at each other," beside themselves from the burden of events beyond the grasp of reason. [13] Without limiting our discussion to a narrow economic determinism, I believe that a decisive factor in unleashing this confused madness of the baroque was the feeling revealed by Barrionuevo's exclamation that "there is no secure property." [14]

A reflection of this madness of the world can be recognized in the bewilderment that many writers revealed regarding the subject of happiness, which was a fundamental theme for the organization of existence. We see a pronounced disorientation regarding happiness in Saavedra Fajardo [15] as well as in Gracián, [16] and those moralists who are more rightly deemed to be witnesses of their time. At bottom it derived from the crisis that was troubling society. The seventeenth century experienced a serious alteration in peoples' social aspirations. If, making recourse to Carlyle's simple and clever formula, we say that happiness is the quotient resulting from dividing achievement by aspiration,[17] it is easy to conclude that — since the baroque century was characterized by a disproportionate increase in social aspirations — the result must have been a generally perceived diminution of happiness. Already considering it in this way, Quevedo in one of his early writings related the madness of the world during his time with the disproportionate claims driving everyone to climb the social ladder.[18]

Therefore, a manifestation of this madness consisted in the effect of displacement that individuals underwent in their customary positions as they were indicated by the traditional ordering of the universe. The effect was judged to be a general befuddlement that put things on their heads and vice versa. Jerónimo de Mondragón's *Censura de la locura humana y excelencias de ella*[19] reveals how the question had slid from its initial Erasmian character to a feeling of disharmony vis-à-vis the world of human beings (in which social positions continued to be taken into account), and then to the point of leaving it upside down. The theme can also be related to certain aspects of the epoch's conservative character and immobilist tendencies.

With this we touch upon the other great topos revitalized by the baroque: the *world upside down*. It was one of the topoi studied by E. R. Curtius who, by means of the data he collected, initially believed it to be a simple rhetorical game of stringing together *impossibilia* that were then used as a satire against the present.[20]

It is possible to assume that the image of the world upside down was the product of a marginal culture of the dispossessed, that is, of a popular counter-culture. This is how M. Bakhtin has suggested it should be conceived for the Middle Ages and the Renaissance.[21] I see it, rather, above all when the topos acquired such a force in the baroque, as a product of the culture of a changing society in which the disturbances that certain groups underwent in their position and function created a feeling of instability, which translated into a view of a staggering disorder. Considered in this way, it would be the result of a conservative or — perhaps better said — traditional valorization. There is no doubt that the theme revealed — and this Rousset has made evident with respect to the French baroque[22] — a feeling of instability and mutability. But if with regard to the assertion that everything changes, one judges that everything in the world is found to be distorted, it is because an underlying rational structure exists whose alteration allows for considering the existence of disorder: if one can speak of the world upside down it is because it can be right-side up. Quevedo's satirical *Discursos* and *Sueños* played on the basis of that structure.

The Spanish baroque retrieved the topos and, probably as a consequence of the intense experience of crisis being lived at the time, gave it a great emphasis. "Everything runs upside down," Luque Fajardo informs us,[23] and he proceeds to list examples that relate predominately to social existence. Suárez de Figueroa observed that today it was "the common style of the world" to see things "functioning upside down everywhere."[24] "There is nothing right-side up in the world from the moment it enters," wrote Fernández de Ribera — everything in it functioned upside down.[25] One of the most interesting works of Quevedo, *La hora de todos y la Fortuna con seso*,[26] contains a free elaboration of this topos in which the author's notion has to do with presenting how things would be in a world that started to function right-side up. Tirso wrote a comedy, *La República al revés [The Republic Upside Down]* that at least helps us to appreciate the theme's popularity.[27] It was also a subject that extended to the popular literature of *Avisos*: "Everything functions upside down," Barrionuevo told his readers.[28] Let us add that the figure of the comedian was also an agent of this inverted world: "I am he who says upside down / all the things he speaks," declared the corresponding character in Lope's comedy *El mejor alcalde, el rey*. In general, these references in context allow us to confirm the topos' conservative character in the same way it manifested its presence in Nieremberg.[29] Notwithstanding, when we come to the chapter Gracián dedicated to the theme in *El criticón*, we encounter such a severe critique that it allows us to insist that Gracián — like Saavedra Fajardo — advanced an ambivalent morality that was at bottom dissenting rather than conservative.[30] Following this lead, on losing the belief (typical of the privileged groups) in the order of objective reason as the keeper of justice and harmony, the "world upside down" topos went on (in the nonprivileged groups, which were more and more nonconformist intellectually) to turn into a formula of social protest.

This view of the world, which was tied to the consciousness of crisis, produced yet another image — or at least its diffusion and exacerbation — that was utilized by baroque writers: the world as a *confused labyrinth*. It is symptomatic that it already constituted perhaps the most repeated topos in mannerism.[31] Later, in the central moment of interest to us, Comenius warned about the risk of losing oneself in "the labyrinth of the world, above all such as it is organized at present"; with these words his thought brings out its connections with an actual and concrete situation from which derived all the force of the topos in the seventeenth century.[32] Comenius dedicated an entire book to the theme: *The Labyrinth of the World and the Paradise of the Soul*. Chlup and Patocka, who have recently presented an interesting anthology of the author, commented that the *Labyrinth* "expresses the situation of a profoundly disrupted society. The work contains, in allegorical form, a critique of human society such as it will appear to Comenius: a pilgrim who desires to traverse the world to elucidate his vocation, he observes the conditions and professions of humankind; everywhere he sees the reign of false appearances and disorder."[33] In the sphere of Spanish literature, one could say something very similar about the trials of picaresque characters.

In Spanish letters, the theme of the labyrinth is found in Góngora and in many others. V. Bodini has made evident the way in which it belongs to the fundamental structure of *La vida es sueño*.[34] Francisco Santos spoke of the "labyrinth of the world,"[35] and Enríquez Gómez asked that we imagine the world to be "an enchanted labyrinth."[36]

A similar topic is the *large plaza* where everybody assembles pell-mell; Comenius's pilgrim even has to go there.[37] Gracián's travelers also go to this "universal plaza" of the world, where all of its confusion is inscribed.[38] Suárez de Figueroa made use of the image for one of his books.[39] In Almansa's *Cartas*, it was said that the court was "like a plaza of the world" because everything going on in the world was known.[40] The theme is also found in Quevedo.[41] These semblances of the reality of that time are so obviously related to those we have previously mentioned that we do not need to add anything else.

The image of the *world as hostelry* more forcefully expressed an idea similar to the preceding; some made use of the image, and Fernández de Ribera extended it throughout an entire book:[42] madhouse, hostelry of the world, the world is "a profound hostelry of humankind." In the goings and comings of people who gather in an inn, in the brief time they spend there, in the variety and confusion of however many people are in it, in the lies and deceptions it is full of, and in its disorder, the image turns out to be extremely adequate as a version of the world comprising our existence: "Human existence is a hostelry where the wise is a lingering pilgrim," but it is also a place to learn all the tricks, deceptions, or other resources to defend oneself from everyone else (according to a baroque view of humankind that we will consider below). Fernández de Ribera called it the "university of students passing through this life."[43] Let us recall that in *La pícara Justina*, López de Ubeda tells us that the hostelry, a suitable center for the pilgrim and picaresque life, is the "university of the world,"[44] the place for learning about the struggle of life, in the conception of baroque pessimism.[45] The theme was present in Quevedo: the "inn of the world," which nevertheless is not to be feared when one follows the right path.[46]

Finally — and we have left it for last in this enumeration because it is the most studied and best-known theme — the *world as a stage* (which was unrelated to the question of the use of the theater as an instrument). The grandiose topos that Calderón carried to its greatest heights, and which for him had multisecular repercussions, meant many things, as we have seen in the aspects summarized above. First is the transitory character of the role that is assigned to each one, and which is only enjoyed or suffered during a representation. Second is its rotation of role distribution, so that what one is today is someone else tomorrow. Third is its condition as appearance, never as substance, whereby what appears to be — above all for the consolation of those enduring the inferior roles — does not affect the ultimate nucleus of the person but remains on the surface of the apparent, frequently in flagrant contradiction with the profound being and worth of each individual. With all of these implications, the topos of the "great stage of the world" became the most efficient means for impeding mobility: there was no reason to raise oneself up in protest because of one's lot in life, and there was no reason to struggle violently to change the positions assigned to individuals because, in the dramatic order itself (and not the geometric order in the mode of an orbit or cycle), the rapid succession of changes was assured. This topos and that of the "world as inn" implied and completed one another. Together, they occupied the place of greatest interest in the baroque repertory: "All the world's a stage," said Shakespeare in *As You Like It*.[47] On the plane of symbolist mentality, which on the whole continued to exist in the baroque generations, this double play effectively contributed to the devalorization of the world and of its pomp, riches, and power, but at no time forcing those who enjoyed these favors to divest themselves of them.

The world is diseased. Wars, famines and plagues, cruelty, violence, and deception dominate the society of human beings and are a threat everywhere. In the anonymous writing (among others) that J. M. Barnadas has made available, allusion is made to the many "afflictions" (thievery and injustices) that were endured; the writer recognized that it would not be easy for the king "to keep there from being so much disorder and so many injuries, which was imposed by necessity; this is a pessimistic view linked to the distressing experiences of a threatening present.[48] "What do you want the world to be other than hardships, shocks and afflictions?" F. Santos asked himself.[49] "A terrible flood of diseases has spread through the world," noted Suárez de Figueroa.[50] But the baroque human being could not simply be asked to limit himself or herself to an ascetic renunciation, no matter how much it was preached, whether in the rousing tones of Quevedo or the wearisome sermonizing of Nieremberg. Between the Middle Ages and the baroque remained the indelible Renaissance, with its experience of growth and economic boom; the malaise that was being suffered was recognized as proceeding from a disproportionate expansion of aspirations.

Without a doubt the baroque, and not only the seventeenth century, was tragic, contrary to what Mopurgo maintained. The list that could be made of "works of doom" in art and literature would be copious indeed. Even longer and more full of doom would be the list of so many grievous events in political life and in the economy. But for the satisfaction of the few who freed themselves from the ills and for the dazzling of those who could seriously protest, the baroque was also the epoch of fiesta and splendor. This other face showed itself — in art, literature, politics, or war — whenever there was produced a certain closeness to the Church, the monarchy, and the most elevated seigniors, a contrast that belonged to the prototype of those observed in the background of baroque works.

Lope, especially, and Góngora to a lesser extent, were entrusted with reflecting this other aspect, although moments of dejection were not lacking in either. The fiesta character offered by the baroque did not eliminate the deep-seated bitterness and melancholy, pessimism and disillusionment, as Calderón's work demonstrates. But although one had to depart from the distressing experience of a state of crisis, and although the baroque was no less obliged to reflect it, these other radiant and triumphal aspects had to be cultivated so as to attract the weary masses and to promote their adherence to the values and persons that were presented. The baroque lived this contradiction, relating it with the no less contradictory experience of the world (which would provoke the images we have just seen) in the form of an extreme polarization of laughter and crying. Quevedo provides us with many examples of this polarization, especially in his poems. The theme of the alternating and counterposed result of laughter and crying vis-à-vis the world was symbolized in the figures of Democritus and Heraclitus, the two philosophers considered so exemplary by seventeenth-century writers: one would laugh and the other would cry in contemplating life and the things that were present for us in it, which came to be evident proof of its disharmony.[51] Antonio López de Vega wrote an entire jumbled-up volume on the theme;[52] Enríquez Gómez also treated it in some of his poems, and Suárez de Figueroa dedicated to it several folios of his *Varias noticias importantes a la humana comunicación*.

A young scholar, Fonquerne, said of Céspedes that "the universe of his creation, while grandiose in many aspects, is almost always hostile, dominated by fatality and occult forces."[53] This characteristic could be attributed to all baroque writers, save those exceptional cases designed to present the attractive side of the system to be maintained, in order to motivate and secure peoples' adherence. Within that universe we find lodged a dramatic, fragile, variable creature, that uncertain and floating creature, as Pascal would call it: the human being, who, suddenly, like Andrenio of Gracián's work, finds himself or herself placed in a world where one has to make oneself and, simultaneously, to succeed in making the world into a secure base from which one can draw support. Just like Gracián's pilgrim, his relative, the pilgrim of Comenius, in resolving to enter the world — "travel through the world and acquire experience" — asks himself "whether something exists upon which he might be able to base himself with certainty."[54] Passages from Pascal express this state of mind very dramatically.[55] With elegant lines, Juan de Arguijo rendered an account of his internal state of insecurity: "Busca sin fruto, entre la niebla oscura / que cerca a la razón, mi pensamiento / segura senda que sus pasos guíe . . . [Amidst the dark fog surrounding my reason, my thought seeks a sure path to guide its steps . . .].[56]

Connecting the aspect of vacillating doubt suggested by the problem of incertitude with the distrust regarding interpersonal relations, Suárez de Figueroa has us notice that "the human condition is uncertain and almost impossible to investigate because of the disparities of its inclination and the rambling manner of its behavior."[57] With that, the theme perhaps reached its fullest baroque rendering; it parted company with a Cartesian scientific formulation and kept itself within the limits of a morality of doubtful application that was derived from a problematic anthropology.

But before going on to treat the parallel conception of the human being corresponding to this conception of the world, we must first refer to other aspects of this world that, instead of granting it a dual status, made it what scholarship would call a *mixture* rather than a mere *composite*. As Ricardo del Turia tells us, "In the mixture the parts lose their form and make a third, very different material, and in the composite each part preserves itself as it was before, without being altered or changed."[58] Well, although the world is bad and adverse, it can also have manifestations of the good and favorable, not because at one extreme is one thing and at the other its contrary, but because very diverse effects can be abstracted from one and the same quality. There are not pessimistic aspects and then different optimistic aspects. Rather one would have to say that, by means of adequately manipulating the pessimistic aspects, favorable results can be obtained.

From this internal state of "mixedness" would derive the consequence of insecurity and uncertainty that the human being always encounters in his or her relations with it. This in turn comes from the fact that in its innermost contexture the world is not a made being, finished and at rest, but possesses a contradictory, unstable, dynamic *consistency* (I am using this word in Ortega's sense). The world is a struggle of oppositions, the place where the most complex network of oppositions is interwoven. This endows it with movement and assures its preservation, "since everything / among natural things / increases with opposition," according to Calderón (*Saber del mal y del bien*). The human being, as Suárez de Figueroa said regarding the world, "is a force that comes to be maintained by a discordant concordance, just as everything that has movement on the universal globe."[59]

Therefore, making use of the reserves of conservatism that every Platonizing solution includes, the baroque mind affirmed — above and beyond the wars and deaths, deceptions and cruelties, misery and suffering — an ultimate concordance of the most opposite elements, not because it eliminated all those ills but because it reciprocally adapted them, as the human being was adapted to them. Therefore, ultimately, all baroque behavior was a morality of accomodation, and Cartesian provisional morality was a baroque morality to the extent that it participated in such a qualification. "Like the harmony of the universe, our life is composed of contrary things," Montaigne assured,[60] and one must recognize that, from mannerism to the baroque (and all individuals of both times felt convulsively shaken to a greater or lesser degree by the economic and moral crisis that made everything oscillate), the appeal to this formula of harmony of contraries masked, even without attempting to, the threat to the conservative ordering of society. There were thus differences in this affirmation of harmony: for some (Lope), it was an eternal manifestation of the order that must be maintained; for others, it was the mere affirmation of movement and therefore of a renewing dynamism that was produced from the impetus of oppositions. As Gracián wrote:

> "I was contemplating this very laudable harmony of the entire Universe, a harmony composed of a strange contrariness that as the world is so large it doesn't seem it would have the power to maintain itself for a single day: this left me baffled, because who would not be astounded by seeing a harmony so strange, composed of oppositions?" — "Thus it is," responded Critilo, "that this entire Universe is composed of contraries and is harmonized by disharmonies."[61]

In this passage it is the scholar who converts the reference to opposition into that of disharmony, accentuating the confusion as a condition of experience; on the other hand, both of the characters participating in the dialogue coincide in stressing the great number of the internal tensions, the great part of the contrariness that is not eliminated, but upon which the baroque imposed its forms of accommodation.

In the pages that follow we will encounter texts similar to those I have just cited, although I shall omit many that could be drawn from Lope for comparison — as imbued as he is, given his conservative character, with popular Platonism. At times we encounter very curious manifestations of this doctrine of instability, which are applied to the strangest physical problems.[62] The human being is placed in the midst of this contradictory, uncertain, deceptive, and radically insecure world, and therein the drama of his or her story must unfold. "In this theater, so surrounded with contraries, so adorned with oppositions, mortals reciprocally see themselves represent their actions."[63]

In having to ask themselves in a much more dramatic way than at other times about the ambience of their existence, inasmuch as they perceived it to be critically threatened, baroque individuals acquired their knowledge of the world and their suffering, pessimistic experience about what the world was; but they also confirmed, with tragicomic simultaneity, that by learning how to play a skillful game they could also aim for positive results. From the notion of this polyvalent mixture of the world, the baroque human being drew the elements to construct his or her own figure (although I am more inclined to think that at bottom it was the suffering and varied personal experience of self and of others that led to the construction of a world view prior to the moment it was assumed).

It seems easy to recognize an immediate and direct connection between the baroque's conflictive character and the pessimism regarding the world and the human being in society, which was expressed at every turn. This was a general historical situation in the terms we have advanced, terms that have a parallel application to the conception of the human being. To maintain that the pessimism of Mateo Alemán in *Guzmán de Alfarache* came from his being a new Christian [*converso*] is to set up an unnecessary hypothesis, just as it would be to consider in any other case that its origin was to be found, for example, in the malfunctioning liver of the author in question. In history, as in science, one must rely on the interpretation that turns out to be more generally necessary, more broadly valid. Very well: pessimism regarding the world and human beings — a pessimism that can ultimately be overcome or, better, compensated by religion, education, by the adequate and opportune intervention of human beings themselves — was the mental attitude of seventeenth-century human beings, and the Spanish were no exception.

According to seventeenth-century thought, human beings are individuals involved in struggle, with all the ills going along with it, and also with all the possible advantages that follow more or less hidden in the wake of suffering. First, they find themselves in internal combat with their own selves, which gives rise to so many concerns, so much uneasiness and even violence that break out from within and are projected into their relations with the world and others. The human being is an agonistic being, struggling against the self, as was revealed in so many soliloquies from the tragedies of Shakespeare, Racine, and Calderón. The presence of this agonistic element in the internal life of the individual was found in the Prostestant mentality no less than in the Catholic following the doctrine of the Tridentine decree *"de justificatione."*[64] "The life of man is war with himself," Quevedo would say. "Our life goes on being nothing more than a continuous and perpetual war, with no kind of truce or peace," Suárez de Figueroa would also write.[65] This apparently ascetic view extended throughout all of Europe, but it became displaced toward an affirmation of domination over the world (in Gracián and others).

But political opposition, revolts and conspiracies, and, above all, the new fact that war had been constituted as a general and persistent way for peoples to relate to each other also provoked a conception of human beings as subjects in a perennial and constitutive struggle with fellow subjects. It therefore became possible, closely dependent upon the moral situation of the time determining the concrete circumstances of crisis, that during the second quarter of the baroque century a curious event took place — perhaps only a small literary phenomenon, but a very significant one. A line from Plautus that for centuries had been read without attracting too much attention — or, at any rate, prompting responses of a contrary opinion[66] — was turned into an accepted topos, into an aphorism that went from mouth to mouth, for in it the epoch's contemporary sentiment found expression. The sentence referred to the aggressive character that, as a consequence of the epoch's pessimism, was imputed to the human being: *Homo homini lupus.* Luque Fajardo wrote about it: "As the discrete preacher said, explaining the ancient proverb: man against man is a wolf; it would have sufficed to say: Man against man is man, which would be high praise because man has no greater contrary than man himself."[67] Adhering to the circulating aphoristic formulation, Hernando de Villarreal made the sentence his own: "Men themselves are wolves to each other."[68] The reason that such a thought has been identified again and again with the singular pessimism of Hobbes could only be the fault of ill-informed historians. Furthermore, in the very year when *Leviathan* was published (1651), the first part of Gracián's *El criticón* appeared, where he affirmed that among human beings, each one is a wolf to the other.[69] It was thus a mode of thought common to baroque Europe, which latched onto an aphoristic formulation because of its easy accommodation to that thought. With the customary platitudes with which they expressed themselves to their public, a Jesuit wrote in a private letter (13 October 1637): "The politics of Satan reigns in the world."[70] Thus he translated the experience of a cunning general struggle involved in contemporary coexistence (frequently within one kingdom and even more so among the kingdoms themselves).

The denunciation of bad human qualities, which oscillated between pointing out human egoism,[71] wickedness, or corruption, had perhaps never been as diffused as in the seventeenth century. If in some cases one hears an archaic echo of the ascetic and medieval theme *de contemptu mundi* as preparation for religious discipline, in the baroque century one commonly observes with regard to this subject a considerable degree of secularization that made everybody seek to draw, from the exercise of distrust vis-à-vis the world and human beings, the appropriate arts for overcoming them to one's own advantage. Thus it is not in moralists and religious writers where one encounters passages against the aggressive or perverse condition of the human being, but among those who wrote about the ways of establishing and conducting oneself with others and even among those who simply wrote literature (which constituted an indispensable field in baroque society): novelists, poets, authors of miscellanies (whom we would call essayists today), and (to a lesser extent) among dramatic authors.

It is important to cite several more references because the diffusion of the theme is an essential fact for comprehending its decisive role in the formation and significance of baroque culture. I will not cite ascetic writers such as Nieremberg, nor the well-known passages (which I include here without quoting) of M. Alemán, Quevedo, Gracián, or others. Let us recall other texts, such as that of Anastasio de Ribera: "The most common enemy of one man is another."[72] A poet who proves very interesting because of how precisely he corresponded to the mentality of the time, Gabriel de Bocángel, wrote very similar words: "One might consider the judgment of another Philosopher who said he saw no animal more contrary to man than another man."[73] A politician would agree with the poets: Saavedra Fajardo, in asserting that man is injurious to himself and others, established the common conclusion of his contemporaries — "There is no greater enemy of man than man."[74] An economist came to have the most severe tone; in effect, Álvarez Ossorio judged with great sorrow that man solicits the ruin of man, meditating about who could escape an enemy of such force, a declared enemy whose malicious nature makes everybody pursue one other "like very savage wolves and tigers."[75]

These references denounced the human aggression and violence that foregrounds the pessimism with which humanity was viewed. Social and public violence in war, in the epoch's penal practices, in homicides, robberies, and other criminal acts committed daily; violence in private, interpersonal relations: news reporters of the epoch related the case where the marquise de Cañete dealt out punishment to three of her servants (such cases explain the frequently proclaimed hate that servants felt toward their masters) so brutal that the king ordered the marquis and marquise arrested, had them condemned to pay a large fine, and banished them from the court for a period of time. The *Noticias de Madrid (1621-1627)* referred the incident to the year 1622. It was a disgusting spectacle that coincided with many others narrated in the novel writing of the time. Montaigne, after rendering an account of the feelings of ambition, envy, superstition, revenge, and cruelty that find refuge within the human being, judged that "our being is held together with debilitating qualities."[76] Affirmations of this type constituted a foundation for many of the constructions of baroque culture. Their echoes were heard everywhere. Jerónimo Yáñez de Alcalá made his character say (a character who remained faithful to the social reality of his time in so many of his commentaries): "The nature and condition of human beings is already so corrupt . . . "[77] Francisco Santos asked that the human being forgive him because, he tells us, "I feel compelled to compare him to the pig."[78]

These elements are woven into the canvas upon which the baroque writer would paint the figure of the human subject's modes of conduct. In 1593 Guillén de Castro pronounced before the Academy of Nocturnals, in Valencia, a "Discurso contra la confianza," which the Academy itself had commissioned (a circumstance that increases the fact's social import); this came to be prophetic of the attitude that would hover over the following century. In the pages of this writing, the author warned against the calamities that confidence in others had brought to the world and the poison that could reside in self-confidence.[79] An author inebriated with Madrid's baroqueness, Liñán y Verdugo, noted that "in his very nature man is terrible, cautious, astute, a friend of his own advantage, desiring of saving himself at the least cost and with the smallest amount of his own work."[80] It seems as though Liñán was seeing people hidden at Madrid's street corners, waiting to waylay each other, to pounce on whoever was unprepared. Barrionuevo recorded this general commentary and observed to his public: "Everywhere there is malice at best, and everybody is trying to deceive each other."[81]

In effect, this basically solitary and agonistic being, engaged in struggle at every moment because of the influence of a principle of egoism and preservation, was the *waylaying human being* such as the baroque mentality conceived it. "We all live expecting to be waylaid by each other," wrote M. Alemán.[82] This is similar to what Saavedra Fajardo would observe: "They arm themselves with cunning against each other and all live in perpetual distrust and suspicion."[83] Therefore in the magnum opus of Gracián, Critilo would tell Andrenio that his teaching was directed "toward your opening your eyes and living always alert among enemies."[84] A lexicographical study on the baroque — which has lamentably yet to be be done — would definitely show a high degree of frequency in the use of such words as *waylaying*, *caution*, and *distrust*.

In chapter one we already discussed subversive violence that led at times to insurrection, a violence nourished in all of Europe by the crisis situation of the seventeenth century. Now let us consider the phenomenon of violence from a very different aspect: the spread of violent sentiments occurring in all the peoples of Europe but perhaps in Spain exhibiting a particular virulence. The agencies of authority not only tolerated these sentiments but frequently fomented them, perhaps to establish an atmosphere for applying their own repressive measures. But in my opinion it was rather to excite the passions of the masses, which authority addressed and on which it based itself, so as to make their adherence more complete, their obedience and acceptance of policies more blind, and their intervention more energetic when it was necessary to go to them in cases of internal or external war.

The gruesomeness, violence, and cruelty so evident in baroque art were rooted in that pessimistic conception of the human being and of the world and which they, in turn, reinforced. The taste for bloody ruthlessness is apparent in many French, Italian, or Spanish works, and only a lamentable lack of information — or worse still, an unconfessed and censurable desire to remain ill informed — can attribute it to the influence of the character of one country or another, since it was a fact that they all held in common and that was peculiar to the historical situation of the baroque in all of Europe.[85] To the references of the picaresque novels of Castillo Solórzano correspond those from the German picaresque novel of Grimmelshausen. For María de Zayas, cruelty was little less than an obsessive aspect in her confrontation with the other sex: "As for cruelty, there is no doubt that it is located in the heart of man and is born of his harshness."[86] The real violence was probably no greater, no more harsh in the seventeenth century than in prior epochs, but consciousness of violence was more acute, as was acceptance of it, which came to inspire an aesthetics of cruelty. A letter from a Jesuit (27 May 1634) relates the case of a hanging as something to provoke laughter.[87] Few references have the force of the one in which friar Gerónimo de la Concepción described his own feelings upon watching the tuna fishing off the coast of Cádiz, where thousands of tuna were taken to be killed, sliced, and salted. The occasion included the brutal spectacle of the creatures fighting with the fishermen or with workers employed to chop off their heads as they were taken from the water. The friar commented with all sincerity: "The entertainment is so pleasurable, for in view of the strength of the brutes, the variety of the harpoons and nets with which they are taken and killed, or the bloodied state in which they customarily leave the sea, there is no bull fiesta to equal it."[88] It is difficult to find a comparable passage of baroque taste in the face of a spectacle of such bloody cruelty.

There is no doubt that the spectacle of violence, pain, blood, and death — a spectacle that was popularly supported and displayed before the masses — was used by the rulers and their collaborators to terrify people and in this way to succeed more efficiently in subjecting them to their place within the order. The chronicler León Pinelo recounted an example of this baroque pedagogy of violence that needs no commentary. Because of the visit to Madrid of the prince of Wales in 1623, the archbishop, as a conciliatory action toward the favorable result of negotiations and to teach the people how they should deal with the affairs of this world, asked the different religious orders to appear in the procession of Holy Friday "with some decent exterior mortifications." Here is the account made by the chronicler of Madrid:

> the Descalzos of St. Gil and of St. Bernard appeared together with the Order of St. Francis; then, the Our Lady of Mercy Descalzos of St. Barbara, the Augustinian Hermits, the Capuchins and the Trinitarian Descalzos, some with skulls and crosses in their hands; others with rough vestments and hairshirts without hoods, and their heads are covered with ashes and crowns of thorns, and are pouring blood; others with ropes and chains at their necks or around their bodies; crosses on their shoulders, fetters in the shape of a cross tied to their feet, piercing their chests with stones, with muzzles on their mouths and the bones of the dead in them, and everybody praying the psalms. Thus they went down the Calle Mayor and by the Palace and returned to their convents in a trek lasting more than three hours, which amazed the Court and left it full of examples, tenderness, tears and devotion.[89]

I believe this explains what we mean in speaking about the baroque pedagogy of the sentiments of violence as a means of repression and subjection.

The fiestas and diversions — for example, the bulls — gave an opportunity for applying an equivalent system of mentality shaping so as to guide it in a similar sense. Because of this, Barrionuevo did not like the bulls — he revealed himself to be a person of opposition in this also — and confessed that he did not go to this stifling and savage spectacle.[90] In their letters the Jesuits recounted a curious anecdote. They were speaking about the arrival of a mission from the king of Denmark, of the courtesies with which its members were welcomed, of how well feasted they were (undoubtedly the Spanish were seeking in the friendship of the Danish king a well-placed counterbalance in the Thirty Years' War); for this reason they tell us that various diplomats of the group showed an interest in attending a bull fiesta. As one Jesuit informs (4 November 1640), in attending it "one Dane fainted on seeing so much blood run."[91] This incident might help one understand the nonexistence of a Danish baroque.

One would certainly commit an error of materialist overstatement to maintain that this literary and artistic cultivation of cruelty (which on occasion offered genuine sacrifices on the stage set — one example among a thousand, *La estrella de Sevilla*) was developed to pave the way for its use as a means of repression by the ecclesiastical and political authorities. In any case, it is terrifying to read some of the methods recommended in the seventeenth century for the extinction of subterranean politico-religious dissidence constituted by the minority of new Christians within the Catholic monarchy,[92] or the program of measures to annihilate the gypsies.[93] The extent of repressive harshness in France, as well as in Germany, is extremely well known; and everywhere the atrocities of the period of wars which provisionally ended with the Peace of Westphalia led to a familiarization with violence, not only in confronting the exterior enemy but also those within — rebels, dissenters, those who are heterodox in some way. Of course, the daily spectacle of repression and war contributed all over Europe to the same inclination toward cruelty. But what interests us is to observe that the ruthless staging of cruelty represented the accomplishment of the objective toward which the entire pessimistic and affective formulation of the baroque was oriented: the necessity of making the human condition evident, to dominate, contain, and guide it.

To attain effectiveness, the baroque had to operate on psychological motivations [*resortes*], had to stimulate and direct them. An exacerbation of the interest in death became the final step of the great task to give sentiments public currency, preferably those of a morbid type. It cannot be doubted that this interest had already existed and that, since the awakening of the energies of modern individualism, the theme of death preoccupied those societies at the threshold of the end of the Middle Ages, when a profound transformation of this theme occurred.[94] But in the baroque it registered still a further intensification. If the fifteenth century had shown a genuine obsession about death, the seventeenth — observed E. Mâle — exceeded even this and succeeded in offering a more frightening and impressing version of it. Whereas in the Middle Ages death was, in art and thought, a theological idea, and in popular spectacles was presented with an impersonal, generally didactic character, now it was the theme of an experience affecting each one individually and causing a distressing revulsion. In the seventeenth century, said Mâle, "after the great doctrinal struggles and the wars of religion, souls still remained stirred up for a long time."[95] Much more profoundly than Mâle himself could have envisioned in his time (by now almost fifty years ago), historical research on the baroque crisis has revealed these aspects under a new and striking light.[96] Above all, we see that it was planned in greater detail. To contain such disquiet, this guiding activity intervened to dominate the sentiments, and very particularly those that the presence of death could awaken. Jean de Sponde wrote his *Stances de la mort* with this concern in mind.[97]

Nonetheless, we find a different accent even in those cases where the utilization of the theme of death preserved its traditional ascetic character. Thus, when Quevedo wrote that "with myself I carry the earth and death . . . ,"[98] or Salas Barbadillo that "the earth and human flesh are the same thing,"[99] their words do not exactly reflect the Christian dogma of resurrection. It is a notion of death, not as a doctrinal preparation for the transition, but as a force adverse to life and thus as a drama of the living that renders itself evident to everyone, demanding to be dealt with in the play of existence.[100] In the figures on medieval tombs and on those that the Renaissance so ostentatiously erected, the decorative elements were an offering to or a recognition of the virtues of the deceased or an attempt to beseech divine benevolence on the deceased's behalf. Now they were not addressed to the one who had passed away, Mâle observed; in the baroque epoch, when the skeleton was introduced as an iconographic resource — which perhaps stemmed from Bernini's initiative — it addressed the still living public that contemplated the funeral monument.[101] And such a spectacle could tell one many things.[102] Its carefully realized representation of how one ends up after death could contain a severe warning about what lies beyond, or also a reminder about what happens when one has not known how to defend oneself from enemies, or perhaps a mere anatomy lesson, or the barbarous confirmation of what the force of those in power can do to one if one dares to confront them. The representation of the skeleton, then, had multiple functions in the baroque, and if we cannot deny that the principal function corresponded to an ascetic-religious meaning, resonances alluding to the dangers of the social and political world were never lacking. Soon we shall see how an entire series of concepts — time, change, decay, etc. — that were fundamentally intertwined in baroque mentality were connected with this event of the transition of death, which Lope articulated in a line of internal and contradictory tension: "Going and staying and, in staying, departing."

Previously we said that attraction toward the macabre could relate to the hardening of the repressive operations that baroque Europe experienced with monarchical absolutism, with the religious intolerance that inspired it and at whose service it was placed. It would be excessive to affirm a wholly direct and mutual dependence; but both aspects undoubtedly related to each other as facts of a determinate historical situation. In any case, violence and the macabre were united in that brutal recommendation that, from the point of view of the technology of repression, Juan Alfonso de Lancina made regarding the silenced efficacy of the seditionary's cadaver.[103]

In our conception, this image of the waylaying human being — characterized by an attitude of both defense and attack which is maintained in all the moments of existence — is the reflection of a spiritual state that possessed a common origin with this other phenomenon of collective violence that consisted of the continuous war between state and state. In the preceding century, Europe inaugurated a stage of successive wars between states that in the baroque century turned into a general and permanent conflagration. Elsewhere I have tried to explain this occurrence, which is much more recent and peculiar to the modern age than one might ordinarily believe. It derived from the collision between the new and the traditional in the situation of these European peoples. What was new is the zeal for gaining power, growing larger, for wealth and expansion; this zeal has served as an impetus for European sovereigns and for particular realms since the technical, economic, and demographic boom at the beginning of the modern age. It is this desire for wealth and power that inspires this repertory of concrete measures — not always coinciding in content, but much more so in their declared finality — that we call *mercantilism*. The political conception deriving from this draws states to acquire the greatest part possible of the goods offered by nature. And here the traditional aspect presents itself for consideration, for unquestionably not everything corresponds to this dynamism resulting from the experience of expansion and mobility, no matter how much this experience has contributed to awakening a consciousness oriented toward the future. Elsewhere I have studied this extensively, and now, more resolutely than at that time, I feel authorized to call it *progressive*.[104] Despite the fact that this conception of the march of human events is undebatably present, and that the ascending social groups based themselves on it from the early Renaissance on, there remains, deeply etched in the consciousnesses, the face of a nature constituted by an unalterable quantity of goods and foodstuffs. This traditional view is typical of agriculturally based cultures (as were those of all the European peoples until the end of the seventeenth century, when some began to move beyond this level).

The result, then, is obvious: if people are stimulated to strive toward possessing more and, at the same time, believe that the volume of available goods does not alter as a whole, they have no option left but to direct themselves toward others so as to succeed in augmenting their own share at the expense of others. Heckscher has brought out a similar attitude in the mercantilists,[105] and I have applied this schema of a dual consciousness to explain the phenomena occurring in the modern state.[106]

As an example of such an attitude formulated in a general sense, I referred on that occasion to the thesis that Montaigne articulated in one of his essays: "One's profit is another's loss."[107] We are now acquainted with an almost exact sentence from another French writer at the height of the baroque, Méré: "One's good fortune might often be another's ill fortune."[108] We can even add a Spanish reference containing the same idea: "There is no benefit without harm to another," wrote Juan Cortés de Tolosa.[109] Using a saying from the street, Barrionuevo wrote: "Some get rich making others poor."[110] The universal confrontation of everybody against everybody else that is articulated in these sentences constituted the basis of this attitude of struggle and violence that was perceived in the baroque everywhere and among all individuals, influencing their pessimism. Individuals of the seventeenth century, losing stability in their estatist position because of the social crisis, wanted to move upward, to be and have more; and being certain, almost without expressing it, that they would not be able to improve or augment their share except by taking from others, they assumed a stance of struggle to take from others what they could and also to defend their own from the surrounding incursions.

One can easily recognize in this view a primitive and confused schema — we might even call it crude — of the society of competition. The bourgeois doctrine of free competition would arise from this base. It seems unquestionable that already in the individuals of the baroque one can see a distant relation with the bourgeois who would be bound up in this schema. The relation has led K. Heger to speak of "mercantile thought" in Gracián as reflected in the acquired meaning of such concepts as value, estimation, appreciation, profit, and utility, which can be interpreted in terms of supply and demand.[111] W. Krauss has indicated the presence of an "economy based on laws," literally, of an *ökonomische Gesetzlichkeit*.[112] This is interesting to recall, but one must add that to a greater or lesser extent one can say something similar about many other baroque writers; furthermore, in these others, as in Gracián, it was merely a matter of a way of thinking that had not yet begun to feel the effects of the intense process of rationalization that would characterize bourgeois mentality.

Certainly when, in the last years of the seventeenth century, the mercantilist mentality of struggle and competition became oriented toward a formula of economic freedom and, along with Colbertism, postulated a free trade, the baroque century would have ended. It is inexplicable that A. Hauser did not recognize any more than the aspects of authoritarianism and interventionism in mercantilist writers and that he merged them with those aspects specific to the baroque and official classicism.[113] But in the seventeenth century there was not only a final Colbertine stage in the sense mentioned above; in the same phase of the authoritarian, interventionist, and mercantilist baroque (characterizing in this way all areas from the economy to religion, passing through literature and others), one must take into account that the baroque was what it was, among other things, because this view of struggle that influenced it, this competitive and "waylaying" point of view, could not occur without the existence of a certain degree of freedom. Precisely because this freedom existed and extended to the conflictive aspects indicated in a previous chapter, the social powers made use of the culture of the baroque to set up specific expedients of containment.

The world of human beings — because of its basic conflictiveness — appeared to the minds of the seventeenth century as complex, contradictory, and problematic. Whatever one wanted to do with human beings required study and needed to be learned in a form convenient for accomplishing it. Because the raw materials that one manipulated were human beings, it was necessary to study the human being in the folds of its interiority.

Let us keep in mind that from the experience undergone by the European minds during the stage of humanist ideals, such as they were understood from L. Bruni to L. Vives, from Erasmus to Montaigne, there remained a keen interest in the study of what pertained to human existence. Attention toward the human being changed in tone and orientation, but it did not diminish, rather, on the contrary, it became intensified and stimulated by the specific dramatism of the epoch. This inclination did not remain based in a gratuitous intellectual concern but came to be included in the crisis circumstances we have recalled in the preceding pages. When one is conscious that the relations between one individual and another and between each individual and the groups of a diverse nature in which he or she is included have suffered a serious transformation; when, in connection with this, one seeks to act upon human beings to reach in their society certain practical objectives that involve an innovation with respect to the recognized meaning of existence: it then becomes easy to comprehend that knowledge about the human being is of the utmost interest and presents itself under a different form than it assumed in the philosophy (*ancilla theologiae*), as well as in the morality and politics, of the medieval centuries under scholastic culture.

"The true knowledge and the true study of man is man," wrote Charron, articulating a general way of seeing things.[114] This was a principle of anthropocentrism that, all the way from theology to morality, from psychology to politics, informed all thought in the baroque. Its presence in art is very evident. The human being was studied by taking one's point of departure from the human being (this was the procedure that Renaissance thinkers had previously taught: Vives, Gómez Pereira, Huarte de San Juan, etc.).

Examples like the following could be repeated in works of greatly differing quality: the Calderonian character of *Eco y Narciso* finds himself in the middle of the forest — in the middle of the world's confusion and obscurity — "not knowing who I am"; upon directing his investigation toward himself, he does not refer so much to his character as a socially defined figure as to his generic being, his human being: "ignorando / quién soy y qué modo tengan / de vivir los hombres" [not knowing who I am and in what way men must live].[115]

The microcosm that was conceived to be the human being was studied in numerous areas (the topos of the microcosm, which come from antiquity, now served to emphasize the autonomous character that such a being was recognized as having).[116] It was studied to know how it was, what turned out to be equivalent to it, and, under the domination of the modern mentality, how it functioned and conducted itself. "I intend to interrogate nature / about who I am," we read in one of the philosophical songs of Enríquez Gómez.[117] Formulated in one way or another, from one or another of the many angles its many-sided structure exhibited, this was a question that resounded everywhere in the pages of countless authors in the seventeenth century, up to the famous passage in *Discours de la méthode*, where Descartes stamped it with a new direction (although one should not forget how it was rooted in the baroque).

For better or worse, rightly or wrongly, with a more or less innovative, more or less conservative aim, in the baroque epoch this zeal for knowing the internal functioning (the metaphor accords with Huarte's psychology, which had so much influence on baroque mentality) of the human being not only was not eclipsed but was intensified. The social crisis was more acute, consciousness of it more profound, its threatening tensions more problematic. Human beings needed, more than ever before, to be able to act in governing all others and their society; therefore, the need existed to know them.

Thus the pressing interest in the functional and social aspects pertaining to human existence led to a consideration of the experience of life. And the value of life increased because it was not viewed as something unchangeable after its beginning, always equal to itself, already over and done with from the moment the individual who lived it became established in the world and in society. It was not viewed as a *factum* but as a process: a *fieri*, a becoming.

Perhaps one would have to say that all reality possessed this condition of not being done, of not having been finished, which undoubtedly facilitates our understanding of this new baroque taste for lines of loosely related words, unfinished painting, architecture that eludes its precise outlines, emblematic literature that requires the reader to bring the development of a thought to an end on his or her own account. One who contemplates a painting or reads some *Empresas* or follows the lines of a building with one's gaze has to collaborate in finishing the work — or at least one's own experience of that work. In the same way, the human being — who is the singular, individual human being — has to proceed making his or her own self. "One is not born made," said Gracián.[118] And with that the fundamental condition of the plasticity or moldability of the human being remains affirmed: by encountering himself or herself always in a process of realization the individual can act on the self, and others can act formatively upon this individual.

Life has to be made and, therefore, it is important to know how one makes it. Let us recall the lines of Rioja: "As the clay given form by the skillful hand, / from the wheel that is driven to movement, / scarcely firm in its figure."[119] Human beings work as potters on their own selves and on others. This is what represents a work such as Gracián's and its most radical significance: the step from a morality to a system of morals, or let us simply say to a reflection on practical behavior, which could not properly be called a *science des moeurs* according to the expression of nineteenth-century positivists but that we can call an *art of behavior* (giving the word *art* its import as a *technique*). (Nevertheless, up to a point there did exist an approximation in some cases to what would later be called a *science des moeurs*; it is perhaps in the baroque Blaise Pascal where this expression is found for the first time.)[120]

The well-known soliloquy of Segismundo leads to the posing of this general question that disquieted the baroque mind: "What is life?" To inquire, to know, to experiment, to make life the final object of all scrutiny. It is simply that life has to be made: it is not something finished but a making, a becoming. Gracián himself offered the reader a work, his fullest and definitive work, *El criticón*, which he tells us is "the course of your life in discourse." Thus we have made evident the interest in the individual's mode of being and life, life's successive character and its condition as a task to be reflexively realized.[121]

The individuals of the baroque advanced along the path of their living, weighted down with the problematic and, as a consequence, dramatic necessity to pay attention to themselves, others, society, and things. The baroque individual was par excellence the *attentive* individual, to use a very Gracianesque word. Life would result from one's attentiveness: "Crece el camino y crece mi cuidado," went a line from Fernando de Herrera. The idea of *cuidado* [concern] was insistently repeated in Góngora, Lope, Villamediana,[122] and more forcefully in Quevedo[123] and Gracián.[124] As a human being Enríquez Gómez called himself a "passenger of concern," seeing his existence riding on concern.[125] An idea such as this would never, according to Vossler, have the character of "religious meditation," "mystical immersion," or "its own philosophical conviction";[126] but it does reveal the uneasy preoccupation of one having to make oneself at every step and, correlatively, to make one's world, in a constant exercise of choice, which is the servitude and grandeur of human existing.[127]

"There is no perfection where there is no choice," affirmed Gracián.[128] Choice was freedom or, better said, it was the version of freedom typical of the modern individual (because of this the archaizing Donoso Cortés would still protest against it). The Jesuit theologians and Descartes were in agreement with respect to it. Unless we bear in mind what choice meant in baroque thought, however trivialized we sometimes find such an idea to be, it is not possible to understand the work of Lope or of Calderón (in *La Dorotea* or in *La vida es sueño* one finds focused statements on the subject). When social or political freedom was reduced or annulled, this feeling of freedom was intensified; it was not a mere interior state but a movement from within that was directed outside: the individual of the seventeenth century affirmed it as the freedom of choice. Choosing meant not only that there were various things to select from but that the option influenced the effective end (but not always in the desired direction). Therefore things could and even had to remain different after being chosen: whoever chose played a part in making his or her world. That granted a decisive value to the individual's recognition of the character of choice that made the self become a becoming and made society a result of innumerable choices being exercised. As an example of what this attitude of choice represented psychologically and morally in the mind of the epoch, consider the role of the image of *bifurcation* that G. Fessard has emphasized in the Ignatian *Exercises*.[129] This image was the fundamental and constant symbol of the option faced by baroque individuals at each instant of their existence. "So much difference and importance can be contained in the *how*," thought Gracián:[130] the how was ultimately the putting into practice of the choice.

But this choice, as the baroque individual conceived of it, was not an act that remained within the subject; rather, it was its nature to overflow operatively toward the exterior. It was reflected in behavior; it realized itself therein. And if we say that it became real, one must also consider that to a certain extent it took on a physical character. Choice was the freedom to guide one's own behavior, and as behavior assumed a mode of working in the outside world, this signified that choice was the equivalent of choosing one's own behavior or at least freely attempting to direct one's behavior physically, following the line established by one's own will. The presence or absence of freedom or choice did not take place only on the level of interiority. It consisted in being able or not being able to do something in the exterior world, motivated by self-determination. All of this serves to show us how far we are from what the medieval moralists called *freedom* and how those who had not gotten beyond the traditional mentality would continue to conceive of it.

For the baroque — in this sense, for the modern — freedom has two faces: on the negative side it is not depending on the other or (which is the same thing) not serving (Jerónimo de Gracián viewed that as the great sin of his time);[131] on the positive side it means doing with one's person what one's own will decides.[132] When one falls short of this it is said that freedom is lacking. Céspedes y Meneses wrote: "I know no other reason for us to call a horse a beast and a brute, except because it neither knows how nor can govern itself so that its will is freely done, because in everything it has to follow the will of someone else and another must rein and guide it." Perhaps these words are not sufficient to clarify what I want to emphasize with respect to the change undergone by the concept of freedom as the baroque mind conceived it — a concept of freedom that abandoned the soul's interiority to project itself into the world of external action. But let us continue reading this passage from Céspedes:

> What difference does it make whether, to escape being in the ultimate misery, you tap the substance of your soul and its natural powers and in your interior being freely live freedom, if on the other hand the use and domination of your body, its members and feelings, and if freedom's command over the ministers and government of this its realm and small world has been tyrannized and occupied by force?[133]

Thus is eliminated the image of Seneca's wise man, who judged himself free in his internal reflection even when behind the bars of a prison. Now, in a change of view that was genuinely scandalous to the traditional mind, freedom was found rather in the anonymous individuals of the people, in the individuals who, remote from where the decisions of sovereignty took place, guided their steps with greater independence, moved at will in that part of the exterior world that belonged to them individually. This character of Céspedes, captive behind prison bars, contemplates the countryside, "envying the free movements of the poor and miserable day laborer and desiring communication with the most rustic and crude herdsman."

But when this freedom did not stop even at the prospect of entering into conflict with the seignior's will, and above all when it was a question not of this illusory wandering through the relatively empty fields of the day laborer or the herdsman, but of the affirmation of independence in their behavior on the part of numerous citizen groups — and therefore of possible criticism and dis-obedience vis-à-vis the rulers' modes of behavior — in such cases freedom became a serious problem for whoever was in command. The fact that the yearnings for freedom, understood in this new way, might spread among broad popular sectors could have serious consequences in the struggle mentioned earlier between those contending among themselves for social and political powers. The freedom to operate socially became extremely dangerous for the privileged society of the seventeenth century. It could not be ignored but must be diminished. The two agencies [*instancias*] of authority and repression, the monarchy and the Church, had to confront it, and they transformed themselves in their internal structure in order to achieve such an object more efficiently. That is what we call seventeenth-century absolutism, which was an essential component of the baroque. Therefore, for the baroque the basic problem would be the living tension between authority and freedom, not only in terms of politics but also in literature, art, and religion.

Chapter 7
Fundamental Concepts of
the Worldly Structure of Life

The ever greater force of the world of real events became evident in the eyes of individuals at the onset of modern times. Autonomy with respect to the supernatural powers that one assumed to endow the events themselves in their appearing and disappearing, in their manner of taking place, shows that the role of experience acquired a relevant import — experience as the way to link the interior of the individual with the environment he or she occupied. Of course this use of the concept of autonomy turns out to be more than debatable when we learn that baroque writers and the public that followed them often revealed themselves to be imbued with conceptions that were full of confused symbolism, religious otherworldliness, and magical occultism, all of which coincided in making those events depend on forces that exceeded the empirical world and robbed it of its self-sufficiency. It is undeniable that the presence of aspects of reality in which one seeks evidence of a (magical or religious) beyond, an otherworld (invisibly determining what becomes present before our eyes), is frequently accentuated to thwart the vigor with which the empirical data of reality assert themselves. In relation with that, something new and interesting happens: even the relations with the transcendental plane are organized and developed by making recourse to means, knowledge, and expedients that belong to and proceed from the world of experience. The Jesuits disseminated certain forms of religious life in which the role of experience proceeding from the plane of the sensible was utilized decisively. On the other hand, the use of magic — which has also been studied — reveals an obvious preference for means taken from natural life. This all falls in the field of experience that thereby embraces the totality of human life.

This predominance of the world of *experience* was of course inherited from the Renaissance, where it acquired a fundamental value for everyone, from the mystics to the physicists, traversing all the writers on art, politics, and medicine. In any of these fields, it expressed the concrete and personal testimony as a basis for mentally organizing the practical relation of individuals with their surrounding world.[1] Very well, regarding the issue at hand it is perfectly licit to apply what we have said about the Renaissance to baroque mentality. Notwithstanding, one might have to make this exception: since for the baroque individual the realm of transcendence was not diminished but rather expanded, this showed a resolute inclination to treat it with the means made use of in the domains of experience. Even to manipulate "natural secrets" one made recourse to experience, as Calderón demonstrated in *La vida es sueño* or in *El mágico prodigioso*; one seized upon means of empirical application even in dealing with providence (the last work cited above by Calderón and his *A Dios por razón de Estado* are good examples of what we are discussing). Writing at the height of the baroque, Calderón serves very well to verify the frequent use of the term *experience* and the decisive role corresponding to this concept in the human being's projection upon the world.[2]

Attention to the condition of the human being, so extensive in baroque mentality, translated into a preoccupation with the course of experience; with experience one may not succeed in possessing the structure of universal knowledge, although ultimately (as with physical laws) it is a universalizable knowledge; yet on no account does experience fail to be valid for organizing the conduct of life. Baroque art gives us the results of a particularizing observation of the human being; therefore, Ribera or Rembrandt went in search of testimony, which was then transformed by them into a plastic document, from aged persons in whose bodies the course of life had had a visible individualizing effect. Simmel pointed out "the remoteness of Rembrandt's art from the universality of human phenomena and its maximum elaboration of the individual."[3] Few have carried the individualization of experience as far as Velázquez: he strove to capture what an individual — himself, Velázquez the painter — had experienced of an object, thing, or person that had appeared within his field of vision. At one time I said that the work of Velázquez was the work of a painter in the first person.[4] This corresponds perfectly with the change from the notion of experience in the Renaissance, which saw in the phenomenal world a manifestation or reflection of an objective reality, to the baroque, which saw experience as the translation of an interior vision. A passage from T. Browne says: "The world that I regard is my self."

Warnke has drawn attention to the baroque's obsession with the contradictory character of experience.[5] In what way can one understand such a contradictory character in the appeal to experience? On the one hand, the baroque mind saw in it a reservoir of events that cannot be abstracted from their individual status, with each one in a certain way being endowed with absolute certainty. On the other hand, it was conceived as a form in which one can see the coincidence of a great number of events; and by means of the repetition present in them, they are seen as valid for supporting statements of a greater amplitude — which, also in a certain way, gives rise to the fact that such events dematerialize, take on a spectral character (baroque individuals perceived science to be a world of events that had become detached from their singularity, generalized, dematerialized, as a sphere of the spectral).[6] One must keep in mind that the contribution of science, with its newly invented apparatuses, had effects even on the vacillating feeling of security with regard to the things that were seen. Contrary to what our senses tell us, Zabaleta and all of his learned contemporaries knew that the Milky Way was not a whitish cloud, but rather the agglomeration of innumerable stars — a discovery made possible by Galileo's "spyglass," of which Gracián and others also spoke.[7] The lack of confidence in what one sees empirically can be derived from ascetic teachings, but it can also be the result of a rigorous scientific knowledge. Let us recall, for example, that one of the objections the baroque anti-Machiavellians leveled against Machiavelli was that he tried to translate a particular, limited experience into maxims of universal value,[8] which did not impede baroque politicians and moralists from writing, basing themselves on singular examples, all sorts of precepts and postulating their general scope, among which was included the very precept that one must abide by the particularity of circumstances.

Therefore, we find in the background of the epoch an appeal to the individualization of experience that led to a feeling of variation and changes that in turn provoked the affirmation of a supposed capacity to channel them. By virtue of that, attention to the human being and society would have to derive from the prominent role of the idea of *movement*. An entire series of concepts playing a role in different aspects of baroque culture were linked to movement as the fundamental principle of the world and human beings: the notions of change, modification, variety, decay, restoration, transformation, time, circumstance, and occasion were all derivations from it. One must certainly refer the idea of movement, which was recognized to function as a universal principle, the mover of whatever exists, to the crisis at the end of the sixteenth and first half of the seventeenth century. From his mannerist point of view (which offered before the fact so many baroque ways of seeing) Montaigne wrote: "our life is nothing but movement"; and he accentuated the thought elsewhere: "Being consists in movement and action."[9] As for Pascal, in his lucid anguish, though no less baroque because of it, he would say that "our nature is in movement," and shortly before he had said of man that "he needs...movement to live," a thesis that in Pascal acquired a certain obsessive character in the reiteration of the original, founding role that corresponded to movement.[10] "Everything comes to be by way of figure and movement," Pascal wrote another time. Since Burckhardt and, more clearly still, Wölfflin, these categories of movement and change are considered necessary to grasp the significance of the baroque. Society was living a dramatic experience of changes that was linked, on the other hand, to the correlate of a varying, protean, changing reality; the human being's striving to grasp that reality engendered baroque culture. Thus L. Rosales was able to note — and for us this serves as a representative case — "the transitive and dynamic force of Góngora's language"; although the transitiveness was based on the semantic evolution of all language, Góngora took it to its extreme and gave it a greater potency — precisely because of his metaphorical methods — and projected it throughout all the levels of his work.[11] In my opinion that was linked to the condition that the baroque deemed fundamental in reality.

"Without movement things neither increase nor are maintained," Saavedra Fajardo affirmed,[12] and this is a principle that inspired the social, political, biological, and physical ideas of the epoch we are studying: as Céspedes y Meneses wrote, "Just as the heavens are in continuous movement, so it seems that the lower things follow them, circling together with them, for we see that they never remain in their state and being."[13] This principle had such a general scope that mere recognition of the dynamic character reflected in a human work was converted into a criterion of aesthetic judgment. Referring to a sculptor, Jusepe Martínez lauded "the movement and grace of his figures."[14] Bocángel, in praising some statues, wrote these lines, and his words tell us the grounds of his judgment: "They keep movement in repose / and their moving is in repose concealed."[15]

Consider the distance separating this from the aesthetic criteria of the purely Hellenic tradition. Suárez de Figueroa wrote: "Joyful and almost divine is he who, imitating the spheres, enjoys himself in his movement as they do."[16] Rousset has cited a line from a French poet from the beginning of the sixteenth century, Motin, that can well serve as an expression of the general principle accepted by everyone: "Everybody's soul is the only movement."[17] The discovery of the circulation of blood, which was coetaneous with baroque culture, confirmed this general law that ruled everywhere, from stars in the macrocosm to the vital center of the heart in the microcosm. Bances Candamo marveled that, in the same way the sun revolves, the heart also "makes, in repeated revolutions, that continuous movement of blood circulation which was discovered by the new Chemical Philosophy."[18] From science to morality, everything spoke to baroque individuals about this universal law of movement. Everything in the world was "either on its way up or on its way down," as the oft-cited *Empresa LX* of Saavedra Fajardo said. "Everything speeds up as it grows," affirms Bocángel. Therefore, everything moves. Even though movement was the fundamental principle of the baroque's world view, it was not striving to exhibit the work of a perfect organism, of an architectonic body, of a systematic treatise, but — as Wölfflin observed — the impression of a happening, a drama, the motion of becoming, grasping a reality always in transit.[19] The physics of Galileo, the economy of the mercantilists, the accommodating or combative morality, the regimen of permanent warring conflicts, the manipulating politics of the rulers, and the works of architects or painters showed themselves to be dynamic formulations in which equilibrium was always at stake and frequently threatened.

Converting this dynamic conception of reality into a principle of political anthropology, Hobbes would write: "That which is really in us, is onely Motion,"[20] and Gracián came to say the same thing (and this is not the only case) when he affirmed that "moving is the definition of life."[21] Even beauty was no longer discovered in the harmony or symmetry of the immutable, but in changing movement; because of this, Quevedo would say: "Puédese padecer, mas no saberse, / puédese cudiciar, no averiguarse, / alma que en movimientos puede verse" [It can be experienced but not known, it can be desired but not investigated, the soul that becomes visible in movement],[22] since beauty is not in repose but it "is fire in its moving." In the baroque society of Louis XIV, a French writer at court, Chantelou, recounted a significant anecdote: Bernini was called to Paris to design the new architecture of the Louvre; also having to sculpt a likeness of the king, Bernini asked him not to pose stationary but instead to move around and walk normally before him so that he could grasp his true semblance. "A man," commented the great Italian artist, "is never so similar to himself as when he is in movement."[23] Of no less importance was the dynamic conception of the art object (in this case, of painting): Rubens succeeded in creating this dynamism with incomparable efficacy in his painting and, at the same time, he did not neglect to theorize about these aspects in relation to the pictorial version of the human figure.[24] Perhaps Velázquez is the one who accomplished with unrivaled success the supreme effort of painting movement itself; other painters, in trying to capture it, had proceeded by painting an object with the distortion that movement imparted to it in a given instant, which in this way became fixed on the canvas. Velázquez tried to take to the painting movement as such, movement directly in action, not represented in one of its multiple instants whose succession gives a dynamic result. The maximum achievement of these attempts is the version of the spinning wheel in the well-known painting of *Las hilanderas*. This most fully attests to what baroque culture was striving for and what the problem of dominating the dynamic reality of the world and human beings signified for it.

Elsewhere I have related the conception of time and space that was typical of early bourgeois mentality with the idea of velocity, which undoubtedly had to be expressed in baroque writers in conjunction with their estimation of movement. From the outset of the seventeenth century, we see a significant frequency in the use of the term: Céspedes y Meneses spoke about wind velocity;[25] Suárez de Figueroa, of the velocity of time,[26] Saavedra Fajardo, of the velocity attained in navigation,[27] all of them with a frankly admiring tone. In this the reference of Suárez de Figueroa could not be more interesting; he may have been the first to reveal the pleasure it provides: "The velocity with which one proceeds to enjoy the world while traveling by sea cannot but be very delightful."[28]

If it has been said that the "age of Bernini" "could effect a great cinematographic theater,"[29] it is because a cinematic image traversed the entire world view of the individuals of the baroque. It informed the universal conception of a "changing reality," which was the principal observation of all the epoch's manifestations. Bocángel affirmed the "successive modification of the world."[30] This modification [*mudanza*] was another of the fundamental principles making up the components of the universe and, like it, the small universe of the human being. "In nature no thing remains as it is," said Saavedra Fajardo.[31] "There is nothing stable in this world," wrote Francisco Santos.[32] Everything changes: things and human beings, their passions and characters, their works. Rodrigo Caro would have us notice that the earth itself, so firm and stable, "at times suffers modification, trembles, shudders and moves," to the point that it does not have today the same figure that it will have tomorrow, nor did it ever have the same figure in other times, a fact that depends "on this lower sphere's hidden and exact laws."[33] A physician who, because of the work of his profession, knew the suffering caused by the plague and starvation during the seventeenth-century social crisis, who reflected and wrote about the causes and aspects of the economic crisis he was witnessing, and who, as a baroque writer, poured out his moral experience in verse, however bad (I am referring to Cristóbal Pérez de Herrera), began his *Proverbios morales* with these words: "Everything is modifiable in the world . . ."[34]

Here we cannot leave out the description from the author of the most renowned baroque song dedicated to ruins, Rodrigo Caro: "Just as there is nothing new under the sun, there is nothing stable, perpetual, nor permanent, because everything has a continuous mutability," a principle, then, that extends to the sphere of things and with incomparable force to the sphere of human beings.[35] "That is mainly subject to modification and ruin which our modifiable and diverse will has for law."[36] Because it was such a central theme, Gracián also could not fail to make it his own: "There is no state other than continuous mutability in everything."[37] The human being is in transit between the modes of the real — what Gracián called a "pilgrim of being." Human beings are changing and shifting. Therefore, to place the immutable before them says nothing. Access to them comes only from the dramatic proof of the mutable, even though it is in order to teach what remains permanent throughout the changes,[38] a point of view with which Góngora and Quevedo concurred. Once again this conception resulted from the transposition on the level of thought and doctrine of a real and concrete, lived experience. Barrionuevo very critically explained it to his public, keeping close to his personal circumstance: "The affairs of Madrid all pass to God for him to dispense what good he will. They abolish tomorrow what they determine today. There is no firmness in anything; each one seeks to further one's own interest and no one the common interest and good of all: thus has everything gone astray."[39]

Although there remained the concept of a permanent nucleus of identity (a foundation that would not be eliminated until the crisis of Aristotelian logic in our time), it cannot be denied that the baroque possessed a very acute consciousness of the multiplicity and variability of the manifestations of the human: "that the works / are not united in man, / though they are all of man."[40]

Nevertheless, this idea of modification became so acute and so decisive in the organization of the baroque world view, that it came to inspire a transitoriness whereby the principle of identity tottered and along with it the very notion of being; this threatened the immutability of the ontological order that traditional thought had left so firmly in place. Suárez de Figueroa tells us that "there is nothing that truly deserves the attribute of being, if everything, as one can see, is undergoing constant modification."[41] The metaphysical order of being, the basis of the traditional doctrine of Scholasticism, seemed to collapse, rendered unsteady by the dramatic existence of mutabilty. Even individuals themselves, swept along by the instability of their changes, could see themselves singularly stripped of their essential condition, of their *substance*, in the Scholastic-Aristotelian sense of the word: and the individual "is never his or her own likeness."

Even the things we deem to be natural change, observed Tirso de Molina: for example the fruits of the trees, thanks to the ingenious grafting work of the orchard laborer; moreover, art changes more than nature, and we see that "in things made by art substance remains the principal base, but the use, mode and accessory vary daily."[42] The baroque, while ultimately respecting the limits of a substantialist conception of the world, made this world enter into a whirlwind of changes, which some of Rubens's paintings might adequately illustrate. If, under the weight of tradition, the baroque could not go so far as to conceive of a reality that might consist purely in changing (i.e., not in a succession of changes but in pure flowing), it nevertheless came to intuit poetically this pre-Heideggerian being of not being anything else than pure passing. Extending the Heraclitean intuition, Bocángel wrote these lines: "Water is forever eternal / but it never repeats itself."[43]

Modification was, then, a great baroque theme. Poets and moralists stressed it; politicians and economists seized it to explain the declines of the states. Lope exalted modification in verse: "Celestial harmony / rests on modification." Even what seems eternal is subjected to mutability. Even the prime mover moves and changes.[44] The permanence of things is based on change itself: its mutability is the reason for its subsisting. In the novel that he wrote about an earthquake he witnessed, Bocángel himself believed that "while everything becomes modified

/ only modification is steadfast."[45] Lupercio Leonardo de Argensola repeated the same doctrine in a line pronounced with a solemn tone: "Thus modification sustains the world."[46]

As for Cellorigo, the reminder of territorial mobility — of the physical displacements that the epoch's crisis (with its positive and negative aspects) helped to instigate — played a role in his accepting the prevalence of a similar principle. For him, the cause of the great intemperance that was observed in persons at the time was "the variation [*mudanza*] in foods and in the nature of the land."[47] And Pellicer focused on a social phenomenon, observing that a year after having risen up against the invading French the Catalonians proceeded to do the contrary; he commented: "Such is the force of hunger and the modification of things."[48] The link between the grave moments of crisis that took place in the epoch and the theme of modification stands out explicitly in these words.

With regard to human beings, this transitory condition was evident and did not leave one unaffected. Céspedes would say that coursing through the accidents of life shows us "its unceasing modifications."[49] Borne by this idea, baroque writers put into play a word that expressed the notion of modification to its highest degree — a word that would acquire a particular prominence in the Ortegan philosophical lexicon (I at one time adumbrated the influence of the baroque lexicon on Ortega). I am referring to the term *peripeteia*. López Pinciano defined it as "a sudden modification of the thing into a state contrary to what it was before."[50] With good reason, language has bound this word to the changes happening to travelers during the course of their journeys. And thus in the baroque it was also bound to the image of the *homo viator* that we see reflected in texts of Cervantes, Gracián, Salas Barbadillo, Comenius, and Grimmelshausen.[51] Suárez de Figueroa would also say that "our life is all pilgrimage."

Mobility, change, inconstancy: all things are mobile and transitory; everything escapes and changes; everything moves, rises or declines, is transferred, gets whirled around. There is no element of which one can be sure that one instant later it will not have changed places or been transformed. *Inconstancy* is a universal and insuperable factor, "as there is nothing constant in men or in nature," maintained Pérez de Montalbán.[52] There is no remedy but to accept it, take it into account, and try to clarify its possibly favorable aspects. One can lament "the natural condition of human inconstancy," as did Céspedes,[53] and one even takes precautions against its most serious changeableness in what Tirso called "womanly chameleons,"[54] proclaiming the pejorative nature of such an estimation; or one can sing the praises of inconstancy from a vantage point of consolation. Thus Lope confronted the world with the question: "In your modifications, who will be constant?"

Calderón dramatized the theme, accepting the burden of a reality that is imposed upon us: "There is no life secure for an instant . . ."[55] The traditional admonition that the moralists and preachers addressed to their listeners regarding the threatening incertitude of the end was extended or, rather, became an extension of the no less disquieting insecurity of things in daily experience, precisely because the baroque human being, who in so many aspects was acquiring tendencies of bourgeois mentality, was concerned with the theme of security.[56] It was known that "the circumstances of our human frailty are as uncertain in their ends as they are insecure in the stability of their steadfastness," noted Céspedes.[57] Modification and frailty correspond to one another. Objects of mutability, inconstancy, and frailty constituted the favorite subject matter of the baroque writer: the cloud, the water flowing by ("O image, O mirror of life!" Villamediana would versify), the brief rose, the rainbow, fireworks. Such objects were used because in comparing them with other objects that appeared steadfast and in verifying that they both shared the same condition, the dramatic nature of change and insecurity was accentuated.

"Things vary, fluctuating in a perpetual growth and diminution," said the political writer Ramírez de Prado,[58] and he took it upon himself to inform us about the inexorable projection of this principle into the realm of the human. "In the human state nothing is steadfast." Similar texts from Fernández Navarrete and other politicians and writers on economic subjects are known.

The natural movement of things has a *rising* phase and another of *decline*. The baroque offers us an unredeemable antinomy on this point. On the one hand, there was the experience of crisis that it endured: "In this decayed age" (as Calderón put it in *Sueños hay que verdad son*), whoever lived with full consciousness tended toward a pessimism about the state of the world. "Every day, as the world keeps getting closer to its end, everything goes from bad to worse," affirmed María de Zayas.[59] Very significant English texts have made reference to this sentiment: among the poems of John Donne, which appeared at the beginning of the seventeenth century, there is one entitled "An Anatomy of the World; Wherein . . . the Frailty and the Decay of This Whole World Is Represented"; in addition, there are passages from R. Burton, from Goodman,[60] and others. On the other hand, what doubt is there that the baroque, considering itself as the time of the moderns, with advantages over any other past time, affirmed its confidence in the present and future, resolving in favor of the latter the famous "querelle des anciens et des modernes"?[61] How does one make the two estimations compatible? From the outset, the baroque writer was concerned with containing the inexorable period of decline, with achieving the best possible circumstances for this decline, with prolonging its end. There was only one way to overcome it: by succeeding in turning whatever was approaching its end into something else. Decay and renewal were complementary elements of the baroque's thematics. "Renewal gives perpetuity to things decayed in nature," maintained Saavedra Fajardo.[62]

Political writers, whose scrutinizing gaze readily saw the declining situation of crisis that the Spanish monarchy passed through, drew a lesson from the experience that accentuated the changing view of things. Republics grow and soon diminish, as do all natural bodies, "because the variety of human things is so uncertain and modifiable that it customarily levels the highest republics."[63] A severe ascetic did not say this, but a writer on economy who was dealing with the ways to enrich a kingdom and its individuals. And baroque writers departed from a similar or equivalent affirmation; making use of this baroque formulation regarding the necessary transforming dynamism that must impel reality, they also found a pretext to propose economic and political reforms in the government — with such reforms they judged it possible to renew and bestow an efficacy on the bulky and inoperative apparatus that the monarchy had become.

In all of this, there was a profound antinomy that permits us to comprehend the baroque as a confused, insufficient, critical, early phase in the formative process of modern mentality. It comprised modification, but underlying it the baroque mind believed in a world ruled by uniform, general laws,[64] a world that God maintains in its perennial order; in the same way, Galileo sought the eternity of the natural laws: "What cannot be eternal cannot be natural."[65] It has been said that Vico's *New Science* strove to extract from history a set of laws equivalent to the geometric laws governing the physical world in the Cartesian system, with that simplicity, uniformity, and generality whereby in the systems of seventeenth-century thinkers — for example, a Malebranche — the concatenation of causes providentially took place.[66]

In this obsession for modification, one would perhaps have to recognize an early version — crude and based on confused inference — of the conception of the world as a succession of phenomena whose order only some minds can come close to grasping, while everyone else remains blind to it. More than a century later, information regarding the conceptual structure of science as knowledge of a phenomenal world would have become widespread; in a writer who to a certain extent was already acquainted with such a conceptual structure, we find this curious matching of the two words *modification* and *phenomenon* (the latter word in the sense of natural science): man, confronted with nature, "in the flowing vicissitude of his state will only see modifications or phenomena."[67] In a certain way, the idea of modifications had been equivalent to the idea of phenomena — specifically for a mind that did not grasp that the order of phenomena was based on laws, even though it might aspire to penetrate this order, a mind that became entangled in the confusion of the changing movements in the empirical world.

This leads us into the final point in this section: a dynamic and changing world is inevitably a varied world. "O common variety, certain modification," wrote Juan de Arguijo in a sonnet to Fortune, linking the two aspects together: *variety* is a condition of reality inasmuch as reality changes in itself. In such a case, variety is a radical condition of reality: "In this image of things no quality is as universal as diversity and variety," affirmed Montaigne.[68] Such is the extent to which it was highlighted in baroque mentality. In the face of the obsession with ideas of unity and perpetuity of the Middle Ages, the attention to and estimation of variety became dominant in the Renaissance. I have indicated the presence of this new aspect in *La Celestina*, and in another context I have referred to the significance of La Boétie's work.[69] "Varied nature," as a character of Cubillo de Aragón called it (*El señor de Buenas Noches*), is what must serve as the point of departure. The baroque made the new formulation more radical and turned variety into perhaps the foremost of the values comprising the world. Manifestations of an ascetic type would not be lacking. Martínez de Cuéllar makes us aware that "thus is life, always variable, never whole, and ultimately nothing."[70] But there remained the reference to variety as an element in itself — an element that was generally judged to be a fruitful and pleasing value.

Exalting "the variety with which the land is adorned," Lope tells us that variety is the most beautiful aspect of the physical nature our eyes contemplate.[71] Suárez de Figueroa also thought that "nature is beautiful because of its overabundant variation...; the noticeable variety of things delights to the highest degree."[72] Even in the prejournalistic literature of the *Cartas*, Almansa propagated the topos: "The beauty of nature consists in its variety."[73] Bocángel assures us that "because the varied in itself has much that is good, we see it in nature, and, furthermore, they even say that nature is good because it is varied,"[74] in such a way that his words appear to offer us an opinion that the author takes for granted as circulating commonly and anonymously. In the pages of *Guzmán de Alfarache* can be read: "Nature is adorned with variety. That beautifies the fields, with the mountains being here, and there the streams and founts of the waters."[75] Finally, the theme entered the literature that strove for a more numerous public, the journalistic *Avisos*: "Variety is the beauty of nature and all the senses crave it, and the understanding is even more inclined toward it," wrote Barrionuevo.[76]

Let me emphasize the positive aspect of the question that we indicated above. Gracián gave it a much greater scope: "All the universe is a universal variety which in the end comes to be harmony"; and going beyond a strict aesthetic valorization, he added: "Variety was always beautifully agreeable."[77] He was able to formulate a general principle: "Uniformity limits, variety expands."[78] These words point out the opposition between the baroque spirit and that of the eighteenth-century Enlightenment; for the latter, uniformity would be precisely the inspiring principle of its entire disposition. For Gracián, on the other hand, as for Pascal,[79] it was a principle that limited and restricted.

The same topos is found in similar terms in political writers; Saavedra Fajardo has us observe that "in variety [nature] wanted to reveal its beauty and power."[80] That general assumption led him to insist on the variety of peoples, regimes, customs, and characteristics; he even established a link between these aspects, which would end up serving as the basic principle for the multiform specificity of the governments, in conformity with the experience of pluralism characterizing the system of the modern state and with the confirmed necessity that, to know individuals and their societies, one must penetrate the inescapable diversity of their characteristics. Saavedra Fajardo linked these points in the following way. First, according to his version of the moral and characterological pluralism of human beings, "not without great wealth, study and experience can one dissect the diversity of talents [*ingenios*] and customs of one's subjects, so necessary in whoever commands"; second, every operation of politically guiding human groups must be based on the preceding assumption of their diversity: "Nations must be governed according to their natures, customs and styles"; finally, this creates a resolution that adapts the modes of government to the varied condition of each group and in a certain way leads to its assimilation: "The prince seeks to accommodate his actions to the style of the country."[81] Thus the consciousness of variety, as a positive aspect that enriches experience and conditions human behavior, informed the baroque conception of politics and society.

The human being, then, is also within the universal dominion of variety. "From childhood to old age everything is variety. Human beings do not have in themselves the same things, nor are they ever their own likenesses, but rather are always renewed, undergoing alteration as much in body, hair, flesh, bone and blood, as in the soul, changing from one instant to the next customs, habits, opinions and appetites." Once again brushing up against the limits of the traditional metaphysical conception of the human being, Suárez de Figueroa was meditating about the difference between peoples and races that results from the whims of nature and that makes the most learned persons philosophize; for all of this uncontainable course of mutations, he sought explanation in the different combinations of the four humors that form the body.[82] From there derives the scientific basis of human "variety," founded on the view of a differential psychology that baroque minds so enthusiastically assimilated: "Not every talent is brought to bear on one field of knowledge or faculty, and there is no talent suitable for all fields, but just as the faculties and professions have their differences among themselves, neither more nor less are there differences in the talent of human beings, that some have abilities for one profession and others for another." In this way Carballo also drew upon the inheritance of Huarte and found an explanation for the fact of unquantifiable human diversity, the consciousness of which had emerged along with the thrust of individualism advancing in the realm of economic life and of society in general.[83] From another angle, Céspedes y Meneses touched upon the psychological foundation of the question, such as he understood it, relating it to the problem of the role of the passions: "There is nothing that gives greater comfort to the soul in its passions than the diverseness of possibilities, because the soul is cheered and relieved by varying entertainment and communication."[84] These words lead us to what the baroque possessed of culture in society, using this expression in a superficial sense, as the secondary product of the baroque's urban character (which we studied in chapter 4). In contemplating the varied and variable world of the economy accompanying the recent and so fickle invention of "stocks" [*acciones*], José de la Vega made recourse to one of its most popular and common manifestations to exaggerate the force of its variety: one must "flatter the palate with a variety of flavors and a diversity of tastes."[85] In the unhealthy extremes of consumerism that seventeenth-century Spanish society experienced during its pathological state of crisis — from opulent ostentation to starvation — Jerónimo de San José also pointed out the enjoyment people received on account of the variety in the creativity and ornateness of dress and other components of personal attire.[86]

The diffusion of the theme was such that it reached all spheres in a common appraisal of its differentiating results. Tirso, confronted with a multitude of people, commented on their "ordered confusion and tranquil variety."[87] That such a commentary could assume a favorable tenor says much about the new mode of appraisal. In the same vein, when Jerónimo de San José referred to letters, he tells us that "the same narration of new and varied things entertains and delights the variable nature of men."[88]

But the principle of variety, whose dominion, much broader than the world of human beings, extends to all of nature, derives from a law where the following rules: to the unity of cause corresponds a diversity of effects (although the baroque would not debunk the traditional principle that there can be nothing in the effect that is not in the cause, as would be done in contemporary thought, such debunking would have been announced long before). Jáuregui formulated in verse that incipient way of seeing:

> Assí con una causa el barro i cera
> siguen discordes fines y contrarios;
> una se ablanda i otro se endurece,
> si a un tiempo el sol en ambos resplandece.[89]
> [Thus one cause drives clay and wax
> toward discordant and contrary ends;
> one becomes soft and the other hard,
> if simultaneously the sun shines on both.]

Variety presupposes variation, and what moves varies. With this we have seen the first set of concepts that, within the configuration of baroque mentality, derive from the role granted to the idea of movement.

Bound to the idea of movement, however, as the other face of the question, is an idea that as a consequence has no less prominence in the baroque world view: the idea of *time*. Although the mechanical clock was invented earlier, the seventeenth century experienced interesting innovations in the art of clockmaking; the impetus stemmed from an obsession with time and the zeal to measure it, which was a mode of beginning to submit it to human domination. With the clock, time became "living and visible," said Bances Candamo;[90] the clock thereby withdrew time from the terrifying region of the unknown and made it an object of sensible observation, which was a way to begin to know it.

From the sphere of economic relations — with the diffusion of the interest loan, speculations regarding merchants' prices, the incipient consideration of conjunctural movements — to the field of science or art, temporality came to be conceived as an element constitutive of reality. When we said that reality was a process rather than a state, we were referring to its ultimate temporal makeup. "Age decomposes and modifies everything," said Jáuregui,[91] which means that time makes and remakes things, takes them from being what they were in the current of a universal mutability and renews them by turning them into something else. "Time finishes off and estranges everything," wrote Quevedo in a harsh line.[92]

If the ultimate reality of whatever exists is its passing, and since passing away is time, this means that time is the ultimate constitutive element of all reality. "Nothing of what is today will be tomorrow," we read in Martínez de Cuéllar. "Everything you see flies with time. Nothing you are aware of remains."[93] Some lines from Bocángel refer to the theme: "El concertado impulso de los Orbes / es un relox de Sol y al Sol advierte / que también es mortal lo que más dura" [The harmonized momentum of the planets clocks the sun and gives it warning that what most endures is also mortal].[94]

Time is the place where everything is encountered, where everything finds itself deposited. In it, things acquire their form and presence and in it they disappear upon passing away, not remaining longer than time because time is what everybody comes to conceive of as solely continuous, permanent: modifying, passing away, changing, and moving. Góngora apostrophized "Tu eres, Tiempo, el que te quedas / y yo soy el que me voy" [You, time, are what stays behind, and I am the one on the way out]. Speaking of these themes, it is never possible to forget the excellent line of Quevedo, in his famous sonnet — translated in part from du Bellay — to the fickle grandeur of Rome: "All that is fleeting remains and endures." Of a reality that unceasingly flows and passes by, that is what remains, the being of its flowing. The human being is defined as a "continuous flowing," a succession that cannot be arrested and at each instant withstands the dramatic anxiety of becoming a future that thereby will pass away to follow in the form of a past. Jáuregui versified to the Sun as it follows its path (one of the most effective baroque symbolizations of time): "Que es vida todo el tiempo que me llevas / y el que me ofreces un mortal cuidado" [All the time you bring me is life, and the time you offer me is a mortal concern].[95] If the human being is a succession of states, it is not the singular state that counts: its nature can be compared, as we are so often told, to transitory dreams. What matters is the structure of succession as such, the ground of the changes that is succession itself — in other words, time.

''My life goes flying away, time runs on,'' said Lope with emotion. And rather than being able to measure in Galilean fashion the past periods of this flowing, what interested the baroque writer was bringing into view the irreducible schema of this temporal course: its *fleetingness*. The course of time is the successive occurrence of the changes, the substitution of things that pass out of existence with others that will later suffer the same fate.

This gave rise to the baroque preoccupation with the theme of ruins. In them, the baroque was striving to encounter evidence of time, which corresponded to the incipient historical consciousness that was being opened up. In this sense, the baroque writer, such as Rodrigo Caro, cultivated archeology. But ruins were also a very adequate material for studying the structure of human work and, therefore, the condition of the life of the human beings who had created it without being able to escape their own fleetingness. They were an evident witness to the struggle between perennial, though changing, nature and the mortal human being who was endowed with the capacity for making things change — for example, for making stone into a palace. Simmel's well-known reflection on the social significance of ruins is perfectly applicable to the baroque.[96] In the baroque, Poussin and Claudio de Lorena, Velázquez and Mazo, tried to capture their human significance. The theme's utilization in so many paintings, in so many novelistic accounts, verifies its diffusion. It is confirmed by recalling the many poems either dedicated to or alluding to the ruins of Troy, Carthage, Rome, Numantia, Sagunto, and Italica: Arquijo, Quevedo, Rioja, Caro, Quirós, and others wrote verses about them. Time, then, is the pure dynamic process of transformations. Since "the passing of time moves mountains," according to a line from Lope, how could the things existing in and through it not also move, in a continuous mutation? "No period has been so obsessed with the depth and width, the horror and sublimity of the concept of time as the baroque," wrote Panofsky.[97] The saturnine images used in its seventeenth-century symbolization correspond to that consciousness of the uninterrupted advance of a universal transformation that annihilates things but also is the source of truth and fecundity. As some lines from the canon Tárrega say: "As time creates it, / time unmakes it all."[98]

"The conditions of time are modifying." Sentences such as this one from Setanti or reference to "the modifications of time" in Tirso, or to the "violence of time" in R. Caro, make manifest the baroque intertwining of ideas around the existence of time and change. "The diversity of times and circumstances varies the effects of equal things."[99] Here we see another idea emerging that is closely connected to those already advanced — an idea to which must be referred the transformations presented to us by reality: *circumstantiality*. If the mode of being of things becomes present in certain circumstances, this means that the changes in the modes of being that we encounter in the passage of time depend on these circumstances. Therefore Gracián would say that "circumstance is as much required in things as substance."[100] Although he, as well as all the other writers of his time, did not renounce the Scholastic-Aristotelian legacy of the notion of substance, he placed the accent of being — which things offer to us human beings in the experience of the earthly world — on its dependence on circumstance (it is of interest to emphasize that Gracián used this concept in the singular; the baroque and Ortegan lexicon also coincide here). If circumstantiality is the mode of things appearing to us in time, the necessarily temporal mode of being in which we encounter things, this means that temporality affects the being of things. With regard to things, their mode of being is their mode of appearing to us, which implies their temporality: the mode varies according to the different situations that take place in time. Things, human beings, are in a circumstance. Their circumstantial presentation affects their mode of being; they are, consequently, time.

It has been said that the works of the baroque are dynamic compositions, manifestations of an art of movement that was cinematographic, engaged in capturing the instant in its instability, in its transitoriness: a four-dimensional art, which in this way introduced the dimension of time.[101] All of the preceding explains that the baroque was a historicist culture, the first of its kind. If the baroque writer could think along with Rodrigo Caro that history was a defense against the "violence of time,"[102] she or he would soon note that this was a false appearance since history was on the way to manifesting and obligating one to take it into consideration as an inescapable datum of existence.

In the baroque, preoccupation with history reached an intensity never before known. There occurred a process of the historification, of the "circumstantialization" of very diverse areas of knowledge that until then had been maintained under a rubric of permanent fields of knowledge: theologians and philosophers recognized a historical character in natural law itself. Politics, with greater validity, moved beyond the boundaries of a perennial moral philosophy to become converted into a historical knowledge. This leads to a very revealing anecdote: Saavedra Fajardo, traveling the roadways of Europe during the Thirty Years' War, related that he composed his *Empresas* "writing in the inns about what I had rambled upon on the road."[103]

This condition of circumstantiality offered by the world is ultimately bound up with another series of ideas that are no less necessary to consider for the study of baroque mentality: *fortune, occasion, gaming [juego]*. "Fortune is various," such is the fundamental sense of the idea itself in the aspect that here concerns us. These words of Francisco Santos contain an estimation of a positive note;[104] others would make an unfavorable judgment of it: Jerónimo de Cáncer spoke about "the varied, black and ugly fortune."[105] But all of them, borne by the obscure consciousness of a dominating insecurity, articulated the characteristic that the people of the baroque emphasized in the myth of classical origin: variability. Céspedes more broadly developed the same topos: "variable fortune, the enemy of all stability and calm."[106] Machiavelli very vigorously renewed the theme of Fortuna, transforming in part the ancient and medieval heritage and adapting it to the necessities of the Renaissance mind.[107] In contrast to the characteristics he gave it, we note that in the seventeenth century the predominant aspect had to do with the disruption of the most steadfast things, the introduction everywhere of unexpected variation, accidental change, contingency. In the second of his *Declamaciones castellanas*, which carries "Contra la Fortuna" as a title, Bocángel called fortune "this continuous disquieter of the world."[108] Accentuating this force that ran contrary to the reasonable succession of things, Calderón (in *El mayor monstruo del mundo*) would denounce "the contingent deliriums / of fate and fortune."

In the seventeenth century, fortune was a rhetorical image of the idea of the world's mutability: it was conceived as the mover of the changes and the cause of the movement that disturbed the sphere of humans.[109] It took its point of departure from a sentiment not of pure chance but of a strange, changeable, and unattainable force in the face of the course of events or, at least, in relation to the particular sphere of human events. In one of his sonnets, Trillo y Figueroa called it "impious providence."[110] But to some extent it was recognized that one might insert oneself effectively in the apparent course of fortune, that is, with a margin of possibility of inclining the result toward one's intended goal. Villamediana once spoke about "the laws of fortune";[111] although with this expression he was probably referring to the inexorability of the dispositions of fortune and not to the regularity of the course established by such dispositions, there nevertheless remains a final resonance of a given order. Céspedes confusedly observed that "it is noteworthy that although the contingent occurrences of nature are so unequal, they sometimes join together so that they seem more effects of coordinated causes rather than of causes that are accidental and without order."[112] He conjectured an unattainable order based on laws. Calderón also seemed to appeal to this when in *De un castigo tres venganzas* he had one of his characters say: "O, how many things, fortune, / are linked and bound together, / all of them possible . . ." Although we may never escape from the sphere of possibility, one discovers a concatenation that allows for inserting human activity into the succession of events at fortune's disposal.

When, many centuries ago, it began to be noticed that the world was a stage of changes, the idea of fortune was seized upon to explain those changes whose succession did not seem to correspond to a rational order. There were many nuances in this idea of fortune: for the ancients, it was a decision of the gods, foreign to human beings — fate; for the Middle Ages, it was an event that providence caused to fall out of the regulated order so as to make the designs of God more inscrutable and frightful; for writers of the fifteenth century, it seemed to signify the manner in which the disorder constitutive of a world in crisis becomes manifest through its own development; at the height of the Renaissance, there was the appeal to the natural forces that fall beyond our voluntary activity, beyond our control; and in the seventeenth century, one can observe that this latter conception — which we can call Machiavellian — turned into the idea of a forward movement of the things of this world, which certainly does not fit into a rational schema but which the informed human being can confront with a strategy, thereby coming to obtain favorable, statistically verifiable results. The opposition of reason and fortune was a theme of Calderón (one finds an example of this type of formulation in the second part of *La hija del aire*).[113] In the sense that reason already corresponds to the regular and predictable order of the natural world, fortune comes to be the contrary. Elsewhere Calderón would consider it in this way: "Because one does not see effects / where fortune and nature / are not opposed" (*Saber del mal y del bien*).

Here Calderón moved in the ambit of a traditional concept of nature, one that was Aristotelian and teleological. But under the influence of the transformation in the concept of nature underway since the Renaissance, the idea of fortune was instead going to envelop the entire area of natural relations that were not a pure connection of means to end, but that presented themselves as relations of a mechanical type of dependency whose raison d'être was not attained, could not be discovered within the divine order of ends. This baroque version came to be the idea, symbolized in one image or another, of a current of changes that could not be arrested; it was innate in nature, but one had no hope of grasping its law because it seems not to exist in the face of its apparent, phenomenal manifestations. What did prove possible was exercising an *adequate* mode of behavior (the term is from J. A. de Lancina, at the end of the epoch we are studying).

This mode in which the real presents itself to us circumstantially, and in such a way that we cannot confront it except by accommodating ourselves to it, tells us that things become present for us on an *occasion*. The occasion is the instrument of fortune, Quevedo would maintain, the circumstance understood fortuitously.[114] It is the mode of whatever appears before us and has not been limited to a simple physical event — in the face of which we have to take up a mode of behavior without counting on universal norms of reason. The occasion (there are similar concepts: the moment [*punto*], the time, the opportunity, but none is clearer and more rigorous) constitutes, therefore, an aspect under which the temporal and changing being of things becomes evident to us. "All things have their time," Juan de Zabaleta tells us, and that time is the occasion; therefore, "the things that lose their moment generally lose their being."[115] Céspedes said that "knowing the state of the times is for those who are prudent and prepared," since "the difficulties and contingencies of the times frequently give laws to nature."[116] Again we find the word *law* in the sense we have seen previously. In *El criticón*'s broad educational repertory with respect to baroque culture, the role attributed to occasion is of central import. To accommodate oneself to the occasion is also the basic principle for a writer such as N. Feret;[117] as for Céspedes, he said that "accommodating oneself to the times is a very great prudence and discretion.[118] "To rely on the occasion," the baroque precept par excellence, meant to count on the way reality presents itself to us as being of a fleeting mode and without any apparent rational structure. This "counting on" signified — abstracting it from the sedimentation of lived experience — operating by knowing how to conduct oneself in a way adequate to the instant wherein the thing enters into our field of action and to attain our intended result. Saavedra Fajardo formulated the idea with clarity: if all things have their rise and fall, their changes, "whoever knows their time will easily overcome them."[119] This explains why for the Tacitists (who offered the most pronounced manifestation of such behavioral techniques as belonged to baroque writers) the concept of occasion had a decisive relevance, as it did in the already cited Gracián and Saavedra, but no less in many others, from Alonso de Barrientos to Juan Alfonso de Lancina. This dependence on the occasion in the way things become present to us gives rise to the fact that our relation with things always takes place in a *conjuncture* and must be resolved in it. This word was also very frequently used in the seventeenth century; in Gracián or Céspedes it would not be difficult to find fifty examples of its use.

The preceding discussion helps us to comprehend the great development in baroque literature of judgmental considerations regarding those who were correct or mistaken in their strategic interplay with the world, with society. They were the victors or the defeated of fortune: in the seventeenth century, much was written about their examples in biographies cultivated by Mártir Rizo, in exemplarizing comedies composed by Lope, A. Coello, Pérez de Montalbán, in the moralizing stories by C. Lozano. They were characters from the ancient world, such as Priam, Dido, Seneca; of more recent centuries, such as Álvaro de Luna, the duke of Viseo, or queen Juana of Naples; or from the very present when the baroque public had them in view, such as Rodrigo Calderón, the count of Essex, Cardinal Wolsey, and Lord Protector Thomas Cromwell.[120] Enthusiasm was especially excited by the examples of those who had known how to dominate the occasion or had failed in their attempts. The idea of fortune, then, did not signify that an inexorable *factum* — favorable or adverse — had descended upon them; nor that pure chance had to be passively tolerated by the human being. In both cases, there would be no need to consider such assumptions, to counsel, give advice, warnings, or to study behaviors, nor would it be possible to attribute merit or unworthiness to the person. In the face of the challenge of fortune, in the face of the difficulty of the occasion, there must always remain a margin of possible personal intervention. To make ready for such intervention, baroque culture assembled the means at its disposal.

With things and human beings, which appear in our life endowed with the indeterminable and scarcely apprehensible reality of the occasion, the mode of operating can be nothing other than gaming. All the very typical products of baroque culture relate to gaming: the casuistic morality, Machiavellian politics, the economy of profits in large-scale commerce, the incipient stock speculations, the artist's trompe-l'oeil technique, the war between princes, and so on. All of Europe played in the seventeenth century, and at times the excessive zeal for playing caused genuine catastrophes, as in tulips speculations in Holland — a case recalled by Sombart when he studied, with great insight, the role of game playing in the early formation of mercantile capitalism.[121] In seventeenth-century Spain there was an unhealthy increase in all sorts of games of chance, but especially in card games. Cards many times represented the ideal image of the type of behavior we want to define here, inasmuch as they were typical of the baroque human confronting a world whose conditions we have described. Everything was a dramatic game, and everybody in Spain played passionately. Since this gaming manifested itself as characteristically baroque, that serves as verification, whatever may be the fact's statistical inadequacy, regarding the diffusion of the baroque in the Spanish society of the seventeenth century.

Let us pass to another issue. A changeable and modifiable world is a pheno-menal world, a world in which things are *appearances*; at least that is what must be taken into account by whoever comes up against them and, taking them into account, has to plan and continue onward with his or her existence. This does not mean that there is not something else behind things. There existed a difference in nuance — although this does not make it less important to understand — between two different and related mentalities that were close in time: the mannerist Renaissance and the baroque, which was saturated with classical knowledge. From the point of view of the first, Francisco de Holanda would maintain that "the bold painter not only has to recognize and paint the way his works are in terms of the external surface that everybody sees, but he even has to know perfectly how all things are in the concealed within that is not shown."[122] From the point of view of the second, what was of greatest concern had to do with what the eye saw, and its active role was recognized. In looking, the eye coats with a dye, everybody functions as "dyers" in observing things, Gracián would say; in contemplating the world, everybody "gives it the tint that is good for them in terms of the deal, the exploit, the undertaking and the event."

Over and above an intellectualist objectivism, typical of medieval Socratism, we thus find a tinted world conditioned by the interests of each person.[123] It was difficult to maintain the antinomy between the objectivity of the real and the gaze that contemplated it. The pilgrim introduced by Comenius in one of his works has some spectacles placed on him: "As I later had occasion to verify many times, they had a peculiar property: they made distant objects near, made distant those that were close, enlarged what was small, reduced what was large, beautified ugly things and made ugly the beautiful, made black what was white and white what was black."[124] Of course this pilgrim ultimately believes that behind all this is the truth and assumes that one can reach a judgment on its terms. Even those most attentive to appearance did not fail to think about what was within, as the Gracianesque characters recognized. In a culture based firmly on the Aristotelian tradition, it would be absurd to deny the vigorous existence of a substantialist conception of things. The restoration of Aristotelianism has been pointed out as something to be taken into consideration when speaking about the seventeenth century.[125] The Lope of the *Arte Nuevo* did not fail to have read Robortello.[126] But what once again draws our attention in the seventeenth century is that, in many cases without taking the trouble to harmonize both conceptions, the sublimation of a crisis experience in a changing world came to underscore the fact that in our operative dealings with things we have to count on their apparent, phenomenal character, just as things are presented to us, swept along by a shifting current of reality. Moreno Villa, with great perspicacity, said that Velázquez painted appearances.[127] In their empirical and personal vision of the world, this was what baroque individuals aspired to grasp. "All the world is sketches," says a sentence from Mira de Amescua,[128] which in the seventeenth century had a topical character, and Barrionuevo, among others, repeated it.[129]

I have written before about about the presence and correlatively the profound alteration of Plato's myth of the cave in Gracián. What is interesting about it relates to the modification the theme undergoes. In Plato, the man closed up in the cave contemplates only phenomenal shadows that he takes for things in the empirical world; when he exits from the cave, he is able to enter the world of full and ultimate reality, that is, the world of ideas. In Gracián, the man exits from a cave of absolute solitude and bursts forth into a world of phenomena presenting themselves to his experience, of appearances whose mode of unfolding he must apprehend to make his life in accordance with that apparent reality.[130] In another place, the same Gracián tells us that "what we first come across are not the essences of things but appearances."[131] The opposition of *appearance-substance* or *manner-being* contains a metaphysical and moral aspect that was frequent in Gracián and in all baroque writers, who took it from tradition — the aspect expressed in the multisecular metaphor of the husk and the core [*corteza y meollo*]. But it also contains a formulation that we could designate epistemological that Gracián and others of the baroque were also incipiently aware of: appearance is the way things reveal themselves to us in experience, what we have access to and know, and thus what we must count on and make use of. To know is to decipher the play of appearances, "redeem the appearances," according to the intention of the modern scientific spirit. Appearance and manner are not falsehoods but something that in some way belongs to things. Appearance and manner are the face of a world that for us, in any case, represents a phenomenal world that we relate to by knowing it empirically and utilizing it. Galileo and Descartes were aware of this, though more as rationalists and scientists than simply because they were of the baroque; but baroque writers confusedly glimpsed this concealed path. Let us note that in the eighteenth century a great scholar of the Enlightenment, Maupertuis, who was a physicist and moralist and director of Berlin's Academy of Sciences, wrote: "We live in a world in which nothing of what we perceive resembles what we do perceive."[132] This sentence seems directly out of the baroque; nevertheless, it expresses the great paradox between science and experience, the affirmation of which gave rise to modern science. In the midst of crisis, the baroque individual felt lost in the face of things and succeeded only in speaking about confusion and disillusion, according to whether this individual became more inclined toward a logical consideration of, or an ascetic disrespect for, this tremendous and, notwithstanding, easily surmountable antinomy between reality and appearance.

According to the baroque writer and to the founder of modern physics it is possible to take a final step that will free up for us the definitive and essential truth of things; but it is a step that will draw us out of the world of experience, although inevitably by a different route. In this world, we find ourselves submerged in an interdependent network of appearances: we must refer to it and we must sketch the conduct of our life in it. "Things commonly do not pass for what they are but for what they appear."[133] Because of this, in an early formulation it was not important to the political or moralistic writer of the baroque to divest reality of the veil that covered it, but to become accommodated (or for us to accommodate ourselves) to that immediate reality. This is the way one of Gaspar de Aguilar's characters formulated the question in *La fuerza del interés*, a comedy with a theme very much in harmony with the epoch's frame of mind: "Don't you see that men judge / what is by what appears to be?"[134]

The topos of disillusion [*desengaño*] would only come to be dealt with at a second moment:[135] not to make the disillusioned individual abandon the world, but rather to teach him or her how to adapt to it. After disillusionment, wrote Martínez de Cuéllar, the human being confronted with things "looks at them as they must be, not as they are"; before, on the contrary, "you looked at the world deluded and thus knew things as they are, not how they must be."[136] The being of things — the previous words tell us, despite being highly charged with asceticism — is its first appearance, even though its secondary and ultimate being — a *must be* or *come to be* — remains behind what we see at first sight. This appearance that we have before us is something that belongs to the thing as much as substance itself, at least in relation to ourselves and to our empirical existing.

The distinction between *appearance* and *essence*, which is normal in Western thought, became accentuated in baroque mentality and constituted the basis for organizing this "tactic of accommodation" reflected in morality and politics. These latter areas are impossible to understand without situating them against the background of the phenomenal conception of the world that we have been advancing. If Velázquez painted phenomena (appearances), Botero and Gracián, Saavedra and Boccalini constructed a politics for a phenomenal world.

The individuals of the baroque, then, considered themselves placed in a world that was, in the words of Suárez de Figueroa, "all perspective." [137] Perspective, as the way for reality to become present to the eyes of the artist, was the notion informing the entire work of painters in the seventeenth century. Perspective is the way whereby the world came into view and and was captured by baroque painting. What we are saying about painting is valid for every type of consideration: for art and for thought. Paravicino, in indicating the central theme of one of his funeral orations, would say: "The entire field of eloquence is foreshortened to this perspective," [138] a text in which the introduction of the concept of foreshortening reinforces the function of the concept of perspective. Lope tells us about "the distant views that perspective reveals to us." [139]

From another angle, this same concept was an aspect of the relativism or circumstantialism of the epoch that was so observable in Saavedra and others. [140] Gracián said: "As each one conceives or perceives, thus the desired color becomes present to one, according to affect and not effect. Things are nothing more than how they are taken." [141] This is how, from a certain perspective, human things are seen and known by the human being. Comenius said that human beings were provided with an instrument called a *perspicillum*, something like a spyglass, that directed one's view backward because it was curved; by using it to see the things done behind their back, they could foresee what would occur up ahead, in the future. But every perspicillum gave a different image, and thus everything was seen according to the perspective of each person: this gave rise to disputes and quarrels, for no one believed more than what could be observed from one's given perspective. [142] The ancient topos so often repeated authoritatively in a Ciceronian sentence now obtained a more rigorous meaning and a much greater importance: the multiplicity of opinions, which derives from the multiplicity of viewpoints, results from the open-faced diversity constituting perspective.

Finally, it is only within the boundaries of perspective that the world of things and human beings becomes visible for us. The baroque confronted a world in terms of perspective. Painting treatises studied the problem technically and debated about linear perspective and what they called aerial perspective. But this manner of seeing was projected onto whatever fell in the human world, even though it was considered something as transcendent vis-à-vis the world as the interventions of divine providence. Don Álvaro de Mendoza, a Franciscan bishop from Jaca, would say in a sermon:

We see that lines are applied to a board by means of the art of perspective,
so that if you look from one direction it seems a flowering garden, from
another, a stormy sea; from one direction, an irate face, from another a
face of love; from one direction a St. Francis, from another a Magdalene.

Then if human industry succeeds in uniting a multitude of such varied and
different views, without either one being dependent on the other, why can
we not concede this to the divine essence in its real and true substance?[143]

The diversity of data that nature presents to human observation and reflection,
the diversity of behaviors that the human being can project and carry out in view
of those data, the diversity of ideas provoked in the human mind, and even the
inexplicable, inaccessible diversity of effects that providence produces directly
in earthly life — these diversities can only make sense when contemplated in the
organization of a perspective.[144]

The preceding reveals the threat of a relativism that began to hover about
baroque consciousness and that since then would continue to increase in the
modern mind. It is therefore comprehensible that Quevedo, like many others,
would force himself to hold to the severe ascesis of appealing to the reason that
judges behind one's eyes: "Farness and proximity deceive sight," perspective
confuses us regarding things. But no less certain was Quevedo's great admiration
for Velázquez, the artist of perspective par excellence; as Quevedo observed,
he did not place in his painting anything but "distant splotches"; and he added
that "in him they are truth."[145] In other words, perspective is truth in certain
conditions or (which is the same thing) in a real given situation — that is, in a
circumstance. Beyond this, that truth disappears, it is a mask. But while the
perspective is maintained, as in the stage representation that it provides, the
manner whereby the real becomes present for us in this circumstance is what
counts. Since our game is accomplished in this life, we must rely on it. Whatever
may be our reserved places in the otherworld, we have to accommodate ourselves
to the game with the appearances surrounding us, that is, to the mode of reality
we must count on. K. Heger has pointed out "the distance between a functional
perspectivism and the relativist renunciation of the unity of thought," limiting
the first to Gracianesque and baroque perspectivism, which would be more of a
method or means of access to reality (as it appears to us) than a conception of
the world.[146]

The pragmatic character of the baroque, in which a system of accommodation
precepts was compartmentalized, gave rise to a mode of behavior that was
somewhere in between agonistic and ludic. This mode of behavior cultivated
ostentation, dissimulation, and other forms that, from the viewpoint of traditional
morality, would be qualified as insincere, even hypocritical. This was dependent
on the baroque's social conditions and on the ends that its cultural instrumentation
pursued in the state of society producing it. Nevertheless, Rousset seemed to
suggest that this has a nationalist link: he has related these aspects with the
character of one people or another. He tells us that the Spanish Gracián and the
Italian T. Accetto opted for the deceptive appearance, with its two faces being
ostentation and dissimulation, whereas the French Feret ultimately preferred to

rely on the truth that was behind or within. But if we consider Quevedo, Rousset's comparison collapses (with Gracián himself it is inappropriate). In the baroque, the theme of the world within did not exclude the other aspects of interest in its façade, and it became trivialized. We can encounter it in plays that intended nothing more than pure diversion: in an intermezzo of Quiñones de Benavente, one character asks another: "And may you teach me the world / all from the inside." Let us recall, on the other hand, the presence of the idea of the *"faussetés déguisées"* that La Rochefoucauld mentioned in his Maxim 282; because of their similarity with truth, he recommended their acceptance and deemed it prudent to allow oneself to be deceived by them.[147] Here we are touching on the fundamental aspects of the practical game of the baroque moral system. Pascal departs from a similar experience that makes one consider the veiled character of whatever one confronts: "Human life is no more than a perpetual illusion . . . Man is thus nothing but a masking, lying and hypocrisy, both within himself and in regard to others."[148] To face this type of environment, there only remains the play of tactics or the wager, which is another form of gaming.

One must recognize that the baroque writer did not fail to emphasize, at times with insufferable and tiresome insistence, the world's phenomenal and, therefore, transitory, shifting character, which was devalued as illusory. The ascetics (whose literature abounded in the seventeenth century and whose influence on the epoch's great writers is unquestionable),[149] using the fiction of making the understanding into a character who judges the world, would have it condemn the world as a deceiving reality that to the truly wise would turn out to be a radical falsehood. The baroque individual, however, who was not always nor by any means an ascetic, recognized the phenomenal condition of reality and played with it.[150] As Suárez de Figueroa said, it was possible for baroque individuals to think that "they endure and will endure until the end of the world, indistinct and confused, veiled and unknown, good and bad, as actors in the tragedy of this life; but once it's over the masks are removed."[151] But from a sentence of this type, one should more generally and effectively draw a final consequence relating to accommodation rather than to a rigorous ascesis. The topos of the world's theatricality is even formulated in such a way that it accentuates and foregrounds the basic contradiction of reality. Céspedes assures us that "all this life and its actions and accidents represent to the living a farce or a comedy in which the characters that yesterday played kings today left slaves, and in a short space of time those we saw in the greatest ruin and disgrace, we soon viewed happy and content."[152]

Baroque individuals based themselves on experience and affirmed its illusory quality.[153] Montaigne stated that "the account one draws from experience is always faulty and imperfect," revealing the distance already separating the Renaissance from the baroque.[154] In Shakespeare and in Calderón, this was obsessive. The theme of the opposition and confusion of truth and lie, shadow and reality, was repeated in Calderón's works and constituted the main notion of some of them, as in the one carrying the significant title of *En esta vida todo es verdad y todo es mentira*, in which the protagonist asks: "How, I again come to ponder, might shadow and reality be reconciled?" This contradiction emphasizes the uneasy instability of the epoch, which was the source of the state of mind it translated. But this did not hamper the attempt — with no small commitment — to show people how to move and how to take part in such a world. The baroque individual of course used the technical means and the scientific discoveries (whose growth was in great part owed to the seventeenth century), but not so much to strengthen the evident reality in the attempt to make manifest that there was no other as to turn them into resources for confronting the world so that effects could be produced upon that world — effects that succeeded in accentuating its condition as illusory. If the individuals of baroque culture believed themselves aware of "how the eyes are deceived" (the title of a comedy by J. B. de Villegas that was put on in 1622), and if some — ascetically — were concerned about unveiling this truth, all were inclined to make use of resources that reinforced deception or entrapped by means of it, whether to guide others from within it or to make its presence, in a given case, stand as an advance warning regarding the constant threat of deception in the course of earthly life. But the widespread practices, especially in art, of "deceiving the eye" had no pretense of making us believe that what we saw prepared by an artist's skillful manipulation was the true reality of things, but of moving us to accept that the world we took to be real was no less apparent. By means of these procedures, the politician as much as the moralist and the artist judged it easier to obtain acceptance for or submission to the Church, the monarchy, the social order (with its distinctions of regimented groups), the power of the rich, and those other discriminations supporting the stability of the system. In other words, they showed people that in relations with the world one must adhere to a game ruled by knowledge and prudence; they told them that, regardless, this world, however apparent it may be, is what confronts one and what must be dealt with; and they reminded them that, precisely because of its condition as illusory appearance, one must wholly enter into the game in terms of whatever becomes present to us.

The techniques for bringing out the apparent and illusory condition of the empirical world thus prove very important. The great development they undergo and their decisive role in all the forms of communication with a public become comprehensible. What in art corresponds to our formulation are the modes of striving for an effect that are used so as to produce a certain degree of indetermination concerning where the real ends and the illusory begins. As examples of effects of this type — to give an idea of what we mean — one would have to cite some of Velázquez' fundamental paintings, such as *Las meninas* or *Cristo en casa de Marta y María*. Let us note that now it was not a matter of the ingenuous virtuosity of copying something with such realism that we could believe what was only a painted image to be a real and living thing. The Velázquez experiment was much more complex: it had to do with multiplying one image among others, which were so functionally articulated that they ended up producing a sort of incertitude concerning the moment wherein this play of images passed from the represented to the real. This gave rise to what we could consider to be the theatrical structure of these paintings, in accordance with what the contemporary theater intended.[155]

To achieve effects of such a nature, the theater offered great possibilities — and more so as the epoch developed technically. The topos of the world as a stage, the human being as an actor, of life as a comedy (whose medieval-classical origin was studied by Curtius)[156] became profoundly renewed in baroque writers, in Lope, in Villamediana (in Suárez de Figueroa and Céspedes we have just seen it), reaching its peak in Calderón. Although "the theater of the world" mentioned by Lope (*Con su pan se lo coma*) — whether in Lope himself, in Quevedo above all, and even in Calderón — preserves a certain character of ascetic negation, it is an image that at the same time possesses a practical import based on what it tells us, by means of a translation whose meaning is easy to grasp, about how we must adapt our behavior to a world whose condition is similar to the stage representation: it is an entity that is transitory, ultimately illusory, but certain and evident while harsh, precisely when we have to organize our relation with this world. Thus is explained, by a type of social conditioning, the fact that in the baroque the boundaries between actor and spectator, between the daily world and the world of illusion come to be very fluid (as Tintelnot observed).[157]

But this baroque sense of the topos of the world as a stage does not incite us to abandon it as our dwelling place — at least this is not the typical and most general direction in its modern usage — but rather it leaves us aware of how we must get along with it to attain what Gracián would call "success." Of course one could go so far as to advocate abstaining from the world and from life (since Christian discipline prohibits the final step of suicide). In this way the neo-Stoic influence repeatedly manifests itself in Quevedo.[158] But these are extreme cases that one feels inclined to attribute to the discontent, vexation, or the chagrin engendered by the sentiment of crisis: to the melancholy or "hypochondria" that were held to be the elegant sicknesses of the time. But this century of discontent was also the century of the quest for self-gain, for success, for the ostentation of wealth, with a zeal to establish oneself in the uncontainable world, in triumphant affirmation on the shifting ground of society.

Rousset's thesis roughly approximates what we have just described: the baroque individual thought that one arrives at one's self through disguise; the character is the true person; the disguise is a truth. In a world of deceptive perspectives, illusions and appearances, it is necessary to meet reality by way of fiction.[159]

All of this presupposes the basic conception that the experience of fiction, unfolding in praxis, is functionally valid to bring us close to understanding the contexture of an apparent, phenomenal world. The inheritance, more

Hellenic than Christian, of an unbreakable belief in the ultimate substantiality of things, takes for granted that in the final moment when the representation falls away, what is revealed is not so much a new world beyond the tomb as the essential and definitive being of things and human beings, the essential being that sensible appearance kept hidden and that becomes unveiled in the beyond.[160]

The application of the image of the stage representation to the experience of the real world thus reinforced the view of the world that we are attributing to baroque mentality. This becomes even more accentuated — whatever may be, on the other hand, the ascetic possibilities that it encourages — if one compares the two levels and reveals the internal plot of the theatrical representation. Such is the significance of one of the many displays of virtuosity typical of the baroque: making theater about the theater. Something similar was done with all the arts possessing a figurative character: painting is painted — Velázquez; narration was narrated — Cervantes, Céspedes y Meneses, and others; fires were set up to cast light, not to provoke admiration for the illuminated objects but for the light's effects themselves; drama was staged wherein the representation of a comedy was represented. The best examples from the theater are a dramatic work by Bernini, *Comedia de los dos teatros* (1637); Lope's *Lo fingido verdadero*; and, under his direct influence, J. Routrou's play on the same theme,[161] a theme that Cáncer and Rosete y Meneses were to treat yet again in their comedy *El mayor representante, San Ginés* (in Cristóbal Lozano the theme even passed to the novelesque account, losing its most characteristic meaning).[162] If reality is theatrical, if the spectators find themselves submerged in the great theater of the world, what they contemplate on the stage is a theater to the second degree. This provides an obvious image of the plot of the scene being lived, but the introduction of the three-leveled complication also lessens the distances between them and softens them; by this means, the psyche is effectively prepared for accepting the phenomenal character of reality. To give greater force to the use of this sort of expedient, the same characters of this reality — the courtiers and the kings themselves — end up going on stage to represent their role: an illusion made real is the most efficient testimony to the illusory character of reality. At least, this was what the artist, the politician, and the baroque propagandist believed, handling their techniques of persuasion with such conviction.

An analogous significance must be attributed to the image of the "dream of life" taken advantage of by Lope, Calderón, Shakespeare, and so many others.[163] The Shakespearean correlation between sleeping, dying, and dreaming serves perfectly the social and moral strategy of the baroque. "Is this sleeping or dying?" asks Calderón's character (*Amar después de la muerte*); the third term, living, is presupposed in this formulation that from the outset is presented on stage.

I believe that this theme also had its starting point in the empirical conditions of the epoch's real existence (it would be too complicated to formulate here how the theme took shape in places other than Spain; perhaps the question became accentuated in Spain because of the specific characteristics with which the ecoonomic crisis — longer, deeper, and more decisive in its social consequences — was present in Spain). We are led to suspect this by those economic writers who characterized the Spanish as pcoplc who seemed only to want to proceed outside of the natural order (Cellorigo and a 1621 anonymous person writing to Philip IV), or by those who characterized their riches as a enchanted treasure (Caxa de Leruela, Barrionuevo). In his *Avisos*, this last author, in commenting on everyone's state of dissatisfaction during the years he was writing, viewed "people walking with such melancholy that it seems they have come from another world, being unable to raise their head."[164] And another interesting economist, Álvarez Ossorio, criticizing the uselessness of such bickering back and forth and falsification in peoples' conduct, noted that whoever led them to behave in such a manner "with the narcotic of caution, makes everybody sleep a dream that seems to offer repose."[165] The "dream of life" was an intellectual elaboration of this experience in the affairs of social coexistence, where one came across individuals who shuffled through life as "human beings under a spell," according to the anonymous writing of 1621.[166] The "chimera," the "dreaminess," were elements of Spanish life that the *arbitristas* fed on.[167]

"Look at our life that is like a dream," advised Enríquez Gómez.[168] The alluring and hammering verse of Lope possessed an influence on multitudes, engraving in the listeners' minds "that our life / is a dream and that everything is a dream"; he would complete the significance of the dream as a picture of life and of the world in pointedly offering his public the well-known topos: "that dreams, dreams are."[169] For the individual of baroque culture, who (except for rare exceptions) had not come to form a new scientific-physical conception of the universe, this world of phenomena, of empirical facts — which, being so forcefully evident, the modern individual cannot deny — presented no way to be interpreted if not as a dream. Thus the necessary dissemination of the image of "life as a dream" and its correlate: the world as a theater. This image alluded to "a common reality that the different characters similarly take part in: that reality is the conflict of reason with the confusion of life."[170] Of reason, let us add, that was understood in the sense of what Gilson has called "Christian philosophy," with its entire system of categories inherited from the Scholastic-Aristotelian tradition. The first clash between a conception of the world based on such transcendental assumptions and one that seemed unable to go beyond the mere empirical verifications of the events had to provoke, in minds that did not yet have the results of Galilean-Cartesian research at their disposal, an interpretation of the world of immanence as a dream. Without a doubt, the theme of life as a dream in Calderón and other baroque writers came from remote and multiple sources.[171] But although it is interesting to know these sources — among other reasons, to appreciate the differences — they did not determine the meaning of the topos as it was used in the baroque. What is of interest in Calderón is the effort he invested in emphasizing the power of the reality presented to us by the dream: "I do not dream, for I touch and believe / what I have been and what I am."

But this itself is a dream. Something as evident as real life is dreamed life. "To touch," "to see as evident," "to view": these words express the channels of the senses offering access to the world of the real; they are expressions that Calderón availed himself of to render an account of the dream experience. Therefore, to understand in all of its profundity the problem that this thesis involved in the baroque, one must realize all the force and fullness that the dream possessed: as if it were another level of reality. Because of this fullness, it can be compared to the plane of reality, can approximate it. As Segismundo said in the Calderonian drama of *La vida es sueño*, in the dream things are presented "as clearly and distinctly / as I am now seeing it."

The adjectives *clear* and *distinct*, as frequently used by Saavedra Fajardo and other baroque writers, have a specifically Cartesian significance. Naturally, in the latter instance they operated in a different network. But let us bear in mind the role of the dream at a critical moment in the formation of Descartes' scientific thought, as well as the import of a certainty on a par with the sensible potency of the real, which those two terms have in this passage from Calderón. The dream, then, belongs to the world of experience: "and experience shows me / that the man who lives dreams/what he is until awakening."

Thus was explained the conflicting and contradictory character of experience.[172] If, in following the means of access to the real that are recognized as such and are guaranteed by experience, one arrives at a dreamed world, the pressure of reality upon individuals striving to observe it leads them to a similar experience of incertitude. This is the key moment of Segismundo's drama (introduced at the peak moment of the crisis lived by baroque consciousness): "Because if I have dreamed / what I saw evident and certain, / what I see will be uncertain."

In connection with the preceding, we need to emend, or at least nuance, the frequently mentioned baroque doctrine of *disillusionment [desengaño]*. Given the idea that the world is a stage, a dream, fiction (with respect to a transcendental essence), the disillusion that it leads us to so that we might apprehend such a truth does not operate by postulating a renunciation or requiring it of whoever recognizes truth. If we all dream reality, this means that we must adequate our mode of behavior to this condition of the real. If in Quevedo, a writer who explored the theme of disillusion frequently and under the most varied forms, we read passages like the following: "I will show you the world as it is, which you do not succeed in seeing beyond what it seems,"[173] this does not mean that the apparent world is annihilated. It remains there, only individuals — having been shown it — can more justly condition their behavior to it. Quevedo formulated the issue in this way to propose that the reader think about the beyond (although this is not always the case in his work). On the same basis, Gracián or Saavedra were striving to influence the modes of behavior that lead to success (although they still exhibited inversely contradictory views of traditional morality). "To live attentive to disillusion and to peril," as Calderón advised, does not signify remaining in a state of resigned abstinence, of passive negation: the word *attentive* says much more, calls for the organization of a strategic attention aimed toward deploying the combat tactics of life.

Among critics limited to mere literary aspects, the baroque passes for an epoch of "disillusionment," understood as a vital negation of the world. Nevertheless, it provided, in rarely equaled number and intensity, references regarding human aggression that we have already seen. It seems clear that the wary and combative individual's radical attitude that was everywhere present proceeds from the fundamental egoism that, already in the seventeenth century, was recognized as the motive for human actions. We must admit, then, that the constant reference to disillusion did not produce attitudes of renunciation but, on the contrary, a common disposition to seek one's own well-being at the cost of another's. Undoubtedly, this view belongs to the basic conditions for survival of the human being, but now it was raised up as a guiding principle and formulated as such by the doctrine of baroque moralists. Disillusion did not signify withdrawal from but adequation to a world that was transitory and phenomenal (and in such a sense one could say that disillusion is made of the fabric of illusions); but it does not therefore stop exerting pressures on the subject, conditioning conduct that, in order to attain its ends, must adapt to the world's unstable and protean presence.

Because of the characteristic of the individual to close upon the self, which was imposed by egoism, and because of the resultant reduction in relations between individuals, who were juxtaposed in mere external contacts that did not overcome each other's isolation, in the baroque world individuals appear on the level of morality as monads. The complete confirmation of this interpretation is found in Gracián and Saavedra Fajardo, as in the picaresque novel.[174] All of Shakespeare's great protagonists — as creations of a baroque anthropology — are beings in a constitutive solitude, secluded in themselves and only tactically related with others: "For each one of them their 'I' is a fortress or a prison," it has been said.[175] Something similar can be observed in Spanish literary creations. A character from Calderón defines his double condition of hermeticism and autonomy, sublimating in these aspects human experience: "king of my own self, / I live with myself alone" (*Darlo todo y no dar nada*). On the other hand, a harsh fact is also clear to us: there was an almost total absence of personal feelings imbued with a certain degree of tenderness in the real life of Spanish baroque society, a sad aspect revealed by so many documents of the time. This isolation gave rise to the fact that the interrelations of some individuals with others — in the so often cruel and inhumane society of the seventeenth century — was reduced to the schema of tactical approaches and retreats, of a game of movements; ultimately to a mechanics of distances, as I have maintained on another occasion.[176] We are confronting a social world composed of individual units that were closed up like incommunicative monads whose interventions could be compared to simple collisions between billiard balls; but in colliding, they could become deformed or destroyed.

The baroque individual as a closed monad relates to the dreaming character that was so frequently attributed to individual existence in the baroque. In the dream, all the manifestations in which life unfolds are directly incommunicable experiences; they do not create a social, collective world. "In the optics of the dream," observed J. P. Borel, "what I do has no meaning except for me, it is not known nor lived by anyone but myself." In the waking state, according to Borel's comparison, my acts necessarily have a social dimension: they are for others, seen by others, undergone by others.[177] But one would have to add that the baroque mind seemingly refused, in a certain way, to see this latter aspect and considered instead that in earthly existence, in empirical life itself, everything transpires as a dream, that we do not escape this in our existence with others, who are limited by their own hermeticism (the ultimate version of this social interplay between isolated individuals may be Malebranche's occasionalism, so pronouncedly baroque in many aspects). But then we have to conclude that, consequently, it is not a matter of a coexistence but of an existence alongside others: whoever is concerned with guiding this existence must inevitably dominate the interplay of forces so as to be able to guide, or at least to take advantage of, what results from the collisions.

Solitude and juxtaposition, egoistic insolidarity and tactical approximation: these extremes tell us the drama of people following after those of a preceding period who had lived expectantly through the experiences of a dawning individualism. Through these experiences, the consequences of a multifaceted crisis imposed upon them, with greater pressure, the shaping action of culture — a greater pressure from the authority dominating the individuals and from the urban milieu that constrained them. The individual was characterized by an unrecognized or denied intimacy (the total lack of intimacy in the baroque's literary creations was acutely pointed out by Tierno Galván).[178] The individual was anonymous vis-à-vis others, closed and without social bonds, whatever may have been the weight of the inert tradition surviving them. And on the other hand, there was the multitude crowded together. This phenomenon of tension between the individual's isolation (rather than solitude) and his or her placement within a multitude has already been pointed out as typical of mass situations in the large city, situations in which the question of guiding modes of behavior acquires a relevant importance.

Thus we can see how the entire conceptual schema of baroque culture, which we have attempted to analyze in the preceding two chapters, wholly derived from and indirectly accentuated the presence of those social aspects discussed earlier.

IV: Baroque Society and the Means of Psychological Effects

Chapter 8
The Technique of Incompleteness

Until now we have sought to clarify the modes of conditioning that issued from the social situation of the seventeenth century, the social aspects that this conditioning impressed upon baroque culture, and the schema of fundamental concepts reflecting that culture's structure. Now, in conclusion, we shall try to be more precise in discussing the presence and significance of the elements arising out of such presuppositions — what they implied for the baroque work, the means for constructing it, and the characteristics that those means impressed upon it. Ordinarily only this last factor is considered, and from there one consequently arrives at a supposed definition of the baroque; but a definition based principally on instrumental or external aspects cannot be sustained and even contradicts these same data. Although it remains indispensable to consider external characteristics, specific morphological data, which are undoubtedly important, we cannot limit ourselves to these data nor can we assume that explaining their raison d'être will allow us to understand what the baroque represented in European and particularly Spanish culture.

Adjectives such as *irrational, irreal, fantastic, complicated, obscure, gesticulating, unrestrained, exuberant, frenetic, transitive,* and *changing* are frequently taken as the expression of the characteristics assumed by any manifestation of baroque culture; they are contrasted with such adjectives as *logical, restrained, real, clear, serene,* and *calm,* which would denote a classical posture. We have already underscored the profound relation of continuity that took place between the baroque period of Europe's modern history and the period of classicism that preceded it. On the other hand, however, the first series of adjectives we have listed brings together all those that Hocke made use of to characterize mannerism prior to the mid-sixteenth century. Hocke has accumulated a great mass of information that reveals mannerist traits already at a time when, until recently, the Renaissance was believed to be at its peak.[1] This makes us realize that, although whatever elements we note as characteristic of the baroque can be found singularly and in isolation both earlier and later, we must consider them within the complex of a historical situation to which they were linked and in connection with which they acquired their meaning. We will try, then, in focusing on an element we submit as being of the baroque, to demonstrate in each case its corresponding situational framework.

Today a general notion comes to mind whenever one haphazardly uses the adjective *baroque*. Since the eighteenth century, the word has been accompanied by a pejorative connotation. According to that view, the decisive characteristic of baroque work would be *exuberance*. And there are current dictionaries, compiled in collaboration with authorized specialists, in which the notion of "baroque" is still limited to little more than exuberance. Thus emerges the tendency in some authors (Wölfflin, d'Ors) to consider every manifestation of exuberance as baroque, regardless of its epoch — so long as its traits correspond to a certain meaning (much more precise in Wölfflin than in d'Ors). Since all cultures have, toward the end of the period in which they develop, a phase of specifically ornate flowering where supplementary elements predominate, these stages of decline would in each case be identified as a baroque phase.

Although we previously said that the baroque was the culture of Europe during the time of striving for a renewal of the monarchy's prestige and a restoration of the socioeconomic powers of the old and new seigniors, one may have to conclude that it was rather a question of an epoch offering creations that accentuated their exuberance and ostentation. The law of ostentation through external signs of abundance seemed to occur in situations such as the one we have indicated. It was not a question of satisfying the taste of those concentrated in the upper reaches of the court. Things were not so simple. After the Renaissance experience — along with the difficulties that some monarchies had to face, the multiplication of media and the expansion of the masses within society, and, consequently, a complexity in the new situation that evoked wonder in everybody and bewildered many — it no longer sufficed to exhibit an external, ornamental wealth, nor was it possible to succeed in surprising and attracting (the intention of all mass culture), to stay within the limits of grandiose ostentation. Ostentation had to be revamped with new methods, utilized with a new technique, and even affirmed or denied in accordance with the demands of the new events.

But baroque art is not characterized by exuberance in the sense of a necessary trait common to all cultural manifestations of the epoch. It is not necessarily typical of Vignola, nor of Giacomo della Porta, of Q. Latour, nor of Perrault. Lafuente Ferrari, with unique insight, has spoken about a "concentrated sobriety" in the great seventeenth-century masters, who frequently cultivated a restrained expression.[2] Italian critics have considered a "moderate baroque," which at that time was formulated by a series of preceptists.[3] A contemporary critic, E. Raimondi, has used the formula "baroque neolaconism" to denote a tendency toward severe sobriety in expression that — despite the fact that some French and Italian writers criticized it even when it was being diffused (while others, such as Malvezzi, followed it to the highest degree) — earned the praise of the Spanish and specifically of writers as unlike as Quevedo and Gracián, being rigorously practiced by Saavedra Fajardo.[4]

After the example of austerity offered by the walls of the Escorial (with its technique of monotonous repetition of the simple), we might allude to the modest architecture of the many small and charming churches in Madrid and elsewhere, whose easy design was repeated in diverse Spanish cities. In painting we might bear in mind the extreme sobriety represented in Sánchez Cotán's or Zurbarán's works. Contrary to what a banal characterization repeatedly claims as typically Spanish, let us recall the many cases such as Martínez Montañés' *Cristo de la clemencia*, in Seville: a scuplture that — without exaggeration, expressive additions and with scarcely more than a few drops of blood on the wounds — even dispenses with the dynamic possibility of dramatization resulting from the lance wound in the side of Christ's body; he appears soberly represented with minimal signs of violence, serenely detained in death.

But let us turn to examples that are more directly of interest. Such is the case of that abbreviated mode of writing that Gracián habitually practiced: the way he takes a known saying, a sentence read somewhere, an idea, sometimes only a metaphor (with elements usually coming from a Biblical or classical source) and collapses its terms to the point of reducing the expression to the ultimate degree of laconism.[5] Saavedra at times opted for modes of expression that approximate the brevity of mathematical theorems, frequently making use of this type of image. Aphorisms, counsels, maxims, and collapsed, brief, rapid formulas are a literary genre very much in line with the taste of the epoch. One author gave his the name of "sparks": "sparks of various conceits [*conceptos*]," as Setanti said; of his own work he commented that "this laconic way of speaking is assuredly not for everybody nor for all occasions."[6] As did so many writers of maxims, counsels, and conceits, Setanti thus applied a severe conciseness that he himself called "laconic speaking."

The preceding would have to be related to the theme of *repetition* that L. Mumford observed in baroque creations; according to him, these repetitive creations have a meaning bound up with the epoch, whether in the case of the uniformity of the series of columns in some buildings, or the series of individuals lined up in the cities' military processions. The series of windows along the Escorial's walls (which M. Pelayo compared in their monotony to the books of contemporary moralists), Bernini's colonnade in Rome, and that of Perrault on the eastern façade of the Louvre seem to correspond to the effects of dynamism and enormousness that a mass culture needs and that, in any case, relate more closely to the characteristics to be dealt with in what follows.

Baroque authors could allow themselves to be carried away by exuberance or could hold to a severe simplicity. Either served their ends equally. To appear baroque, the use of one or the other required the fulfillment of no more than one condition: that in both cases abundance or simplicity take place in the extreme. *In the extreme*: this was one means of psychological action on people, one that was closely bound to the assumptions and goals of the baroque.

It was not a question of exuberance or simplicity in itself, but in either case by virtue of its extremeness, its exaggeration. "A knight in the extreme," Cervantes called don Quijote. In the same way, so were seventeenth-century Spaniards and many other Europeans. The humble cosmogony reflected in the paintings of Sánchez Cotán is an extreme formulation, as is the abundant wealth of things that Rubens's paintings offered with incomparable exuberance; the almost monochrome painting of Rembrandt, or Poussin's soft and varied chromatic repertory is also a mode of extremeness. As we know by his own testimony, what one baroque artist admired in an earlier sculptor was a similar quality he observed in some aspects of the work he was praising: in the sculptor Ancheta, Jusepe Martínez emphasized as worthy of note that "he made his figures with fierce postures."[7]

Expressionist art, art of the extreme: E. W. Hesse spoke about the "baroque aesthetic of exaggeration and surprise, invented to evoke wonder in the public."[8] Ultimately, it is a culture of exaggeration and, as such, a violent culture, not because it proposed violence and was dedicated to demonstrating it (although there was also much of this) but because the presentation of the world offered to us by the baroque artist strives to make us feel amazed, moved, by the instances of violent tension that occur and that it holds: landscapes darkened by stormy violence; human figures in "fierce postures"; ruins that tell us of the uncontainable destructive force of time upon the solid work of the human being; and violence grasped in its suffering and tenderness, which grants a greater vibrancy to the baroque creation.[9] All of this can, in part, be mannerism — there is no doubt that the baroque movement inherited many things from mannerist attempts;[10] but now, although gesticulation remains very important, the dramatic element of expression takes precedence, to the extent that expression openly articulates instances of extreme tension in the human experience of things and of other human beings.

This explains the role of antitheses and means of a similar structure in baroque rhetoric, with its thousand plays of extreme opposition (for example, fire-ice, shining-darkening, etc.).[11] One cannot fail to take into account what rhetoric and the very diverse use of its multiple means signified at this cultural moment. Rhetoric's step into first place among the arts of expression (although statistically the number of those cultivating poetics may have been greater) and the return to Aristotelian rhetoric are phenomena tied to the European development of the baroque, as studied by Mopurgo-Tagliabue.[12]

I believe that there was an ultimate rhetorical justification in the widespread Italian practice of rendering Petrarch "as a god," an activity that in Spain would be developed imitatively with Garcilaso. Chronologically it corresponded instead to the mannerist period, and it (in this case also) was undoubtedly in advance of what would be baroque taste.[13] At the height of the baroque we encounter something similar: the repeated utilization of literary genres much cultivated in the epoch and born of a rhetoric applied to matters of nature, politics, and so forth, that were transferred to a divine subject. This is what happened with emblematic works and other types of symbolic or enigmatic literature; we come across some rather extreme cases making use of the esotericism that such genres contained.

Corresponding to the criterion of judgment that we have been describing, when Gracián praised the Escorial what he admired was its extremeness.[14] The first letter of the *Cartas de jesuitas* (of the published series) commented on the new Retiro palace that it "is striking because of its magnificence."[15] The "magnificence" of the "miraculous" Aranjuez astounded Almansa.[16] In another realm, it would perhaps be even easier to cite in the theater extreme cases where the staging was capable of disrupting the minds of the spectators in a very violent fashion: examples, from different authors, would be *La estrella de Sevilla*, *La serrana de la Vera*, *El castigo sin venganza*, and hundreds more. One can cite situations like this in the novel as well (aside from the manifestations of "deviance" in the picaresque novel), above all in the courtly novel of Céspedes y Meneses. Many of these extreme cases correspond to genuine hagiographic, heroic examples. Heroic material — cultivated in the novel and theater — is very adequate for offering extreme representations. The heroic is an extreme case, although the baroque version of the hero as a person of discretion would be very different from the hero as knight in previous stages. The "heroic virtues" of St. Teresa, according to Jerónimo Gracián, made her a type of saint well suited to impressing the baroque psyche.[17] Let us recall as well the "eroici furori" exalting the figure that itself was "heroic" à la baroque, in the very important *Diálogo* of Giordano Bruno.[18]

The mannerists, both theoretically and practically (i.e., Vasari and Michelangelo), understood that what was unrestrained, taken to the extreme, possessed an ability to impress: by exploding its proportions, it came to have a forceful impact on the psyche. The word *terribleness* expressed this condition very well. Vasari spoke about Michelangelo's "terribilità."[19] *Terrible* does not mean something that incites fear and that, because of this feeling, annihilates the possiblity of admiring what is being contemplated as such. Of course, the word appears in this sense not only today but in some texts of the sixteenth century: thus when we find "terribleness" used in *El Crotalón* it is in reference to death.[20] In this sense, it is unfavorable: the condition of that which terrifies and to a certain extent blinds, as happens in the spectacle of death at a time when the estimation of death had greatly changed, despite the well-known topoi of Christian asceticism. But very much on the contrary, in the baroque the terrible was positively valorized as an aspect of a work because it denoted what *in its extremes* or (expressed with a Spanish formulation that about that time passed to the Italian lexicon) what *grandiosely* attracts us with an irresistible force in whatever we are viewing. Referring to Michelangelo — whose work probably originated the new use of the word — Céspedes emphasized his "grace and terribleness."[21] Carducho praised those painters who made use of "that jovial and terrible manner." Carducho himself spoke about the "very heroic works" he admired in Rome, and in another passage, alluding this time to poets, he tells us of his taste for those "who sang most heroically and sweetly."[22] This compatibility of terms — sweet, heroic, terrible, graceful, jovial — helps us comprehend what underlay their simultaneous use: allusion was made to disproportion, to the extremeness that, outside of all law, all prosaic reasonableness, was capable of awakening one's taste and admiration (and what the baroque called *astonishment* and *wonder*) in confronting a human work, this lack of proportion, nevertheless, could not go so far as to annul the faculties of pleasing [*gustosa*] contemplation.

When Paolo Beni said that "poetry should not be either clear or precise, it ought to be only magnificent," the baroque was calling for this magnificence not only in the poetic work but also in architecture, politics, and the arts of war.[23] In commenting on the preceding sentence, Mopurgo linked it to the baroque's loss of restraint, a consequence of the disappearance of every mimetic norm in the rhetoric of the time.[24] Of course, magnificence-unrestrainedness-terribleness-extremeness are closely connected to one another; yet one does not have to view that as a pure and simple consequence of a rhetorical game: this rhetorical game, with its possibilities of acting upon the psyche of the addressee, occurred in relation to the epoch's situation that we are here describing. That is to say, the baroque ceased imitating, lost restraint, took pleasure in the terrible, and sought to cultivate the extreme, all to impress a public more forcefully and with greater freedom.

The extremeness was linked to what was already observed by Wölfflin: the baroque did not want to manifest a satisfied and becalmed existence, but rather a state of excitation, of turbulence.[25] Wölfflin interpreted this internal movement as an aspiration to the sublime, an idea very close to magnificence in the judgment of the seventeenth century. In this respect, recall Schiller's affirmation: beauty is the enjoyment of a happy people, whereas those who do not feel happy seek to attain the sublime. This sublimeness is a manifestation of sensibility: it belongs to the class of terribleness, extremeness; the feeling of unhappiness (in Schiller's fine observation), not inevitably one of misery, would provide the impetus for it — a feeling provoked by the state of crisis and instability in the baroque epoch.

In accordance with the effects of this play of sensibility, in the judgment of people in the baroque, the author capable of giving his or her works this "terrible" quality possessed a condition or faculty whose reference was drawn from classical sources, although now it came to acquire a greater force and underwent a semantic alteration: I am alluding to the word *furor*. López Pinciano referred it to Plato's *Phaedo*,[26] and Lope de Vega also cited the Platonic origin of the idea.[27] In the theoretical realm of mannerism, this term's renewal was already known to Vasari.[28] One more reference expresses what this doctrine became in the second phase of sixteenth-century Italianism: that is, when the first notices of the theme appeared, for example, in Du Bellay, who mentioned it in Sonnet IV of the *Regrets*.[29]

When the preceptists of the baroque period repeated doctrines of Renaissance classicism, but with a new accent (which one has not always been able to read in them, thus preventing an adequate perception of the baroque phenomenon), we are confronting a full-blown development of the theory of furor that is linked to the different aspects related to extremeness. Carducho characterized it as an original, spontaneous factor, contrary to something learned, that moves the artist (and we might even say that moves the human being in general who is making something): "a natural furor prevailed over studies."[30] Lope, clearly, could not fail to accept the doctrine of furor as a grace that makes itself known at the margin of the opposition between nature-spontaneity and artifice-learning. For him it had what we have just described with the word *grace*. Lope attributed to poetry "a divine and rare furor."[31] But López Pinciano gave a complete definition whose import is of great interest (combining perfectly with the reasons that I, from my point of view, find in baroque culture): "Furor is an alienation in which the understanding separates itself from the beaten path."[32] Let us refrain from a facile and untenable gesture of admiration with regard to the author's advance use of the word *alienation*, central in Marxist thought; but let us recognize that here we have the key of this extremeness we have been discussing: the baroque creator, in attempting to resolve one of those situations that the seventeenth century considered to be without precedent, felt thrown out of, beside himself, alienated. In such a sense baroque culture led human beings to be other than themselves, to go outside of the beaten path, and this technique of alienation — we also have no reason to refrain from using the word — provided the basis to bring to bear upon such subjects a culture of estrangement, a guided culture. The basis for the baroque to be a guided culture is revealed in the fact that it was fundamentally a culture of alienation.

The baroque preceptist Carballo, in *Cisne de Apolo*, after various passing references dedicated five chapters of its last dialogue to the theme. Carballo spoke about "a divine furor and an inspiring grace and natural inclination." They are not identifiable concepts but are approximate and related. The poet can do nothing "without a certain breath of furor." It is a question of a "furor and ecstasy." But how does this force operate on whoever undergoes it? "Furor draws one forth as if out of oneself and transforms one into another nobler, more subtle and delicate mode of thinking; one is elevated and enthralled in it to such an extent that it is possible to say that one is outside of oneself and has no knowledge of the self." Thus we have once again come across this alienating state, which extends from the ecstasy of the mystic to the exploitation of the worker in the capitalist order. In the middle is located the state of those seventeenth-century Spaniards described by the economists as going outside of the natural order, crazy, enraptured, in a state of furor — let us now say — similar to what was said about poets.

At the outset, this alienation — this being drawn outside of oneself — was expressed about the thousands of poets singing the praises of the entire social system of values sanctioned by the baroque monarchy and its periphery; it descended as well on the public that was estranged from itself by the effects of the verses clamoring for their attention, especially in the theater. If we bear this in mind, it will be easily understood that this baroque alienation performed the function of taking over and guiding the masses, in accordance with the objectives we have attributed to the culture of the epoch. Carballo added that the poet, "with his imagination [a species of furor] comes to feel his body inflamed as if with anger, and with this inflammation and ardent furor, almost disengaged from his spirit and as if outside of himself, comes to plan and compose such a variety, not only of lines and stanzas but a thousand lofty and elevated inventions."[33] The theme was so common that many other statements could be discovered similar to the following, which Juan de Zabaleta made in passing: "Men compose [verse] while outside of themselves."[34] Recording the final echoes of the baroque in this as in so many aspects, Bances Candamo wrote: "Seized by furor they pronounce sentences and things exceeding human study, which, once tranquil, not even they understand."[35]

Bearing in mind this state of the poet — not forgetting that the poet had a shaping and integrating social function equivalent to that of today's journalist (the commentator or editorialist) — we see that this situation, which applied to those who composed verses for social consumption, which was estranging and designed for mass guidance, became an almost general state of mind that was widespread in baroque society and particularly in Spanish society, which greatly exaggerated its characteristics. The economist Martín G. de Cellorigo described this state of mind: "It seems that the desire has been only to reduce these kingdoms to a republic of bewitched individuals who live outside of the natural order."[36] It was the result of the activities performed by all those writers, poets, and novelists (the novel was then a form of poetry) who perceived themselves as thrown out of the "ordinary course of understanding." Ultimately it was an active and passive furor, a collective surrender to every form of extremeness. It was the consequence of a social condition, of a society where one daily heard it said, even by the king himself (referring here to Philip IV), that everything seemed on the verge of going to ruin.

But what we have just called passive furor, which seeks effects of extreme efficacy in whoever contemplates a work (that is, in a very numerous public) received in the seventeenth century a name that has a very modern appearance: *suspension*. This word was probably used with one of the highest degrees of frequency; it alludes to psychological effects that end up coming very close to the current technique of *suspense*. In the seventeenth century, there were those who made reference to the efficacy with which, in one sense or another, suspense operates on the mind. Céspedes y Meneses noted that "whenever we see a great resistance, a suspended and interrupted emotion violently suffocates the senses and debilitates and weakens its strength."[37] The effort to cut short a feeling at once provokes a reaction that alters the normal course of the person's affective development and, according to the author, weakens his or her resistance. But something else can occur: the utilization of similar techniques may not lead to negative effects; instead, maintaining itself to an adequate degree, it might, after having produced a transitory and provisional weakening (which means the course of attention and feeling will become reestablished, being only momentarily cut short), provoke the reaction of a more energetic affection. This procedure functioned as if it contributed to fixing and encouraging the forces of the psyche that follow, making it part of an event that takes place wholly in the psychological realm.

Jankelevitch referred to the "mannerist" applying this term not to people in the sixteenth century but to all those for whom "appearance" and "manner" prevail over "truth," to all those who, recognizing the ground of truth, play with "manner" (which applies to the baroque in the highest degree). He maintained that in becoming aware of this opposition or dissymmetry and noting the means it provides and the power its studied use represents, whoever knows how to manipulate it is tempted to exploit — and this was what happened with whoever made baroque productions — the propensity of human beings to feel surprised and in awe.[38] Thus by means of extremeness (according to the concept we have put forth) and its derivative or connected manifestations, there was the attempt to accomplish specific effects conducive to evoking awe: such was the goal of this "cutting short" or suspense that put a momentary halt to what the baroque work seemingly attempted, only to unleash a greater effectiveness — that is, to attract and subject more avidly those it addressed. The baroque artist, pedagogue, and politician appealed to a technique of suspense that intensified, in a second moment, the influencing and guiding results they pursued.

López Pinciano commented that "the new thing delights, and the amazing more so, and the marvelous and wondrous even more."[39] Whoever the addressee was (the spectator, the reader, the subject who must obey), he or she was left full of wonder by the qualities that Pinciano gradually articulated (whether in a natural phenomenon, a human action, a work of art, or the majesty of the king). We have already seen the emphasis E. W. Hesse placed on the role of wonder and surprise. If the Aristotelian theory regarding the role of wonder was read in the Renaissance and continued to be read and remembered in the baroque, in this latter period one finds in the notion of wonder — a word frequently joined with *astonishment* — the idea of something different from an introduction or access to knowledge. The idea was rather that of a psychological effect that for a few instants brings the forces of contemplation or admiration to a halt so as to let them act more vigorously when they are afterwards released. Therefore this helps explain the taste for the new, the unusual, the marvelous, the awesome, for that which astonishes, in the sense that its magnificence or strangeness offers itself as a surprise.

All these effects were achieved with studied means, by manipulating motivations [*resortes*] within the human being that were acted on to arrive at this transitory situation of suspense. Suárez de Figueroa knew that the "suspended admiration" soon unleashed more forceful effects.[40] The preceptist Carballo counseled the dramatic author in particular to endeavor to "have the listeners' psyches *in suspense*, now happy, now sad, now amazed, and with a desire to know what will happen in the end, because the greater this *suspense* and desire, the more agreeable after the end."[41] An author of comedies who belonged to the Valencian group, Carlos Boil, proposed the utilization of those themes in which "el énphasis que se muestra / suspende, y la suspensión / de un caballo al vulgo cuelga" [a shown emphasis suspends, and a horse rearing up at the people leaves them hanging];[42] suspense (a means preferably applied to the mass, to numerous and anonymous common people) arrests one's attention in a state of anxious instability so as to reinforce the consequence of emotional effects.

Here was all that the baroque author expected from the technique of utilizing the expedients [*resortes*] we are discussing. Lope, as novelist, noted that one must proceed in one's narration by counting "on the suspense of what is expected, for the greater pleasure [*gusto*] of whoever listens."[43] Villamediana admired in the poem "the suspense whereby it estranges [*enajena*]," a curious linking of this expedient with the technique of alienation. And if the question was eminently posed in relation to the theater (the baroque art par excellence), it was no less applicable to other aspects of culture, such as the novel, poetry, or music, including even painting or the actions of a politician, as we will discuss below.

A French writer formulated no less clearly the advice we have just read in Carballo. In a passage from his tragedy *Andromire* (1641), Scudéry asked that each scene present "something new that always leaves one's spirit in suspense [*suspendu*]."[44] Putting the psyche in suspense: there lies the secret. Without seeking a systematic explanation or being aware of the fundamental connections we are proposing here, one of the French scholars on the subject has conjectured an interpretation similar to ours, if only remotely. In reference to seventeenth-century French tragedy, which every day is of greater interest in terms of the lack of restraint in its feelings and the exuberance of its means, Lebègue maintained that in its independence and novelty vis-à-vis the precepts of the ancients, its intention was to cause surprise, and that was linked to a fifth characteristic that this historian indicated: the quest for extreme emotions. The characteristics of the correlative extremeness and suspension coincided, then, as we have seen, with aspects that today are being noticed in the French baroque.[45]

Specific modes of behavior present in the political sphere, modes serving to introduce the majesty of the kings in seventeenth-century absolute monarchies, must also be referred to such characteristics. Kings who knew how to operate as they should, including every great personage who intelligently ruled his conduct (to put it succinctly, everyone having the pretense of heroic "splendor" in his manner of acting), typically left in suspense those who hung on their every word, who were present at and busy with their governmental activities. Such was the doctrine of Gracián, repeated in *El héroe*, *El político*, *El oráculo manual*, and other places. Gracián was perhaps the greatest expounder of the doctrine of suspension, which in his work acquired a central place in his psychology and in his moral system. It would be worthwhile dedicating a study to this theme.[46] Other writers — now referring only to political writers — also took the theme as their own. One of them, Ramíriz de Prado, spoke about the suspension produced in people as an efficient, indispensable resource of the ruler.[47]

Secrecy, suspense, and imposing the force of majesty by extrarational means were elements that were bound up with one another in the advice that Gómez Tejada gave to the rulers: "The secrecy of the Prince makes him more closely resemble God and, consequently, gains him majesty and reverence, puts his vassals in a state of suspense, perturbs his enemies."[48] "Make his Majesty mysterious" was the advice of J. A. de Lancina: "Whoever wants to evoke suspense in the common people makes his activities mysterious; the more one displays one's activities, the greater the resulting curiosity, and arcane doings cause veneration."[49] Especially among the Tacitists, the doctrine of secrecy went hand in hand with that of suspense, and both constituted key elements in their elaborated doctrine of the prince's behavior; they disseminated it in their pages, and it became a basic principle of monarchical absolutism, as it was insistently preached to its subjects. Words such as these from Calderón's *La gran Cenobia* were heard on stage: "en secretos misteriosos, / obedeced los efetos / sin examinar el cómo" [in mysterious secrets obey the effects without examining the "how" of their coming about]. The very conception of majesty contained an echo of the idea of suspense; this conception was enveloped by a renewed charismatic sense whose plan entailed the discussion of whether it was proper for the king to be frequently present before his people and become familiar among his subjects or, inversely, whether he should keep himself far removed, enveloped in a halo of mystery without anyone being able to penetrate his thoughts. Such came to be the notion of the *arcana imperii* originated by the Tacitists and developed by the absolutist writers: it cannot be translated by the contemporary expression *state secrets*, which has become an ordinary version typical of a bureaucratic government in a world whose relations have remained without magical content. On the contrary, the *arcana* appealed to extraordinary effects and to the beguiling action of the *potestas* by means of magic, although it was clearly a matter of natural magic (something like possession of certain psychological knowledge that is rarely present), which in the seventeenth century the Cartesians themselves cultivated for amusement.

This technique of suspense in the theater and novel and in politics also applied to the art of painting, with its well-known social objectives in the epoch. The practice of incompleteness, as it occurred in Velázquez and others, has not been sufficiently stressed. It is a process of suspension wherein one expects the contemplating eye to end up supplying what is missing and to supply it somewhat in its own fashion. All painting of "splotches" or "smears," of distant brush strokes, is to a certain extent an *anamorphosis* that calls for spectator intervention to recompose the image. In all of these cases, what Baltrusaitis has written applies: "The optic beam is not the passive conductor of a sensation produced by an object; it recreates it, projecting its altered forms in reality."[50] In relation to this aspect a very eloquent parallelism has been observed between an example taken from literature and another from painting; both examples are very famous and are approximately from the same time, in the early years of the seventeenth century. After having already written a dozen works, among which were his most grandiose tragedies, the works that Shakespeare produced later seem more carelessly done, as if they were not polished or gone over for the last time. Some critics have tried to see esoteric reasons for this difference, reasons of occult symbolism. Others have chosen to assume that the author had become fatigued and that this weariness had led him to become careless in his work. Doesn't it seem more appropriate and congruent with the circumstances of the case to relate this fact with the baroque sensibility and with its taste for the incomplete? In view of the evidence we have, there is no reason to limit our consideration of the plays to a judgment evaluating them as "imperfect"; in no instance is there reason for considering them necessarily imperfect, although on occasion (as in so many of Lope's works) both judgments can overlap. In an appraisal better fitted to the epoch's circumstances, I believe, then, that we are confronting a Shakespearean application of a more and more baroque procedure: a procedure wherein the incomplete serves as the means for leading to a state of suspension, to the public's active intervention, and to contact with and psychological action upon this public, thus inclining it toward certain desired objectives.

The other example of the technique of incompletion is offered by Velázquez's painting, among other examples. Today it has become customary to remark upon its character of being unfinished, careless painting. Ortega greatly stressed this aspect of Velázquez's work.[51] Keeping within the boundaries of biographical explanation, the attempt was made to see this as a loss of interest on the part of the painter, who was distracted from his task by preoccupations other than painting. Let us not go into the personal question. We are interested in its historical grounds. Formulating it in this way we find that Velázquez's procedure was not unique, but had a place among the general current of painters of his time (with cases as distinguished as Rembrandt's), who enthusiastically practiced the painting of "smears" or of painting "boldly" [*a lo valiente*], which Gracián was representative in admiring. The most interesting facet for us has to do with what was seen during the epoch: when Gracián himself praised Velázquez in this sense, and when Quevedo viewed his work as praiseworthy, they did not see certain profiles or colors carefully and fully placed on the canvas, but rather discontinuous and incomplete "splotches." Quevedo thought that this was much more "true" in the picture than a refined finish. Some years before, a writer as informed and appreciative of painting as friar José de Sigüenza threw in the face of the Spanish painters their way of leaving the work so well finished, vis-à-vis the liberal assurance of painting "boldly" that he admired in the Italian artists.[52] This helps us to understand that Velázquez's technique of incompletion — aside from the distinctiveness of its application — was neither exceptional nor original in him, nor did it fail to correspond to an entire historical process: it represented a high point in procedures of the baroque.

In the practice of Saavedra Fajardo, another enthusiast and good sampler of the "smeared" paintings of his time, what was the literature of *empresas* but an incomplete and open-ended way of writing? The frequent utilization of allusions and evasions in the pages of Quevedo himself probably corresponded to the same notion.[53] A degree of sloppiness, with its rigorous historical significance, entered into the baroque aesthetic, which in the most extreme cases gave the impression of brazenness.

Carelessness had its set of precepts. The value conferred on the studied practice of carelessness sublimated the function we are here attributing to the so-called technique of the incomplete (i.e., within the baroque perspective). "Carelessness is clothed in finery," wrote Bocángel,[54] and Calderón made the doctrine his own: "in carelessness there is beauty" (*La Sibila de Oriente*). Applying a judgment formulated even in terms of the most quotidian aspects of life, Cubillo de Aragón had one of his characters say that "you must praise carelessness in the spectacle" (*El señor de Buenas Noches*). This role of carelessness (which extended even to the point of attributing an aesthetic value to ugliness)[55] was not opposed to the cultural judgment of the baroque; on the contrary, it appeared as one of its elements. Pellicer de Tovar formulated the principle in all its rigor: "Carelessness is perhaps indicative of greater skill than a lack of it."[56]

The receivers of the baroque work, being surprised at finding it incomplete or so irregularly constructed, remained a few instants in suspense; then, feeling compelled to thrust themselves forward and take part in it, they ended up finding themselves more strongly affected by the work, held by it. In this way they experienced an incomparably more dynamic influence of the work being presented, with a much greater intensity than when other tacks were taken. It is not a matter of ultimately obtaining the public's intellectual adherence so much as moving it; therefore, this state of suspension was used to serve as the expedient to launch a more firmly sustained movement. And that was the question: to move.

Such was the meaning of this baroque technique: to suspend by making use of the most diverse means, so that after this moment of provisional and transitory arrest the mind was more effectively moved, given impetus by the detained and concentrated forces that are then set free but after always having been situated in such a way that they followed along a channel that guided them. The technique of suspense relates to the utilization of resources that are mobile and changing, resources of unstable equilibrium, of incompleteness, of the strange and the rare, of the difficult, of the new and never before seen. As Céspedes de Meneses said of one of his characters: "He became somewhat suspended by the unforeseen novelty [impensada novedad]."[57] Let us concern ourselves now with one of the most decisive of these points: the utilization of the obscure and the difficult.

The extremeness constituting the basis of the baroque and the suspension that it strove to manipulate skillfully as a resource led it to make use of the notions of difficulty and obscurity (the second by virtue of the first). In the early times of mannerism and cultism, Luis Carrillo went so far as to say that "making things somewhat more difficult are effects of good speaking," although one must reject obscurity and discreetly make use of difficulty with moderation;[58] some years later, however, López Pinciano would not hesitate to assert that "what is beautiful resides in what is difficult."[59] Lope, in having some of his characters dispute the subject, had one of them say (in La dama duende) that poetic expression must be "obscure even to rare spirits [ingenios]." Pellicer de Tovar offered us the normative principle of this new judgment: "Being hidden is a condition of what has value [lo precioso]."[60] And Gracián perceived it as a general criterion: "The difficult was always esteemed."[61] A. Collard devoted a chapter of her work to the subject of obscurity and difficulty in seventeenth-century literature and indicated that a Renaissance text — Boscán's translation of Castiglione — already intimated participation of a reading public stimulated by the means that were used to achieve that very objective. The author did not belabor this point, which for me is the essential aspect of the question and the one that led me to pose it (in the preface to my 1944 book). Through the many passages she cited — even though many that I note here and that I consider more interesting for my purposes are omitted — A. Collard posed the question as to whether there was a decisive difference between an obscurity in terms of meaning or content (Gracián, Quevedo, etc.) and one in terms of external form or expression (Góngora, Carrillo, Bocángel, Trillo). Such a differentiation had been accepted in general terms (by Menéndez Pidal, among others), but the author saw no reason to maintain this point of view. Of courses, this discussion has little significance in terms of the theme's meaning for us, and the possible consideration that each of the different types of difficulty was aimed toward distinct publics (as F. Lázaro proposes) does not change matters. It would be relevant, however, if we discovered that the second mode of obscurity (difficulty of expression) was aimed toward more prominent, rich and cultured publics. This was probably the case, but it still remains to be studied. I believe that in both instances these two modes of obscurity — although other aspects can be observed in their duality — operated on the public in the same way: attracting the public, holding its attention, making it participate in the work and use its forces in deciphering that work, thereby guaranteeing the work's influence on the reader.[62]

In the seventeenth century there was repeated praise of difficulty, and it was formulated pedagogically: good and effective teaching has to make use of the difficult and therefore of the path of obscurity in order to obtain a more solid anchoring of knowledge. A passage from Carballo is of great interest for understanding this question and appreciating its scope and, in passing, for becoming aware of how certain values, such as clarity in classroom teaching, are not absolutes but products of a historical judgment. According to Carballo, one must admit that

> very clear things engender a certain tediousness accompanied by a loss of attention; thus a student will read four pages of a book, and when the book is clear and about ordinary things, he does not pay attention to what he reads. But if its style is difficult and extraordinary, this itself incites him to work to understand it; we are naturally inclined toward understanding and knowing it, and one contrary expends its force on another — thereby with difficulty the appetite for knowledge increases.[63]

This is not a solitary reference. Decades later, Gracián would analogously maintain that "when the meaning is more obscure, the greater difficulty gives greater satisfaction to the reason [*discurso*] in finding it."[64] The pedagogical method of the difficult had in Gracián — perhaps the most eminent preceptist of the baroque — its staunchest supporter: "The more difficult truth is, the more agreeable, and knowledge that costs something is greater esteemed."[65]

There were undoubtedly diverse reasons for the currency of a taste for what could be understood at a price. According to Highet, the tendency toward an obscuring distortion and complication would, in the seventeenth century, come from Greek and Latin influences: for example, in the style of Góngora, Marino, and Milton; Jáuregui had to lean toward Gongorism in translating *Pharsalia*.[66] But why did this influence come about, why did it become generalized and achieve a central role in the system of baroque culture?

There were doubtless trivial reasons — such as those giving rise today to the diffusion of crossword puzzles (which does not mean it is a trivial theme in sociological terms). José de la Vega, wanting to render an account of the mediocre state of culture in his time, wrote that "it never fails that one admires what one does not comprehend, whether because one has not come to understand that one has not understood or whether because awe is generally the fodder for ignorance."[67] Certainly some specific forms of difficulty conform well with the midcult and correspond to its mass character. This was undoubtedly one of the reasons at work in the seventeenth century.

Of course, in the baroque there was a common inclination toward the difficult and obscure that reached to the lower social levels. But in the very precepts of the moment, these qualities were defended and their cultivation by the author was desired. This attitude, then, belonged to the mentality that made and guided the culture of the seventeenth-century baroque: it is the aspect we have to try to explain. In my opinion, the texts of Gracián, Carballo, and many others do not admit any other interpretation: it was considered a procedure to focus attention better and to make a work or spectacle leave a deeper impression on the spirit of its receivers. Many manifestations of seventeenth-century social life required obscurity, which reinforced the state of suspension and translated into difficulty, including a doctrine that captivated and left a permanent impression, a work of art that introduced the public in its world and moved this public, a political power that astonished and imposed itself.

On other occasions I have tried to show that emblematic literature and all the other genres related to it and utilized for religious, political, and educational ends or simply for pleasure corresponded to this characteristic of baroque culture. As stated by Saavedra Fajardo, the most illustrious writer of *empresas* in the Spanish language, the final goal of this mode of writing, which necessarily led to a high degree of difficulty, resided in that "the reader retain pleasure in understanding them in themselves."[68] As if pronouncing a precept to be rigorously applied, Lope said that "an enigma is an obscure allegory that is understood with difficulty."[69] Carballo asked that literature "be very difficult to understand."[70] And not only literature: all art was an esoteric and difficult language that was read and understood beneath the apparent signification of the symbols utilized.[71] Some time ago, I wrote that the public ceremonies and fiestas, arches, carriages, and other public manifestations of an artistic nature had the symbolic value of genuine emblems or hieroglyphics, which were utilized to take advantage of the educational and guiding role attributed to difficult obscurity.[72] León Pinelo tells us about funeral catafalques or triumphal arches decorated with hieroglyphics and carried through the streets.[73]

Within the realm of art, one must refer to a type of work that was very widespread in the seventeenth century, although its origin dates much further back to Plato's considerations of perspective. We are referring to the so-called anamorphoses, whereby with a play of reshaping and distortions performed upon the object one strives to make that object, at first glance, disappear or, better, to make it approximate in appearance or resemble a very different thing; then when the eye of the spectator contemplates it from a determinate point of view, it reestablishes itself in the sensible form of its own reality. These plays of perspective were always used, but in the Renaissance they began to become more widespread because of the conjunction of a greater geometric knowledge and an intense curiosity about magical effects; they become very frequent in the baroque, being an exercise of virtuosity in the geometric science of perspective that was much enjoyed in the seventeenth century.

Thus we must consider anamorphosis as one of the most interesting and complicated manifestations of the precepts of difficulty. It was the application of a calculated knowledge that, although it partook of natural magic (inasmuch as it was a manipulation of natural expedients that were difficult to grasp), was at the same time a rigorously geometric knowledge. Therefore it came to constitute an area where the baroque and rationalism approximated one another. G. Rodis-Lewis studied this aspect of the theme, informing us that it was a genre cultivated by engineers, mathematicians, and philosophers of the Cartesian school.[74] Baltrusaitis has recently studied the theme of anamorphosis in an intensely interesting book, and its conclusions coincide with and support our formulations.[75] He has pointed out the anamorphic works in France of Salomon de Caus, J.-F. Niceron, and Maignan. Niceron published a work under the title *Thaumaturgus opticus* (Paris, 1646). Maignan was a secondary figure of Cartesianism, whose name is of interest because that intellectual current entered Spain principally by virtue of this author.[76] The origin of the word *engineer* has been attributed to Salomon de Caus, although I have cited facts elsewhere demonstrating that at that point the word had been known in Spain for some time.[77]

The procedures of anamorphosis were applied — according to inferences from the extensive repertory of examples collected by Baltrusaitis — to the representation of every sort of theme: biblical, hagiographic, political, heroic, or those of natural phenomena. The high point of anamorphosis was apparently situated between 1630 and 1650; Paris became the center for the study and dissemination of this genre of optical combinations, which was cultivated among personages close to the court.[78] That helps to demonstrate the connection that Paris had with baroque culture, contrary to what has so often been asserted. With anamorphosis, taste for the difficult took a new and outlandish turn, entirely in accord with the mentality of the epoch.

In the baroque world view, various factors entered into play: an interest in rationally manipulating expedients for channeling and guiding the public's movements; with this in view, a utilization of the effectiveness possessed by the technique of suspension; the tendency to extremeness; and the use of the pedagogical force offered by the "challenge" of difficulty. Above all, however, the art and politics of the baroque were a *decipherment*, which evidently presupposed an interplay with difficulty and obscurity. Thus arose the role that in the baroque must inevitably be attributed to the series of elements entering into play — that is, the group of factors organized around the concept of artifice.

Chapter 9
The Social Role of Artifice

The taste for the difficult occupied a preferential position in baroque mentality; in judging any work whatsoever, it gave a prominent role to the qualities of novelty, rarity, outlandishness, the breaking of norms. All these traits (as present in the conceptions of seventeenth-century individuals) were connected in that they each derived from a longing for novelty, just as this longing in turn originated from the tendency to seek out difficulty.

"Whatever amazes brings novelty" is a sentence we read in Céspedes y Meneses, but we could find similar statements in any other writer of the baroque century.[1] In the eyes of these writers, there is a natural, innate inclination that pulls the human being toward the new. Lope's Dorotea, in the work that bears her name, relates that "difference causes novelty and awakens desire," which for Tirso was "the property of all that is new, for our changing inclination ordinarily holds the newly arrived in higher esteem."[2] The tendency to consider whatever one wants to encourage as a product of nature clearly shows itself on this point: "The desire to know about new, strange, amazing and diverse things, and inquire into their causes, is natural in everyone."[3] The chain of adjectives linked in this text is typically baroque. Examination of all sorts of things (since mannerism, although it becomes accentuated in the baroque) used words such as *new*, *original*, *capricious*, *rare*, and *outlandish*, and they all represented a highly positive judgment; this is not to be seen as a manifestation of Spanish taste but as a phenomenon common to broad sectors of the European seventeenth century, as Wölfflin already showed.[4] In an extensive study regarding the meaning of history principally in the Spanish Renaissance, I examined at length the role played by this interest in novelty. There I pursued the formation of a topos that the seventeenth century inherited and strengthened as a condensed formula for expressing one of its deepest tendencies: "Everything new gives pleasure."[5] To the numerous references given there about this aphorism's presence in texts of the sixteenth and seventeenth centuries, I can add still another, this one taken from one of María de Zayas y Sotomayor's novels: "As the common people say, the new gives pleasure";[6] a passage from Agustín de Rojas confirms its trivialization in the form of a proverb.[7]

The role of novelty underwent profound change from the sixteenth to the seventeenth century. During the Renaissance century it gave impetus to social life in numerous aspects, and although it was only found in certain strata of the urban population (never among the rural population, nor in many sectors of the cities), it came to be a vital principle that stimulated the ascendant social groups. When monarchical absolutism firmly closed its ranks in defense of a privileged social order, it saw itself threatened with collapse by the changes coming in the wake of the sixteenth-century spirit and its economic and demographic boom. That provoked, in this second phase we are indicating, a serious distrust vis-à-vis novelty. It was excluded from all manifestations of collective life that might affect the fundamental order and was confined to those areas judged to be innocuous or at least of no consequence for the political order. That practice came to be adopted by all regimes of force occupying the government of peoples (as we have occasion to see even nowadays). Perhaps one has to view this reaction as indicative of the state of anxiety in the face of change that threatened to break up the traditionally organized social life, an anxiety awakened at the time by a general feeling of crisis. A rejection of the new that was threatening everywhere emerged in those who feared possible damage to their privileged positions. "Everything is calm," Pellicer warned his readers (8 March 1644), "and time is very much pregnant with novelties that they say will soon be born."[8] In his gazetteer tone, Barrionuevo translated what we have just described with the following words: "Monstrosities are seen and heard every day in Madrid";[9] at the very least, his news sheets on the whole indicated overwhelming confusion, both when it occurred and when it was corrected.

Thus the seventeenth-century individual, and particularly the Spaniard, did not expect anything favorable (I refer, of course, to those integrated in the system). Consequently, for them it was a matter of blocking the way to all novelty (in politics, religion, philosophy, and morality) precisely because of the fact that, even though undesirable, it appeared by virtue of the disorder of the times. "In politics there are novelties every day," commented a letter of the Jesuits (2 March 1638),[10] and Barrionuevo informed his public that "in this place we see new things every day" (19 August 1654).[11] Therefore, this was what the sector of those integrated into the system, who mounted the "propaganda campaign" in its baroque rendition, wanted to avoid or at least to neutralize in terms of its possibilities for revolt. But since, after the Renaissance experience and after hearing how much had been said in its favor for more than a century, the public spirit would not so easily reject the attraction of the new, free reign was now given to those areas where the accompanying threat to the order would not be serious or would turn out to be so remote that there would be no problem in stifling its excesses in time. Art, literature, and poetry continued exalting novelty, and certain social groups' taste for the new could be siphoned off by these activities. (However, if a ten-line ballad or any minimal stanza contained a suspicious allusion to the dealings of any minister, it would suffice for the author to be jailed without charge for years; such was the case of Adam de la Parra.)[12]

The baroque proclaimed, cultivated and exalted novelty. It recommended it: "According to this it will be good for us to follow another path abounding with novelty, so that benefit might be gained."[13] There was the desire to maintain it as a universally valid principle: "everything in this world is novelty," said Fernández de Ribera, although in universalizing it in such a way he obviously made it lose all of its virulence.[14] Baroque declarations in favor of the new were no less fervent than those of the sixteenth century, but to the extent that they were permitted they were be limited to poetic game playing, literary outlandishness, and trick effects machinated on stage, which evoked wonder in and suspended the depressed psyche of the seventeenth-century urban inhabitant. Nothing of novelty, let me repeat, so far as the sociopolitical order was concerned; but, on the other hand, there was an outspoken utilization of the new in secondary, external aspects (and, with respect to the order of power, nontransferable ones) that allowed for a curious interplay: the appearance of a daring novelty that enveloped the creation on the outside concealed a doctrine — here the word *ideology* would not be out of hand — that was inflexibly anti-innovation, conservative. A force reconstitutive of traditional interests was smuggled in by means of the novelty that one was attracted to for enjoyment.

Because of this, the baroque writer was very interested in novelty. It was a way to provide for the smooth ingestion ("pleasing," according to the norm of the sempiternal Horacian precept) of an entire system reinforcing the monarchical-seignorial tradition. Because in the baroque the pedagogy and all modes of directing human behavior endeavored to reach the individuals' extrarational levels and from there to move them and integrate them into the supporting groups of the prevailing social system, one of the most important means was attracting attention through the *suspense* of novelty whenever no risk was involved. The new pleased, the never-before-seen attracted, the invention making its debut fascinated; but this would only be permitted in apparent challenges that would not affect the underlying foundation of beliefs holding up the absolute monarchy's social framework. On the contrary, in making use of these novelties as a vehicle, the persuasive propaganda in favor of the established order was more easily introduced.

We already know that the baroque placed little trust in strictly intellectual arguments, in Scholastic thought shaped by traditional society, which criticism had eroded in many spheres during the preceding three hundred years. It preferred to appeal to extrarational means that moved the will. And novelty is a very forceful means: it charms one's taste and will into following it. "Novelty draws one's eyes and they, one's will," said Céspedes y Meneses.[15]

Thus preceptists and practitioners of different arts were in agreement about seeking novelty in one fashion or another because without obtaining it nothing would be successful (with the understanding that it was a question of arts that were in themselves inoffensive). Carballo requested that the poet make an effort to invent "rarer and more amazing" things.[16] When an author's work was praised, as Setanti did with that of J. Merola, its positive quality resulted from "its rarer invention,"[17] and the author himself very inappropriately boasted about it. A theoretician of history, Jerónimo de San José, would admiringly inform us about "the grace of innovation which is rarity."[18] Even in those arts characterized not by verisimilitude but by truth (above all, history), where the truth was always demanded of whoever practiced it, we now find that this advice to follow truth was curiously nuanced. In effect, Cabrera de Córdoba clearly recommended the baroque writer's subordination to the demands of the new: "The truth must be about what is noteworthy, to teach and delight because of its singularity and strangeness."[19]

This path toward captivating the will, toward making use of the new, thus gave force to the unique, to what remained outside of the norm. It related to the tendency toward a greater freedom from precepts, a freedom characterizing authors and the public in baroque society; at the same time, this society saw the reinforcement of the absolute power with which the prince could impose his mandate on collective life. All the authority withdrawn from Aristotle was given in manifold to the absolute king.[20] When Lope proposed a disavowal of the laws of classical poetics (never mind that he, without saying so, came to set up another system of precepts), it was to assure that whatever the king wanted was law and that if everybody could make the literary norm an object of personal judgment and rejection, on the other hand nobody had the capacity to examine critically the royal mandate before which nothing was possible but blind obedience.

To the extent that the area of novelty, of the extraordinary and the strange, was so severely curtailed, thereby restricting the area accessible to personal examination and taste, and to the extent that in other spheres personal evaluation remained subject to an indisputable authority, the free energies accompanying the desire for the new were unleashed more forcefully in the realm allotted to them. Whatever this culture had of a gesticulating or capricious quality emerged from this interplay of harsh constriction and permitted expansion, depending on which realm one was dealing with, a duality that we find at the base of baroque society. This led to the out-of-the-ordinary and free enthusiasm for outlandishness, a final and unhealthy manifestation in the exercise of freedom that, for the individuals of the seventeenth century, remained possible in one sector of existence.

Even those who would seek other paths, for reasons of personal preference, displayed a tendency to give themselves over to outlandish novelties. The seventeenth-century writer had to recognize (as López de Vega noted, although not without a certain personal ill humor) that "given the general corruption of our century the realm of the outlandish still retains a greater appearance of virtue than blame."[21] Therefore, he confessed that "being determined to introduce something new into the light of the public, I made a unique selection of paradoxes." To secure a "good sale" [*buen despacho*] for what was printed, it was necessary "to attract the readers' attention with something outlandish."[22] But there were those who not only recognized that taste for the outlandish was widespread in the public, but also admitted it in the system of precepts, although with certain requisites. In effect, one of the defenders of the new theater (that is, of baroque theater proper), González de Salas, admitted the outlandish in extraordinary cases as a manifestation of superior genius — "the novelty, the outlandishness and even the temerity that the genius can be permitted."[23]

This state of mind invaded all of life. And passion for the outlandish, where it was permitted, developed monstrously among peoples who found their ways blocked to a rational criticism of social life. Ortega, in his essay on Velázquez, made an inventory of outlandish events taking place in the Spanish seventeenth century; they were attested to in the epoch, and we have no recourse but to accept them. But in commenting on these pages from Ortega, Mandrou made it clear that, once again, it was not an exclusively Spanish event. The outlandishness, the frenzy that went from inconceivable crime to the most nonsensical tales of miracles, was common to all of Europe in the seventeenth century, whose first newspapers (such as the *Mercure français* or, certainly, the Spanish *avisos*) included the most outlandish or unlikely stories about apparitions, violence, death, miracles, all corresponding to a mental atmosphere that was the same everywhere.[24] Beyond its basic accounts of the continuous construction of convents and churches, enthronements of religious images, and processions, León Pinelo's *Anales de Madrid* are full of stories about martyrdoms, miracles, and absurd events.[25] "In this monarchy prodigious things have happened," said Almansa, and he was referring to some genuine hallucinations.[26] "Miracles and rare prodigies have recently been seen," recounted Pellicer (7 May 1641).[27] "One sees portents and what are almost miracles," Barrionuevo said (12 September 1654), but all in all he was more prudent in introducing the adverb *almost*.[28] As in Spain, people all over Europe were inclined to hope for magical effects, for extranatural events to bring them hope or confirm its loss.[29] A Jesuit told how people felt themselves drawn to hope for magical novelties by the appearance of some "reddish clouds" (perhaps an aurora borealis). In telling his correspondent about it, he included this explanation: "The house mathematicians have not made it out to be anything new, nor do they reveal that there is any particular mystery"; but he, who must not have been very knowledgeable in the natural sciences, added as his personal impression: "It could be more than it seems."[30] The renewal of magical forms of thought, fomented by the most characteristic instruments of baroque culture, was universal at this time. It was something that L. Febvre had already seen beginning, in a rising tide, at the end of the sixteenth century, but in the seventeenth century it acquired an unusual vitality and diffusion, giving rise to the transformation of novelty into an unimaginable outlandishness when novelty found the channels for reasonable development cut off.[31]

Of course, despite all the mechanisms of control that were used to contain this eagerness for new, surprising and extranatural effects, such an exceptional state of mind was created that it gave rise to the unrestrained development and substantial alteration of a phenomenon that in the Renaissance had been encouraged by the impulse to dominate nature: magic.[32] I am referring now to the new transformation of magic or sorcery into witchcraft and to the enormous development of witchcraft in all of Europe beginning with the final years of the sixteenth century.[33] An increase in witchcraft trials occurred in France,[34] in Italy,[35] and in England, where Trevor-Roper has spoken of a witchcraft epidemic.[36] Its presence in Spain is well known, above all after the studies of Caro Baroja.[37] In Spain, the auto-da-fé of the witches of Logroño made history and incited the indignant protest and severe rational criticism of Pedro de Valencia.[38] In 1632, León Pinelo told about a burning of thirty-two condemned by the Inquisition and seven backsliders [relajados].[39] In France, phenomena that were equal in number or even more numerous are not as well known; nevertheless, it is possible to cite them, and it is an aspect that should not be overlooked in speaking of France in the early modern centuries. F. Buisson has given some striking references in this respect.[40]

Despite the mechanisms of repression that were set in place (sentences from Inquisition tribunals, deaths from torture, civil executions by royal order and without a trial), it was unavoidable that the passion for the unknown, for the new and extraordinary, and, finally, for its corruption in the outlandish would go to such extremes, already beyond the permitted limits — limits that would also be broken by mystics and heretics on the one hand (recall Miguel de Molinos) and those rebelling against political authority on the other (the movements of revolt and of separatism in Andalusia). The case of Quevedo is exemplary: not being satisfied with his "rarities," with his novelties or freedoms on the literary plane, he ultimately tried to use his freedom to criticize the government. This attempt was already a step outside of what was permitted, and as a consequence he had to undergo a long imprisonment.[41]

There is a seemingly insignificant example that because of its very limitations renders an eloquent account of the changes of sensibility occurring in seventeenth-century society (changes given impetus and encouraged by the rulers of baroque culture; changes that expressed the new direction taken by taste for the "rare invention"). Since the end of the sixteenth century, many passages in Spanish literature had offered a judgment on Bosch. This judgment was generally positive and refined, but in the sixteenth century his work had been viewed as a complex of symbols that allowed one to read the world of nature (symbols that for the most part continued to prevail in the following century; for example, Suárez de Figueroa's mention of hay, which was the protagonist of one of Bosch's paintings).[42] But in this later time period, what excited enthusiasm were the strange elements. Although a French neoclassical writer such as Félibien viewed Bosch as the author of "figures boufonnes,"[43] in the baroque epoch he was viewed in a very different way: José de Sigüenza admired him as a "strange man in painting";[44] Quevedo was interested in him because of his "strange postures";[45] Lope was enthused with him, holding him to be "a really excellent and inimitable painter";[46] and Jusepe Martínez (who deemed it necessary to write an entire book on such an original painter) related his ingenuities to those of Quevedo's *Sueños*.[47]

At times novelty, which was liable to outlandishness by dint of being pursued by the seventeenth-century public, turned into the most banal caprice. To that would correspond the introduction of exotic and ephemeral vogues in men's and women's clothes and in their personal appearance: beards and long hair for men, uncommonly high shoes for women, and many other novelties in their dress — even extending to the capricious taste for lap dogs, which around that time were introduced in feminine circles, something criticized by Francisco Santos.[48]

This widespread expansion of the expedients that baroque culture utilized to reach vast strata of the population, including the lower social levels, is further confirmation of the mass urban character (appealing to the numerous common people of the city was normal) in the culture's products. Jerónimo de San José's reference is very clear: "It is something to be considered that the strangeness or outlandishness of style that used to be of interest to odd persons and scholars, is today not as interesting for them as for the multitude at large and the ignorant common people."[49] Let us not forget that in reference to the theater, Racine would say, without excluding his own exquisite tragedies, that it was written for the "vile populace."[50] There is no doubt that utilization of such expedients would have to be found in close congruence with the conditions of baroque society.

Interest in novelty translated into genuine — although superficial — enthusiasm for invention. The baroque individual, who always preferred nature transformed by art to simple nature, would agree with the words Martínez de Mata used to close his *Discurso VIII*: "Nature never produces anything for the benefit of man that is not in need of his art and ingenuity to perfect it."[51] Martínez de Mata was an economist who exalted manufacturing and foresaw an age when industry would predominate, something that almost none of the Spanish writers imagined. But whether giving the expression a serious or banal meaning, all of them were nevertheless inclined to prefer the products of art or technique — that is, the work of human invention. The appearance of a new product of human invention enthused many people, and when nothing better could be obtained, this enthusiasm was placed in the banal invention of, for example, a new stanza form. León Pinelo tells us that in public fiestas, other "inventions" were seen together with comedias, costumes, and dances.[52]

Clearly the heritage of the Renaissance was not dead, although it was diverted and subjected to an energetic control; thus the conception of nature retained a basis of confused mechanistic inspiration (not incompatible with the continued existence of a strong magical conception). This underlay the general satisfaction awakened in active groups of seventeenth-century culture by the appearance of any mechanical invention showing itself to be a copy of the natural world, as recreated by the human being. The presence of this mental attitude would be much stronger in France and Italy because the controls opposed to the rational development of knowledge, while existing, did not succeed there in imposing themselves with indisputable superiority. In Spain the contrary happened, although the continuation of the spirit revealed by Huarte de San Juan[53] was not completely interrupted, as we can see in Gallego de la Serna[54] and others who had started preparing the way for the reception of modern science in Spain in the second half of the seventeenth century.[55] At the least, there was admiration for what was done outside of Spain. With respect to an innovation he had heard about, which the English had introduced on their ships to make them unassailable, Barrionuevo commented that "human ingenuity can do anything."[56] But while, in Italy, Torricelli invented the barometer; in France, Pascal established the principles of the hydraulic press; and in England, the epoch of mechanization was set underway: in Spain, José de Zaragoza — who could have been a valuable man of science — had to limit himself to using his ingenuity for the construction of some mechanical toys that, placed in a luxurious box, would serve as a gift offered to entertain the child king Charles II on the occasion of his birthday.[57]

The diffusion of the word *engineer* (which I have dealt with on another occasion)[58] continued in the decades of the baroque. The myth of Vulcan was interpreted in terms of this new concept, becoming the "greatest engineer of the gods," according to B. de Vitoria.[59] Calderón expressed the value of possessing "artifice" (to which was given the name of "science") in the myth of Prometheus: "that whoever gives light to people / is the one giving them science / . . . that whoever gives sciences, gives / voice to the dust and light to the soul" (*La estatua de Prometeo*).

The clock represented that mechanical ingenuity admired by the baroque human being and also symbolized inexorable time, thereby uniting two decisive aspects of baroque culture. Calderón made the clock the most complete image of mechanization (in *De un castigo tres venganzas*), and Bances Candamo admired it for the same reason.[60] Other examples where technical inventions were valorized occurred in relation to printing, the mariner's compass, and artillery.[61] Nevertheless, we have already shown how the situation of Spanish society, with the economic interests of the new classes and their new industrial activities being choked off, was accompanied by a redirection of the innovative capacity; simultaneously, the taste for human artifice was limited to banal manifestations of a capricious curiosity. I don't know if the word *tracista* [designer], which in the epoch became equivalent to "engineer," translates this minimum degree of technical development.

In any case, the Spanish mentality of the baroque epoch had the general quality of deriving satisfaction from all artifice, from whatever ingenious invention of human art that appeared, in terms of the novelty it offered. What Céspedes y Meneses said about his able character could be said about anybody capable of such achievement: "His skill and artifice suspended them and evoked their wonder," a sentence in which novelty and suspension once again appear intertwined.[62] The same author gives us a curious example of how a construction of this type amazed: "Thus this awesome and secret artifice was endowed with such rare ingenuity, with so much subtlety, that no one without particular knowledge of it would fathom its working; it was a scheme from a German engineer."[63]

One of the reasons for the theater being a seventeenth-century spectacle was its artifice, and as such it was specifically adaptable to the baroque's objectives. References to theatrical activities that could be cited in this connection are practically inexhaustible in the collections of writings that circulated during the epoch. As much in the *Cartas de jesuitas* as in the sheets of the *avisos*, one can find mention of comedies staged to celebrate all sorts of events, because the theater offered multiple possibilities for obtaining the expected effects in accordance with the varied nature of the events. Its role in seventeenth-century society could not be any greater. Almansa provides us with a curious fact: among the numerous properties that Rodrigo Calderón possessed at the moment of his fall (titles, public offices, honors, jewels, and money) it was recorded that "he had a lifetime theater box in Valladolid's houses of comedy, and another in the open-air theater of the Cruz de Madrid."[64] Premieres were announced, texts were sent back and forth; the "mounting" of a comedy (as it was then called) always awaited great fiestas, much talked about events (Carnival, Shrovetide, the Night of St. John, Corpus Christi, visits of great personages to Madrid), the days for celebrating saints and birthdays of royal persons, or other days of special significance. "Two great comedies of majestic ostentation" were given for the king's birthday (1622); in hopes that the queen would rapidly recover her health, a comedy about the fable of Perseus was presented (1653) in the Buen Retiro.[65] Barrionuevo tells us (24 November 1655) that the marquis de Heliche had twenty-two new comedies prepared and divided them among eight companies to celebrate when the queen gave birth.[66] "They are already putting the stage machinery in order for a grand and festive comedy that is ordered for when the Queen gives birth," announced the same Barrionuevo on a later occasion (the reader was informed about this one on 28 November 1657) for the arrival of the Prince of Wales, the duchess of Mantua, and the duchess of la Chevreuse.[67] The Jesuits spoke about comedias in the palace, in the Buen Retiro, and about the new theaters being constructed. Comedies were also performed in the houses of seigniors; according to a Jesuit, the cardinal of Borja offered one in his palace, and León Pinelo mentioned one that was performed in honor of an aristocrat's anniversary. They were also put on in convents and schools, such as the comedies that the Jesuits organized in the fiestas commemorating the founding of the Society, which the king attended.[68]

Every year during the days of Shrovetide there was much theatrical activity, as in the year 1632 when León Pinelo related that there were three comedies repeated every day at the palace.[69] The Night of St. John was another a propitious occasion: in reference to 1640, the writer tells us that he himself prepared "a comedy presented on the large pond, with machines, stage props, canopies and lights, all resting on boats."[70] Plays were also put on in Madrid, Barcelona, Valencia, Bilbao, and Seville.[71] There was ultimately no more visible or influential way to take a greater part in baroque social principles than in theatrical representations. There was no better way to emphasize the grandeur, the splendor, and the power, and this was already an expedient of effective psychological action on the multitude. Therefore, this effect was the essential aim of the use of the theater, and the fact that on consecutive days the people were allowed to enter royal locations to attend comedies did not correspond to democratic inclinations of the Austrian monarchs. In a way, the performances were done for the purpose of their attending. When a Jesuit tells us that "stage machinations and comedies of the Retiro communicated freely with the people because of the generosity of His Majesty," it indicates the major objective of this animated stage life.[72]

Díez Borques has studied the structure of theater locales — that is, of the permanent theaters at the beginning of the seventeenth century — with their highly differentiated range of tickets and prices. The mass character of the spectacle becomes obvious in his study; in considering how inexpensive tickets were for people of the lower class, while those destined for the elite public remained high, he wrote: "Keeping this price was undoubtedly a concern so as to make the theater accessible for the great majority, in accordance with its function as a mass spectacle destined not for reflection but to disseminate ideals that were intended as collective ideals."[73] Barrionuevo offered a curious news item: "Every day the comedy has been put on it has earned one thousand ducats...and every day the comedy was put on in the Retiro the king earned five thousand reales, the coliseum or pantheon being filled by five o'clock in the morning."[74] In this way it helped allay the expenses, sometimes nonsensical, entailed by the stage set, expenses whose total corresponded to the dominant principle of ostentation typical of baroque society: as one approached majesty, it was necessary to raise expenses to totals worthy of all the people's admiration. Barrionuevo (23 January 1655) recounted that the comedy under preparation in the theater for the king would cost fifty thousand ducats; two years later (23 January 1657) he wrote about another comedy in La Zarzuela, at a cost of sixteen thousand ducats. On 26 December 1657, he said that the grand comedy of the Retiro, prepared in honor of the queen's giving birth (which in his news sheets had been announced for months), would cost, with all its complements, 600,000 ducats. The political plan behind the theater campaign counted on the fact that these things would be said, without a doubt; but in the midst of baroque society such a plan also had to assume that some, like Barrionuevo himself, would make further comments: "All this comes about very purposely designed for the present misfortunes and calamities."[75]

Probably one must consider that this unrestrained activity in stage representations (the commentators never spoke of their literary value but of their magnitude, cost, the almost insuperable difficulty of setting them up, and so on) was not developed to satisfy the tastes or personal frivolities of kings and rulers, but to stun and attract the public mass. Barrionuevo again tells us that because of some serious political difficulties to be overcome, "there has been put together a grand comedy of San Gaetano, using all of the Court's best ingenuities, with trick stage machinery and devices." Given the circumstances, and full of suspicion about what might be said in such a comedy, the Inquisition requested it for review and retained it until finally, because of the queen's support, it was staged in an amended version. Hence on this occasion the gazetteer commented: "the assembly of the people is a day of judgment and there were so many people who went to see it at the prince's open-air theater that as they left one man was caught underfoot and smothered to death."[76] In response to the announcement about a comedy's public opening in the Retiro, so that everybody might see it in the following days, Barrionuevo predicted that the "uproar of people going will be infinite."[77]

Aubrun has written something in this regard that we must take into account. According to him, "when someone from Madrid crosses the threshold of an open-air theater, he or she loses his or her qualification in society as a merchant, servant, son or daughter, adventuress or picaro; they are transformed into a spectator with the same title as their neighbors and along with them share the same demands, the same mentality, the same *morality* of the theater."[78] One must add, however, that such procedure would serve precisely to ensure that on leaving each one would feel more in one's own social status, judging oneself to be in agreement with nature and thus able to function with confidence. We might also ask whether this "estatist promiscuity" elevated the laborer or downgraded royalty, as we might assume by some of the crude diversions to which royalty devoted itself.[79]

One of the things having the greatest influence on this development of dramatic art (unprecedented perhaps since ancient Greece) is the fact that — apart from other motivations — the stage setting of theater allowed recourse to the use of surprising artifices. At the end of the baroque's experience of theater, Bances Candamo admired the stage poem or comedy for its "manufacture," its "interior artifice," for the "ingenious machine of its contexture":[80] the theater satisfied the quotidian and banal taste for invention. In a short and packed study, Alewyn showed how the stage representation of baroque theater was based on the broadest utilization of sensible expedients: "the arts of the mimic, the painter, the musician, the set designer, and the machinist are joined here to assault all the senses simultaneously, so that the public cannot escape." The development of means of lighting, allowing stage representations to abandon the day for the night, added the effects of illumination to the repertory of theatrical representation, thereby multiplying its possibilities.[81]

Here occurred a seeming historical contradiction of the baroque. In one aspect there was an apparent instance of medievalization, even in the theater that had the pretense of being one of its most modern creations (and baroque individuals presumed themselves to be modern). Like the theater of the Middle Ages, the baroque theater again incorporated the upper parts of the scenic space; it unfolded in a vertical sense, trying to take over that part of the world that is nearest to heaven. But although this continued to give them cause to exalt their feelings about the otherworld, the individuals of the seventeenth century used such means to demonstrate a domination of nature whereby these effects of wonder are achieved. The technical difficulty of artifice was alien to the medieval human being, whereas its appreciation was decisive for the baroque: whoever manifested this type of domination succeeded in persuading, attracting with regard to what was proposed. By virtue of technical resources, such as the more skillful and calculated use of pulleys, the seventeenth-century individual was successful in having the public see actors representing divine persons, saints, the kings and their allegories, and superior beings who colonized the upper spaces;[82] in the eyes of the public, this artifice produced a sensible verification of their superiority.

The lighting effects were of great importance for achieving surprise and collective reaction, that is, for moving the public extrarationally, which was their purpose; without them, the other expedients could not have been manipulated, at least could not have attained the force they were acknowledged to have. The light itself, with all of its changes, frequently performed the action. Barrionuevo commented on a comedy using stage machinery that was presented before the king and queen: "The apparatus is superb, even the lights are exquisite."[83] The light medium expressed what the artist predominantly made use of in the epoch.

The successes of artifice were probably greater in this realm (correlative to the development of the science of optics, despite the great distance separating the artist or stage designer from a knowledge of optics). The effects that one can attain with light when it is ingeniously manipulated were taken into account, including its entire technical basis, in the theater. A similar development took place in painting, and — metaphorically at least — in poetry; I would even add, allegorically, in politics, around the image of majesty. Caravaggio praised Jusepe Martínez for being a "great naturalist" (that is, for dominating the effects of nature); in his paintings "the figures received a fierce light of great rigor."[84] With a light such as this in so many of the epoch's paintings, in many theatrical representations that were put together, the illuminated object came to be a pretext or support for the resplendent and dazzling effects of illumination itself.

Lighting, along with so many other expedients acting upon the senses, activated the changing and wondrous play of effects in the theater and, to a different extent, in painting and the other figurative arts, whose relation with baroque theater has been pointed out by Tintelnot.[85] The idea of a similar play of effects combined with the basic aspects of the baroque world view. In a changing, varied, reformable world, the taste for changes and for the metamorphoses was satisfied in stage effects and the enthusiastic interest in artifice by recourse to stage machinations.[86] There was a genuine development of stage engineering; admiration for it is reflected in many pamphlets dedicated to describing the dazzling effects of certain representations that became famous.

From the first decades of the seventeenth century, the English public sought ingenious productions in the theater. The role of the *metteur en scène* took on great importance, as demonstrated by the preserving of an infinity of drawings and projects, and the important artist Inigo Jones made drawings for sets during the second period of Shakespeare. There were Shakespearean works, such as *The Winter's Tale*, in which surprising set effects played a great role from the time of its first presentations: when the protagonist, turned into a statue, suddenly appears before the spectators, she begins to come to life, impressing them with the "trick theatricality" of the stage director.[87] In Spain it has been observed that Lope was against the use of artifice in the theater;[88] but, despite some irony on his part, it is certain that *artifice*, *inventions*, *appearances*, or (according to the new word that began to be used at that time) *tramoyas* [stage machinery] were acquiring an always greater portion of the stage and having greater importance in the presentations.[89] There is information about the great engineering apparatus used in staging Lope's *La selva sin amor* and also about the performance of the great "machinist" Cosme Loti in the theater established on the royal site of the Buen Retiro.[90] Let us observe that references to stage effects in the margins of manuscripts began to multiply and become more complicated. A large study now underway will undoubtedly reveal the great wealth of set inventions in the Spanish theater of the seventeenth century.[91] Certainly, from Cervantes's *La*

Numancia to so many works of Calderón (citing no more than the chronological extremes of interest), stage machinations reached a great sophistication, with instances of mechanical apparitions, strange illuminations, rocks that opened up, palaces that were contemplated in vast overviews, transformed landscapes, meteors, and serious accidents of nature that were imitated to the astonishment of the spectator — not to mention the ships, horses, and wild animals that move on stage, all showing the complex development of theatrical techniques. Blanco White referred to his still having seen an ancient comedy on a religious subject in exaltation of the Franciscan order; it was so bizarre and full of nonsensical effects machinated by the stage machines that the Inquisition prohibited it by 1804. It was a work by Luis Belmonte, *El diablo predicador*, which was presented in Madrid in 1623 before Philip IV.[92] To all this must be added the means used for the realization of allegory and ideas (which are discussed in the appendix to this work).[93]

But for us it is of interest to confirm the consciousness of the role of technical artifice in the theater, of its importance and extent, which gave rise to the linguistic phenomenon that the words *comedia* and *tramoya* were frequently used together; in many cases, the second term served to express the idea of the first. We have read the reference to *tramoyas* and *comedias* in a passage from León Pinelo and in the paragraph cited earlier from one of the Jesuit letters. In taking note of a comedy in the Teatro Nuevo del Retiro, another Jesuit letter related: "They say that the stage machines [*tramoyas*] it has are huge." Both are references to the years 1639 and 1640. Around the same time, Pellicer also informed his public about comedies in the Retiro, commenting about them only that they had "many stage machines."[94] In later years, Barrionuevo included items that were roughly equivalent: "a comedy of stage machines" in the Retiro; days later he gives this curious reference yet again: "It is all stage machinery"; and still later: "It is said that the apparatus of the Retiro comedy is huge and exquisite." "The industry can do anything,"[95] he commented, as if it were a matter of some of those industrial inventions that were appearing, above all in England — those that were going to revolutionize the world and, along with it, its distribution of power. Let us notice that in the way of "literary" comments there is not even a word on this, nor on hundreds of other examples. The Jesuits and, later, Barrionuevo continued to give accounts of works having stage machinery and apparatuses.[96] Barrionuevo tells us that the marquis de Heliche, who was very familiar with the subject, dealt with such machinery and was assisted by a person called "Bacho the 'tramoyista.'"[97] Let us recall that passage from Fontenelle where the philosopher explains to the marquise, his interlocutor, why Phaeton in the theater rises to the upper reaches of the stage set. If a scholastic, he says, were to treat the matter, he would maintain that it is because the end of occupying the upper regions of space belongs to Phaeton's essence; but a modern, Cartesian physicist knows that if Phaeton is ascending on stage it is because behind the backdrop some weights are falling. Thus although the marquis de Heliche was not a profound Cartesian physicist but only a baroque engineer of stage machinery, he was acquainted with the secret and knew how to make clouds, horses, or saints ascend and descend: Barrionuevo said that to prepare his work "the Marquis de Heliche summoned Diego Felipe de Quadros, a lead contractor, and requested 300 hundredweights for the machinery's counterweight."[98] Here is one more instance of the "rationalization" of the baroque mind.

People of their time, the Jesuits also took an interest in this type of theatrical representation, wherein the motives of mechanically producing wonder predominated. They tell us that for the fiestas of the Centennial, several suggestive comedies and dialogues were put on in Madrid and Guipúzcoa. We have information about a work written by Valentín de Céspedes with the title — very indicative of an inflated confidence for the purposes of integration and propaganda — *Las glorias del mejor siglo*. What we know about others can be summarized in a commentary of this type: "It is an extraordinary thing because of the excellence of the stage and the multitude of the machines."[99] The Jesuits used mechanical devices to call forth strong emotions, as when, in the middle of a sermon, a curtain is unexpectedly drawn that reveals a dramatic religious scene in real life and makes those in the congregation break out in wailing and crying.[100] And there were still more examples, everywhere: according to Pellicer, the count of Lemos financed a fiesta in the parish of Santiago that had many apparatuses "of clouds and other machines."[101]

We have at our disposal several very interesting examples in France that incidentally serve to confirm the extent of baroque culture in the country. In a comedy about St. Ignatius's vocation, which was staged in a French Jesuit school, many fantastic elements were presented, among them apparitions and transformations, ascensions and falls, explosions, and other effects provoked by all kinds of devices. Nevertheless, in the play's text this annotation figures in at the end: "The saint appeared above the adjoining roof and was descending with the help of machines as if he descended from heaven."[102] We see that a similar machinery, a perfect piece of engineering, served to obtain apologetic effects. Of course the hundredweights of lead were destined to be used as counterweights or in similar mechanical effects, as we saw in the case of the aristocrat who directed the royal theater in Madrid. The first French journalist of the seventeenth century was T. Renaudot, who, like his contemporaries, felt a great passion for the theater. He recounted a presentation of *Orpheus* for the king and queen in which Victory was seen slowly descending from the sky in her chariot; while the spectators were wondrously asking how she could remain so long suspended in air, she sang verses in honor of the king's weapons and the queen's virtues.[103]

To accentuate these effects before a public of courtiers and even on occasion a broader public, the royal persons themselves or persons of high status participated in the theater — no longer for the enjoyment of confusing illusion and reality, but to attract to human grandeur all the possibilities of admiration and captivation at the disposal of artistic effects. These stage diversions of the grandees are well known. Rennert has related data about them, even regarding the participation of the king himself.[104] Deleyto mentioned theatrical representations, first in chambers in the royal palace designed for effect, then around 1630 in the palace of the Buen Retiro in rooms constructed, precisely for the interplay of machines and stage machinations, where such "tramoyistas" as the Italian Cosme Loti, the Valencian Candi, and others stood out.[105] Tintelnot collected similar information about Versailles, Vienna, and the Polish court.[106] The presentation of Bocángel's *El nuevo Olimpo* — one instance among many (and more could be drawn from the French court) — reveals their utilization to deify the grandees. In the play, which was performed to celebrate the queen's birthday, the infanta was given the role of the Mind of Jupiter presiding over the fiesta that was presented on stage, and all the other roles were distributed among persons of the nobility (the work was published in 1649). Let us recall that Tirso boasted that "the greatest powers of Castile" themselves liked to play the role of the principal character of *El vergonzoso en Palacio*.[107] All of this came to create, on the level of reality, the amazing effects that the theater's mechanical, verbal, and optical resources unfolded before the suspended attention of the spectator.[108]

With respect to an epoch that was about the same as the one here under consideration, it has been said that mercantilism was liable to contradictions within its own system: it accepted machines and the introduction in general of technical inventions even though in the economic realm this was opposed to its policy of creating possibilities of employment. In doing so it was responding to the taste for the new, typical of the Renaissance mentality that mercantilism had in part — like the individuals of the baroque — assimilated and that influenced its attitude toward manufacturing. "Put in other terms," added Heckscher, "mercantilism had opted for technical inventions, affected by its general conception of society."[109] In the middle of the seventeenth-century crisis in Spain, this opting for machines would not apply to the exploitation of agriculture, nor to the textile industry or others, despite the outcries of Sancho de Moncada, Martínez de Mata, Álvarez Ossorio, and others for factories. In some cases the very word *fábrica* [factory] attains, in the Castilian linguistic area, its modern meaning. But although modern manufacturing establishments were built on peninsular soil only by way of exception, and although according to Cellorigo "every kind of manufacture necessary to the kingdom" was lacking, the machinated effects set up for the plays of Calderón or of many others corresponded in part to a similar inspiration that was related to the general movement of society even though it was incapable of affirming its new ends. But neither did the activity of manufacturers gather momentum in France or Italy under the weight of a crisis we discussed in preceding chapters. It is explicable that a country with a vigorous baroque, inasmuch as this must develop under the pressure of conservative interests, would have a belated industrial takeoff; but it is also comprehensible that the baroque was not in itself what stifled the voices of those economists who, like Sancho de Moncada or Martínez de Mata, did not tire of demanding what we today call "industrial activity."

All the myths containing an exaltation of the creative or transforming capacity of the human being, which at bottom were linked to the preference for novelty and artifice, were extensively developed in the baroque. Such was the case of the myth of Prometheus, which has resonances in Gracián's work and, among other examples, gives us Calderón's comedy *La estatua de Prometeo*.[110] The myth of Circe must also be mentioned: Lope devoted one of his major poems to her, and frequent reference to her is found in many other works, even to the point of producing allusions of a humorous sort.[111] Besides some partial approximations, the figure of Faust emerged in the works of both Marlowe and Calderón.[112] The myth of Proteus, of Adam (this above all), and of others also awakened special interest during the epoch.[113]

Within this area of problems related to the transforming enthusiasm of the baroque, one would have to make a final reference to fiestas. To understand the importance of the theme, let us begin by recalling that Quevedo cried out against the fiesta and diversion, preaching to the prince a professional morality that Aranguren has called "the absolutism of concern" — that is, surrendering all of one's living hours to being preoccupied with and concerned about governing well.[114] Fiestas became so widespread in baroque society, especially in Spain, that they threatened to lead to the abandonment of the most urgent and indispensable public obligations.

Burckhardt drew attention to the role of fiestas in the Renaissance, and even in his writings we can verify that the Renaissance fiesta was a resplendent manifestation of the pleasure of life. Yet because the seventeenth century was in general a time of sadness and crisis, and although despite this the baroque retained an element of pleasure (the Jesuit conformists commented that the great amount of work demanded the rest of the pleasing fiesta), other aspects predominated in the baroque fiesta. Its show of wealth and artifice was proof of the grandeur and social power of whoever gave it and at the same time proof of his or her power over nature, whose course one is always striving to change in some way. Baroque fiestas were held for ostentation and for evoking admiration. They had to be celebrated in urban population centers and were prepared "so that everyone may view them," as the *Noticias de Madrid* observed on one occasion (referring to the fiestas that were organized in September 1627 to celebrate the cure of the king). The motives varied greatly. These social manifestations of the baroque fiesta were prominent in themselves, and together they served as a measure of the power of whoever made it possible.

To strive for certain effects — a momentary pleasure or surprise — those staging fiestas used abundant and costly means, expended a vast effort, made large-scale preparations, and set up a complicated apparatus. In wonder, the spectators asked themselves what would be beyond the power of whoever did all this to achieve what was apparently such a small thing, for a few instants of pleasure.[115] Regarding one of the imagined fiestas that he liked to recount, Tirso commented that "the fiesta had been interesting and ostentatious" and that its visual aspect was worthy of "the abundant wealth" of the person who gave it.[116] This type of commentary was probably the one that whoever organized such an ostentatious manifestation was trying to obtain. It happened this way even in religious fiestas: Almansa never emphasized their devotion but admired that "in them one has seen countless riches."[117] On the occasion of a procession that the Jesuits organized in honor of their new saints, the *Noticias de Madrid* told its readers that the Jesuits went "richly adorned with many jewels."[118] With respect to processions or the Way of the Cross, León Pinelo related that the multitude "has converted what is penitence into a fiesta." In this way they evoked greater admiration. During the stay of the Prince of Wales in Madrid, Pinelo said of the procession of Corpus Christi that it was "the greatest, most grave and ostentatious procession that has been seen in Madrid and in Castile." About the fiestas on the occasion of the choice of the king of Romanos (1637), he related that they were so extremely solemn that "in the Court they have never been equaled by any fiesta of their kind"; in them a construction was erected that "evoked amazement that in one month could be assembled in Madrid as much wood as contained in this grandiose building, which was made of nothing else."[119] And this took place in a country where for lack of wood, among other reasons, the navy found itself suicidally incapacitated.

In Spain and in all of Europe, the procession played a large role in the epoch's fiestas because it conjoined its mass character with the fact that it was an appropriate occasion for the display of grandeur. Whether for giving thanks, for supplication, or for making amends, the processions' devotion, unction or internal religious sentiment was never emphasized; rather, they were noted for their rich splendor, which was increased by the custom of erecting costly altars in the street to evoke people's wonder. In one case, León Pinelo tells us that there were "seven very rich and lavish altars," "there were fourteen altars of great riches, curiosity and ornamentation," "there were many rich altars, costly ornamentation in the streets and a great crowd":[120] both the divine power and the civil power that supported and honored it on earth remained sublimated.

Manifestations whose goals were to suspend and attract became general and frequent in the baroque. "These diversions are really necessary to be able to withstand so many adversities," Barrionuevo sarcastically commented.[121] The same Barrionuevo criticized the "thousand diversions in Madrid, whether at the highest or lowest levels" that one saw every day.[122] In the *Cartas de jesuitas* there are constant references to them: entertainments, comedies, contests, public tauntings, games, light shows, and so on. "Today there is a masquerade of all the seigniors and among others the admiral comes out dressed as a woman," said one letter.[123] Pellicer, who was always cautious, dared to call attention to the fact that fiestas of great pomp were being organized (in the year 1640) with so many people and such festive dress, as if there were not a war knocking at the door; on a similar occasion, he repeated "that it seemed as though there were no unrest and no war movement anywhere in Spain."[124] The companies of nobles formed in Madrid to go to the war in Catalonia entertained themselves with galas, banquets, and parties at night.[125] "Around here it is a question of nothing but enjoyments and pleasures," Barrionuevo said harshly; "they spend their time doing this while our enemies refine the gunpowder of their grievance to blow us away." This comment is from 1655.[126] The following year he would repeat: "Given that there are always fiestas, they get roused up about this and not about seeing how we have to defend ourselves from so many demonic enemies who will not let us alone."[127] When the year 1657 arrived he painted a serious picture and showed how broadly it applied: after speaking about the distressing situation in Seville, he said that on Saturday and Sunday of Shrovetide the king and queen had three or four meals, made more amenable with one-act farces, intermezzos, dances, music, and witticisms; on Monday there was a great comedy and, after dining, more entertainment until dawn; on Tuesday other diversions continued. Speaking of fiesta after fiesta, he commented that the king was present at some of them, accompanied by grand seigniors and those of less prestige, "with so many people present that the streets could not hold them."[128] In 1658 he insisted again and again: "great festivities," "everthing is fiesta and rejoicing," and with rancor toward the situation he commented that "the fiestas become grand at the expense of our flesh."[129] Nevertheless, he pointed out more than once, in passing and with respect to diverse occasions, the affluence of the public.

For the monarchy perhaps the most important thing was to be shielded in the face of the discussions and hostilities that so many critics stirred up from within. Against these critics it made use of the means for producing the irresponsible, stunned, and blind adherence of the masses. One of the best means was to maintain that adherence in fiestas; we know that for this reason the public was allowed to enter the fiestas of the Retiro. If elaborate fiestas already characterized the epoch of the Renaissance, now, at the same time that they were more costly and surprising, they were displayed before a greater mass of spectators, although those who took an active part continued to be a limited group. Perhaps, however, it was not the spectators' diversion that counted so much as the people's wonder in the face of the "magnificence" of the rich and powerful. Let us say with Barrionuevo that "all is fiestas and rejoicing," but the historian who would interpret this as a mere manifestation of frivolity would be committing a serious error. "There was never in Spain such an intense and prolonged fever for spectacles and merrymaking," commented Deleyto, "as during the forty-four years of the reign of the poet king."[130] To the grand fiestas of the court must be added the saints' festivals, the dances, mock war games on horseback, the bulls, and masquerades:[131] the organization of festivities represented an attempt to distract the people from their ills and to stun them into admiring those who were able to command such splendor or such enjoyable entertainment. The fiesta was a diversion that stunned both those who commanded and those who obeyed: it made the latter believe, whereas for the former it created the illusion that wealth and power still remained.

In the monarchy of the Spanish baroque, the fiesta was thus converted into an institutionalized celebration. Attending a fiesta and receiving an appropriate gift there became part of the stipend and perquisites of certain public employees. In the times of Philip III and Philip IV, the Royal Council, the Juntas of Reform and other special juntas, the personal reports of experts, the petitions of judicial boards, and other local authorities spoke out against fiestas and bestowals that were distributed in them. In 1619, the Junta of Reform proposed that the king do away with the custom introduced in the councils that consisted of "distributing among themselves certain benefits at Church festivals and bullfight fiestas," and the Sala de Alcaldes de Casa y Corte warned Philip IV that the assets of the ministries of justice and treasury "are eaten away little by little in the tribunals and juntas because every judge receives thirty thousand maravedis and more at every bullfight fiesta and others, and another large quantity goes to the ministers and officials, which comes to be a great sum of money because they are so numerous."[132] This institutionalization of the fiesta reveals its linkages with the social system and with the means of integration on which the baroque monarchy was based.

Thus fiestas were a characteristic aspect of baroque society. Poets versified about them and other writers recounted them, praising their magnificence and exalting the power of the seigniors and the glory of the monarchy. "The poets, players, dancers, comedians and the actors of farces are very eager to show off the beauties of their professions," related one of the *Cartas de jesuitas*.[133] Poets and writers of prose celebrated some of these manifestations from the literary point of view, usually in deplorable writings.[134] The most important writers cultivated this genre. Their occasions were marriages, births, victories, peacemaking, canonizations, and even the deaths of royal personages, which were treated with glorifying circumstance. Argensola, Lope, Bocángel, Góngora, Calderón, and others contributed to this occasional literature, which also occurred in other countries. It is curious that in his *Gazette* Renaudot also included accounts about fiestas in honor of illustrious personalities, undoubtedly because this re-flected public taste.[135] In reference to the very baroque characters of the novels in which Céspedes liked so much to describe fiestas, Fonquerne pointed out that individuals of the noble and rich class were moved by a taste for luxury, osten-tation, and the fiesta;[136] but let us note that this always required a numerous surrounding public to contemplate it, a public to whom his admiring narrative was addressed. Because of this, the fiesta — even when realized in a nearby country setting, as Tirso or Céspedes imagined it — nevertheless assumed a connection with an urban milieu that corresponded to the baroque's social aspects that have been brought out above.[137]

As with all products of baroque culture, fiestas were an instrument, even a weapon, of a political nature. Kings and ministers were aware of this; they spent more on fiestas than they could afford. The political and economic writer Martínez de Mata explicitly formulated it when he recorded that "the statesmen counsel that the prince have means for the people to divert themselves because melancholy does not give rise to producing novelty in the psyches." And Pascal, who devoted several pages to considerations regarding the possibilities of divertissement, understood to what extent it could be used to make human beings avoid thinking about themselves and their problematic surroundings. La Bruyère knew well that the governments (those he defined) were interested in ''letting the people benumb themselves in fiestas, spectacles, luxury'';[138] if they did not enjoy such diversions directly, they dreamily contemplated them, even though in others. Moreover, if in producing merriment the fiesta could simultaneously fill the spectator with admiration regarding the magnificence of whoever gave it or whomever it was dedicated to, it could be a means not only of distraction but also of attraction. The rulers of Spanish baroque society made use of precisely this aspect, not always with the results they desired.

The seventeenth-century fiesta had to count on some invention, an ingenious mechanism, an unusual artifact, an architectonic construction that, with paste-board and wood or similar materials, resembled an impressive grandioseness (the more fragile the materials, the more amazing the effects obtained with them). To this notion corresponded the construction of pools and canals in the gardens of the Buen Retiro so that aquatic fiestas could be organized there in imitation of the Romans (Pellicer called them *naumachias*, as did the Romans)[139] to signify that the Spanish monarchy was about to equal or surpass the historical greatness of Rome. These fiestas were also repeated so that the people could attend. At one time the absurdity included the construction of an armed galley, a ship, and other small vessels. Barrionuevo, with a strong dose of irony, related that the king and queen relaxed in the galley: "The gondolas and a ship go in front, it appears to be an armada, and in the stern, seated on a rug, the favorite and his son at the royal feet. They pretend to be battling, artillery and muskets go off, they go around three or four times, night falls and everything is over." This item comes from 18 July 1657. On 13 February of the following year, he reported that the king had gone to the Retiro "where they gave him a royal salute with the artillery of the galley and ship of the pools." Months went by and the king and queen continued to relax, sailing in the pools of the Retiro in the galley and ship (the galley was apparently called "La Real de España"). Barrionuevo could do nothing more than write paragraphs full of bitter desperation: there was no money to arm the ships and endow them with artillery and ammunition; there was no money to pay the soldiers; the fleet or solitary ships that came from America or traveled the coasts of the peninsula were seized by enemies; England claimed to have placed a permanent maritime blockade around Spain. In the Retiro, meantime, as a means of diversion for the king and queen and their retinue, the pools and canals were made longer and bigger, a new galley that was "a big thing," carried artillery and musicians; other vessels accompanied them, and the king, queen, grand seigniors, and courtiers took their place in this sad entourage and played war.[140]

But probably a mass — at least between explosions of emotion — gullibly admired the king's taste for the things of war, his gallantry in the midst of armed fire that baroque rhetoric would call "terrifying," and the magnificence of power that could so transform nature as to pretend that there was a sea at the court's back door. An entire system to stimulate admiration and adherence was set at play in this ridiculous (for us as well as for lucid and liberal minds in the seventeenth century) masquerade of the galley of the Buen Retiro.

Still another aspect of the fiestas fulfilled perfectly the required conditions of wealth, ingenuity, surprise, and brevity. Fireworks [fuegos de artificio] were a very adequate sign of the splendor of whoever ordered them because of their very artifice, their difficulty, the expense in human labor and in money that they implied (which the rich and powerful had at their disposal for nonproductive purposes); at the same time, they corresponded to what we already know as a taste for invented artifice ("inventions of fire," said Tárrega, recounting the great fiestas in Valencia).[141] They constituted a characteristic manifestation of the baroque fiesta.[142] It was an adequate spectacle for display before the wonder of the public, "with the festive uneasiness of the plebeian people," said Tirso.[143] We know that the Spanish court was very much taken with fireworks, whose art, wondrous in the epoch because of its technical complication and no less because of the costly transitoriness of its performance, was admired by the duke of Saint Simon in his day. The Noticias de Madrid give us copious references: in the fiestas of the Carmelites in honor of St. Teresa, there were "great fire inventions" (June 1622); when the Prince of Wales passed a night in Segovia, the same thing happened, and also when he arrived in Santander, on the way back to his country they set up "fire inventions"; when the king visited Seville, "the whole city burned with great fire inventions" (March 1624); in the fiestas for the health of the king, the Council of the Indies "spent many ducats on fire[works]" (September 1627); the laying of the first stone of the Almudena could not happen without them.[144] The Cartas de jesuitas speak about fiestas with "engines of gunpowder and rockets";[145] Pellicer rendered an account of fires and fiestas with rockets and gunpowder inventions;[146] Barrionuevo repeatedly mentioned fiestas with light shows and fireworks,[147] and one can also find mention of this in León Pinelo.[148] Let us recall that when Campanella, a typical writer of the baroque mentality and of the world of the Hispanic monarchy, exalted the power of the human being, he did not do it, as did another Renaissance thinker, because of the creative power of human hands (Campanella noted that monkeys and bears also have hands); rather, he cited human knowledge and the human capacity to dominate the arts of fire: "The art of fire is unique to man." [149] With their illumination, the arts of fire were the answer to the zeal to replace night with day, overcoming the night's obscurity by means of pure human artifice. The subject took the form of a genuine topos.

Let us examine how the theme is presented in three representative novelists whose stories tell us what the epoch's public opinion expected and admired. Pérez de Montalbán, recounting a fiesta in the context of one of his novels, said: "Night came or, rather, did not come because the ladies and lights were so numerous they were able to deny it." [150] In a story from one of the episodes on the outskirts of Toledo, Tirso remarked positively about "the night so well protected by lights that in Toledo the light of the sun was missed but little." [151] Céspedes exalted the marvelous fiestas that took place at an imagined anniversary in his novelesque world, "making the darkest night over into day." [152] The *Noticias de Madrid* tell about a costume festival organized by the admiral that ran through the streets of the capital; the lights in it were so numerous that the night seemed like broad daylight. [153] Later, in reference to a fiesta in the Retiro (this time a royal fiesta, thus implying its grandeur), one Jesuit wrote to another: "It seemed more like the light of day than the dark of night." [154] This capacity to transform the order of the universe, however fleeting it might have been, showed overwhelmingly the greatness of whoever had so much power over natural and human resources as to achieve such effects. [155] In a world like that of the baroque, ruled by prudence, those effects were sufficient to make people reflect on the advantage of continuing to adhere to such a powerful personality.

Appendix

Appendix
Sociopolitical Objectives
of the Use
# of Visual Media

Given the objectives of dissemination and effective action sought by baroque culture (though in saying this I am not irrevocably affirming that it succeeded), one can understand the interest in the manipulation of visual elements, the preponderant role granted to the optical function within the scope of the culture. On the other hand, appealing to the efficacy of the visual image is typical of societies where a guided mass culture develops. From both perspectives, then, the baroque had to be a culture of the sensible image, as it effectively was. In paraphrasing a fragment from Aristotles's *Poetics*, when an author as intellectualized as Racine articulated the necessary components of a tragedy, alongside decoration he would include "everything that is for one's eyes."[1]

By utilizing artistic media, seventeenth-century culture could more fittingly accomplish its propagandistic ends. Once again it is essential to refer to these ends to understand the aspects here under consideration. If the epoch's art was animated by a spirit of propaganda and if it took its point of departure from the fact that the image was an effective means for obtaining its objective, then one can maintain with Argan that "there is no attempt to conceptualize the image but to offer the concept made into an image" — that is, to provide the concept with a force that is no longer demonstrative but of practical application, a force typical of the image.[2] In reality, all of the preceding is valid not only for art but for all the manifestations of culture that address a public with the intention of captivating it; therefore, the same thing said about art can be said about politics, morality, and religion. Elsewhere I have written about the role of emblems from a point of view coinciding with what I have just put forth, in particular their mixture of doctrine and plasticity in didactic baroque literature.[3] In baroque cities, triumphal arches, tombs, altars, and artificial fountains were built to celebrate or commemorate an event, to highlight its importance; as with the widely diffused emblems, this was a product of the collaboration of the plastic arts to achieve effects of social significance. Complementing the magnificence of those monuments of a provisional architecture (no less praised as instructive because of this) were the hieroglyphics and other pictures that were drawn on their surfaces. Even sermons used printed or etched hieroglyphics, pictures to be deciphered, all of which reinforced the call addressed to the spectator or listening public, and opened up a channel in their attention for the penetration of a doctrine or feeling of amazement, suspension, or stupor that would facilitate the public's captivation.[4]

Calderón's method was to make visible, with all the force that the evident has within the field of vision, the principles and precepts of the doctrines—or at least of those that pragmatically appeal to human behavior and strive to guide it. That doctrinal content, inasmuch as it shares in the "truth" (in an Aristotelian sense), possesses a certain permanence. But unlike the person of the Middle Ages, the baroque person had insufficient confidence in the attracting force of the pure intellectual essence and thus strove to coat it with those sensible elements that indelibly engrave it in the imagination. Such a formulation was based on a recognition of the method indicated by the following verses from Calderón:

> Y pues lo caduco no
> puede comprehender lo eterno
> y es necesario que para
> venir en conocimiento
> suyo, haya un medio visible. . .
> *(Sueños hay que verdad son)*

[And thus the transitory cannot comprehend the eternal, and to come into its knowledge, one needs a visible means.]

Concerning this assumption, the entire question — for Calderón as well as for all baroque artists (and also for politicians and moralists)—resided in how one succeeded in passing from one plane to another, in what means one used for a given doctrinal content "to pass over into a practical concept / from an imagined one," as the work above puts it.

The value of the efficacy of visual resources was unquestioned in the epoch. The dispute about the superiority of the eye versus the ear in communicating knowledge to others had a medieval foundation. Whereas the Middle Ages opted for the second method, modernity has sided with the first, that is, with the method of seeing.[5] In the Renaissance, this was completely confirmed; on one occasion, we have referred to the defense that Galileo, among others, made of seeing. This dispute was reproduced and even intensified during the baroque. It was widespread among French writers of the time,[6] and in Spain Suárez de

Figueroa made a declaration that conforms perfectly to our point of view, considerably reinforcing it: according to him, both the eyes and ears are valid modes of access for knowing things, but "in sum, among the senses that serve the soul, it is the eyes through which many affects enter and exit."[7] Let us note that in this preference for the sense of sight, the role performed by the eyes in the constitution of experience was very much involved; ultimately, the theme was linked to the transformation of the concept of experience that took place with modernity (and which we discussed in chapter 7). The baroque considered that even our eyes can deceive us. In the seventeenth century, this theme came to infiltrate the everyday stream of commentary. Pellicer counseled "believing only what we see with our eyes, and they should not always be wholly believed."[8] This was written in one of the journalistic *avisos* of the time. Such advice to individuals who, then, already belonged to modernity, advanced the notion of not placing total, limitless confidence in the testimony of sight; but it also implied that since we do believe in something, and insofar as we have access to reality, this object of belief cannot be recognized except by way of our eyes.

But to this aspect of physical experience the baroque added what we might call the aspect of psychological experience: the eyes are the most direct and effective means that we can make use of in questions of affections. They are linked to feelings, as feelings are linked to them. To move the psyche, which we have seen to be what the baroque strove for, the most effective means are visual.

Individuals of the baroque thus knew that direct vision of things was important beyond measure. Igniting movements of affection, adherence, and surrender depended upon it. Direct presence—or at least the presence of symbolic representations most faithfully united in repeating the represented—had an incomparable force. To have certainty of things "seen and not things heard" was, therefore, what they strove for. For this reason, a typically baroque person, the Count-Duke of Olivares, achieved the effects of captivating people by resorting to direct, visual media whenever possible and, when not possible, to effects of faithful plastic representation. A Jesuit letter tells us that Olivares was trying to assure the public dissemination of his image as a pious ruler, able to attract the benefits of heaven because of his religiosity, which was how he wanted to appear before the small world of the court and before the opinion of the general public. He sought, then, to obtain a visual image of himself in others, one formed by the testimonies derived from those who had in some way or another viewed him in person: "Every morning, from five until six, he is most devotedly on the dais of Nuestra Señora de Atocha and, in effect, he is so great, as manifest by his pious and loud words and his sobs while hearing mass, that those who hear him, and there are many, leave very edified." This was how one Jesuit referred to it in a letter from 6 August 1639.[9] When Olivares, on the other hand, wanted to be viewed as a victorious general, since it is not easy to have recourse to people who were directly present at military scenes in Fuenterrabía, he had himself represented with all the visually convincing, impressive force that derived from painting in the specific way it was being cultivated by the great baroque artists—in this case, no less than Velázquez.

Of course this use of the visual did not stand in the way of baroque writers (especially those dedicated to the theater) who did not want to reject the possibilities that hearing also offered, comprehending what voice and music could contribute toward successfully moving the feelings. This explains why the musical factor was being more and more incorporated, above all in works that, perhaps because of their strong allegorical nature, called for a heightened action of extrarational elements on the public.[10]

Returning to our point of departure, there is no doubt that utilizing the plastic arts for the effects of teaching had a very remote origin: the tympana, the capitals, the stained glass of medieval churches, with their iconographic totalities, are examples. Many centuries before, in the ancient sculptured remains of the civilizations of the Near East, elements of this type were present.[11] In the sixteenth century, painting and sculpture having a heavy symbolic charge were still considered to be an appropriate language for those who did not know how to read.[12] Because of this, the art of the retables, which had reached its early splendor in the fifteenth century, continued to be cultivated in the sixteenth century and underwent an expansion in the seventeenth; in this phase, however, instead of anecdotal elements that were figuratively represented to be "read," the aspects of grandioseness predominated (the dynamism of the lines, the reflections of gold, the dramatics of the gestures, and so forth).

On the one hand, not only did the Church make use of these resources, but they were also utilized in civil society by politicians and others who strove to attract a mass to their ideological positions, implying such a quantitative change that it presupposed a transformation in the very nature of the method. But on the other hand it was not solely a matter of teaching but rather of reaching what we have seen the baroque writer calling a "practical concept," that is, a concept that embodies action. Around the turn of the seventeenth century, those who were beginning to reformulate the question in the way we are indicating were also writers close to the Church and artists working for it, reflecting about the way (given the conditions of the epoch) in which a work can develop with the greatest efficacy.[13] But their discovery would immediately come to be generalized in all realms of culture. One of the ultimate representatives of baroque pedagogy, Comenius, would conceive his work as the result of a method of plastic representation: such was the significance of his work *Orbis sensualium pictus* (1657).[14] Thereby, those who are taught not only are provided with certain knowledge but are also captivated and effectively driven toward the actions expected of them.

In the baroque, the tendency developed for certain scenes—the viewing of which could awaken religious or political feelings (or both at the same time, since they are so intertwined), attracting the viewer toward the subject provoking these feelings—to unfold in the street for a greater public viewing. Not only the taste for the anonymous parade, as we saw earlier in the words of L. Febvre, but the interest in its plastic force for shaping behavior by means of the emotions it awakened was one of the reasons why the procession was so widespread in Spain and from there went abroad. Moreover, when these street manifestations passed by the monasteries or even in other places, artistic tableaux were set up that, in the much more frequent case of events or fiestas having a religious character, were richly adorned altars incorporating an entire representation of doctrinal scope (whose meaning was more or less explicit or hidden, as in the figures of literature or emblems). The altars represented a collaboration of the plastic arts of painting and sculpture, of course, but also of architecture, which in these cases took on a greater importance. During a a fiesta oriented just as much toward the Church as the palace, a Jesuit related (15 March 1638) that of the monuments set up in the various places of Madrid (on this occasion, by monks and nuns), "the architecture of all of them was good, although ours surpassed the others," along with an enthusiastic comment about the one prepared in the convent of the Descalzas Reales,[15] whose significance in baroque Madrid has been mentioned above. In chapter 9 we saw these altars praised for their wealth and ostentation. But it was a question of obtaining the infiltration of a doctrinal content by means of every type of plastic representation.

Nevertheless, it is significant that painting predominated within the whole of the arts. Even the political writer, to render account of his work, made use of terms of comparison with the work of the painter. The other forms of expression were subordinated (or at least this was the intention) to the laws of painting. We can compare the different position it occupied in the Renaissance to understand better the novelty that was introduced afterward. In effect, sixteenth-century preceptists maintained that painting ought to be subject to the work of the architect; because of this, painting was often accomplished in black and white "so as not to injure the order of Architecture." But if one wanted to use colors and other media, they had to conform with the external environment so that "one copies and naturally simulates [finja] everything outside of the building that can be seen through any openings or windows."[16] It was precisely this formulation that changed decades later. Among baroque writers like Paravicino and many others, painting was deemed to be first among the arts and those who were learned in it gained in social prestige;[17] yet in the common opinion of the seventeenth century, painting was also held up as a role model for all the other arts (including literature), which all tried to approximate it. This becomes manifest in noting the scope of the use of the neologism *pintoresco* [*picturesque*], a word that was introduced around that time in the Romance languages. This word, which expressed the mere fact that something pertained to painting, turned into an attribute of quality as much for painting itself as for any other artistic form.[18] It served to qualify in terms of praise that which deserved to be treated by painting or that which was effectively treated in the mode of painting by other arts or by literature: it helped in referring to a greater animation and a freer interplay of lights and shadows, with a very suitable condition for rendering movement.[19]

It is not happenstance that the attention to painting and to the work of the painters of their time took up so much space in the pages of writers from Galileo to Huyghens. Among Spanish baroque writers, let us recall Sigüenza, Góngora, Paravicino, López de Úbeda, Lope de Vega, Quevedo, Gracián, Calderón, and Saavedra Fajardo. It has been said that the poems of some French baroque writers constitute a poetic version of Poussin's paintings.[20] The connection—with respect to themes, problems, and procedures—between Velázquez and Calderón has been observed by E. W. Hesse.[21]

In reality, this "picturesque" transformation of poetry and the other forms of expression proceeded from the consequences of mannerism. In Spain it was announced, with the coming to fruition of Michelangelo's influence and at the same time as its general Renaissance formulation, in a passage from Francisco de Holanda, who manifested many pre-baroque elements: painting is of greater efficacy than poetry to the extent that its nature is "to cause greater effects and to have much greater force and vehemence, so as to move the spirit and soul to happiness and rejoicing, as well as to sadness and tears, with the most effective eloquence."[22]

It was in the baroque when the topos *ut pictura poesis* would find its fullest meaning and also when it would become most widely diffused.[23] Lope became its proclaimer in many well-known passages from his comedies of a popular scope and no less in his learned poems.[24] The application of such a topos, broadened in general to all written expression, had a curious manifestation at the beginning of the original edition of Saavedra Fajardo's *Idea de un príncipe político y christiano*, where a letter was published (and reproduced in the following editions) from a Fleming praising the work of Saavedra in these terms: "Cedant picturae aliae, hic nobis Apelles est, qui ingenio et lineas et colores omnes vincit." The work's author in turn responded to the words in praise of his friend's quill, the painter of his ingenuity.[25] Salas Barbadillo, playing with the metaphor in baroque fashion, would tell us that he painted or wrote his figures in his novels with "the lines from this brush and the lines of words from this quill."[26] In the seventeenth century, similar texts were very numerous.

What was the source of this interest in painting and the recognition of its predominance? Why did the moralist, the politician, the pedagogue, and the poet want to approximate the way in which a painter operated? I believe that once again this phenomenon must be referred to the conditions of society that we have already put forward: a society that, in view of the situation, found that its ruling classes needed to attract and act upon mass opinion by means of extrarational channels; in such circumstances, it made use of painting and granted it a preeminent place because of the efficacy with which it was thought to affect the psyche's motivations [*resortes del ánimo*], impressing it directly by means of the sense of sight. One writer said it admirably at the very threshold of the epoch: "There is nothing better than painting to give delight and make something slip more smoothly into one's psyche [*âme*], nor to engrave it more deeply in one's memory, or more effectively prompt the will to set it going and energetically move it."[27] Fernández de Ribera tells us about a monseigneur who "had many animated inducements painted, for they customarily penetrate better when painted than when heard."[28] There is no doubt that this person must have been a good representative of baroque mentality.

The first demand that the preceptists postulated for painters (and that they demanded from those who imitated them in their labor) was to cultivate this aspect of their art. And thus Carducho would say that painting "must teach, move, speak and delight always and with all types of people," to the point that, although one must respect the substantial facts of reality, it was possible to introduce alterations in the modes and circumstances in order to accentuate this capacity to move.[29] The role that baroque thinkers recognized for painting was grounded in its capacity to work on a broad public in this way: that was what was most characteristic about it, its "efficacy and force," as Jáuregui wrote.[30] The numerous topoi and oft-repeated anecdotes relative to the efficacy of painting's psychological and moral action—capable as a consequence of having a decisive influence on human behavior—were gathered together in a curious work that Félix de Lucio Espinosa published under the title *El pince* [*The Paintbrush*] near the end of the epoch under consideration.[31]

Baroque writers insisted that the force of painting was in its possibility to grasp life. The reality that the baroque was concerned about penetrating and dominating was not to be found in the Platonic realm of the essences but in the dramatic and changing sphere of life. Painting, Jáuregui would also say, "does not strive only for breadth of body, but for lives and spirits."[32] The reference to the "living image" as the object that an art tries to maintain became common;[33] the portrait came to be its preferred manifestation. We cannot omit the reference in Lope: "You will see a great painter, / manifesting his ingenuity, / make a living image" [*El perro del hortelano*].

If in the Renaissance a profound antinomy occurred between its severe precept of the imitation of nature and its aesthetic of beauty, given that it is possible for the natural not to be beautiful,[34] in the baroque we find an even greater antinomy between the struggle to grasp living reality and the weight that the aesthetic placed on ideal representations based on an abstract conception of the social hierarchies. Despite its apparent and violent naturalism, what the baroque offers us never remains a pure and simple realism. Even the portraits themselves share

an entire gamut of generalized, typical elements, and they reflect group characteristics that were considered to affect the beings not because of their real indi-
viduality but because of their social position as doctrinally defined. Accordingly,
some are distinguished, others common, some beautiful, others ugly, others well
proportioned, others deformed—not in their individual being, but by necessary
derivation from their hierarchical place on the social scale, a scale that was
conceptually considered to be natural. But by keeping within a general conception
of estatist nature, the baroque, rather than rendering this conceptually, made
attentive use of an entire series of ornamental elements; the role of these elements
was to make evident before one's eyes the magnificence of the personages who
appeared in their midst and, at the same time, to present as an unquestionable,
positive fact their possession of the appropriate qualities, given their social status.
This has been verified in Bernini himself and was common to baroque artists,
politicians, and writers.[35] It was not a question, then, of pure realism. The
remains of idealism, of Neoplatonism appeared everywhere (they are easy to
confirm in Lope, for example). The Renaissance had accentuated the traits of
idealism; now, in the baroque, they would join with the mental heritage of an
estatist conception of society (corresponding to the strongly conservative character
of Platonism), encouraging it, permitting it to be extended to eighteenth-century
classicism, up to the eve of the social crisis of the French Revolution.

But, in conjunction with what we have said, the baroque artist and writer
knew that the world was not ruled by the mental schemata of a reason understood
in the way of Scholasticism; nor did they share in the *esprit de géométrie* (closer
to the former than it perhaps appears), although it was possible to make occasional
use of the possibilities of calculation, as did the merchant, the soldier, and the
artist and politician as well. The world and society could continue to be maintained
within a final rational order whose law could be expressed in terms of a teleological
conception of nature in the Scholastic-Aristotelian mode or (in mathematical
terms) in accordance with the well-known words of Galileo; nevertheless, to
operate among human beings it was necessary to accede to a specific concrete
reality, full of dramatics, charged with passions, and affected by psychological
motivations [*resortes*] that had to be recognized in order to dominate and channel
them.

Beyond any set of precepts of Aristotelian inspiration, the portrait would then
be considered not as a document of beauty nor as the contrary, according to
established aesthetic values, but rather as an attestation of psychology, an object
of observation for knowledge of the profound and multiform human being. The
broad gamut of the portrait corresponded to this transformation: previously it
was only of principal and heroic figures (Calderón still commented with irony
that some common women aspired to being portrayed), whereas now the repertory
of persons was wide-ranging, a crowded and moving world of superiors and
inferiors that swarmed before the spectator, even changing their relative posi-

tion—perhaps placing those from the lower levels in the foreground as the protagonist, as in *Las hilanderas*, or inverting their roles, as in *Los borrachos*.

But in reducing human subject matter to a painting object and subjecting it to techniques so it could be captured did not imply a direct, ingenuous, "copying" realism; it constituted instead an opening to reality by a knowingly manipulated technique of access, by an indirect means or to the second degree. In praising painting, one had said before that it exactly reproduced what was delimited (thus the anecdotes about confusions between the picture and the real object). Now that was not the case. A painting was painting, that is, a medium of access to the world that was knowingly used, that was ostensibly situated between the eye and the representation. Relying on this distance between the eye and the representation, one took a leap to the real, which was always a version, a study, a manipulation.

This is how painting, for the people of the baroque, became an especially apt medium for rendering an account of the experiences of human reality, of the living.[36] Despite the aesthetic symbolism preserved in the thought of the epoch, and in the midst of the ancient Hellenic heritage weighing upon painters and their critics,[37] a treatment of new themes and a new manner of confronting them nevertheless forced its way in: a new manner that neither strove to beautify them nor was resigned to imitation. Painters sought to study them and to offer them up to be recognized as testimony of the real. They they gave themselves over to an enthusiastic and repeated investigation of those aspects of the real that were uniquely present in the ugly, the deformed, the distorted. In the baroque, individuals' interest in this obscure side of things was undoubtedly prepared for by their own violated position, which in the society of the epoch was subject to a deforming pressure. From this level a consciousness of the grotesque and twisted could be acquired, and the minds of the epoch exercised their possibilities in grasping it. They learned that the real was much more complex than their received intellectual inheritance would have them believe. And it was possible in this way to note that, contemplating things in a foreshortened perspective, from the violated point of view of the irregular, the outlandish, or the abnormal, one ended up obtaining an enriched view of reality that the baroque mind came to judge as varied and changing.

From the visual angle of what we have just described, it would be interesting to consider one of the more specific characteristics of baroque painting: its procedure of "distant splotches," of the "smears" or "thick brush strokes," in the diverse terminology of the epoch, a procedure whose invention was at that time attributed to Titian. There are many texts that describe this. Let us select that by Jerónimo de San José because it already gives us an interpretation of the matter: "Since Titian was weary of the ordinary way of painting in the sweet and subtle fashion, he invented another way, so strange and lofty, of painting in thick brush strokes, as if they were carelessly done smears."[38] We ask ourselves what reasons sustained the general opinion in the seventeenth century toward this Titianesque manner of painting:[39] it was judged that this way alone gave an authentic rendering of the living. It was a painting of what was incomplete, shifting, and unstable, a painting adequate for grasping the human being and life. Such an adaptation is explained by saying that the human does not possess a being that has become, but a being becoming—a *fieri*, not a *factum*;[40] consequently, a being incomplete and in continuous change.

This, then, proceeded from the baroque's interest in obtaining a more fitting way to penetrate the real so as to ensure its directive grasp. These attempts frequently had a technical basis; in terms of their being an experiment, they implied a mechanization. In the preceding instance we see that by a physical (and easily disseminated) procedure—such as applying paintbrushes in a certain manner, that is, in a "thick" and careless manner—one discovered that painting necessarily increased the capacity to apprehend the living world.[41] In the realm of painting, the interest in what it is proper to call *experimentations*, with mirrors, plays of perspective, and light and color corresponded to what we have indicated. The same distortions that these studied combinations were able to provoke in the view of things came to constitute a method (or way of access) to approach the real. In his *Vite*,[42] Vasari recounted that Parmigianino took hold of a barber's mirror to make a self-portrait, contemplating himself reflected in it and noting the strange distortions of things because of the roundness of the mirror. "Gli venne voglia di contrafare per suo capriccio ogni cosa" [There came to him the desire to make a counterimage of everything through his caprice], and this aspiration to recreate the real made him reach a new verism: the truth of a reality whose most proper condition was that of changing—for example, the fact that an object increased or diminished as it neared or became farther from the mirror. In this way, forcing himself "to investigate the subtleties of art," the painter succeeded in ascertaining new aspects of the real that could be attested to in the painting, giving form to his personal experience in it.

If the cultivation of painting aroused the interest of baroque individuals up to such a point, it was not because using paintbrushes made it possible for one to acquire a capacity to imitate nature; rather, in manipulating them the artist obtained the ability to re-form and remake that which was given in nature. This theory, which once again manifested the manufacturing basis inspiring the baroque work, was articulated by one of the most representative of Spain's seventeenth-century poets and preceptists: Jáuregui.[43] It was necessary to take one's point of departure from the fact that what in art is superficially called "imitating" never becomes limited to a mere reproducing: "Art can hardly form / the very being of the thing." We must always take into account the constitutive limitation that art cannot go beyond a mode of fiction: "Sculpting or painting / must inevitably be fiction."

Certainly their role "is to simulate [*fingir*] the natural," but that cannot be understood as copying. Not only is it impossible to copy a natural model, but the intervention of the artist always has an active character as well, introducing a new element, making the model other than what was offered up to personal observation. The object cannot be grasped "unless the paintbrush re-forms it." It is necessary for the painter's operation to transform the object so as to introduce it into the world of art.

The baroque century repeatedly defined painting as a poetic activity in the etymological sense of the word, that is, as a creative activity. This qualification was what proved attractive for those writing about it in the seventeenth century and what they emphasized above all: its possibility of creating a world of beings who live the life of art correlatively to the world of natural beings. The preference for painting was based on the fact that this activity is more in the foreground. Painting has fewer means than sculpture or architecture because it cannot rely on the third dimension of the natural world, that is, it cannot physically make use of bulk; nevertheless, it better demonstrates the reach of the human creative force. By finding itself further removed than other arts with respect to nature, it is able to imitate it better than any other. This estimation reveals the significance of the preference that human beings of baroque mentality showed for pictorial art, to the extent that it was a human activity capable of remaking its natural models. Galileo's remark is the most interesting in this respect: he succeeded in formulating the estimation underlying the baroque preference for painting. "Nature itself gives light and shade to sculpture, and art gives it to painting; for that reason, therefore, an excellent painting is more worthy of admiration than an excellent sculpture." The reason for this recognition of excellence is found in the principle that "the greater the distance separating the means with which one imitates from the things being imitated, the more awe the imitation evokes."[44]

Thus painting remakes and re-forms nature, but in turn painting itself becomes the object of a similar process: painting is a re-forming instrument of what is naturally given because it rectifies and re-forms itself. The possibility of moving on this double plane of correction, multiplying the knowing and calculated action of the human being, ends up bestowing on painting the highest degree of superiority. Now a politician and political writer (many of whom dealt with painting in the seventeenth century) tells us that for him a painter is great because he "corrects a flawed painting with four brush strokes and a couple of shadows."[45]

I am going to refer to a final question that I dealt with years ago while trying to explain certain "modern" aspects in baroque mentality, a question that does not contradict but rather nuances the recognition of the fundamentally conservative character of the objectives that such a mentality exhibited. There was an attempt to reach certain socially conservative results, operating within circumstances of a modern character. In relation to this, I now want to show that the baroque painter and public came to a significant reformulation of the debate over preference for color or drawing.[46] A. Hauser was absolutely correct in attributing an immediate and direct political meaning to this theme, but he was completely mistaken in trying to interpret it because in his book Hauser practically neglected to study the baroque. In effect, Hauser assumed that at the high point of the baroque (which he confused with the Colbert era under Louis XIV) there was a choice made in favor of the drawing, whereas "the decision for coloring implied a stand against the spirit of absolutism, rigid authority, and the rational regimentation of life."[47] Hauser listed Watteau and Chardin as representatives of this new attitude, but he neglected to bring out sufficiently what had already been done much earlier by Rubens, Velázquez, Poussin, and others. I have no intention of composing a history of art, but rather a history of the mentality of the baroque epoch. Therefore, rather than what the painters did (something that is otherwise very evident), what is of interest here is to inquire into how the polemic concerning drawing and color really developed in the seventeenth century.

In my study of Velázquez I cited the explicit remark of El Greco, who denied that Michelangelo knew how to paint because he was unaware of color. Now let us note a few additional facts. Already in the sixteenth century, in a work of Celestina literature (which as such was representative of the mental change that was underway) we discover a solid choice in favor of color over line.[48] At the beginning of the new epoch, when one spoke about the painter's instruments it would be normal to mention nothing more than paintbrushes and colors.[49] It is symptomatic that great Spanish baroque poetry opened with someone like Góngora, about whom D. Alonso (the one most knowledgeable about him) has written: "If one were to make a tally of all the adjectives referring to color occurring in his poetry, one would be amazed to see that there is no stanza, and scarcely a line, that does not offer some hint of a color."[50] Jáuregui, realizing the common preference for color, would also attempt to offer an explanation. He referred to the sensibility he found in his surroundings, to the values that baroque artists and writers wanted to record in their works: the reason for the primacy of color and for the superiority granted to painting because of its use, did not derive from an increased capacity to copy what was natural, external, but from the fact that it allowed translation of "a thousand internal passions."[51] Color and movement of the soul went together; therefore Bocángel would say — in his work the attention to painting is also relevant—that the goal of the great portraitist was "to color the soul with passions."[52]

One more name has special relevance because it is of a political writer, perhaps the one of greatest significance in the culture of the Spanish baroque: Saavedra Fajardo posed the question of the dispute regarding color and drawing, deciding in favor of the first, as was normal in seventeenth-century Spain. Saavedra Fajardo, an author who utilized artistic elements in his work, a baroque writer who liked painting and introduced appraisals of it in his diverse writings (that is, a good representative of seventeenth-century culture, who drew prestige from his understanding of painting), would express this opinion: color "is what gives things their ultimate being and what most reveals the movements of the psyche."[53] It had to be a politician who made manifest this final and definitive aspect of the question.

This lyrical engineering of the human world culminated here—the engineering that the individuals of the baroque expectantly strove to cultivate, despite the insurmountable contradiction entailed in its own terms. The opinions regarding painting express everything at issue in this epoch with respect to knowing how to penetrate psyches and wills and, as a consequence, with respect to knowing how to move and guide the anonymous multitudes of people. It would seem that by virture of painting, all of those whose concern with human modes of behavior related to the practical end of governing it (that is, politicians, moralists, pedagogues) would be able to succeed in their objectives. The key to adapting to the internal motivations [*resortes*] that affected individuals, in pursuing their mass integration in the social system, resided in the manipulation of painting's resources. The desired direction to impress on those groups bearing the brunt of this operation undoubtedly pointed toward the restoration and preservation of values that came from the seignorial tradition; but in the sixteenth century, the modern and individualist experience undergone by European societies was not in vain. Instruments of greater efficacy would have to be used, instruments capable of influencing individuals who recognized their freedom; a complex regime of social control, organized in the shadow of the absolute monarchy, strove to maintain these individuals actively integrated in a conservative society of traditional privileges.'

In this way, the society of the seventeenth century—biting its own tail—revealed the grounds of its own crisis: a process of modernization that was contradictorily set in place to preserve inherited structures. This way of posing the question explains that relationship in the mode of a historical law: if a society in the seventeenth century showed itself to be well adapted to baroque culture, whenever we consider its baroque richer, we shall necessarily discover that such a society's future would also be more closed.

Notes

Abbreviations in Notes

AFA	*Archivo de Filología Aragonesa* (Saragossa)
AHE	Archivo Histórico Español
BAE	Biblioteca de Autores Españoles
BHI	*Bulletin Hispanique* (Bordeaux)
BN	Biblioteca Nacional (Madrid)
BRABLB	*Boletín de la Real Academia de Buenas Letras de Barcelona*
CC	Clásicos Castellanos
CODOIN	Colección de Documentos Inéditos para la Historia de España
CSIC	Centro Superior de Investigaciones Científicas
MHE	Memorial Histórico Español
NBAE	Nueva Biblioteca de Autores Españoles
RABM	*Revista de Archivos, Bibliotecas y Museos* (Madrid)
RBAM	*Revista de la Biblioteca, Archivo y Museo de Madrid*
REP	*Revista de Estudios Políticos* (Madrid)
RFE	*Revista de Filología Española* (Madrid)
RSH	*Revue des Sciences Humaines* (Lille)

Notes

FOREWORD. THE CHANGING FACE OF HISTORY

1. Arnaldo Momigliano, "History in an Age of Ideologies," The American Scholar (Autumn 1982), pp. 495-507.

2. Ibn Khaidun, The Mugaddimah: An Introduction to History, 2d ed., translated from Arabic by Franz Rosenthal (Princeton, 1967).

3. Immanuel Kant, "The Idea of Universal History from a Cosmopolitical Point of View," in On History, edited by Lewis White Beck (Indianapolis, 1963), pp. 11–26.

4. Mandrou, De la culture populaire au XVIIe et au XVIIIe siècles (Paris, 1964); Magistrats et sorciers en France au XVIIe siècle (Paris, 1968).

5. Duby, Les trois ordres ou l'imaginaire du féodalisme (Paris, 1978; English ed.: The Three Orders: Feudal Society Imagined, translated by T. N. Bisson [Chicago, 1980]) and numerous other works.

6. Ariès, Essais sur l'histoire de la mort en Occident (Paris, 1975; English ed.: Western Attitudes towards Death from the Middle Ages to the Present, translated by Patricia M. Ranum [Baltimore, 1974]); Vovelle, La mort et l'Occident de 1300 à nos jours (Paris, 1982).

7. Carlo Ginzburg, Il formaggio e i vermi: Il cosmo di un mugnaio del '500 (Turin, 1976; English ed.: The Cheese and the Worms: The Cosmos of a Sixteenth-Century Miller, translated by John and Anne Tedeschi [Baltimore, 1980]).

8. Francisco de Quevedo, "La España defendida," in Obras completas: Prosa, edited by F. Buendía (Madrid, 1961), pp. 488-526.

9. J. N. Hillgarth, The Spanish Kingdoms, 1250-1516 (Oxford, 1976-78).

10. Sánchez-Albornoz, España, un enigma histórico (Buenos Aires, 1956).

11. Translated by Edmund King (Princeton, N.J., 1954).

12. See especially Eugenio Asensio, La España imaginada de Américo Castro (Barcelona, 1976), pp. 34-40; and Sánchez-Albornoz, España.

13. Asunción Domenech, "Entrevista a José Antonio Maravall," Historia 16 (December 1980), pp. 109-14.

268 □ NOTES TO PP. xvii–xxxi

14. *Poder, honor y élites en el siglo XVII* (Madrid, 1979).
15. Maravall, "From the Renaissance to the Baroque: The Diphasic Schema of a Social Crisis," translated by Terry Cochran, in *Literature among Discourses: The Spanish Golden Age,* edited by Wlad Godzich and Nicholas Spadaccini (Minneapolis, 1986), pp. 3-40.
16. The Structure of Spanish History, p. 41.
17. See Heinrich Wölfflin, *Renaissance und Barock* (1888); Werner Weisbach, *Der Barok als Kunst der Gegenreformation* (Berlin, 1921); and Frank Warnke, *Versions of Baroque: European Literature in the Seventeenth Century* (New Haven, Conn., 1972). For an overview of the literature in this area see Gerald Gillespie, "Renaissance, Mannerism, Baroque," in *German Baroque Literature,* edited by Gerhart Hoffmeister (New York, 1983), pp. 3-24.
18. See this volume, p. xxxiii.
19. Cf. Maravall, "La cultura de crisis barroca," *Historia 16,* extra 12 (December 1979), pp. 80-90.
20. Ibid., p. 82.
21. Ibid., p. 89.
22. Cf. Maravall, "Seminario sobre la cultura del barroco," *Actas del II° Coloquio del Grupo de Estudios Sobre Teatro Español* (GESTE), Toulouse, 16-17 November, 1978, pp. 21-22.
23. See Nicholas Spadaccini, "Cervantes' Aesthetic of Reception in the *Entremeses,*" in *Critical Essays on Cervantes,* edited by Ruth E. Saffar (Boston, G. K. Hall, forthcoming).
24. Maravall, *Honor, poder y élites,* pp. 14-15.

TRANSLATOR'S INTRODUCTION: THE TRANSLATING MECHANISM

1. A. Gramsci, *The Modern Prince,* in *Selections from the Prison Notebooks,* translated and edited by Quintin Hoare and Geoffrey N. Smith (New York, 1971), p. 130.
2. Machiavelli, *The Prince and the Discourses,* translated by Luigi Ricci (New York, 1950), p. 64.
3. See the introduction to Gramsci, *Selections from Prison Notebooks,* pp. xiii-xiv.
4. Vol. 14, p. 187b.
5. It is significant that Maravall links the emerging role of *suspense* in cultural artifacts with the notion of alienation (213-16). Elevation of alienation or estrangement as the characteristic of all art (in terms of "literariness," for example) can only occur against the backdrop of a (literary) history that is already in place.
6. The discussion of *ressort* in the *Encyclopédie* accentuates this causal origin:

Springs [*les ressorts*] draw all their energy from the elasticity of matter; although that property is universally known and even palpable in almost all matter [*corps*], we are nevertheless still left in a profound ignorance regarding the cause that produces it; thus in this article I propose to treat it only by means of its effects, and above all by means of the use clockmakers make of it in deriving the moving force and the regulating force (vol. 15, p. 474b).

Because of the inevitable absence of cause, of essence, the *Encyclopédie*'s preferred image to describe *ressort* is the inner workings of the clock, the eighteenth-century mechanism of historical conception. Even so, the distinction between a regulating and moving force, here made possible through recourse to an underlying "mover," cannot be maintained unproblematically. Compare, for example, the following formulation: "The force of inertia on the regulator is opposed to the moving force that starts it going" [*s'oppose à la force motrice qui l'anime*] (vol. 14, p. 36a); this entire introduction could be considered a gloss of this sentence.
7. Jameson, "Postmodernism, or the Cultural Logic of Late Capitalism," in *New Left Review,* no. 146 (July- August 1984), p. 63. Interestingly, the topic of this issue is "The Impasse of Euro-Socialism."
8. Heidegger, "Der Ursprung des Kunstwerkes," *Holzwege* (Frankfurt am Main, 1950), p.

50; English ed., "The Origin of the Work of Art," *Poetry, Language, Thought*, translated by Albert Hofstadter (New York, 1975), pp. 61-62.

PREFACE

1. These and the quotations given below are from my *Teoría del saber histórico*, 3rd. ed. (Madrid, 1967), pp. 87, 134, 189.

INTRODUCTION. BAROQUE CULTURE AS A CONCEPT OF EPOCH

1. See López Piñero, *Introducción de la ciencia moderna en España* (Barcelona, 1969); he distinguished periods for the crisis of Spanish historical thought that are close to those established here.

2. J. Baltrusaitis, *Le Moyen Âge fantastique* (Paris, 1955).

3. See J. Puig y Cadalfach, *Le premier art roman* (Paris, 1928).

4. See my *Concepto de España en la Edad Media* (Madrid, 1954); examples cited are on pp. 403ff.

5. See Gómez Moreno, *Las iglesias mozárabes*, vol. I (Madrid, 1919).

6. Ossowski, *Estructura de clases y consciencia social* (Madrid, 1944).

7. See my *Teoría española del Estado en el siglo XVII* (Madrid, 1944).

8. R. Huyghe, "Classicisme et baroque dans la peinture française du XVIIe siècle," *XVIIe Siècle*, no. 20 (Paris, 1953).

9. From Weisbach, Gothein, and many others, to the French translator of my work cited in note 7, who attempted to introduce the thought studied there "dans ses rapports avec l'esprit de la Contre-Réforme." On the theme of baroque metaphysics and theology, see L. Legaz, *Horizontes del pensamiento jurídico* (Barcelona, 1947), pp. 93ff.

10. *Las ideas y las formas* (Madrid, n.d.).

11. Sánchez Cantón, who did not think it inappropriate to broaden the concept to the liberal arts, instead asked for the closest chronological delimitation possible in "El barroco español: Antecedentes y empleo hispánicos de *barroco*," in *Manierismo, Barocco, Rococó* [Convegno Internazionale, Rome, 1960], (Rome, 1962).

12. *The City in History* (New York, 1961), p. 351. Referring to the new epoch, L. Mumford makes this characterization: "The new pattern of existence sprang out of a new economy, that of mercantilist capitalism; a new political framework, mainly that of a centralized despotism or oligarchy, usually embodied in a national state; and a new ideological form, that derived from mechanistic physics, whose underlying postulates had been laid down, long before, in the army and the monastery" (p. 345). This is without a doubt an essential aspect of the question: the utilization of rational and mechanical elements that scientific thought and modern technology allocate for accomplishing magical, extrarational objectives, which in the Baroque was formulated with calculation. This is the epoch's double perspective that I have been insisting on for many years.

13. *Baroque et classicisme* (Paris, 1957), p. 26.

14. Joyce G. Simpson, *Le Tasse et la littérature et l'art baroques en France* (Paris, 1962), p. 112.

15. *Estudios sobre el barroco* (Madrid, 1964), p. 62. The passage comes from the study on "Los estilos generacionales de la época: manierismo, barroco, barroquismo."

16. Ibid., 106.

17. P. Francastel, "Baroque et classicisme: histoire ou typologie des civilisations," *Annales: Économies, Sociétés, Civilisations* 14, no. 1 (January-May 1951), p. 146. Tapié's response in the same journal recognizes the large part played by Spain, whose shadow, according to his own words, was cast over the entire book. His subsequent monograph, *Le baroque* (Paris, 1961), corrected to a certain extent the previous absence, but it didn't prove satisfactory in terms of his general posing of the question. One can see that Tapié is insufficiently acquainted with Spanish sources.

18. *Southern Baroque Art* (London, 1924) and *Spanish Baroque Art* (London, 1931).

19. E. I. Watkin, *Catholic Art and Culture* (London, 1942).

20. Hatzfeld, *Estudios sobre el barroco*. See in particular the article "La misión europea de la España barroca."

21. See Gerhardt, "Rembrandt y Spinoza," *Revista de Occidente* 23, 1929.

22. Hatzfeld, *Estudios sobre el barroco*, pp. 467-68.

23. On Scholasticism in Spanish mysticism, see A. A. Ortega, *Razón teológica y experiencia mística* (Madrid, 1944); and Garrigou-Lagrange, "Saint Jean de la Croix," *La Vie Spirituelle*, supplement, 1930. For a formulation in terms of the baroque, A. A. Parker, "Calderón, el dramaturgo de la escolástica," *Revista de Estudios Hispánicos*, nos. 3-4 (1935), 273-85, 393-420.

24. *Avisos de don Jerónimo de Barrionuevo* (see the correspondence on 2 October 1655), BAE, 221, vol. I, p. 199.

25. *Cartas de jesuitas*, in MHE, vols. 13-19, published by Gayangos. The quote comes from vol. 13, p. 24.

26. In chapter 3, we note a curious statement contained in *La Pícara Justina* that shows that the taste for hagiographies was not as common as has been supposed. The very fact that many of the stories and comedies of saints contain such a great percentage of grotesque realism — think about *Santo y sastre*, the title of one of Tirso's comedies, in which hagiography made its appearance at the theater with St. Homobono ascending to the sky with his cross — reveals an undebatable realist erosion of supernatural elements.

27. *De l'influence du Concile du Trente sur la littérature et les beaux-arts chez les peuples catholiques* (Paris, 1884).

28. *Crescimiento y desarrollo* (Barcelona, 1964), p. 438.

29. González de Celleorigo's declaration that "every kind of manufacture necessary to the realm" was lacking because the increase in population already represented an incipient consciousness of it (*Manual de la política necesaria y útil Restauración a la República de España* [Madrid, 1600]. fols. 12, 2).

30. I am utilizing Tönnies' categories, though only approximately.

CHAPTER 1: SOCIAL TENSIONS AND THE CONSCIOUSNESS OF CRISIS

1. "Lamentos apologéticos...en apoyos del Memorial de la despoblación, pobreza de España y su remedio," in *Memoriales y discursos de Francisco Martínez de Mata*, edited by G. Anes (Madrid, 1971), p. 374.

2. It was published in 1587 in Madrid and is reproduced in part in BAE, 65.

3. Included in *La Junta de Reformación*, AHE, 5 (Madrid, 1932), p. 228. In my *La oposición bajo los Austrias* (Barcelona, 1972), I quote other data concerning a similar mode of discussing the issue that on occasion expressed itself with frank resentment against the kings.

4. *French Absolutism; The Crucial Phase (1620-1629)* (London, 1968).

5. See my "La imagen de la sociedad expansiva en la consciencia del siglo XVI," in *Hommage à Fernand Braudel*, vol. I (Toulouse, 1972), pp. 369ff., and *Antiguos y modernos: La idea de progresso en el desarrollo inicial de una sociedad* (Madrid, 1967).

6. *Memorial de la política necesaria y útil Restauración a la República de España*, fol. 16.

7. *Comentarios políticos*, edited and with a preface by J. A. Maravall (Madrid, 1945), p. 36.

8. See my "El primer proyecto de una Facultad de Ciencias Políticas en la crisis del siglo XVII (El Discurso VIII de Sancho de Moncada)," collected in my *Estudios de historia del pensamiento español*, series 3, *La época del barroco* (Madrid, 1975).

9. We are not concerned here with related themes (better characterized in terms of individual morality), some of which have been brought together under the title "La comedia y los problemas sociales," in E. W. Hesse, *La comedia y sus intépretes* (Madrid, 1973), pp. 180ff.

10. See George M. Foster, *Traditional Cultures and the Impact of Technological Change* (New York, 1962).

11. See my *Estado moderno y mentalidad social: Siglos XV a XVII*, part 3, chap. 1 (Madrid, 1972).

12. For the crisis in general, see A. Gil Novales, "La crisis central del siglo XVII," *Revista de Occidente*, no. 115 (1972). When the upheaval of the seventeenth century was already underway, the Thirty Years' War accentuated the crisis, as Trevor-Roper maintained: the burden of taxes, oppression by the soldiers, the grave losses of military defeats, the difficulties of commerce, unemployment and violence, impertinence and mutiny of the troops — all that produced everywhere a popular discontent that translated into disorder. Chancellor Séguier's ongoing accounts of the peasant insurrections in France are now known (*The Crisis of the Seventeenth Century* [New York, 1967], p. 48). Nevertheless, I believe that the basic conflictive nature of the seventeenth century, which proved capable of creating the baroque's "superstructure" (allow me to use this term for the purpose of clarification) came from other spheres (specifically urban ones, as we shall see).

13. "de 1560à 1660: La chaîne des hommes," in *Le préclassicisme français*, edited by J. Tortel (Paris, 1952).

14. H. Koenigsberger, "The Reformation and Social Revolutions," in *The Reformation Crisis*, edited by J. Hurstfield (London, 1971), pp. 83ff.

15. *Las comunidades de Castilla, una primera revolución moderna*, 2d ed. (Madrid, 1970).

16. B. F. Porshnev, *Les Soulèvements populaires en France de 1623 à 1648* (Paris, 1963).

17. *Fureurs paysannes* (Paris, 1967).

18. *Alteraciones andaluzas* (Madrid, 1973).

19. Robert Forster and Jack P. Greene, eds., *Preconditions of Revolution in Early Modern Europe* (Baltimore, 1970).

20. See the last of the studies in my *La oposición política bajo los Austrias* (Barcelona, 1972).

21. In *Preconditions of Revolution*, p. 124.

22. See, for example, Juan Alfonso de Lancina's work, whose title is already revealing: *Historia de las revoluciones del Senado de Mesina*, 1692. Barrionuevo's *Avisos* (vol. 2, pp. 34, 49, 114, etc.) also offer some comparable examples.

23. Porshnev, dealing with the richness of France, has maintained that new investigations prove that

seventeenth-century French absolutism was a nobiliary state and the French society of that time a feudal society, or at least feudal and aristocratic to a greater degree than in the eighteenth century . . . The seventeenth-century bourgeois economy was perceptibly less developed than in the following century, and the bourgeoisie as representing the capitalist modes of production could not even be considered anywhere near power.

The general conclusion drawn from incursions into the social and economic order of France is clear: it was, broadly speaking, still a feudal society, characterized by the predominance of feudal relations of production and feudal forms of economy; "capitalist relations, as a structure, were disseminated by means of this mass feudalism" (pp. 35, 39 and 43). The preserved remnants of feudalism do not allow one to speak unequivocally of a feudal society: monarchical-nobiliary society is something different — from the outset, the people had to be taken into account in a different way. Therefore chivalry and the baroque are not interchangeable concepts.

24. According to which the seigniors were created, given a title and invested by kings, and the seigniors' jurisdiction and rights depended on the latter. This is completely different from the feudal conception of seignior and vassal, and because of this I am opposed to the use of the word *sovereignty*. The notion of sovereignty as an integral piece of absolutism was present in the baroque but transcended it. On this subject see Castillo de Bobadilla, *Política para Corregidores*, vol. I (Barcelona, 1624), p. 600.

25. See my *Estado moderno y mentalidad social*.

26. R. Mousnier, "L'évolution des institutions monarchiques en France et ses relations avec l'état social," *XVIIe Siècle*, nos. 58-59 (1963), p. 71.

27. See R. Mousnier, J. Labatut, and Y. Durand, *Problèmes de stratifications sociales: deux cahiers de la noblesse (1649-1651)* (Paris, 1965).

28. See B. Schnapper and H. Richardot, *Histoire des faits économiques, jusqu'à la fin du XVIIIe siècle* (Paris, 1971), p. 226.

29. This point of view is amply documented in my *Estado moderno y mentalidad social*.

30. See R. de Arco's anthological collection *La sociedad española en la obra de Lope de Vega* (Madrid, 1942).

31. See my *Teatro y literatura en la sociedad barroca* (Madrid, 1972).

32. G. Bénichou, *Morales du grand siècle* (Paris, 1948), pp. 16 and 53.

33. W. W. Rostow, *Politics and the Stages of Growth* (Cambridge, Press, 1971).

34. *Avisos*, vol. I (4 November 1654), BAE, 231, p. 79.

35. See my *Estado moderno y mentalidad social*, vol. 2, p. 36.

36. On the less known reference to the Catalan nobility, see J. H. Elliot, "A Provincial Aristocracy," in *Homenaje a J. Vicens Vives* (Barcelona, 1965). López de Madera informed Philip IV: "In substance everything that is bad comes from bad administrators" (*La Junta de Reformación*, AHE, 5, p. 102). Regarding the ills of the country, Barrionuevo observed: "All the administrators who have a hand in it are causing it, with no one feeling a twinge of sadness at the common loss, nor dealing with anything other than one's own interest" (2 June 1657), BAE, 222, p. 87.

37. *Discurso en razón de muchas cosas tocantes al bien, prosperidad, riqueza y fertilidad destos Reynos y restauración de la gente que se ha echado dellos* (Madrid, 1610).

38. *Idea de un Príncipe político y cristiano, representada en Cien Empresas*, in *Obra Completa* (*OC*), edited by González Palencia (Madrid).

39. *Gobierno político de agricultura* (Madrid, 1618).

40. See A. Decouflé, "L'aristocratie française devant l'opinion publique à la veille de la Révolution (1787-1789)," in the volume by various authors, *Etudes d'histoire économique et sociale du XVIIIe siècle* (Paris, 1966).

41. *Discurso*, fol. 7.

42. *La sociedad española del siglo XVII*, vol. 1 (Madrid, 1963), p. 267.

43. A document (from about 1621) from the Sala de Alcaldes de Casa y Corte to Philip IV, in *La Junta de Reformación*, p. 211.

44. Anonymous to Philip IV, from about 1621, influenced by Cellorigo, in ibid., p. 225.

45. C. Viñas Mey, in *El problema de la tierra en España, en los siglos XVI y XVII* (Madrid, 1941), has put together an interesting anthology of seventeenth-century texts about swindles and acts of force endured by the peasants. The theme of farm worker unrest, to which Lope de Deza would dedicate the lengthy work mentioned in n. 39, indicating no less than fourteen reasons for the ruin of the Spanish countryside, was a theme that became disseminated as a topic of literature: examples can be seen in works such as *El pasagero* of Suárez de Figueroa, among others. In observing the growing strength of seignorial pressure already during the last quarter of the sixteenth century, T. Mercado very angrily denounced the increase in hunting reserves.

46. R. Carande wrote:

Some exemptions granted to the farmers, such as declaring their working livestock, equipment and products free from attachment and seizure for debts owed, and other analogous policies, ended up being very insufficient to free them from a poverty that devastates villages and stimulates a rural exodus to the battlefields, to the Indies and otherwise to the city where they seek accommodation in the great houses as hirelings or domestic servants (*Carlos V y sus banqueros*, vol. I [Madrid, 1965], pp. 134-35).

47. The characterization Cañizares gave of the phenomenon of the formation of masses — which were seen as proto-proletarian, with subversive tendencies, although he referred them to the moment of the *comunero* conflict — must be understood as the way their situation was viewed during the time when the author wrote (I comment on Cañizares' text in *Estado moderno y mentalidad social*, vol. 2, p. 368).

48. *Restauración de la abundancia antigua de España* (Naples, 1631).

49. See R. L. Kagan, *Students and Society in Early Modern Spain* (Baltimore, 1974); also my *Poder, honor y élites en el siglo XVII* (Madrid, 1979).

50. Thus came about, according to Domínguez Ortiz, the fact that "notwithstanding the very bad financial situation, pensions and living allowances continued to be lavishly offered, for more or less justified reasons." This tendency became accentuated during the calamitous reign of Charles III, to the point that Federico Cornaro, the ambassador to Venice in 1678-81, wrote in his *Relación*: "There is scarcely anyone who does not live from the king's treasury or who in the absence of royal pensions would be able to support oneself with one's own income . . ." There is much truth in the witty sentence another ambassador to Venice, Foscarini, wrote in 1686: The previous kings summoned the grandees to the court in order to ruin them; "now they [the grandees] are destroying who destroyed them." Effectively, the upper aristocracy's residence at court produced many expenses for the kings; on the occasions of the royal emergency tax, the kings had obtained great sums from the aristocracy, but since its members were incapable of creating wealth and tried to make the nobility's subsistence indispensable to the monarchy, it was ultimately this latter, i.e., the nation and the Royal Treasury, that had to support it (*Alteraciones andaluzas*, pp. 244-45).

51. *Cartas de Andrés de Almansa y Mendoza. Novedades de esta Corte y avisos recibidos de otras partes (1621-1626)*, letters 14 (18 November 1623) and 15 (3 February 1624), printed in *Libros raros y curiosos* (Madrid, 1886), pp. 234 and 261.

52. *El Antiguo Régimen: los Reyes Católicos y los Austrias* (Madrid, 1973), pp. 355-56.

53. *Avisos*, vol. I (5 September 1654), BAE, 221, p. 56.

54. The Church supported a nobiliary social morality that, as some observed in the epoch itself, contradicted the evangelical message. This was verified in the theater, which was almost wholly produced by priests, with the Church's consent and in its and the monarchy's service. In this context, an example drawn from Cubillo de Aragón's work proves interesting: during a dispute regarding whether one should or should not accept the family duty of vengeance, the representative of nobiliary judgment — which in the comedy is put forth as generally conceded — directs these words to whoever maintains a more humanitarian thesis: "Believe that you would better be found / less Christian, but more honored" (*Las muñecas de Marcela*, ed. A. Valbuena Prat [Madrid, 1928], jornada II, p. 60). It doesn't seem that the Inquisition was in any way disturbed by this juxtaposition of "honrado" and "cristiano."

55. Ph. Butler, *Classicisme et baroque dans l'oeuvre de Racine* (Paris, 1959), pp. 52, 54. See the synthesis that E. Préclin and Tapié offered in similar terms in *Le XVIIe siècle* (Paris, 1949).

56. K. Vossler, *Lope de Vega y su tiempo*, translated by Ramón de la Serna, 2d ed. (Madrid, 1940), p. 268.

57. On the other hand, the continued existence of estatist society was normal in all of Europe, England included (see Laslett's work cited below in chap. 5, n. 32). The difference was in the fortifications with which this society defended itself.

58. Vossler, *Lope de Vega*, p. 293.

59. Letter 16, no date, p. 302. Since the *Noticias de Madrid (1621-1627)*, edited by González Palencia (Madrid, 1942), refers to the events, we know that they took place on 5 July 1624.

60. From the *Memorial* already referred to; the passage is cited in the anonymous *Memorial* to Philip IV, from 1621 (*La Junta de Reformación*, p. 231).

61. *Restauración política de España*, discurso 1, p. 4.

62. Unedited manuscript from 1621, cited by Carrera Pujal, *Historia de la economía española*, vol. 1 (Barcelona, 1943), p. 481.

63. Cited by Viñas Mey in *El problema de la tierra en España*.

64. The *Avisos* (ed. *Semanario Erudito*, 31, p. 87) say that they had executed two and expected another; nine had been arrested and seventy accused. Other references include *Avisos*, p. 92, etc., and Barrionuevo, *Avisos*, BAE, 221, p. 35. The *Noticias de Madrid (1621-1627)* had already offered the information that on one day five young men were condemned to the stake for homosexual practices and, on another day, two boys (pp. 43 [Dec. 1622] and 133 [March, 1626]). Other data collected

274 □ NOTES TO PP. 37–43

by Horacio Salas appear in *La España barroca* (Madrid, 1978). In Jeroni Pujades's *Dietari* (vol. 3 [Barcelona, 1975], pp. 225-26) can be found, with reference to Saturday, 13 September 1625, the information that about forty sodomites "del floret de la ciutat y alguns doctors del Real Consell" were discovered and encarcerated in Venice.

65. A report from the Consejo Real to Philip III (9 January 1620), in *La Junta de Reformación*, pp. 34, 35.

66. *Varias noticias importantes a la humana comunicación* (Madrid, 1621), fol. 74.

67. *Avisos* (27 September 1656), BAE, 221, p. 320.

68. *La Junta de Reformación*, pp. 12, 18.

69. Ibid., p. 539. This declaration of the king referred to August 1627. Things would become much worse.

70. V. L. Tapié, *Baroque et classicisme*, pp. 60-61.

71. H. Hauser, *La pensée et l'action économique du Cardinal de Richelieu* (Paris, 1944).

72. *Obras*, edited by Benítez Claros, vol. 1 (Madrid, 1946), p. 84.

73. F. Braudel, *La Mediterranée et le monde méditerranéen à l'époque de Philippe II*, vol. 2, 2d ed. (Paris, 1966), pp. 76ff. (English ed.: *The Mediterranean and the Mediterranean World in the Age of Philip II* (New York, 1973), v. 2, pp. 735ff.)

74. CODOIN, 40, pp. 292ff.

75. See the last chapter in my *Oposición política bajo los Austrias*.

76. *Avisos*, 2 (8 November and 13 December 1656, February 1657), BAE, pp. 15, 35, 59.

77. *Avisos*, 2 (7 March 1657), BAE, p. 66.

78. *La Junta de Reformación*, pp. 95-96.

79. *Avisos* (26 March 1641), ed. *Semanario Erudito*, 32, p. 20.

80. *Cartas de jesuitas* (1 December 1639), MHE, 15, p. 374.

81. *Avisos* (13 December 1639), ed. *Semanario Erudito*, 31, p. 104.

82. Ibid., p. 106.

83. Ibid., p. 178.

84. *Cartas de jesuitas* (19 June 1640), MHE, 15, p. 451.

85. Ibid., p. 149.

86. *Avisos*, vol. 2 (17 January 1657), BAE, 222, p. 51.

87. *Avisos* (21 July 1643), ed. *Semanario Erudito*, 33, p. 39.

88. Letter 16, n.d., p. 298. Also on this occasion the *Noticias de Madrid (1621-1627)* recorded the event in these terms: "On this day the King's chamber assistants failed to supply the food, and the Count of Olivares ordered guards to arrest all of them in their homes" (p. 102).

89. *El pasagero*, p. 87.

90. Céspedes y Meneses, *Fortuna varia del soldado Píndaro*, BAE, 18, pp. 347, 353.

91. I give some data in my *Carlos V y el pensamiento político del Renacimiento* (Madrid, 1958).

92. *Día y noche de Madrid*, BAE, 33, p. 147.

93. J. M. Barnadas, "Resonancias andaluzas de la decadencia," in *Archivo Hispalense*, nos. 171-73 (Seville, 1973); the document is reproduced on pp. 112-15.

94. According to my interpretation, that is one of the faces of the historical problem in the formation of monarchical absolutism. See my *Estado moderno y mentalidad social*.

95. The collection is one of those preserved today in U. S. libraries. See Lindsay and Neu's *French Political Pamphlets 1547-1648* (Madison, 1969).

96. "Algunas reflexiones sobre la sátira bajo el reinado de los útimos Austrias," *Revista de Estudios Políticos*, no. 15 (1944).

97. *Avisos*, 2 (7 March and 28 November 1657), BAE, 222, pp. 67, 118.

98. *La Junta de Reformación*, p. 219.

100. *Cartas de jesuitas* (19 January 1638), MHE, 14, p. 291.

101. Ibid., (1 December 1637), p. 261.

102. *Día y noche de Madrid*, BAE, 33, p. 147. It deals with an unpublished manuscript that belonged to his collection; one would hope that it will one day be published.

103. *Avisos*, 2 (31 January 1657), BAE, 222, p. 57. Saavedra Fajardo, on the other hand, wrote: "Vice has no greater enemy than censorship . . . And thus, although grumbling is in itself bad, it is good for the republic, for there is no greater force over the magistrate or the prince . . . Grumbling is an argument for the republic's freedom, because under tyranny it is not permitted" (*Empresas*, 14, in *OC*, pp. 232-33).

104. *Avisos*, 2 (on different dates in the years 1657 and 1658). The reference to friar Nicolás Bautista is from 24 April 1658, BAE, 222, pp. 63, 67, 169, 172. In the anonymous *Sumario de las nuevas de la Corte*, published as an appendix to the edition of Almansa's *Cartas*, it is affirmed, in an attempt to idealize the figure of the monarch, that he told the clergy's preachers "that they should never tire of nor shrink from telling him truths, because he would never grow weary, neither of hearing them, nor of making corrections as he heard" (pp. 347-48). Weariness of the criticisms and apprehension because of them must have, nonetheless, come about very quickly.

105. "La rivolta anti-spañola a Napoli," p. 55.

106. *Noticias de Madrid (1621-1627)*, p. 72 (August 1623); see also "La oposición político-religiosa a mediados del siglo XVI: El erasmismo tardío de Felipe de la Torre," in *La oposición política bajo los Austrias*, p. 53.

107. *Diez lamentaciones del lamentable estado de los atheistas de nuestro tiempo*, edited by P. O. Steiggink (Madrid, 1959). The idea of "freedom" vis-à-vis the Church was the great sin of the epoch that J. Gracián emphasized and condemned, revealing the duality of its origin in the political and the religious.

108. *Noticias de Madrid (1621-1627)*, June 1621, p. 3; September 1621, p. 11; July 1624, pp. 98-100.

109. *Margarita. Oración fúnebre en las honras de la Serenísima Infanta* (Madrid, 1633), fols. 32v to 35v. The clergyman Paravicino wanted to punish the authors of the placards with blood and death, whereas Álamos de Barrientos and Saavedra Fajardo — the Tacitist politicians — recommended tolerating and being indulgent with them.

110. From the comedy *Tanto es lo de más como de menos*, cited from Jaime Asensio's study of it in the journal *Reflexión* 2 (January-December, 1973 [Ottawa]).

111. *Avisos*, 1 (23 September 1654 and 24 April 1655), BAE, 221, pp. 61, 131.

112. *Cartas de jesuitas* (3 June and 18 July 1634), MHE, 13, pp. 57, 81.

113. Ibid. (8 July 1638), 14, p. 450.

114. Ibid. (19 June 1638), p. 431.

115. *Avisos*, 1, BAE, 221, pp. 75, 209, 275, 304, 246 (the dates run from 1654 to 1656).

116. Pellicer, *Avisos* (24 July 1640), ed. *Semanario Erudito*, 31, p. 190.

117. Ibid. (13 May 1642), 32, p. 258.

118. Barrionuevo, *Avisos* 1, 2, BAE, 221, p. 46; 222, pp. 95, 134.

119. *Cartas de jesuitas* (12 and 19 June 1640), MHE, 15, pp. 446, 447, etc. See also Pellicer, *Avisos* (12 June 1640), 31, p. 175. The Jesuits began their references to the uprising in Portugal in these terms: "In Portugal there have been some popular riots, though of little importance," yet when they increased and became more damaging in the following days, the information transmitted became more alarming (letters from 12 and 20 September 1637), MHE, 14, pp. 189, 191.

120. See J. H. Elliot's contribution to Forster and Greene's *Preconditions of Revolution in Early Modern Europe* and my *La oposición política bajo los Austrias*.

121. BAE, 126, p. 23.

122. A. A. Sicroff, *Les controverses des statuts de pureté de sang en Espagne du XVe au XVIIe siècles* (Paris, 1960); as an example of what is here under discussion, see friar Jaime Bleda's *Crónica de los moros de España* (Valencia, 1618).

123. Although the figure of the foreigner offered favorable aspects in other, more immobilist

epochs, now, with seventeenth-century prenationalism, with the uninterrupted and general system of international wars, with the greed of mercantilism and perhaps the advantages of seeking someone to blame for all the misfortunes that were being suffered, the foreigner came to be — except in individual cases — an undesirable figure. The theme was already found in such writers as Quevedo, Mateo Alemán, and Ruiz de Alarcón, and in such economists as Sancho de Moncada, Martínez de Mata, Lope de Deza, and Gondomar. Ruiz Martín's forthcoming book about the Genovese will greatly clarify this phenomenon. What is of interest to us is the character of an internal and social conflict present, for example, in a writer like Murcia de la Llana: "How certain it is that the foreign nationals residing in Spain are mainly motivated to get rich by making deals and contracting by sea; then what reason is there for the poor native of Spain to be working with his sweat and blood to keep [its riches], so that the foreigner pluck it away with his dealings?" (*Discurso político del desempeño del Reino* . . . [Madrid, 1624], fol. 12.) Among the rich, on the other hand, we already have evidence of another attitude: "Something being from a foreign artisan is enough to give it value" (Francisco Santos, *Día y noche de Madrid*, pp. 396, 409).

124. This is a subject that has not yet been studied as it deserves. There are some references in P. W. Bomli, *La femme dans l'Espagne du Siècle d'Or* (The Hague, 1950). María de Zayas wrote a few sentences full of bitterness about the woman's state of submission. Some more data can be seen in the book I am currently preparing on the picaresque novel.

125. Some interesting data can be found in P. A. Sole's *Los pícaros de Cónil y Zahara* (Cádiz, 1965).

126. A few paragraphs above we have already seen a reference to the theme of long hair, indicating vaguely its protest significance, in a text by Francisco de León. Juan de Robles also spoke about it, commenting ironically about its abundance, in *El Culto Sevillano* (I discuss this passage in my *Antiguos y modernos*, p. 100). María de Zayas observed: "Throughout time men have been fond of long hair, although not as much as now" (*Amar sólo por vencer*, ed. cit., from her *Novelas ejemplares*, 2d part: "Desengaños amorosos" [Madrid, 1950], p. 216). Also Lope in *La Dorotea* spoke ironically about the vogue of men's long hair (E. S. Morby's edition, 1958, p. 179).

127. *Avisos*, ed. *Semanario Erudito*, 33, p. 147.

128. *Avisos*, 2 (13 December 1656), BAE, 222, p. 33.

129. Saavedra Fajardo observed "the aversion that some estates of the republic have against others, like the people against the nobility" (*Empresas* . . ., 89, in *OC*, edited by González Palencia [Madrid, 1946], p. 619).

130. *La Méditerranée*, vol. 2, pp. 75ff. (English edition, vol. 2, p. 734ff).

131. P. Vilar, *La Catalogne dans l'Espagne moderne*, vol. 1, p. 625.

132. R. Villari, "La rivolta anti-spañola," pp. 67ff.

133. Pellicer, *Avisos* (1644), ed. *Semanario Erudito*, 33, pp. 163, 176.

134. These last references, in Barrionuevo's *Avisos*, refer to the year 1655 (BAE, 221, pp. 108, 195, 225). Another very theatrical reference about a bandit priest is found in *Noticias de Madrid (1621-1627)*, p. 157 (March 1627).

135. *El bandolerisme català del Barroc*, 2d ed. (Barcelona, 1966), pp. 187-88.

136. J. Reglà, "El bandolerismo en la Cataluña del Barroco," *Saitabi*, 16, 1966.

137. On the literary scope of the theme, see A. A. Parker, "Santos y bandoleros en el teatro español del Siglo de Oro," *Arbor*, nos. 43-44, 1949.

138. Regarding those principles, see my *Teatro y literatura en la sociedad barroca* (Madrid, 1972).

139. BAE, 54, p. 577.

140. See my study "Reformismo social-agrario en la crisis del siglo XVII: Tierra, trabajo y salario según Pedro de Valencia," *Bulletin Hispanique* 72, nos. 1-2 (1970).

141. *Memoriales y Discursos de Francisco Martínez de Mata*, edited and introduction by G. Anes (who emphasized the protest character of these writings) (Madrid, 1971).

142. See Caxa de Leruela, *Restauración de la antigua abundancia de España* (Madrid, 1627), p. 54; also my *Estado moderno y mentalidad social*, vol. 2, p. 510, n. 177.

143. *La Junta de Reformación*, pp. 395-96.
144. Domínguez Ortiz, "La movilización de la nobleza castellana en 1640," *Anuario de Historia del Derecho Español*, 1955.
145. *Cartas de jesuitas* (14 May 1639), MHE, 15, p. 248.
146. Ibid., 16, p. 22.
147. *Noticia general para la estimación de las artes...* (Madrid, 1600), p. 319.
148. *Engaños que causa el vicio*, in María de Zayas, *Novelas ejemplares*, 2d part: "Desengaños amorosos," ed. cit., vol. 2, p. 455.
149. *Avisos* (1656 and 1658), BAE, 221, p. 266; 222, pp. 41, 145.
150. *Discurso universal de las causas que ofenden esta Monarquía y remedios eficaces para todas*, added by Campomanes in his appendices to the *Discurso sobre la educación popular de los artesanos*, vol. 1, p. 426.
151. The nobiliary obligation to give oneself militarily over to the king's service was ignored to such an extent that one of Ruiz de Alarcón's comedies (*La verdad sospechosa*) tells us about some nobles who, when their firstborn son dies, make their second son leave his studies at Salamanca and go, not to a battleground, but to Madrid,

> . . . donde estuviere
> como es cosa acostumbrada,
> entre ilustres caballeros,
> en España, pues es bien
> que las nobles casas den
> a su rey sus herederos.

[Where he might be, as is a customary thing in Spain, among illustrious gentlemen, since it is good for the noble houses to give the king his inheritors.]

The mere glittering of a courtier retinue increased the glow that, according to baroque methods, played the role of blinding the people who contemplated its majesty.
152. *Tiberio ilustrado con morales y políticos discursos* (Saragossa, 1645).
153. See my study "La corriente doctrinal del tacitismo político," collected in my *Estudios de historia del pensamiento español*, ser. 3.
154. Published by G. Anes as an appendix to *Memoriales y discursos de Francisco Martínez de Mata*, p. 491.
155. Álvarez Ossorio, *Discurso universal de las causas que ofenden esta Monarquía*, pp. 408-9.
156. P. M. Skrine stressed the unrest and political instability underlying baroque society. "Then what is rebellion?" he asks. The thematic connection established with such representative works as Wondel's *Lucifer* (1654) and Milton's *Paradise Lost* (1667) helps us to understand the cosmic character that the baroque human being fearfully attributed to the problem of the subversion of order. (Skrine, *The Baroque: Literature and Culture in Seventeenth-Century Europe* [London, 1978], p. 112.)
157. See my *Estado moderno y mentalidad social*, vol. 2, pp. 563ff.
158. *Política para Corregidores*, vol. 1, p. 597.
159. *Avisos* (14 July 1643), ed. *Semanario Erudito*, 33, p. 29.
160. Paz y Melia, *Papeles de la Inquisición*, no. 543, p. 209.
161. *El viaje entretenido*, edited by I. P. Ressot (Madrid, 1971), p. 88.
162. "Relación de la Cárcel de Sevilla," in *Colección de libros raros y curiosos*, edited by B. J. Gallardo, vol. 1, cols. 1341-1342 (the "Relación" is from 1585, and the process increased uncontrollably from then on).
163. *La Junta de Reformación*, p. 213.
164. The references gave in these paragraphs from Barrionuevo are found in his *Avisos*, I (1654-56), BAE, 221, pp. 77, 191, 253.
165. Published in Valencia, 1574.

278 □ NOTES TO PP. 53–61

166. See R. Huyghe, "Classicisme et baroque dans la littérature française au XVIIe siècle," *XVIIe Siècle*, no. 20 (1953), pp. 284ff.

167. See Mandrou, "Le baroque européen: Mentalité pathétique et révolution sociale," *Annales*, 1960, pp. 898ff.

CHAPTER 2. A GUIDED CULTURE

1. See George Herbert Mead, *Mind, Self and Society*, edited by Charles W. Morris (Chicago, 1934), p. 33.

2. W. W. Rostow, *Politics and the Stages of Growth* (Cambridge, 1971).

3. L. Febvre, "De 1560 à 1660: La chaîne des hommes," in *Le préclassicisme français*, edited by J. Tortel (Paris, 1952), pp. 18-23.

4. The use of the formula "reason of state" in the sense of motivations of propriety that rule individual behavior was frequent in the novel and the theater. For an example, see J. Pérez de Montalbán's *La hermosa Aurora*, the first novel of the volume *Sucesos y prodigios de amor* (Madrid, 1949), p. 27. Several other diverse examples are commented upon in my article "La cuestión del maquiavelismo y el significado de la voz *estadista* en la época del barroco," in *Beiträge zur französischen Aufklärung und zur spanischen Literatur; Festgabe für Werner Kraus* (Berlin, 1971); this article also appears in my *Estudios de historia del pensamiento español*, ser. 3.

5. *El curioso y sabio Alejandro, fiscal de vidas ajenas*, in *Constumbristas españoles*, vol. 1, p. 135.

6. Mopurgo-Tagliabue, "Aristotelismo e barroco," collected with works from various authors in *Retorica e barocco* (Rome, 1955), pp. 156-57. The author invoked the names of M. Pellegrini, Tesauro, Gracián, etc.

7. Racine, *Principes de la tragédie*, edited by E. Vinaver (Paris, 1951), p. 27. Reproduced in a broader context, the passage says the following: "Mores or character are found in all sorts of conditions, because a woman can be good and a slave can as well, although ordinarily woman is of a lesser goodness than man, and the slave is almost absolutely bad." This is an Aristotelian formulation that in the baroque would be given a specific nuance.

8. M. Weber, *The Protestant Ethic and the Spirit of Capitalism*, translated by Talcott Parsons, 2d ed. (London, 1976), p. 81 [trans. modified].

9. *Les caractères* (Paris, 1950), p. 208.

10. See E. Gilson, "La connaissance de soi-même et le socratisme chrétien," in *L'esprit de la philosophie médiévale*, 2d ser. (Paris, 1932); R. Richard, "Notes et matériaux pour l'étude du socratisme chrétien chez Sainte Thérèse et les spirituels espagnols," *Bulletin Hispanique*, 50, no. 1 (1948).

11. Self-knowledge, in an ascetic sense that comes from the patristic tradition and is renewed by the Jesuits, has been pointed out in baroque writers and specifically in Calderón by B. Marcos Villanueva in *La ascética de los jesuitas en los autos sacramentales de Calderón* (Deusto, 1973), pp. 177ff. We are principally interested in the new *operative* sense that the theme displays: knowing oneself to remake oneself.

12. *El discreto*, in *OC*, edited by A. del Hoyo (Madrid, 1960), p. 80.

13. *Oráculo manual*, edited by Romera Navarro (Madrid, 1954), p. 482. On page 479 we read that "if one doesn't know one doesn't live."

14. Ibid., pp. 451-52.

15. *Cisne de Apolo*, vol. 1, pp. 42, 161.

16. Suárez de Figueroa, *Plaza universal de todas ciencias y artes* (Perpiñán, 1630), fol. 336. In *El pasagero* (page 55), he applied the same doctrine to novels in particular.

17. *Arte de la pintura; su antigüedad y grandezas*, edited by Sánchez Cantón (Madrid, 1956), vol. 2, p. 146. It is absurd for Schevill to maintain that making use of moralizations — for example, regarding Ovid and others — would correspond to the desire to protect oneself from being condemned by the Inquisition. A great deal must be negatively referred to the Inquisition, but in this case it has

to do with a long tradition of remote origin, which was maintained in the sixteenth century and "modernized" in the seventeenth. Adapting to the times these procedures of formulating the cultural expedients in moralizing form belonged decisively to baroque culture (Schevill, *Ovid and the Renascence in Spain [Berkeley, 1913]*).

18. Ch. V. Aubrun, "Nouveau public, nouvelle comédie, à Madrid, au XVIIe siècle," collected with writings of various authors in *Dramaturgie et société* (Paris, 1968). Aubrun has also written that as a moralist Gracián "limits himself to proposing to man rules of behavior applicable within his historical conjuncture and psychological and physical conditioning" ["Crisis de la moral: Baltasar Gracián, S.J. (1601-1658)," *Cuadernos Hispano-Americanos*, no. 182, February 1965].

19. *Baltasar Gracián und die Hofliteratur in Deutschland* (Halle, 1894).

20. *El discreto*, in *OC*, p. 92.

21. Cited by Hippeau, *Essai sur la morale de La Rochefoucauld* (Paris, 1957), p. 137. There is a recent reedition of Méré's works.

22. *Guía y avisos de forasteros que vienen a la Corte*, in *Costumbristas españoles*, vol. 1, p. 46.

23. *Varias noticias importantes a la humana comunicación*, pp. 143ff.

24. See my *Teoría española del estado en el siglo XVII*, pp. 243ff.

25. *Discursos memorables del nobilísimo arte de la pintura*, edited by V. Carderera (Madrid, 1866).

26. B. Croce y Caramella, *Politici e moralisti del Seicento* (Bari, 1930).

27. *Réflexions ou sentences et maximes morales* (Paris: Garnier), p. 33.

28. Introduction to *Retables baroques de Bretagne et spiritualité du XVIIe siècle*, pp. 19, 37.

29. See his *La dialectique des Exercices spirituels de Saint Ignace de Loyola* (Paris, 1956). Much has been said, and on good grounds, about the Machiavellianism that saturated the moralism of the epoch's Christian writers. With regard to this, L. E. Palacios (in his article "La vida es sueño," *Finisterre*, 2, no. 1 [1948]) tried to bring out a profound difference that he wanted to see symbolized in the figure of Segismundo, an example of prudentialism in the Christian as opposed to the Machiavellian mode. Nevertheless, I believe that prudentialism, resulting from the exaggeration and displacement of the position of prudence in traditional morality, ends up granting a greater emphasis to the problems of efficacy and tends to mechanize its solution.

30. *Máximas políticas de Baltasar Gracián*, in *Estudios jurídicos y políticos* (Madrid, 1884), pp. 129-33.

31. In 1948 I published a brief note, "Barroco y racionalismo" (in *Finisterre* 2, no. 34), where I already indicated this aspect of the question. Of the various points articulated in my interpretation, this is the one that has been most debated. I believe that my theses are fundamentally reinforced by the recent and discerning study of C. Vasoli, *L'enciclopedismo del Seicento* (Naples, 1978), which demonstrates the sources of the epoch's myth of method and univocal science. The correspondence published by M. Batllori, S.J. ("Lettres de J.-Ch. della Faille, S.J., cosmographe du roi à Madrid, à M.-F. van Laugren, cosmographe du roi à Bruxelles, 1631-1645" [extract from *Archivum Historicum Societatis Jesu*, vol. 46 (1977), Rome] reveals the intertwining of a taste for novelty, of a zeal for invention, of an aspiration — which had an extrascientific origin — to arrive at univocal science and the passion to dominate technically the surrounding world, all of which paradoxically characterized the baroque at the same time.

32. His work, already cited, contains an appendix with a series of geometric figures that illustrate his essay; these figures represent an attempt to translate the structure of St. Ignatius's work.

33. F. Picatoste, *Calderón ante la ciencia; concepto de naturaleza y sus leyes* (Madrid, 1881). But let us not exaggerate this point. In Calderón what predominated was the idea of science as a contemplative speculation of nature:

> La muda naturaleza
> de los montes y los cielos,
> en cuya divina escuela

la rethórica aprendió
de las aves y las fieras

[The mute nature of the mountains and heavens in whose divine school he learned rhetoric from birds and beasts.]

(*La vida es sueño*)

Yo, viendo la obligación
en que te pone el retiro
que profesas, de saber
los secretos escondidos
de la gran naturaleza

[I see the obligation your professed seclusion places you in, to know the hidden secrets of grand nature.]

(*Darlo todo y no dar nada*)

This type of science, of a symbolist naturalism, inspired to a great extent the baroque's emblematic literature.

34. Céspedes y Meneses made a reference to the "angulists" in *Fortuna varia del soldado Píndaro*, BAE, 18, p. 303.

35. V. L. Tapié, "Le baroque et la société de l'Europe moderne," in Retorica e barocco (Rome, 1955), p. 231.

36. Karl Mannheim, *Ideology and Utopia*, translated by L. Wirth and E. Shils (1936; New York, 1977).

37. H. R. Trevor-Roper, *The Crisis of the Seventeenth Century*, p. 47.

38. *El Celador Universal para el bien común de todos*, included by Campomanes in his appendixes to the *Discurso sobre la educación popular de los artesanos*, vol. 1 (Madrid, 1775), p. 290.

39. Prologue to his *Tácito español, ilustrado con aforismos* (Madrid, 1614): "One cannot rigorously call this State prudence science, for its conclusions are not certain and evident at each and every moment, nor is the occurrence precise that one expects and predicts by means of them"; it was a "science of contingencies" whereby one might be unsuccessful in knowing any specific case, but a science whose predictions were valid in a general sense. See my pamphlet *Los orígenes del empirismo en el pensamiento político español del siglo XVII* (Granada, 1947), pp. 39-40, collected in my *Estudios de historia del pensamiento español*, ser. 3.

40. On the utilization of these symbols in Saavedra Fajardo and others, see M. Z. Hafter, *Gracián and Perfection; Spanish Moralist of the Seventeenth Century* (Cambridge, Mass., 1966), pp. 49ff.

41. Cited by M. Iriarte, S.J., *El Doctor Huarte de San Juan y su "Examen de Ingenios"* (Madrid, 1939), pp. 292-93.

42. *Restauración política de España* (Madrid, 1746) [originally from 1619].

43. Chastel, "Le baroque et la morte," in *Retorica e barocco*, pp. 33ff. The stagnation undergone by the studies of medicine and anatomy in seventeenth-century Spain—as López Piñero made manifest in "La medicina del barroco español," *Revista de la Universidad de Madrid*, 11, nos. 42-43 and in *La introducción de la ciencia moderna en España* (Barcelona, 1969) — would be a phenomenon parallel to the sclerosis in the second half of the Spanish baroque, a correspondence I deem highly significant.

44. *Memorial*, fol. 11.

45. P. Hazard has brought out the topical character of the belief in the differences of national characters as an essential factor of seventeenth-century thought (*The European Mind, 1680-1715*, translated by J. Lewis May [New York, 1963], pp. 53ff.).

46. *El pasagero*, p. 78.

47. Saavedra Fajardo, *Empresa* 46 *OC*, p. 378.
48. See my "La concepción del saber en una sociedad tradicional," *Estudios de historia del pensamiento español: Edad Media*, 2d ed. (Madrid, 1973).
49. *Le problème de l'incroyance au XVIe siècle; la religion de Rabelais* (Paris, 1947), pp. 445ff.
50. BAE, 33, p. 48.
51. *De l'art de la tragédie*, edited by West (Manchester, 1939), p. 24.
52. Mopurgo-Tagliabue formulated the problem in these somewhat banal terms: "This predominantly bourgeois public had made themselves an imaginary morality deriving from their nobiliary nostalgia. It conceded that individuals had a life driven by the passions, but it wanted the nobles, who were invested with public responsibility, to have a superior morality and liked to see it represented in the theater" ("Aristotelismo e barocco," p. 181). But this was not the issue: the baroque was not the result of an ideal that nostalgia for the past suggested to the bourgeois, but rather a complex of expedients, psychologically studied and manipulated with artifice, designed to imprint the broad lines of a mentality that accorded with the interests of the powerful groups in the urban population and, occasionally, in the rural population. To a certain extent, this summarizes the present book's thesis.
53. F. Braudel noted that the baroque "civilization" — according to his preferred terminology — was an agonistic civilization and that its art was a "guided art" of an instrumental nature (*La Méditerranée et le monde méditerranéen*, vol. 2, p. 160; English ed.: vol. 2, p. 832).
54. *Didactica magna* (written in 1638); from the French translation with the title *La grande didactique* (Paris, 1952), p. 19. About this aspect of the author's work, see P. Boret, *J. Amos Comenius* (Geneva, 1943).
55. Maxim 43, *Réflexions ou sentences*, p. 9.
56. "La vida es sueño," *Revista de la Universidad de Buenos Aires*, 4, 1946.
57. *Défense et illustration de la langue française*, p. 121.
58. *Avisos*, BAE, 221, p. 225.
59. *Cisne de Apolo*, vol. 2, pp. 188, 216.
60. *Empresa* 2, *OC*, pp. 175ff. Elsewhere Saavedra pointed out the factors that permitted an active, guiding control: "Freedom, education, discipline, religion, customs, place, obedience, prudence and an infinite number of other contingent factors remove or correct one's inclinations" (*República literaria*, in *OC*, p. 1179).
61. As an example, see Suárez de Figueroa, *El pasagero*, p. 114; also Gracián, in *El criticón*, *Oráculo manual*, etc., where examples abound.
62. *Día y noche de Madrid*, p. 413.
63. *Avisos*, ed. *Semanario Erudito*, 32, p. 6.
64. *La retorica e l'arte barocca*, p. 23.
65. See Pierre Guerre, "Pouvoir et poésie," in *Le préclassicisme français*, pp. 79ff.
66. *Avisos* (2 July 1641), ed. *Semanario Erudito*, 32, p. 89.
67. *Cartas de Andrés de Almansa y Mendoza. Novedades de esta Corte y avisos recibidos de otras partes (1621-1626)* (Madrid, 1886), especially pp. 53, 117, 246. This edition in the *Colección de libros raros y curiosos* includes at the end a short text of a similar nature, *Sumario de las nuevas de la Corte* (pp. 341-51); it exalts the figure of the king, who is presented as one who carefully dispenses justice, levels oppressive inequalities, severely administers public expenditures, and follows an inflexible morality in his private life. Above I have already shown Andrés de Almansa to be a defender of the system. Nevertheless, one year after the first edition of this work, John Elliott wrote me to point out that the *Dietari de Jeroni Pujades* spoke about an Andrés de Mendoça, recording this interesting piece of information dated March 1626:

Thursday the 26th. Imprisoned in irons, Andrés de Mendoça, Castilian by birth, arrived by brig at Rosas; in a letter from the Viceroy and the Duke of Cardona, Count de Empúries, it was ordered that Captain don Pedro de Tapia keep him in prison and well guarded. They say he was arrested *for discoursing* [*por hazer discursos*]. That is, in the debates of the Cortes he responded against the Memorials the Royal Majesty was intending to offer to the Kingdoms. He was already exiled from Castile because of it; they grabbed him in Barcelona at night and did not let him take clothes or anything else.

The passage can be found on p. 43 of vol. 4 of the *Dietari*, edited by Fundació Salvador Vives Casajuana (Barcelona, 1976). Pujades added that he spoke about him earlier on 11 December, but I cannot find the reference. Elliott asked whether this person might not be the same Almansa y Mendoza whose *Cartas* I repeatedly use, and Elliott commented to me that in this case he would not be as much of a supporter of the regime as I have represented him.

Of course, it seems that the person — who Pujades tells us "was well-versed in all sciences and a great poet" (p.44) — was undoubtedly the same, since the original editions of his *Cartas*, published separately during the life of the author, were sometimes signed Andrés de Mendoza and other times Andrés de Almansa y Mendoza. With the help of my erudite colleague and friend, the marquis of Siete Iglesias, I have located some of the author's discourses among the documents of the Colección Salazar kept in the Biblioteca de la Real Academia de la Historia (Siete Iglesias y B. Carretero, in their edition of the Colección Salazar Index, noted that some of Almansa's pages are missing; they have been torn out and have either been lost or are in the hands of unknowing collectors). Of the three discourses I have been able to examine, not one fits in with what the information above attributes to him. The "Discurso de Andrés de Mendoza contrapuesto al de Pedro Mantuano sobre la jornada de Francia dado a los Consejos reales de Estado y Gobierno" (Col. Salazar, N-4, fols. 118-28) is nothing more than a relatively banal writing in praise of the absolute monarchy ("It is not good for the common people to know reserved and arcane subject matters"; "matters dealing with reputation are a principal component of the reason of State"). Another discourse, dated 23 November 1624 in Madrid, is dedicated "Al Duque de Medinasidonia, mi señor, del Consejo de Su Majestad" and is written in praise of the nobility: "The knightly order was and is the nerve of the republics" (fols. 166-69). The third, printed under a pseudonym, is entitled "Relación de la muerte de don Rodrigo Calderón..." (fols. 185ff., printed); it concerns a piece of edifying literature, lacking in interest, that is limited to praising the virtue and resignation of a person in his last days before being executed.

The passage from Almansa that is cited in note 51 of chapter 1 and that is quoted in the text offers extraordinary praise of the politics of reward on the part of the kings in favor of the nobles. It is well known that in his "Memorial de mercedes" (now included by J. H. Elliott and J. F. de la Peña in their edition of the *Memoriales y cartas del Conde-Duque de Olivares*, vol. I [Madrid, 1978]) the Count-Duke severely advocated a completely opposed policy that summarily restricted patrimonial concessions on the part of the king; in that *Memorial* he condemned the excesses of liberality that used up the taxes paid by the poor, a concern that was repeated in many other of Olivares's writings. That leads me to think that Almansa was an exalted supporter of the absolute monarchy or, rather, of what I insist upon designating as the regime of monarchical absolutism, based on a pact of mutual support between the sovereign majesty and the nobility; therefore, Almansa was opposed to the Count-Duke's position. As a consequence I believe that Almansa, along with the upper aristocrats, would be for the king (he seemed to confirm it in his dedication to Medina Sidonia) in the party hostile to Olivares, which would be the cause of his imprisonment. Because of this I maintain my characterization of Almansa as an very avid defender of royalty, nobility, and religion; I am, however, eliminating the reference I made here in the first edition to the Count-Duke, a reference I believe inadequate. On the other hand, in his *Gran memorial*, Olivares, distrustful of the nobles, insisted that it would not be permitted for anyone, from either their upper or middle ranks, to assume leadership of the *populares* because in becoming attached to those who were so numerous and in stimulating and trying to channel their disquiet, the nobles presented themselves as defenders of the people and incited them to oppose granting some tax [*servicio*] when the king requested it (in *Memoriales y cartas*, p. 62). Would Almansa in this sense represent the interests of the noble faction, fomenting the rejection of the royal propositions in the Cortes that were being celebrated in Madrid during these years? In any case it doesn't seem to bear any relation to the project of the "Unión de armas," the other point of conflict of the Count-Duke's politics. In one way or another, it has to do with serving the nobles' pretensions over against the favorite, pretensions that did not prove very favorable for the king.

68. Almansa himself declared his apprehensions about the publication of his *Cartas*, confessing that "our correspondence has perturbed many who have tried to obstruct it," and he excused himself by saying that it was not he but the printers who were making them public (pp. 71, 117).

69. *The Social History of Art*, vol. 2, p. 190.

70. "Popular Culture in Perspective," in *Literature, Popular Culture and Society*, 2d ed. (Palo Alto, Calif, 1968), p. 11.

71. See C. Dejob, *De l'influence du Concile de Trente sur la littérature et les beaux-arts chez les peuple catholiques* (Paris, 1884).

72. J. Sánchez, *Academias literarias del Siglo de Oro español* (Madrid, 1961).

73. See Guerre's "Pouvoir et poésie."

74. See my *Teatro y literatura en la sociedad barroca*, pp. 119ff.

75. *Segni e simboli nella "Vida es sueño"* (Bari, 1968).

76. *Paradoxas racionales*, edited by E. Buceta (Madrid, 1935), p. 86.

77. *Discurso al Rey*, fols. 13, 14.

78. About these aspects of the social structure, see Domíguez Ortiz, *La sociedad española del siglo XVII*, vol. 1 (Madrid, 1963).

79. *Sociología*, Span. trans. (Madrid, 1927), vol. 3, p. 13.

80. *La retorica e l'arte barocca*, pp. 11-13. The baroque technique, like rhetoric, was a method rather than a system: "It doesn't investigate nature, it doesn't set out to increase the accumulation of concepts; it investigates, with an almost scientific coldness, the human psyche and elaborates all the means that might serve to awaken its reactions."

81. See my *Teoría española del estado en el siglo XVII*, pp. 319ff.

82. *Arte nuevo de hacer comedias en este tiempo*, edited by Juana de José Prades (Madrid, 1971).

83. "I thought that novels have the same precepts as comedies, whose goal is for the author to give the people contentment and pleasure [*gusto*], even though art is left by the wayside" (*La desdicha por la honra*, in *Novelas a Marcia Leonarda*, edited by F. Rico [Madrid, 1968], p. 74). In both cases — theater and novel — it is a matter of sacrificing art to the people so as to impose more effectively an ideology, counting on their inadvertent collaboration.

84. Let us also observe that whereas the Gothic or Renaissance façade "is adapted to the structure and has as its principal task to reveal the internal articulations to the outside," in the baroque one seeks "by means of the façade the conquest of exterior space" (Rousset, *La littérature de l'âge baroque en France* [Paris, 1953], p. 168). Wölfflin already wrote that "there exists the tendency to present the painting not as a piece of the world that exists for itself, but as a transitory spectacle in which the spectator had the good fortune to participate for a moment" (see his *Principles of Art History*). And Hauser noted that by virtue of the introduction of the spectator's point of view, "the element of space [is] a form of existence which belongs to him, is dependent on him and, as it were, created by him" (*The Social History of Art*, p. 176).

85. *Philosophía antigua poética* (Madrid, 1953), vol. 1, p. 249.

86. *Rinascimento e barocco*, pp. 51-52.

87. *Traité des passions de l'âme*, 48.

88. *Oeuvres de M. Régnier*, pp. 53-62.

89. *El pasagero*, p. 114.

90. There exists a published version of this interesting document: "Copy of a letter from Martín de la Naja (S.J.) to the Doctor Gaspar Martín" (Saragossa, March 1654).

91. *Avisos*, BAE, CCXXI, p. 91.

92. *De l'art de la tragédie*, p. 41.

93. Cited by Hippeau, *Essai sur la morale de La Rochefoucauld*, p. 162.

94. *Arte de la pintura*, vol. 1, p. 387.

95. *Diálogos de la pintura* (Madrid, 1865). The theme of tears constituted one of the various aspects in which the baroque prefigured romantic sensibility. It extended to the point of declaring crying to be proof of masculinity. Agustín de Rojas (*El viaje entretenido*, ed. J. P. Ressot [Madrid, 1972], p. 125) would maintain that "crying is not timidity when it is born of the soul's piety or of one's own nature." Pérez de Montalbán (*La fuerza del desengaño*, the second novel of *Sucesos y prodigios de amor* [Madrid, 1949], p. 64) would see that even in this the position of man is privileged with respect to woman's, since man "at least has the freedom and time to cry." St. Peter's well-known evangelical episode would be a great Baroque subject: L. Tansillo wrote in royal octaves *Le lagrime di san Pietro* (Venice, 1589); in imitation, Malherbe published in 1607 *Les larmes de Saint Pierre*; and Fernández de Ribera composed a long poem in redondillas, *Las lágrimas de San Pedro* (Seville, 1609).

96. *Oráculo manual*, no. 40, p. 88.

97. *El héroe*, discurso 12, in *OC*, p. 23.

98. *Arte de galantería* (Lisbon, 1670), p. 16.

99. *El museo pictórico y escala óptica*, vol. 1 of *Theórica de la pintura* (Madrid, 1715), p. 35.

100. Mopurgo-Tagliabue, "Aristotelismo e barocco," p. 167.

101. In his *Rhetórica eclesiástica* (2, xi), friar Luis de Granada wrote that "it consists as much in instructing as in moving the listeners' psyches" (p. 104). The attitude, therefore, was already defined in mannerism.

102. *Arte poética española* (Salamanca, 1592), p. 9.

103. *Política española*, edited by M. Herrero García (Madrid, 1945), p. 47.

104. *El pasagero*, p. 27.

CHAPTER 3: A MASS CULTURE

1. *Relaciones geográficas de los pueblos de España ordenadas por Felipe II: Relaciones del reino de Toledo*, edited by C. Viñas Mey and R. Paz (Madrid, 1963), part 2, vol. 1, p. 180.

2. *Memorial de la política necesaria y útil Restauración a la República de España* (Madrid, 1600), fol. 12.

3. *Restauración política de España* (Madrid, 1746) [originally from 1619], discurso 2: "Población y aumento numeroso de la nación española," pp. 44-51.

4. *Extensión política y económica*, the second of the *memoriales* reproduced in the appendixes to Campomanes's *Discurso sobre la educación popular*, vol. 1, p. 42. Álvarez viewed as very obvious the necessity to bring the kingdom up to a level where society was overflowing with people and, correlatively, to increase production for these masses; thus he wrote in another work: "The sole remedy for the entire monarchy is to sow all the fields" (*Discurso universal de las causas que ofenden esta Monarquía*, in the appendixes, p. 356). Naturally the decisive step would not be taken without industrialization: Sancho de Moncada and Martínez de Mata already knew this in the seventeenth century, and it was a common idea in the eighteenth.

5. The textbooks of the history of economic doctrines customarily antedate to the eighteenth century the appearance of the notion that advantages are to be derived from the country's having a large population. In reality, there were medieval texts already saying this, but although one might consider in such cases that this sort of affirmation was foreign to the economy and corresponded to the evangelical maxim of going forth and multiplying, it cannot be denied that since the second half of the sixteenth century the populationist notions were repeated with a distinctly economic character. See my *Estado moderno y mentalidad social*, vol. 1, pp. 114ff.

6. Cellorigo, in the prologue to *Memorial de la política necesaria*.

7. The Royal Council's report to Philip III (1 February 1619): the prince should continue "considering his patrimony's greatest earnings and his empire's most outstanding greatness and activity, the people of its estates, in which the Kingdom most consists" (*La Junta de Reformación*, AHE, 5, p.15.). Philip IV's letter to the cities having a vote in the Cortes (28 October 1622): "The

lack of people and the diminution of and decrease in the towns is the greatest injury of all and what has placed this monarchy at greatest risk" (ibid., p. 390).

8. See my "Reformismo social-agrario en la crisis del siglo XVII: Tierra, trabajo y salario según Pedro de Valencia," *BHI*, 72, 1-2, 1970.

9. About the increase in the number of students, let us recall that in one of the Jesuits' letters it was said that when confronted by a serious military difficulty and fearing invasion, resistance was put up by "withdrawing students from the Universities," along with other measures (MHE, 14, p. 209, letter from 12 October 1637).

10. See Clement Greenberg, "Avant-Garde and Kitsch," *Partisan Review* 5 (Fall 1939), p. 39.

11. Dwight Macdonald, "Masscult and Midcult," *Partisan Review* 2 (Spring 1960) and 4 (Fall 1960); see p. 204.

12. Lazarsfeld and Merton, "Mass Communication, Popular Taste and Organized Social Action," in *Problems in the Communication of Ideas*, edited by L. Bryson (New York, 1948), pp 95-118.

13. The anticipation of the kitsch phenomenon in seventeenth-century culture can be understood with this observation from L. Giesz himself: "From the horrifying story to the epic theater, enjoyable curiosity and the enjoyment of kitsch are united in awe. Fundamentally and from an anthropological point of view, it has to do with the same substratum of experience that becomes active in what is sensational as much as in kitsch (*Phänomenologie des Kitsches*, 2d ed. [Munich, 1971], p. 39). Let us observe that 1700 is frequently indicated as the date of the great explosion of the reading public, of the public interested in art and demanding culture; although there may be important quantitative differences, the expansion and "popular" distortions of certain forms of culture making up kitsch were already openly occurring in the seventeenth century. Consider the widespread discussion in the epoch regarding two concepts that were closely tied to a recognition of superior and inferior levels of culture — that is, the levels of "taste" and of the "common people" [*gusto* y *vulgo*].

14. *Historia de Segovia* (republished in Segovia, 1920).

15. On the difference that is being dealt with here, I am relying on the concepts established by D. Macdonald in his "Masscult and Midcult."

16. If we were concerned with another epoch — for example, the nineteenth century — we would perhaps have to take up such names as Balzac, W. Scott, Dickens, Pérez Galdós, and Zola (focusing on the century's most authentic art, the novel). There is neither a necessary separation nor incompatibility between high culture and kitsch: the same ones who create the first can manufacture the second; the same ones who finance the second can be patrons of the first; and even readers or spectators of a great work go to be distracted or thrilled with kitsch. Even more serious is the fact that a country's art or literature textbooks offer the conventional praise of Rembrandt or Michelangelo, of Miró or Kandinsky, without that influencing the system of values, beliefs, aspirations, and tastes that dominate in the social education subject to a kitsch criterion. Moreover, these same artists and their great works can be utilized as kitsch, as in those business calendars that try to appear learned by reproducing on every month's leaf a painting of the greatest quality for its most inadequate contemplation. It has been said that to a certain extent kitsch needs a great cultural tradition that it can parasitically live from. In any case, it is a *common* culture — not *popular* in the sense of produced by the people — of low quality, and if it is produced in this way it is not because of the necessary incapacity of the artist employed, for the artist can be highly skilled in his or her profession. Nor need the "producer" of kitsch believe in the critical incapacity of the receptive public. If cultural creation lapses into little less than a mechanized production, if it is possible to speak about a "culture industry," it occurs for well-defined reasons that have very serious social consequences. I must confess to the reader that while I have been writing this note I have had in mind the *Arte nuevo de hacer comedias*, which is a perfect kitsch recipe book written by Lope himself.

17. Suárez de Figueroa, *Varias noticias importantes a la humana comunicación*, fol. 234: "It is not unknown that in this way one can put out more work in a single day than many learned writers in a year." This author also dealt with the theme in his *Plaza universal de todas ciencias y artes*

(Madrid, 1615). I have collected similar references (in which views of printing's mass production reflect the image of a growing society) in my *Antiguos y modernos: La idea de progreso en el desarrollo inicial de una sociedad* (Madrid, 1967) and in my "La imagen de la sociedad expansiva en la conciencia castellana del siglo XVI," *Hommage à Fernand Braudel* (Toulouse, 1972). This is one of the aspects in which the baroque not only continues but accentuates a tendency of the Renaissance.

18. G. Francastel, "De Giorgione au Titien: L'artiste, le public, et la commercialization de l'oeuvre d'art," *Annales*, nos. 15-16 (November-December 1960).

19. Hauser, *The Social History of Art*, vol. 2, pp. 222-23.

20. *Arte de la pintura*.

21. *La prudente venganza*, in *Novelas a Marcia Leonarda*, BAE, 38, p. 32. In relation to this let us recall the reference to the street of the *Ropería* [clothing trade] that F. Rico pointed out in *Guzmán de Alfarache* (2.1.1.).

22. Manufacturing: "Producing in a workshop on the basis of free workers, who labor without utilizing mechanical energy, but who are assembled and subjected to a disciplined labor." M. Weber added two other conditions to this Marxist definition: the lack of fixed capital and the absence of a capitalist accounting [see *Economy and Society*, edited by G. Roth and C. Wittich, translated by Ephraim Fischoff et al. (Berkeley, 1978)]. Yet one must still refer to the fact that in such an industrial system a level of the division of labor as such has not yet been reached. A remote glimpse of this regimen of industrial labor in the time of the baroque can already be found in Caxa de Leruela (see my *Estado moderno y mentalidad social*, vol. II [Madrid, 1972], p. 395).

23. Let us again refer to Macdonald's study, p. 214.

24. Croce said this in commenting on W. Scott's "mechanical method." Cited by Macdonald, "Masscult and Midcult," pp. 221-22.

25. Ibid., p. 211.

26. *Phänomenologie des Kitsches*.

27. *Les catactères*, p. 232.

28. *La Junta de Reformación*, p. 100.

29. *Empresa*, 46 *OC*, pp. 377ff.

30. *Group Psychology and the Analysis of the Ego*, standard edition, translated and edited by J. Strachey & Anna Freud, vol. 18 (London, 1955), p. 88.

31. *Revista de la Universidad de Madrid*, 11, nos. 42-43, 1962.

32. *Retables de Bretagne*, p. 20.

33. *Memorial*, fol. 29.

34. See MHE, 15, pp. 23, 178, 278.

35. Here are some examples in Pellicer's *Avisos: Semanario Erudito*, 31, pp. 104, 117, 213; 32, p. 96; 33, pp. 15, 130, 159.

36. "Las *Soledades* de don Luis de Góngora: Algunas características de su estilo," in *Premarinismo y pregongorismo* (Rome, 1973), pp. 72-73.

37. "De 1560 à 1660: La chaîne des hommes," p. 27.

38. About twenty years beyond our chronological limit, La Bruyère had already seen this phenomenon in baroque societies: "In society reason is the first to submit; the wisest are often led by those who are most mad and most bizarre" (*Les caractères*, p. 105). This incomprehensible storehouse, with its emotive character and opposition to all rational substance, served the baroque ruler who set about to operate upon a group: from it he had to draw his resources to move and lead the group.

39. "Aristotelismo e barocco," p. 143.

40. A. Collard, *Nueva poesía: Conceptismo y culturanismo en la crítica española* (Madrid, 1967), p. 10.

41. Edited by I. P. Ressot (Madrid, 1972), p. 67.

42. *Philosophía antigua poética*, II, p. 208.

43. *El pasagero*, p. 50.

44. See my *Estado moderno y mentalidad social*.

45. *La Junta de Reformación*, pp. 23, 67-68, 78, 134, 393, 450, 451. Some members of the junta disagreed in their opinions (see p. 86).

46. BAE, 42, p. 111.

47. He published a work on the subject (L. Lowenthal, "Biographies in Popular Magazines," in *Radio Research 1942-1943* [New York, 1944]). I have not been able to examine this article; I only know it from references.

48. See my preliminary study to the author's *Norte de príncipes* and *Vida de Rómulo* (Madrid, 1945).

49. "De Cervantes y Lope de Vega," *RFE*, 22, 1935. I don't find the word in his work on the *Arte nuevo* (although the idea hovers over the writing), and I think it must be a question of personal recollection, of an expression I heard him use at some time.

50. *The Social History of Art*, vol. 2, p. 163.

51. *La littérature de l'âge baroque en France* (Paris, 1953).

52. *Recherches sur le thème paysan dans la "comedia" au temps de Lope de Vega*, p. xvii.

53. *Aventuras del bachiller Trapaza*, in *La novela picaresca española*, p. 1513.

54. *Obras de Guillén de Castro*, edited by E. Juliá Martínez, vol. 2 (Madrid, 1926), p. 492.

55. *Poetas dramáticos valencianos*, edited by E. Juliá Martínez, vol. 1 (Madrid, 1929), pp. 624-25.

56. *Teatro de los teatros de los passados y presentes siglos*, edited by D. W. Moir (London, 1970), p. 82.

57. Díez Borque gave interesting data about ticket prices in the excellent preliminary study to his edition of *El mejor alcalde, el rey* (Madrid, 1973).

58. See my *Teoría española del estado en el siglo XVII* (Madrid, 1944).

59. *Empresas* 20 and 31, *OC*, pp. 259, 313.

60. *El rey don Pedro en Madrid* (Madrid: Aguilar), p. 611.

61. Ruiz de Alarcón also formulated the question in these terms (*Los pechos privilegiados*, BAE, 20, p. 428): "Al fin, es forzosa ley / Por conservar la opinión / Vencer de su corazón / Los sentimientos el Rey" [In the end, it is an obligatory law that for the king to maintain public opinion, he must win over its heartfelt feelings].

62. In his *Comentarios políticos*, p. 31. That was the thesis of Álamos, Saavedra, and the Tacitists. Lancina would also write that "sovereignty among men consists in opinion" (p. 98).

63. *"De corpore politico" or the Elements of Law, Moral and Politic* (London, 1650).

64. *Oeuvres de Pascal*, vol. 4, *Pensées*, pp. 37-38 (the editor confessed to not being able to identify this work); the second reference in *Pensées*, 1, p. 129.

65. *Cartas*, p. 147 (from November 1622).

66. M. N. Grand-Mesnil, *Mazarin, La Fronde et la presse 1647-1649* (Paris, 1967).

67. Not even a minimally noteworthy study has been done about the beginnings of printing in the Spanish seventeenth century. A valuable contribution has appeared with M. Cruz García de Enterría's *Sociedad y poesía de cordel en el barroco* (Madrid, 1973).

68. *Historia de los movimientos y separación y guerra de Cataluña* (1645), BAE, 21, pp. 478-79.

69. *Historia de una polémica y semblanza de una generación* (Madrid, 1949).

70. *Cartas*, 5 (14 October 1621), p. 72.

71. E. Varela Hervías, *Gazeta Nueva* (Madrid, 1960).

72. *Cartas de jesuitas* (MHE, 13-19) contain many references to matters of this type, as we have been seeing.

73. See my *El mundo social de "La Celestina"*.

74. *Cartas de jesuitas* (13 November 1640), MHE, 16.

75. Besides the information given us by the Tacitists (Álamos, Lancina, etc.), see an example in the *Cartas de jesuitas* (18 November 1640), MHE, 16, p. 62.

76. *Historias*, p. 353.

77. 3, p. 151.

78. E. Shils, "Mass Society and its Culture," in *Culture and Mass Culture*, edited by P. Davidson, R. Meyersohn, and E. Shils, vol. 1 (Cambridge, 1978), p. 209n.

79. R. Klein, "*Giudizio e gusto* dans la théorie de l'art au Cinquecento," in *La forme et l'intelligible* (Paris, 1970).

80. In depreciating some objects of adornment, Dorotea, the exquisite protagonist of Lope's novel, says "they are richer than they are of good taste" and appeals to what she calls "the law [*premática*] of good taste" (*La Dorotea*, edited by E. S. Morby, 2d ed. (Madrid, 1968), p. 174.

81. Here are some references: "Taste has no law" (Ruiz de Alarcón, *Los pechos privilegiados*); "No one is obliged to obey in such matters" (Pérez de Montalbán, *Los primos amantes*, BAE, 33, p. 541); "Its criterion of beauty does not suffer the domination of precepts" (Calderón, *La hija del aire*, 1).

82. B. W. Wardropper, "Fuenteovejuna: El gusto y lo justo," *Studies in Philology*, no. 53, 1956.

83. Carlos Boil, another of the Valencian writers of Lopesque comedies, tells his reader (in *Poetas dramáticos valencianos*, vol. 1, p. 628): "El lacayo y la fregona, / el escudero y la dueña, / es lo que más, en efecto, / a la voz común se apega" [The attendant and the scrubbing maid, the nobleman and the lady are, in effect, who most join in a common voice]. Let us note that he does not integrate farmers, herdsmen, day laborers, and people with rural occupations, where the sociological phenomenon of massification cannot take place.

84. *Política española*, edited by M. Herrero García, p. 119.

CHAPTER 4. AN URBAN CULTURE

1. *La Méditerranée et le monde méditerranéen*, vol. 2, 2d ed., p. 163 (English ed. vol. 2, p. 835 [trans. modified]).

2. About this political phenomenon, compare my *Estado moderno y mentalidad social* (Madrid, 1972).

3. The settings for the series *Sucesos y prodigios de amor* take place in Madrid (two), Seville, Valencia, Alcalá, and Ávila.

4. Madrid, Barcelona, Valencia, Segovia, Valladolid, Toledo, Salamanca, Saragossa, Murcia, Seville, Granada, Jaén, Lisbon, Milan, and Naples.

5. Saragossa, Seville, Córdoba, Toledo, Lisbon, and Madrid appear in his *Historias peregrinas y ejemplares*.

6. Segovia, Madrid, Saragossa, Seville, Córdoba, Granada, Valencia, and others are mentioned in *El español Gerardo*, generally praised with the adjective "big."

7. "Le baroque et la société de l'Europe moderne," *Retorica e barocco*, pp. 225ff.

8. V. L. Tapié, *Baroque et classicisme* (Paris, 1957), pp. 134ff.

9. *Le baroque* (Paris 1961), p. 53.

10. Tapié, Le Flem, and others in *Retables de Bretagne*, which has already been cited.

11. Out of this mass of rural Breton retables, only 16 percent were built before the year 1660; 80 percent were built between that date and the beginning of the French Revolution, and only 4 percent after that event. These data can be found in Pardailhé-Galabrun's part of the study in *Retables de Bretagne*.

12. Many isolated data can be gathered from the volumes of *Ars Hispaniae*, edited by D. Angulo Iñíguez (15) and M. E. Gómez Moreno (16). M. Sagues Subijana has recently published an article on "Cuatro retablos barrocos guipuzcoanos," *Boletín de la Real Sociedad Vascongada de los Amigos del País*, 28, 1, 1972: those retables, set up in rural milieus, are from the very end of the seventeenth century.

13. "Limites chronologiques, limites géographiques et limites sociales du baroque," in *Retorica e barocco*, p. 57.

14. George M. Foster, *Traditional Cultures and the Impact of Technological Change* (New York, 1962), p. 47.

15. B. Schnapper and H. Richardot, *Histoire des faits économiques* (Paris, 1971), p. 206.

16. Some data have been collected in my "La imagen de la sociedade expansiva en la consciencia castellana del siglo XVI," *Mélanges en l'honneur de Fernand Braudel*, 1 (Toulouse, 1973), p. 373.

17. Compare N. Salomon, *La campagne de Nouvelle Castille à la fin du XVIe siècle* (Paris, 1964).

18. *Gobierno político de agricultura* (Madrid, 1618), fol. 37.

19. Compare J. Heers, *L'Occident au XIVe et XVe siècles* (Paris, 1963), p. 93. Depopulation and absenteeism were the aspects insisted upon again and again in the documents, the aspects reflected upon by the baroque rulers Philip III and Philip IV.

20. C. Viñas Mey, *El problema de la tierra en la España de los siglos XVI-XVII* (Madrid, 1941), p. 125.

21. *Restauración política de España*, 1619. I am citing from the 1742 edition, p. 49. This became the general argument of the council's recommendation.

22. Domínguez Ortiz, *El Antiguo Régimen. Los reyes católicos y los Austrias* (Madrid, 1973), p. 349.

23. *La Méditerranée et le monde méditerranéen*, vol. 1, pp. 169-70 (English ed.: vol. 1, pp. 188-89).

24. Domínguez Ortiz, *La sociedad española del siglo XVII*, p. 117.

25. *La Junta de Reformación*, p. 16. Domínguez cited different texts in this same sense.

26. Carande, *Carlos V y sus banqueros*, vol. 1, p. 60.

27. Respectively, *Restauración política de España*, discursos 1 and 2, especially the reference on p. 49; *Libro de las cinco excelencias del español* (Pamplona, 1629), fols. 170ff.; *Gobierno de agricultura*, fols. 21, 22.

28. Compare Heers, *L'Occident au XIVe et XV siècle*, p. 149. In the mid-seventeenth century, Martínez de Mata maintained that urban consumption was the principal aspect of the peasant economy and the only aspect that kept it in a favorable situation; on this he based his defense of protecting the city's factories: "If the manufacturers are diminished in the cities, it is the ruin of farming and produces a surplus that would have to be consumed" (*Memorial en razón de la despoblación y pobreza de España y su remedio*, in *Memoriales y discursos*, edited by G. Anes, p. 290).

29. *Cigarrales de Toledo*, edited by Víctor Said Armesto (Madrid, 1914), p. 49.

30. *El Antiguo Régimen*, p. 139.

31. *El pasagero*, p. 364.

32. Many of these plays appeared to be performed only on family occasions (see E. Cotarelo, *Entremeses, Loas, Bailes, Jácaras y Mogigangas*, vols. 17 and 18 in NBAE).

33. There are many examples of this literature of the stove (as opposed to the peasant hearth, with a chimney and high bell). Among them are Andrés del Prado's series, *Meriendas del ingenio y entretenimientos del gusto* (BAE, 33); Mariana de Carvajal, *Navidades de Madrid y noches entretenidas*, eight novelettes of a familial and *costumbrista* nature (Madrid, 1663).

34. Lope de Deza, *Gobierno político de agricultura*, fol. 26.

35. *La Junta de Reformación*, AHE, 5, p. 23.

36. Ibid., p. 24.

37. I owe this reference to Le Flem, who is doing an extensive study of the social world of the Mesta.

38. Compare the treatise *De tranquillitate animi*, 2, 10-13 (Latin-French ed. of "Les Belles Lettres," pp. 77-78).

39. BAE, 42, pp. 287 and 310 respectively.

40. Ibid., pp. 366, 369. We are referring to songs 2 and 4.

41. Grace L. Morley, *Le sentiment de la nature en France dans la première moitié du dix-septième siècle* (Nemours, 1926). One could write an excellent book about this subject in Spanish literature.

42. *Empresa* 1, *OC*, p. 170.

43. *La Cintia de Aranjeuz* (Madrid, 1945), p. 126.

44. *Paradoxas racionales*, p. 16.

45. Vossler, *Lope de Vega y su tiempo* (Madrid, 1940), p. 100.

46. *La novela picaresca española*, edited by A. Valbuena Prat (Madrid, 1946), pp. 1346, 1357.

47. V. Espinel, *Vida del escudero Marcos de Obregón*, edited by S. Gili Gaya, CC, 1 (Madrid, 1922-23), p. 124.

48. *Forasteros y extranjeros en el Madrid de los Austrias* (Madrid, 1963), p. 15.

49. "Amar sólo por vencer," in *Desengaños amorosos*, *OC*, 2, p. 213.

50. *Día y noches de Madrid*, p. 378.

51. *Aventuras del bachiller Trapaza*, in *La novela picaresca española*, p. 1515; and *El sagaz y sabio Alejandro, fiscal de vidas ajenas*, in *Costumbristas españoles*, 1, p. 155.

52. *El español Gerardo*, p. 124: "common and universal mother of diverse people and remote nations."

53. *Cigarrales de Toledo*, pp. 197-98.

54. Mateo Alemán, *Guzmán de Alfarache*, edited by S. Gili Gaya, CC, 5 (Madrid), p. 91.

55. *El disfrazado*, BAE, 33, p. 249.

56. *El viaje entretenido*, pp. 197-98.

57. Edited by J. Millé, CC, 1, p. 189.

58. *El soldado Píndaro*, p. 303.

59. "Réalités économiques et prises de conscience: Quelques témoignages sur le XVIe," in *Annales*, 1959, p. 735.

60. In response to the questionnaire ordered by Philip II, the "relación" of Toledo stressed this urban aspect, noting that at the end of the workday not a single farmer nor any farming equipment was to be seen passing through the doors of the city (*Relaciones de los pueblos de España, Reino de Toledo*, edited by C. Viñas Mey and R. Paz [Madrid], part 3, p. 506).

61. Jerónimo Yáñez de Alcalá, *El donado hablador*, BAE, 18, p. 503.

62. Navarrete y Ribera, *Los tres hermanos*, BAE, 33, p. 369.

63. *El donado hablador*, p. 1310.

64. *La burlada Aminta y venganza del honor*, in *Novelas amorosas y ejemplares*, vol. 1 (Madrid, 1948), p. 83.

65. *Memorial sobre la política necesaria*, fol. 5.

66. From Gracián Serrano, cited by Domínguez Ortiz, *El Antiguo Régimen*, p. 38.

67. Liñán y Verdugo, *Guía y avisos de forasteros que llegan a la Corte*, in *Costumbristas españoles*, vol. 1, p. 55.

68. *El soldado Píndaro*, p. 367.

69. *Cartas*, 2 (16 May 1621), p. 30.

70. *Libro de las cinco excelencias del español* (Madrid, 1626), p. 161.

71. *La Junta de Reformación*, p. 29. In his letter to the cities, Philip IV took measures against the excesses of ostentation (ibid., p. 390). Rousset, in the work I have mentioned so frequently, *La littérature de l'âge baroque en France,* dedicated part of a chapter to "L' ostentation" pp. 219ff.

72. V. L. Tapié, *Baroque et classicisme*, p. 87.

73. Because of a warped perspective that today would be untenable (that is, because of his failure to notice what was happening in other countries, which today is considered to have also happened in France), R. Huyghe said that the baroque was a decentralizing, provincial art hostile to the monarchy ("Classicisme et baroque dans la peinture française au XVIIe siècle," *XVIIe Siècle,* no. 20 [Paris, 1953]). Francastel recognized the role that corresponded to the French monarchy, but he did not sufficiently appreciate the position of Paris because he took into account solely the plastic arts (and, moreover, somewhat arbitrarily); compare this author's "Limites chronologiques" and "Baroque et classicisme: Histoire ou tipologie des civilisations?," *Annales* (January-March 1959), pp. 142ff.

74. Ph. Butler, *Classicisme et baroque dans l'oeuvre de Racine* (Paris, 1959).
75. See my *Estado moderno y mentalidad social*, vol. I, p. 149.
76. *Doctrina política y civil* (Toledo, 1621), no. 286, fol. 102.
77. This is the title of his work on the epoch's art, published by Skira; see pp. 34ff.
78. Domínguez Ortiz, *El Antiguo Régimen*, pp. 129ff.
79. *De cómo se remediarán los vicios de la Corte y que no acuda a ella tanta gente inútil*, BN, ms. 8755. The administration displayed a lot of activity on this matter. Various documents are collected in *La Junta de Reformación*, AHE, 5.
80. Fernández Navarrete (*Conservación de Monarquías*, discurso 14: "De la despoblación por venirse mucha gente a vivir a la Corte") maintained that the court grew larger "with deformity and excess," relating it to the zeal to manifest grandeur that I have alluded to (1805 ed., pp. 74-77; the work was written in 1612 and published in 1625). Saavedra Fajardo observed that the court was the main reason, among others, for depopulation, which was owed to "the pomp of the courts, their comforts, delights, the earnings of the arts, the opportunities for rewards" (*Empresa* 66, *OC*, edited by González Palencia [Madrid], p. 510).
81. For example, bankers, merchants, functionaries, etc. See my *Estado moderno y mentalidad social*, p. 150.
82. *La Dorotea*, 2, iv, p. 163.
83. González Dávila, *Teatro de las grandezas de la villa de Madrid* (Madrid, 1623), p. 11.
84. Nuñez de Castro, *Libro histórico-político. Sólo Madrid es Corte y el Cortesano en Madrid*, ms. 1675, fols. 9, 11, 24.
85. Sánchez Cantón, *Don Diego Sarmiento de Acuña, conde de Gondomar (1567-1626)* (Madrid, 1935), p. 35. The letter had been published in the appendix to Cabrera de Córdoba's *Relaciones* (Madrid, 1857), pp. 620-22.
86. Cited by Ch. V. Aubrun, "Nouveau public, nouvelle comédie a Madrid au XVIIe siècle," included in the collection *Dramaturgie et société* (Paris, 1968).
87. *Historias peregrinas y ejemplares*, p. 354; the passage cited comes from *Los dos Mendozas*.
88. *The City in History*, pp. 360-61.
89. *Cartas de jesuitas* (20 October 1637), MHE, 14, p. 203.
90. Ibid., 15, p. 311.
91. Edited by González Palencia, pp. 88, 152, 154, passim.
92. *Avisos*, ed. *Semanario Erudito*, 31, p. 21 (31 May 1639); 32, p. 103 (30 July 1641); ibid., p. 283 (1 July 1642).
93. *Avisos*, BAE, 222, p. 13 (25 October 1656); ibid., pp. 16-19 (8 and 15 November 1656); ibid., p. 63 (23 February 1657); ibid., p. 191 (5 June 1958) and passim. Treachery must have been similar on both sides: along with the truculent news items that Barrionuevo repeated in lamenting the state of the city, he also commented on one occasion when those being persecuted killed some magistrates and a mayor: "Not that it bothers me, for these people commit so many infractions in the name of authority that I am not surprised by anything that happens to them" (BAE, 221, p. 303, 9 August 1656).
94. Viñas Mey, "La estructura social-demográfica del Madrid de los Austrias," *Revista de la Universidad de Madrid*, 4, no. 16 (1955), pp. 476-77.
95. "Of Friendship," in *Essays*, English text and French translation, edited by M. Castelain (Paris, 1948), p. 134.
96. *La soledad en la poesía lírica española* (Madrid, 1941).
97. G. Formichi, "Bibliografia della novella spagnola seicentesca," collected in the volume *Lavori ispanistici*, ser. 3 (Messina-Florence, 1973).
98. *Paradoxas racionales*, edited by E. Buceta (Madrid, 1935), p. 15.
99. Constandse (in *Le Baroque espagnol et Calderón de la Barca* [Amsterdam, 1951], pp. 45-47) cited various examples, such as Hurtado de Mendoza's *Elogio de cuerno* and Quiñones de Benavente's *El marido flemático*.

100. *Cartas* (May-July 1621), pp. 19, 31, 35.

101. Ibid., p. 345.

102. *Verdades morales en que se reprehenden y condenan los trages vanos, superfluos y profanos, con otros vicios y abusos que oy se usan, mayormente los escotados deshonestos de las mugeres* (Madrid, 1678).

103. *Breve satisfacción a algunas ponderaciones contra los trajes, que sin más fin que el de ser acostumbrados usan las mujeres en España* (Seville, 1684). Although the first work has more than 350 pp., this response has no more than 38.

104. *La Méditerranée et le monde méditerranéen*, p. 469 of the 1st edition. This paragraph, which was contained in one of the parts of the work that underwent extensive alteration, was omitted in the second edition (Paris, 1966; compare vol. 1, pp. 545ff. [English ed.: vol. 1, p. 602ff.]) because the author changed his ideas about the role of Sicilian wheat in the alimentary crisis of the mid-seventeenth century. In any case, the ground of the question continues to be, in general terms, the same; because of this I am citing the passage as it appeared in the first edition. Concerning the serious Sicilian disturbances, compare H. G. Koenigsberger, "The Revolt of Palermo in 1647," in *Estates and Revolutions: Essays in Early Modern European History* (Ithaca, N.Y., 1971), pp. 253ff.

105. Let us bear in mind the data we reviewed in the first chapter.

106. *Alteraciones andaluzas* (Madrid, 1973).

107. F. Montblanch, *La segunda germanía del reino de Valencia* (Alicante, 1957).

108. *Les soulèvements populaires en France*, p. 153.

109. Bernard Barber, *Social Stratification* (New York, 1957), p. 382.

CHAPTER 5. A CONSERVATIVE CULTURE

1. Barber, *Social Stratification*, pp. 213, 239-46, 264-67, 283ff., passim.

2. Lazarsfeld and Merton, "Mass Communication."

3. See my *Antiguos y modernos. La idea de progreso en el desarrollo inicial de una sociedad*, especially the first part, "La estimación de lo nuevo," pp. 27-110.

4. Ibid., p. 97.

5. *El duque de Viseo*, act 1. Another example is found in *El caballero de Olmedo*, act 3: "Fue siempre bárbara ley / seguir aplauso vulgar / las novedades . . ." [It was always a barbarous law for novelties to obey commoner applause]; also in *Porfiando vence amor*, act 1: "el vulgo, inclinado a novedades" [the common people, inclined to novelties].

6. See "Moral de acomodación y carácter conflictivo de la libertad (Notas sobre Saavedra Fajardo)," collected in my *Estudios de historia del pensamiento español*, ser. 3 (Madrid, 1975).

7. *La Cintia de Aranjuez*, edited by J. da Entrambasaguas (Madrid, 1945), p. 125.

8. Compare my studies on Gracián and Saavedra Fajardo in *Estudios de historia*.

9. Published in Madrid, 1625.

10. *De rege et regendi ratione* (Madrid, 1627).

11. *Doctrina política y civil* (Madrid, 1621).

12. *Varias noticias*, fol. 19.

13. *La Junta de Reformación*, AHE, 5, p. 30.

14. Ibid., p. 69.

15. *Restauración política de España*, pp. 2-4. In *Noticias de Madrid*, an anonymous work published by González Palencia, a curious comment is transmitted about Sancho de Moncada, one already referred to by P. de Gayangos in *Cartas de jesuitas* (MHE, 14, p. 248): "The doctor Moncada, so well known for his printed recommendations [*arbitrios*] regarding the restoration of Spain, has composed a very learned work on this subject, proving on various grounds that if someone knew how to make silver, it would not be to Your Majesty's advantage for him to make it" (7 November 1637).

16. *Varias noticias*, fols. 143ff.

17. *El criticón*, edited by Romera Navarro, vol. 2, p. 267.

18. MHE, 19, p. 220.
19. Barber, *Social Stratification*, p. 7.
20. Suárez de Figueroa, *El pasagero*, p. 50.
21. *La Junta de Reformación*, AHE, 5, pp. 28 and 452-53 (see also p. 386).
22. "Relación de la Cárcel de Sevilla," col. 1364.
23. *Fiel desengaño contra la ociosidad y los juegos*, edited by M. de Riquer, vol. 2, p. 37.
24. *Varias noticias*, fol. 109.
25. *Día y noche de Madrid*, pp. 417ff. and 434.
26. I develop this aspect in *Teatro y literatura en la sociedad barroca* (Madrid, 1972).
27. *Lope de Vega y su tiempo*, p. 305.
28. *Estado moderno y mentalidad social*, vol. 2, pp. 3ff.
29. *Memorial*, fols. 41, 42.
30. Carballo, *Cisne de Apolo*, vol. 2, p. 121.
31. *Memorial*, fol. 16.
32. *Discurso al Rey*, fol. 23.
33. *El pasagero*, p. 32.
34. *Aventuras del bachiller Trapaza*, in *La novela picaresca española*, p. 1486.
35. See Mousnier, *Les hiérarchies sociales de 1450 à nos jours* (Paris, 1969).
36. *Discurso*, fol. 16.
37. R. Mousnier, J. Labatut and Y. Durand, *Problèmes de stratification sociale: Deux cahiers de la noblesse (1649-1651)* (Paris, 1965).
38. P. Laslett, *The World We Have Lost* (New York, 1966).
39. See Ch. Hill, *El siglo de la Revolución* (Madrid, 1972).
40. See his "De 1560 à 1660: La chaîne des hommes."
41. *Pensées*, vol. 1, pp. 147-48.
42. *Memorial*, fols. 15, 16.
43. *La Junta de Reformación*, AHE, 5, p. 246.
44. In chapter 1 I already referred to the generalized idea of strengthening an intermediate level.
45. *Estado moderno y mentalidad social*, vol. 2, pp. 19ff.
46. See E. Lousse, *La société d'ancien régime*, 2d ed. (Louvain, 1952).
47. *Discurso*, fols. 5, 6.
48. Suárez de Figueroa, *El pasagero*, p. 78.
49. "The conservative proposal to save culture by restoring the old class lines has a more solid historical basis than the liberal-cum-Marxism hope for a new democratic, classless culture," Macdonald said on p. 625 of "Masscult and Midcult." Only, he says, it is absurd in a world under the hegemonic control of societies like the Soviet Union and the United States, which are becoming more and more industrialized and massified. Nevertheless, if we take into account the results that such a thesis obtained in the Assembly of Troyes in 1651 and in the Assembly of the French nobility in 1788, we will understand that whatever possessed repeated and ancient historical antecedents did not because of that gain strength in modern society. In the seventeenth-century crisis, we see how it experienced a slow erosion, perhaps, but one that was constant.
50. To understand what the nobles' abandonment of their military duties, which Domínguez Ortiz has demonstrated, signified for the collapse of the system, recall what would be demanded by the doctrine of the nobiliary statute that Calderón was still describing: "that the blood of the nobles is, / rightly and justly, / the patrimony of the kings" (*No hay cosa como callar*).
51. Compare my *Estado moderno y mentalidad social*, vol. 1, pp. 345ff.
52. *Varias noticias*, fol. 106.
53. *La Junta de Reformación*, AHE, 5, p. 27.
54. We already have a documented study about an interesting case in the time of Philip II: Maribel López Díaz, *La venta de la villa de Nestares: Un ejemplo vivo de la desamortización de 1574* (thesis from the School of Political Science and Sociology at the Universidad Complutense of

Madrid). This policy continued in the seventeenth century. Moreover, the sale of settlements of the Crown to nouveaux riches had the characteristics of civil disentailment.

55. Friar Juan de Salazar expressed the zeal for Church economic domination in a crude manner. He excited the kings' greed so as to lead them to honor God, and he made use of this inclination to satisfy the greed of the ecclesiastical group: "He, God, gives the princes kingdoms, lands, property and wealth; and they, the princes, acknowledging and grateful, return it to him, offering everything very liberally to serve him, to the churches and monasteries" (*Política española* [Madrid, 1945], p. 72).

56. On this process of broadening the commitment in the privileged order, see my *Teatro y literatura en la sociedad barroca*.

57. *Genio de la historia* (Vitoria, 1957). This comes to be a topos in the epoch that was used to mark the dividing line imposed on matters of innovation, as it was formulated in *La Dorotea*: "living with past customs and speaking with present words" (4, iii).

58. *Agudeza y arte de ingenio*, discurso 51, *OC*, p. 458, and *El criticón*, 2, p. 140. See Romera Navarro, *La preceptiva dramática de Lope de Vega* (Madrid, 1935).

59. *Diálogos practicables del nobilísimo arte de la pintura*, edited by Carderera (Madrid, 1866), p. 187.

60. *La littérature française à l'âge baroque*, p. 233.

61. *Oeuvres complètes* (Paris, 1958), pp. 56, 62.

62. *Conceptos fundamentales en la historia del arte* (Madrid, 1952), p. 226.

63. Ph. Butler, *Classicisme et baroque dans l'oeuvre de Racine*, pp. 38ff.

64. Ibid., p. 44.

65. Compare L. Rosales, *Pasión y muerte del conde de Villamediana* (Madrid, 1969).

66. *La Junta de Reformación*, AHE, 5, p. 183.

67. "Whoever is from the upper realms owns everything," Francisco Santos would say (*Día y noche de Madrid*, p. 379). In terms of this, the theater goes to the greatest extremes (see my *Teatro y literatura en la sociedad barroca*). One might ask why the political and moralist writers, especially the Jesuits, did not follow this line. Probably it was in the interest of the ecclesiastical monarchy not to deify the civil monarchy too much.

68. Dámaso Alonso's study, "Lope en vena de filósofo" (*Clavileño*, no. 2 [1950]), offers an interesting contribution to Lope's Neoplatonism, whose presence in the greater part of his work and in a group of sonnets with philosophical pretensions reveals his attempt to cultivate a philosophical poetry. It serves us to demonstrate the presence in him of a firm ideological base and his response to the commitment of a conservative ideology, which is the social meaning of Neoplatonism (see K. Popper, *The Open Society and Its Enemies*, 5th rev. ed. [London, 1966]).

69. With respect to the doctrine of the French political writers, E. Thuau has spoken about a "religion of obedience" (see his *Raison d'Etat et pensée politique à l'époque de Richelieu* [Paris, 1966]).

70. C.-G. Dubois, in his book *Le baroque, profondeurs de l'apparence* (Paris, 1973), maintained that there was a sphere of freedom in baroque society precisely to the extent that on no account did one oppose the sovereignty of authority, but rather exalted it, and thereby the baroque appeared as a "society of obedience" (see p. 242). For the most part, my theses approximate those maintained in his book.

71. *Margarita o Oración fúnebre en las onras de la Serenísima Infanta del Imperio de Alemania* (Madrid, 1633), fol. 6. Paravicino made a curious declaration: he considered it admissible to represent a royal person in purgatory but never in hell, which would be an offense only dared by the ancients; "[I] out of respect would not designate them in such a place, nor could I come to such a thing by means of reason." His argument was that whoever can do more can remedy more; therefore, the omnipotent kings always attain the greatest merits that correspond to the magnitude of the remedies they perform (fol. 28).

72. *Sermón de las Exequias de la Reina nuestra Señora* (Saragossa, n.d.); the citation appears on an unpaginated folio, at the beginning of the last third of the booklet.

73. *Declamación panegírica en el dichoso nacimiento del Serenísimo Príncipe Don Felipe el Próspero* (Saragossa, n.d. [the dedication is signed January 1658]), fol. 23. The author added the force of a magical, symbolist naturalism to the sacralization: "The things of nature tell us that when the stems begin to flower, the snakes, basilisks and scorpions and every kind of noxious and poisonous vermin forsake the territory; they cannot tolerate the flowers' fragrance"; therefore, queen Mariana, abundantly giving forth fruit, like the Biblical grapevine, would scare away the enemies of the Spanish monarchy (fol. 34).

74. *Le Tasse et la littérature et l'art baroques en France* (Paris, 1962), p. 17. The deified character of royalty is in every sector normal in the seventeenth-century political conception. See P. M. Skrine, *The Baroque*, chap. 6, pp. 90ff., where he emphasized what Routrou's dramatic work represented in elaborating this doctrine for the public.

75. *Le Tasse et la littérature*, p. 128. Although it had many failings and insufficiencies from its own point of view, the French monarchy reached its ultimate degree of centralization and authority with Louis XIV; many present this monarchy as the model and source of classicism, which was already eliminated in the baroque, yet Joyce G. Simpson viewed it as an example of the baroque, the moment in which the French baroque fully triumphed. Moreover, although Tapié followed this "classical" notion — which no scholar could do today — and supposed that Versailles was the expression of rational good taste, Simpson judged that the palace's lack of restraint and proportion made it baroque, despite its classical elements: "One can perceive neither the plan of the palace nor of the park; one becomes lost there; magnificence turns into megalomania" (ibid., p. 112).

76. "Aristotelismo e barocco."

77. In another aspect, Cubillo de Aragón exalted "being seigniors, whom / the commoners adore and respect," but the author was not concerned about making the development of his work congruent with such a sentiment (*El señor de Buenas Noches*, in his *Teatro*, edited by A. Valbuena Prat [Madrid, 1928], p. 215).

78. *Retables de Bretagne*, p. 35.

79. Out of an abundant literature, let us recall friar Juan de la Puente, *Conveniencia de las dos Monarquías Católicas, la de la Iglesia Romana y la del Imperio español*, 1612; López Madera, *Excelencias de la Monarquía y Reino de España*, 1617; Carlos García, *Oposición y conjución de los dos grandes luminares de la Tierra*, 1617; friar Juan de Salazar, *Políitica española*, 1619.

80. See my *Estado moderno y mentalidad social*, where I give relevant examples from different countries and from several sectors of social life.

81. See J. Sczncc, *La survivence des dieux antiques* (London, 1940).

82. It was something well known in Spain, England, and Italy with Lope, Shakespeare, and Tasso (to limit ourselves in each case to a representative example among the hundred that could be recalled). Recently France is where the question has been most emphasized, precisely because it had appeared more foreign to this movement. See M. Edelman, *Attitudes of Seventeenth-Century France towards the Middle Ages* (New York, 1946).

83. *Artistic Theory in Italy (1450-1600)* (Oxford, 1956), chapter 9 and conclusion.

84. "Propositions sur le baroque et la littérature française," *Revue des Science Humaines*, nos. 55, 56 (July-December 1919).

85. G. Piovene, "Anacronismo della Venezia quattrocentesca," in the collective volume *La civiltà veneziana del Quattrocento* (Florence, 1957). Also in France — in Paris, Nantes, Orléans — churches or parts of churches were built with a fully Gothic character. It has not been possible for me to consult Leu-Lloréns' book, *Les éléments médiévaux de l'architecture baroque* (Lausanne, 1944).

86. England soon undertook to follow another route, and France would also begin going that way with Colbert.

87. R. Romano, "Tra XVI e XVII secolo: La crisi del 1619-1622," *Rivista Storica Italiana*, 74, no. 2 (1962).

88. Ph. Butler, *Classicisme et baroque* pp. 31, 74.

89. See my *Antiguos y modernos*.

CHAPTER 6: THE IMAGE OF THE WORLD AND HUMAN BEING

1. *La tradición clásica* (Mexico City, 1954), pp. 406-7.

2. In a study published in the volume *Retorica e barocco*, pp. 192-93. The following citation from this author also comes from these pages.

3. *El soldado Píndaro*, p. 285.

4. See Hippeau, *Essai sur la morale de La Rochefoucauld* (Paris, 1957). About the significance of the mentioned text, see A. Adam, *Histoire de la littérature française au XVIIe siècle, I: L'époque d'Henri III et de Louis XIII* (Paris, 1948), p. 305. As a man of letters and an anti-Cartesian thinker, the author ended up in the service of Richelieu.

5. Doctor López de Villalobos, *Los problemas del Doctor*, BAE, 26, p. 425.

6. *Oeuvres de Mathurin Régnier* (Paris: Classiques Garnier), p. 189.

7. The passage appears in the polemical writing *Lince de Italia o zahorí español*, in *Obras completas: Prosa*, edited by Astrana Marín, p. 621.

8. *OC*, edited by González Palencia (Madrid, 1946).

9. In one of Cubillo de Aragón's comedies (*La muñeca de Marcela*) we read (p. 135): "What do you expect, seignior, from a madman / if not madnesses like this?" In a certain way the seignior keeps him at his side for assistance in facing the world. I know of no study on the social character of the *gracioso*. Works such as Ch. D. Ley's *El gracioso en el teatro de la península* (Madrid, 1954) prove rather disorienting. Montesinos's famous and undoubtedly ingenious study is entirely "aseptic."

10. Barrionuevo, *Avisos*, 1 (BAE, 221, p. 246).

11. Ibid., pp. 58 and 74.

12. *Avisos*, ed. *Semanario Erudito*, 32, p. 255.

13. *Avisos*, 2 (BAE, 222, p. 5).

14. *Avisos*, 2 (BAE, 221, p. 106). Thus repeated reference to the multiple bankruptcies, clearly a phenomenon of social instability.

15. *República literaria*, in *OC*, p. 1177.

16. *El criticón*, edited by Romera Navarro, 3, pp. 369ff.; see my study "Las bases antropológicas del pensamiento de Gracián," collected in my *Estudios de historia del pensamiento español*, ser. 3.

17. *Sartor Resartus*. It would be interesting one day to study Spanish seventeenth-century society and its great creations — theater, novel, and painting — on the level of a sociology of aspirations.

18. *Genealogía de los modorros*, which is one of Quevedo's early works (1597), *OC*, pp. 2ff. From this date on, few topoi became as widespread.

19. Printed in Lérida in 1598.

20. E. R. Curtius, *European Literature and the Latin Middle Ages*, translated by W. R. Trask (Princeton, N. J., 1953), pp. 96-97.

21. See his *Rabelais and His World*, translated by Hélène Iswolsky (Cambridge, Mass., 1968). I don't know whether this formulation has been influenced by consideration of the topic's later development, so popularly diffused until fifty years ago, although without connotations of protest. H. Grant recently dedicated a brief and interesting study to the theme, proving its long span of existence, since he collected data from medieval and baroque sources up to most recent Catalan games [*aucas*]: "El mundo al revés," in *Hispanic Studies in Honour of Joseph Manson* (Oxford, 1972).

22. *La littérature de l'âge baroque en France*, p. 26.

23. *Fiel desengaño contra la ociosidad y los juegos*, vol. 2, p. 81.

24. *El pasagero*, p. 66. He repeated the theme in his *Varias noticias importantes a la humana comunicación*, fol. 42: "Almost since its inception it has been the proper condition of the world to direct everything upside down, to make everything disfigured."

25. *Mesón del mundo*, edited by Carlos Petit Caro (Seville, 1946), pp. 26, 29.

26. *Obras: Prosa*, pp. 267ff. Compare H. Ettinghausen, *Francisco de Quevedo and the Neostoic Movement* (Oxford, 1972), pp. 76-77.

27. Tirso de Molina, *Obras dramáticas completas*, vol. 1 (Madrid, 1969), pp. 382ff.

28. *Avisos*, 1 (BAE, 221, p. 80).

29. *Epistolario*, edited by N. Alonso Cortés, CC (Madrid).

30. First part, "Crisi VI"; the formula is enunciated on p. 210 (vol. 1).

31. G. R. Hocke, *El Manierismo en el arte europeo* (Madrid, 1961). Many of the references given by the author fall entirely within the baroque.

32. *Jean Amos Comenius, 1592-1670: Pages choisies* (Paris, 1957), p. 42 (an anthology published by UNESCO with an introduction by J. Piaget). The quote comes from the work cited in the text.

33. Ibid., p. 39.

34. *Segni e simboli nella "Vida es sueño"* (Bari, 1968).

35. *Día y noche de Madrid*, BAE, 33, p. 399.

36. BAE, 17, p. 364.

37. *Jean Amos Comenius*, p. 48 (from *Labyrinth of the World*).

38. *El criticón*, 2, p. 10.

39. *Plaza universal de todas ciencias y artes* (Perpiñán, 1630).

40. Letter 9 (16 November 1622), p. 139.

41. The structure of the *Sueños* and the satirical *Discursos* also correspond to this idea.

42. See *Mesón del mundo*. According to Rennert (*The Spanish Stage in the Time of Lope de Vega* [1909; reprint New York, n.d.], p. 310), Riquelme's company put on an *auto* in Seville entitled *El mesón del alma* that would certainly have some relation with the topos here under consideration and that demonstrates its rootedness in a milieu as baroque as Seville.

43. The texts appear in the prologue and on p. 37 of *Mesón del mundo*.

44. BAE, 33, p. 69.

45. In Pascal, man knows the world, "de ce petit cachot où il se trouve logé"; and in the following he makes what he is referring to more precise: "j'entends l'univers" (*Pensées*, 1, p. 22).

46. *El sueño del Infierno*, in *Obras completas: Prosa*, p. 173. The topos of the hostelry was cultivated specifically by writers of picaresque literature or by those who, with the aim of condemning, wrote literature against evil scheming.

47. The first chapter of P. M. Skrine's inventive book (*The Baroque; Literature and Culture in Seventeenth-Century Europe* [London, 1978]) starts off with the title of this line from Shakespeare, basing the surprising and overriding interpretation of the world as a stage principally on Calderón's work, relating it with a passage from Milton and with the view of the Plaza Navona in Rome.

48. Barnadas has edited the document as an appendix in his article "Resonancias andaluzas de la decadencia."

49. *Día y noche de Madrid*, BAE, 33, p. 434.

50. *Varias noticias*, fol. 1, v.

51. See M. Z. Hafter, *Gracián and Perfection* (Cambridge, Mass., 1966), pp. 78ff., where many references are concisely given.

52. *Heráclito y Demócrito de nuestro siglo* (Madrid, 1612; republished in 1641).

53. In the preliminary study to his edition of Céspedes y Meneses's *Historias ejemplares y peregrinas* (Madrid, 1970), pp. 47-48.

54. *Jean Amos Comenius*, p. 43.

55. *Pensées*, 1, p. 26.

56. Poem [*silva*] with the number 67 in S. B. Vranich's edition (Madrid, 1972).

57. In the prologue to his *Varias noticias*.

58. *Apologético de las comedias españolas*, in *Poetas dramáticos valencianos*, edited by Juliá Martínez (Madrid, 1929), vol. 1, p. 623. Ricardo del Turia described the indicated distinction to prove that the "tragicomedy" corresponded to a mixed quality, which helps us to understand its adequacy in the baroque mentality for expressing the complex mixture of reality.

59. *Varias noticias*, fol. 11.

60. *Essais*, III, xiii.

61. *El criticón*, 1, iii, p. 137.

62. We read this paragraph in a writer on economic matters, José de la Vega: "Ignoramuses become astounded about the fact that when boiling a glass of water on the fire the bottom of the glass doesn't get hot; but if they knew the continuous war that... contraries wage in this life, their astonishment would turn into contentment." José de la Vega's work, dedicated to explaining the "stocks" used to gain capital in certain types of society, bears this very baroque title (as the book is baroque through and through): *Confusión de confusiones* (Amsterdam, 1688; facsimile ed., Madrid, 1958), p. 124.

63. Suárez de Figueroa, *Varias noticias*, fol. 9.

64. See my *Teoría española del estado en el siglo XVII* (Madrid, 1944).

65. *El pasagero*, p. 360.

66. See, for example, L. Vives's and, much more directly, Vitoria's, in my *Carlos V y el pensamiento político del Renacimiento* (Madrid, 1958).

67. *Fiel desengaño contra la ociosidad y los juegos*, vol. 2, pp. 30-31.

68. Cited by Azorín in *El pasado* (Madrid, 1955), p. 77.

69. *El criticón*, 1, p. 148. I commented on this passage in "Las bases antropológicas del pensamiento de Gracián."

70. *Cartas de jesuitas* (October 13, 1637), MHE, XIV, p. 223.

71. In his *Memorial*, Cellorigo made this comment on the occasion of the epidemic that Vallodolid was suffering: "The little support that the healthy places have given to the sick has very much been revealed in Spain" (fol. 7). Probably the insuperable fear that descended upon people, a fear deriving from the plagues that ravaged the seventeenth century, was at the root of the baroque characteristics we have been describing.

72. *Obras*, edited by R. de Balbín (Madrid, 1944), vol. 2, p. 47. The text corresponds to a *vejamen* in the Academia de Madrid, a very representative place and occasion in baroque society.

73. This fragment comes from his *Prosas diversas*, in *Obras*, edited by Benítez Claros (Madrid, 1946), vol. 1, p. 141.

74. *Empresa* 46, p. 378.

75. *Extensión política y económica*, in A. Ossorio's *Obras*, edited by the Count of Campomanes, Appendix 1 to *Discurso sobre la educación popular*, p. 8.

76. *Essais*, III, i, p. 8.

77. BAE, 18, p. 533.

78. *Día y noche de Madrid*, p. 408.

79. *Obras de don Gaspar de Castro y Bellvis*, edited by Juliá Martínez (Madrid, 1927), vol. 3, pp. 573ff.

80. *Guía y avisos de forasteros que vienen a la Corte*, "Aviso VI," in *Costumbristas españoles*, edited by Correa Calderón, vol. 1, p. 91.

81. *Avisos*, 1 (BAE, 221, p. 138).

82. *Guzmán de Alfarache*, 1, ii, 4, edited by S. Gili Gaya, CC, vol. 2, pp. 53-54.

83. *Empresa* 43, p. 369.

84. Vol. 1, p. 172.

85. Weisbach, in *El Barroco, arte de la Contrarreforma* (Madrid, 1948), brought together some interesting references (see p. 85). Rousset also gathered some examples of macabre art from diverse places in *La littérature de l'âge baroque en France*, p. 91.

86. *Novelas ejemplares y amorosas*, edited by González de Amezúa, vol. 2, p. 109. Some other references: "With the cruel and hardened hearts of men neither good nor bad works are worth anything" (p. 167); "In anything having to do with cruelty, men are terrible" (p. 208).

87. *Cartas de jesuitas* (MHE, p. 55).

88. *Emporio del Orbe* (Amsterdam, 1690), p. 86; cited by P. A. Sole, *Los pícaros de Cónil y Zahara* (Cádiz, 1965), p. 31.

89. *Anales de Madrid*, edited by Fernández Martín (Madrid, 1971), p. 249.

90. *Avisos*, 1 (BAE, 221, p. 162).

91. *Cartas de jesuitas* (4 November 1640), MHE, 16, p. 40.

92. See Sicroff, *Les controverses des statuts de pureté de sang en Espagne*, pp. 75ff., where the especially interesting opinion of friar Alonso de Oropesa figures in; but at a later date, other opinions could be seen that were no less harsh. For example, see friar Jaime Bleda, *Crónica de los moros de España* (Valencia, 1618).

93. See doctor Juan Quiñones's *Discursos contra los gitanos*, addressed to the king and printed in Madrid in 1631.

94. Tenenti (*La vie et la mort à travers l'art du XVe siècle* [Paris, 1952]) was concerned with this question. We have also dealt with it, considering it a decisive point for understanding the human problem of *La Celestina*; see my *El mundo social de "La Celestina,"* 3rd ed. (Madrid, 1973).

95. *L'art religieux de la fin du XVIe siècle, du XVIIe siècle et du XVIIIe siècle* (Paris, 1951), p. 227.

96. In the exposition "La nature morte; de Bruegel a Soutine," Bordeaux, 1978, figuring into the seventeenth century were no fewer than six painters on the theme of "Vanitas" who included an edifying skull (and perhaps in a worldly sense) in their paintings: S. R. de Saint-André, J. Hupin, J.-F. de la Motte, D. Lhomme, Ch. Luyekx, and P. Piterman. In Spain, the splendid exposition of Antonio de Pereda (Madrid, 1979) assembled material for study that was of great interest; see the catalogue by A. F. Pérez Sánchez, *D. Antonio de Pereda y la pintura madrileña de su tiempo*.

97. A. M. Boase, *Jean de Sponde, un poète inconnu* (Geneva, 1939).

98. *De los remedios de cualquier fortuna*, in *Obras: Prosa*, p. 887.

99. *El curioso y sabio Alejandro, fiscal de vidas ajenas*, in *Costumbristas españoles*, p. 139.

100. Rousset, who was very concerned with the theme of death and with the obsession it came to constitute for many in the baroque, cited a curious example: some bourgeois from Paris organized their attendance at their own burial (*La littérature de l'âge baroque en France*, p. 102). This was attributed to Charles V and was frequently identified as being the result of Spanish influence; as it turned out it was a practice — probably somewhere between the pious and economic — of rich French bourgeois who were imbued with baroquism.

101. E. Mâle, *L'art religieux*, p. 216.

102. See M. Vovelle, *Mourir autrefois* (Paris, 1974): the great ceremony of death, lived by and for others with an exemplary value, was charged with personal sentiment (the death lived by each one, death suffered), but it preserved a secular significance proper to estatist society in which it was the final act of "decorum" wherein each one's rank and position was reflected, along with the way each one had carried out his or her role; it was an act of social morality. (In 1962, I formulated these differences in *El mundo social de "La Celestina.*") See also the suggestive study of Ph. Ariès, *Essais sur l'histoire de la mort en Occident* (Paris, 1975).

103. *Comentarios políticos*, edited and with an introduction by J. A. Maravall (Madrid, 1945).

104. *Antiguos y modernos: La idea de progresso en el desarrollo inicial de una sociedad* (Madrid, 1967). In this work I devoted many pages to the study of how, in the most varied areas of culture (from medicine to navigation, accounting to music, nutrition to the arts of war), a view of history as advancing, in evolutionary progress, was being constituted. Important notions of the concept of progress were lacking, including the word itself, which became diffused in the Castilian lexicon at the beginning of the sixteenth century but did not go beyond signifying a mere notion of movement in the sense of rising and declining. But now I can offer a curious passage in which the word is established for the first time as meaning a movement whose direction is given a positive value, although it is used to reject the positive interpretation as its permanent meaning in the march of human events. In effect, after referring to an opinion that he attributed to Seneca, according to which human things neither worsen to a great extent nor get much better, Suárez de Figueroa added: "Everything continually is found in the same situation and will remain there, although with a small

amount of either progress or decline [*disminución*]" (*Varias noticias*, fol. 240). Therefore progress is a movement that opposes decline as the inverse of its advancing course. In what follows we will see that the historical view proposed by Suárez de Figueroa had progressive tendencies.

105. E. F. Heckscher, *La época mercantilista* (Mexico, 1943), pp. 469ff.

106. *Estado moderno y mentalidad social*, vol. 2, pp. 122ff.

107. *Essais*, I, xxii, p. 147.

108. Cited by Hippeau, *Essai sur la morale de La Rochefoucauld*, p. 135. There is a modern edition of this author's works in three volumes (Paris, 1930).

109. The passage can be found in his *Novela de un hombre muy miserable llamado Gonzalo*, in *Lazarillo de Manzanares* (along with five other novels), edited by G. E. Sansone (Barcelona, 1960), vol. 2, p. 181.

110. *Avisos*, 2 (BAE, 222, p. 9); the sentence is from 1656.

111. *Baltasar Gracián; Estilo y doctrina* (Zaragoza, 1960), p. 138.

112. *Graciáns Lebenslehre* (Frankfurt, 1947), p. 119.

113. *The Social History of Art*, vol. 2, pp. 191-94.

114. *De la sagesse* (I am citing from the Amsterdam edition, 1782, vol. 1, p. 1).

115. See E. W. Hesse's study, "Estructura e interpretación de una comedia de Calderón: *Eco y Narciso*," *Boletín de la Biblioteca Menéndez y Pelayo*, no. 39 (1963).

116. Francisco Rico, *El pequeño mundo del hombre* (Madrid, 1970), an interesting book on the meanings of myth and its presence in Spanish literature.

117. BAE, 42, p. 368.

118. See my "Las bases antropológicas del pensamiento de Gracián."

119. *Obras de Francisco de Rioja*, edited by C. A. de La Barrera (Bibliófilos Andaluces, 1872); the lines cited come from the poem numbered 39 in the collection, p. 222.

120. *Pensées*, 1, p. 20.

121. See W. Krauss, *Graciáns Lebenslehre*, and my "Las bases antropológicas del pensamiento de Gracián."

122. Linked to a consciousness of crisis, the word is no less frequent in the political and economic writers. Leaf through, for example, Cellorigo's *Memorial*.

123. See Laín Entralgo, *La vida del hombre en la poesía de Quevedo*, in *Obras* (Madrid, 1965), pp. 883ff.

124. My article on Gracián ("Las bases antropólogicas del pensamiento de Gracián") brings together some valuable passages that demonstrate the concept's connection with the human being making himself or herself through living experience.

125. BAE, 42, p. 363.

126. *Lope de Vega y su tiempo*, pp. 117ff. This is debatable with respect to Lope but inadmissible with respect to Quevedo, no less to the writer of prose than the poet, or to Gracián.

127. Contrary to the banality with which some, lacking sufficient information, endeavor to characterize this concept, let us not fail to note that beginning with Gil Polo "concern" went hand in hand with the "anguished spirit"; see *Diana enamorada*, edited by R. Ferreres, CC, p. 78.

128. *El discreto*, discurso 10, p. 103.

129. *La dialectique des exercices spirituels de Saint Ignace de Loyola* (Paris, 1956), p. 191.

130. *El discreto*, discurso 22, p. 137.

131. *Diez lamentaciones del miserable estado de los ateístas de nuestro tiempo* (1611); I am citing from P.O. Steggink's edition (Madrid, 1959).

132. See my *Las Comunidades de Castilla, una primera revolución moderna* and *Estado moderno y mentalidad social*, where I have assembled and commented on numerous data concerning the modern concept, necessarily political and social, of freedom as it emerged in the beginnings of the epoch we are here studying.

133. *El español Gerardo*, p. 208. The following citation from this work is from the same place.

CHAPTER 7. FUNDAMENTAL CONCEPTS OF THE WORLDLY STRUCTURE OF LIFE

1. See my *Carlos V y el pensamiento político del Renacimiento*, introduction, chap. 3, esp. pp. 48-49.

2. There are numerous examples in the comedies we have mentioned and in others, such as *No hay cosa como callar*, *En esta vida todo es verdad y todo es mentira*, etc.

3. *Rembrandt*, Spanish translation (Buenos Aires, 1950), pp. 48-49.

4. See my *Velázquez y el espíritu de la modernidad* (Madrid, 1960), p. 140.

5. F. J. Warnke, *Versions of Baroque* (New Haven, Conn., 1972), p. 22. The quote from Browne appears in the same place.

6. Except in banal cases of an asceticism with scarcely any intellectual import, when baroque authors warned against experience they were equally against considering it as a negation of falsehood and as truth of an essential reality. Even Calderon's famous lines end up affirming this intermediate, phenomenal level of experience (close to the phenomenal level that is of interest to modern science). Let us once again repeat these lines (despite their being so well known and having a topos quality, Calderón made them his own):

> that perhaps our eyes
> are deceived and represent
> very different objects
> than what they see, thus leaving
> the soul tricked. What greater
> reason, truth, self-evidence
> than the blue sky we see?
> Might there be someone who doesn't
> commonly believe that sapphire is
> what displays beautiful rays of light?
> Thus it is neither sky nor is it blue.

(Saber del mal y del bien)

It is not sapphire nor the sky, but it is this region of the heavens and place where meteors originate that, on the other hand, has been recognized as playing such a role in Calderón's theater and in all baroque comedy. It is in this that the so-called contradictory character of experience would come to be resolved. On the topical character of this idea, see O. H. Green, "'Ni es cielo ni es azul'; a note on the barroquismo of Bartolomé Leonardo de Argensola," in *RFE*, 34, 1950, pp. 137-50.

7. J. de Zabaleta, *Errores celebrados*, edited by M. de Riquer (Barcelona, 1954), p. 75. Gracián's mention of the Galilean "spyglass" appears in *El criticón*, 3, p. 305.

8. See my *Teoría española del estado en el siglo XVII* (Madrid, 1944), p. 398.

9. *Essais*, II, viii, p. 80, and III, xiii, p. 225.

10. *Pensées*, pp. 28 and 54.

11. "Las *Soledades* en don Luis de Góngora: Algunos caracteres de su estilo," *Atti del Convegno Internazionale sul tema: Premarinismo e pregongorismo* (Rome, 1973), pp. 80ff.; the quote is on p. 91.

12. *Empresa* 82, *OC*, edited by González Palencia (Madrid, 1946), p. 594.

13. *Fortuna varia del soldado Píndaro*, BAE, 18, p. 333.

14. *Discursos practicables del nobilísimo arte de la pintura*, edited by Carderera (Madrid, 1866), p. 162.

15. *Obras de don Gabriel Bocángel y Unceta*, edited by Benítez Claros, vol. 1 (Madrid, 1946), p. 201.

16. *El pasagero*, edited by Rodríguez Marín (Madrid, 1913), p. 3.

17. Rousset, *La littérature française de l'âge baroque* (Paris, 1953), p. 124.

18. *Theatro de los theatros*, p. 98.

19. *Rinascimento e barocco*, italian translation (Florence, 1928), p. 85.

20. *Leviathan*, edited by C. B. Macpherson (Penguin Books, 1968), 1, vi, p. 121.

21. *El criticón*, 2, p. 259.

22. *OC*, edited by Astrana Marín (Madrid, 1932), 1, *Poesía*, p. 23.

23. M. Raymond recorded this anecdote in *De Michel-Ange à Tiépolo* (Paris, 1912), p. 181. Its great interest has been pointed out by Rousset, *La littérature française*, p. 139, and V. L. Tapié, in *Baroque et classicisme* (Paris, 1957), pp. 190ff. Bernini's failure at the court of Louis XIV and his return to Italy was attributed to France's rejection of the baroque. One should instead view in this episode the victory of nationalism that the baroque frequently inspired, especially in France.

24. P. Rubens, *Théorie de la figure humaine, considérée dans ses principes, soit en repose, soit en mouvement* (pamphlet printed in Paris in 1773).

25. *El español Gerardo*, BAE, 18, p. 170.

26. *El pasagero*, p. 266.

27. *Empresa* 68, p. 519.

28. *El pasagero*, p. 150.

29. Rousset, *La littérature français*, p. 39.

30. *Obras*, vol. 1, p. 64.

31. *Empresa* 60, p. 477.

32. *Día y noche de Madrid*, BAE, 33, p. 382.

33. *Obras*, Bibliófilos Andaluces (Seville, 1883), vol. 1, pp. 5,6.

34. BAE, 42, p. 241.

35. Rodrigo Caro, *Obras*, vol. 1, p. 5.

36. Ibid., vol. 2, p. 348. We have just encountered the allusion to a "law of nature." For Suárez de Figueroa modification also proceeds from a universal law and is engendered everywhere — the planets with their revolutions; the sun and moon whose paths engender birth and death; renewal and transformation of things in the nether world, just as the combinations and changes in the four elements composing them (all this understood according to Aristotelian physics): "Neither can one find anything on earth that would be perpetual," and even human activity comes to increase the unceasing number of alterations (nothing else results from human labor and effort). Modification is a cosmological principle: customs, laws, languages, religions, wars, etc. — all is subordinate to its domination (*Varias noticias importantes a la humana comunicación*, fols. 7ff.).

37. *El discreto*, 17, in OC, p. 123.

38. See G. Poulet, *Etudes sur le temps humain* (Paris, 1950), p. xviii, with reference to a wonderful passage from Nicole: "We are like birds in the air, birds that cannot remain there without movement, nor even in the same place, for their support is not at all solid."

39. *Avïsos*, 1, BAE, 221, p. 100. The comment is from 2 January 1655.

40. Lope de Vega, *El rey don Pedro en Madrid*.

41. *Varias noticias*, prologue and fol. 17.

42. *Cigarrales de Toledo*, edited by Said Armesto (Madrid, 1916), p. 127.

43. *Obras*, 1, p. 320.

44. Lope, *Obras en verso*, Aguilar edition, pp. 102ff.

45. *Obras*, 1, p. 95.

46. Sonnet 61 in *Rimas*, edited by J. M. Blecua, CC (Madrid), p. 121.

47. *Memorial*, fol. 7.

48. *Avisos*, ed. *Semanario Erudito*, 31, p. 227.

49. *Historias peregrinas y ejemplares*, edited by Y. R. Fonquerne (Madrid, 1970), p. 307.

50. *Philosophía antigua poética*, edited by Alfredo Carballo Picazo, CSIC (Madrid, 1953), vol. 2, p. 26.

51. Some of these names must be added to the references that A. Vilanova gave in his excellent article "El peregrino andante en el *Persiles* de Cervantes," *BRABLB*, 1949, pp. 97ff.

52. *Sucesos y prodigios de amor*, p. 339.

53. BAE, XVIII, p. 216.

54. *Cigarrales de Toledo*, p. 61.

55. *El mayor monstruo del mundo*, in *OC*, *Dramas*, edited by Valbuena Briones (Madrid: Aguilar), p. 323.

56. See my *Estado moderno y mentalidad social*, vol. 2, pp. 215ff.

57. BAE, 18, p. 266.

58. *Consejo y consejeros de príncipes* (1617). I am citing from the abridged version (Madrid, 1958), p. 6. The author drew this conclusion: therefore, the rulers' decisions "have to be modified every day, every hour and even at every moment" (p. 10).

59. *Engaños que causa el vicio*, in *Obras*, edited by G. de Amezúa (Madrid, 1950), p. 457.

60. The curious work of G. Goodman is entitled *The Fall of Adam from Paradise Proved by Natural Reason and the Grounds of Philosophy*; it was published in 1616 and its success led to a second edition in 1629.

61. See my *Antiguos y modernos; La idea de progreso en el desarrollo inicial de una sociedad* (Madrid, 1967).

62. *Empresa* 66, p. 504.

63. Cellorigo, *Memorial*, fol. 2.

64. See my *Orígenes del empirismo en el pensamiento político español del siglo XVII*.

65. *Opere*, Edizione nazionale, vol. 7, p. 669.

66. See L. Giuso, *La filosofia de G. B. Vico e l'età barocca* (Rome, 1943), pp. 241, 271, passim.

67. G. M. de Jovellanos, *Oración sobre el estudio de las ciencias naturales*, edited by Caso González (Madrid, 1970), p. 236.

68. *Essais*, III, xiii, p. 179. Elsewhere he spoke about "that continuous variation of human things" (I, xlix, p. 217).

69. *El mundo social de "La Celestina*," 3rd ed. (Madrid, 1973).

70. *Desengaño del hombre en el tribunal de la Fortuna*, edited by Astrana Marín (Madrid, 1928), p. 76.

71. *Obras en verso*, p. 51.

72. *Varias noticias*, prologue and fol. 4.

73. At the beginning of letter 15 (3 February 1624), p. 249.

74. *Obras*, 1, p. 132.

75. *Guzmán de Alfarache*, vol. 3, p. 82.

76. BAE, 221, p. 131 (24 April 1655).

77. *El discreto*, 6, in OC, pp. 94, 95.

78. *Agudeza y arte de ingenio*, in *OC*, p. 240.

79. *Pensées*, p. 43.

80. *Empresa* 81, p. 580.

81. *Empresa* 4, p. 186; 81, p. 584; and 59, p. 468.

82. *Varias noticias*, fol. 17.

83. *Cisne de Apolo*, vol. 1, pp. 69-70.

84. *El español Gerardo*, p. 214.

85. *Confusión de confusiones* (1688). I am citing from the facsimile reprint (Madrid, 1948), p. 142.

86. *Genio de la historia* (Vitoria, 1957), p. 331.

87. *Cigarrales de Toledo*, p. 92.

88. *Genio de la historia*, p. 239.

89. *Orfeo*, at the end of canto 1, edited by P. Cabañas (Madrid, 1948), p. 34.

90. *Theatro de los theatros de los pasados y presentes siglos*, edited by D. W. Moir (London, 1970), p. 78.

91. BAE, 42, p. 104.

92. *Poesía* volume, p. 19.

93. *Obras*, p. 123.

94. *Obras*, vol. 1, p. 60.

95. BAE, 42, p. 105.

96. "The Ruin," in *Essays on Sociology, Philosophy and Aesthetics*, edited by Kurt H. Wolf (New York, 1965), pp. 259-66.

97. *Studies in Iconology* (New York, 1967), p. 92.

98. The *loa* preceding the comedy *El esposo fingido*, in *Poetas dramáticos valencianos*, vol. 1, edited by Juliá Martínez (Madrid, 1929), p. 229.

99. Setanti, BAE, 57, pp. 525-26.

100. *El discreto*, 22, in *OC*, p. 135.

101. See Ph. Butler, *Classicisme et baroque dans l'oeuvre de Racine* (Paris, 1959), p. 21.

102. *Obras*, 1, p. 8.

103. *Empresas*, Reader's Prologue, p. 166.

104. *Día y noche de Madrid*, p. 442.

105. BAE, 42, p. 431.

106. *El español Gerardo*, p. 144.

107. See especially *Il Principe*, chap. 25.

108. *Obras*, vol. 2, p. 56.

109. "These are the changes of fortune, some falling from their heights and others rising to the top," wrote Cristóbal Lozano, *Historias y leyendas*, vol. 1 (Madrid), p. 211.

110. BAE, 42, p. 49.

111. Sonnet 21 in *Obras*, edited by J. M. Rozas (Madrid, 1969), p. 97.

112. *El soldado Píndaro*, p. 293.

113. "You have reason and I fortune / and you will see I am without envy," in episode 2 of the comedy. Calderón's thesis, within his Christian morality based on providence, was nonetheless the inverse of what this character enunciates.

114. *La hora de todos y la fortuna con seso*, in *Obras*, edited by Astrana Marín (Madrid, 1932), vol 1: *Prosa*, pp. 269ff.

115. *Errores celebrados*, edited by Martín de Riquer (Barcelona, 1965), p. 85.

116. *El soldado Píndaro*, pp. 337-38.

117. See P. Mesnard, "Baltasar Gracián devant la conscience française," *Revista de la Universidad de Madrid*, 7, no. 27 (1959); and Rousset, *La littérature française*, p. 614.

118. *El soldado Píndaro*, p. 360.

119. *Empresa 88*, p. 614.

120. This literature was avidly read and doled out by the gazetteers to their public; see, for example, Almansa's Letter 6, which relates the execution of Rodrigo Calderón (22 October 1621).

121. *El burgués* (Madrid, 1972).

122. *Diálogos de la pintura antigua*, edited by E. Tormo (Madrid, n.d.), p. 43.

123. *El criticón*, 3, p. 172.

124. In the anthology published by UNESCO, *Jean Amos Comenius, 1592-1670; Pages choisies* (Paris, 1957), p. 45.

125. See E. Raimondi, *Letteratura barocca: Studi sul Seicento italiano* (Florence, 1961).

126. He quoted it explicitly, revealing a direct knowledge. See lines 142-44 and 350 (edited by Juana de José Prades [Madrid, 1971], pp. 290 and 299; this edition has an excellent preliminary study very much of interest for our concerns). The renewed presence of the Aristotelian doctrinal legacy in seventeenth-century literature has been pointed out by E. Moreno Báez, *Lección y sentido del Guzmán de Alfarache* (Madrid, 1948).

127. *Velázquez* (Madrid, 1920).

128. *La casa del tahur*, edited by V. G. Williamsen (Madrid, 1973), line 465.

129. *Avisos*, 1 (27 September 1656), BAE, 221, p. 321.

130. See my "Un mito platónico en Gracián," collected in *Estudios de historia del pensamiento español*, series 3 (Madrid, 1975).

131. *El discreto*, 22, in OC, p. 135.

132. Cited by J. Ehrard, *L'idée de nature en France à l'aube des lumières* (Paris, 1970), p. 103.

133. Gracián, *El discreto*, 13, in *OC*, p. 109.

134. Published in *Poetas dramáticos valencianos*, 2, p. 170.

135. See L. Rosales, *El sentimiento del desengaño en la poesía barroca* (Madrid, 1966). Many elements about the subject can be found in B. M. Villanueva, *La ascética de los jesuitas en los autos sacramentales de Calderón* (Deusto, 1973).

136. *Desengaño del hombre*, p. 108.

137. *El pasagero*, p. 30.

138. *Margarita; Oración fúnebre en las honras de la Serenísima Infanta* (Madrid, 1633), fol. 3.

139. *Pastores de Belén; Obras en verso* (Madrid: Aguilar), p. 1222. The "distant views" were the great problem of Baroque technique.

140. Baquero Goyanes has focused on the study of the subject of perspectivism in representative authors of baroque mentality. See his *Perspectivismo y sátira en "El criticón" de Gracián* (Saragossa, 1959) and *Visualidad y perspectivismo en las "Empresas" de Saavedra Fajardo* (Murcia, 1970).

141. *El criticón*, 3, p. 172.

142. This passage from *The Labyrinth of the World and the Paradise of the Heart* was pointed out and translated from the Czech by my friend and colleague Prof. J. Volec.

143. *Sermón en la Festividad de la Purísima Concepción* (Saragossa, 1630), fol. 11.

144. In his penetrating study on perspective, Panofsky made some statements that mesh perfectly with our thesis inasmuch as they bring out the problematic of the substantial and objective order of the world and the subjective, transforming and reconstructive rendering of reality in accordance with the human being's capacity; and inasmuch as the appearance of this problem is neither happenstance nor dependent on mere intellectual formulations. Perspective, of course,

> seeks a distance between human beings and things...but it again suppresses this distance inasmuch as it in a way absorbs in the human eye the world of things existing autonomously vis-à-vis the human being; on the one hand it reduces artistic phenomena to solid and exact mathematical rules, but on the other hand makes them dependent on the human being, on the individual, to the extent the rules are based on the psycho-physiological conditions of the visual impression and to the extent that its mode of operation is determined by the position of a subjective point of view chosen at will.
>
> * * *
>
> Perspective is an order, but an order of visual appearances. Taking it to the extreme, to accuse such an order of abandoning the *true being* of things in favor of their visual appearance or to accuse it of establishing itself in a free and mental representation of form instead of in the appearance of things seen, is no more than a question of emphasis.

But this modern formulation, which was already present in the baroque and was related to what began to be discovered in the crisis of the ancient world, was not a purely artistic or intellectual phenomenon: "Therefore it is not happenstance that during the course of the evolution of art this perspectival conception of space has become dominant on two occasions: once as the sign of an end, when the ancient theocracy perished; again, as the sign of a beginning, when the modern anthropocracy emerged" (E. Panofsky, *La perspectiva como forma simbólica* [Barcelona, 1973], pp. 51 and 55-56; German original, "Die Perspektive als symbolische Form," *Vorträge der Bibliothek Warburg, 1924-1925*, pp. 258ff.).

145. "Silva al pincel," in *Poesía*, p. 556.

146. *Baltasar Gracián; Estilo y doctrina* (Saragossa, 1960), p. 67.

147. *Réflexions ou sentences et maximes morales* (Paris: Classiques Garnier), p. 52.

148. *Pensées*, p. 47.

149. See B. M. Villanueva, *La ascética de los jesuitas*, passim.

150. It is of interest to bear in mind these two lines from Calderón that I have never seen quoted:

"que es en su concepto rey, / si piensa que es rey, un loco" [that he is king in idea, / if he thinks he is king, a madman] (*La gran Cenobia*).

151. *El pasagero*, p. 30.

152. *Historias peregrinas y ejemplares*, p. 263.

153. Warnke, *Versions of Baroque*, p. 67.

154. *Essais*, III, xiii, p. 187.

155. Commenting on Velázquez's *Las hilanderas*, D. Angulo wrote: "It contains a crepuscular and plebeian story in the foreground and a brilliant and aristocratic story in the background. They are something like the gallery and stage of a theater" (*Velázquez; Cómo compuso sus principales cuadros* [Seville, 1947], p. 55).

156. *European Literature and the Latin Middle Ages*, pp. 138-44.

157. "Annotazioni su l'importanza della festa teatral per la vita artistica e dinastica nel barocco," in *Retorica e barocco*, p. 236.

158. H. Ettinghausen, *Francisco de Quevedo and the Neostoic Movement* (Oxford, 1972).

159. *La littérature de l'âge baroque en France*, p. 54.

160. This can serve as the basis for resolving in a traditional sense the conflict between the image of "life as a dream" (which we will consider in what follows) and the affirmation of the human being's moral reality, a problem studied by E. M. Wilson in *Critical Essays on the Theater of Calderón*.

161. A. Adam, *Histoire de la littérature française au XVIIe siècle*, vol. 1, pp. 570ff.

162. This comedy by Lope de Vega has been studied in other aspects that reveal the work's complex interest; see H. Bermejo Hurtado in "La representación en *Lo fingido verdadero* de Lope de Vega," in *El sueño y su representación en el barroco*, edited by D. Cvitanovic (Bahía Blanca: Cuadernos del Sur, 1969).

163. Other aspects of the theme are discussed in the books of Hocke and Constandse (already cited).

164. *Avisos*, 1 (1 January 1656), BAE, 221, p. 234.

165. *Discurso universal de las causas que ofenden esta monarquía y remedios eficaces para todas*, edited by Campomanes, p. 315.

166. *La Junta de Reformación*, AHE, 5, 1621(?) document, p. 234.

167. J. Vilar, *Literatura y economía; La figura satírica del arbitrista en el Siglo de Oro* (Madrid, 1973), pp. 257ff.

168. BAE, 42, p. 362.

169. The first quote is from *El castigo sin venganza* and the second from *La Arcadia*; see *Obras en prosa y verso* (Madrid: Aguilar), pp. 1055-56. The same line appears in one of Quiñones de Benavente's *loas*, published in his *Entremeses*, edited by H. E. Bergman (Salamanca, 1968), p. 31. See other examples in E. M. Wilson and J. Sage, *Poesías líricas en las obras dramáticas de Calderón* (London, 1964), pp. 135ff., where other references appear.

170. See A. L. Cilveti, *El significado de "La vida es sueño"* (Madrid, 1971), p. 83.

171. Already studied by A. Farinelli in *La vita è un sogno* (Turin, 1916), which contains an extensive bibliography.

172. One of Calderón's characters (*En esta vida todo es verdad y todo es mentira*) asks himself the following question: "if I have seen what I dreamed? / if I have dreamed what I saw?"

173. *El mundo por de dentro*, in *OC*, vol. 1: *Prosa*, pp. 197-98.

174. See my "Bases antropológicas del pensamiento de Gracián."

175. See P. Quennell, *Shakespeare et son temps* (Paris, 1964), p. 335.

176. "Bases antropológicas del pensamiento de Gracián."

177. J. P. Borel, *Quelques aspects du songe dans la littérature espagnole* (Neuchatel, 1965), p. 13.

178. E. Tierno Galván, "Notas sobre el barroco," in his *Escritos* (Madrid, 1971).

CHAPTER 8. THE TECHNIQUE OF INCOMPLETENESS

1. *El Manierismo en el arte europeo de 1520 a 1650* (Madrid, 1961).

2. From the preliminary study to his translation of Weisbach's book, *El barroco, arte de la Contrarreforma* (Madrid, 1948).

3. See references in H. Hatzfeld, *Estudios sobre el barroco*, pp. 46ff. The reference centers on the poet G. Chiabrera, who — along with other belated Petrarchists of the time — led to the coining of the concept I give in the text.

4. "Polemica in torno alla prosa barocca," in *Letteratura barocca* (Florence, 1961), pp. 184ff.

5. J. M. Blecua has indicated this in his "El estilo de *El Criticón* de Gracián," *AFA*, ser. B, 1 (Saragossa, 1945).

6. BAE, 45, p. 523.

7. *Diálogos practicables del nobilísimo arte de la pintura*, p. 182.

8. "Calderón y Velázquez," *Clavileño*, no. 10 (Madrid, 1951), p. 9.

9. Concerning this last point, see Ph. Butler, *Classicisme et baroque*, p. 21.

10. Many of the formal — or, better said, apparent — elements occurred in common, which has given rise to confusions about who is to be included in which category. See, in addition, the cited works of Hocke (*El manierismo*) and A. Blunt (*Artistic Theory in Italy*) and A. Hauser's *Mannerism; the Crisis of the Renaissance and the Origin of Modern Art*, translated by Eric Mosbacher (with author) (New York, 1965).

11. Some examples from Lope: "Etna de amor que de tu mismo hielo / despides llamas.../ el fuego con que me hielas, / el hielo con que me abrasas" [Etna of love, you shoot flames from your very ice..the fire with which you freeze me, the ice with which you burn me] (*Las fortunas de Diana*). Rousset also collected various examples of these rhetorical figures in French literature.

12. "Aristotelismo e barocco," pp. 119-197.

13. See Wardropper, *Historia de la poesía a lo divino en la Cristiandad occidental*. Among others, he cited the works of Malipiero, *Petrarca espiritural con canciones de amor divino* (1536, with ten successive editions), and Salvatorino, *Tesoro de la Sagrada Escritura sobre rimas de Petrarca* (1590); there were analogous cases, such as Fano's *Decamerón espiritual*, 1594. In Spain, Sebastián de Córdoba wrote his *Eglogas de Garcilaso a lo divino* (1575).

14. *El criticón*, 1, p. 361.

15. MHE, 13, p. 4 (3 January 1634).

16. Letter 12 (15 August 1623), p. 206.

17. *Diez lamentaciones sobre el miserable estado de los atheístas de nuestro tiempo*, p. 79.

18. *Gl'heroici furori*; I am quoting from P. H. Michel's edition — preceded by a valuable study — with the Italian text and French translation (Paris, 1954).

19. In his corresponding *Life*; on the subject see Weisbach, *El barroco*, p. 98.

20. *El Crotalón*, p. 157.

21. See Ceán Bermúdez, *Diccionario histórico de los más ilustres profesores de las Bellas Artes en España* (facsimile ed., Madrid, 1965), vol. 5, p. 307.

22. Carducho, *Diálogos de la Pintura* (Madrid, 1865), pp. 35, 73, and 34, respectively.

23. One of the first works expressing baroque sensibility in terms of the aspects here under consideration is probably Fernando de Herrera's *Relación de la guerra de Cipre y suceso de la batalla naval de Lepanto* (Seville, 1572).

24. "Aristotelismo e barocco," p. 141.

25. *Principles of Art History*, p. 118.

26. *Philosophía antigua poética*, vol. 1, p. 222.

27. *La Dorotea*, act 4, scene 2, pp. 327-28, n. 108. The passage probably stems from López Pinciano's passage that we have just cited. E. S. Morby gives other references.

28. For some data concerning the theme in relation to the supercession of the Aristotelian doctrine of "imitation," see F. Flora, *Storia della letterature italiana*, vol. 2 (Milan, 1940), p. 261.

29. *Les antiquitez de Rome et les regrets*, edited and introduced by E. Droz (Paris, 1947), p. 40.

30. The passage, which comes from the *Diálogos*, is reproduced with commentary in C. Justi, *Velázquez y su siglo* (Madrid, 1953), p. 232.

31. *La Arcadia*, book 5, BAE, 38, p. 430.
32. *Philosophía antigua poética*, vol. 1, p. 222.
33. *Cisne de Apolo*, edited by A. Porqueras (Madrid, 1958), vol. 2; see especially pp. 193 and 216 (the other references are found on pp. 184, 186, and 202).
34. *Errores celebrados*, edited by Martín de Riquer (Barcelona, 1954), p. 56.
35. *Theatro de los theatros*, p. 94.
36. *Memorial sobre la política necesaria*, fol. 25.
37. *El soldado Píndaro*, BAE, 18, p. 293.
38. "Apparence et manière," a fragment of his *Le je-ne-sais-quoi et le presque-rien*, in *Homenaje a Gracián* (Saragossa, 1958), pp. 125ff.
39. *Philosophía antigua poética*, vol. 2, pp. 57-58.
40. *El pasagero*, p. 356.
41. *Philosophía antigua poética*, vol. 2, p. 19. It is unnecessary to explain that *agreeable* doesn't have the banal meaning that it has today: it meant that which pleased, even though it be the distressing end of a sad play.
42. *Poetas dramáticos valencianos*, vol. 1 (Madrid, 1929), p. 628, appendix 2: "A un licenciado que deseaba hacer comedias."
43. Lope, *Las fortunas de Diana*, in *Novelas a Marcia Leonarda*, edited by F. Rico, p. 60.
44. Collected by Rousset (*La littérature de l'âge baroque en France*, p. 269), who nevertheless failed to pose the question we are dealing with here. The quote appears in the work's prologue.
45. See M. Lebègue, "La tragédie," *XVIIe Siècle*, no. 20 (1953), dedicated to the baroque.
46. Some pages on the subject can be seen in Krauss's *Graciáns Lebenslehre*, pp. 116-17.
47. *Consejo y consejero de Príncipes* (Madrid, 1958), p. 25.
48. *El filósofo* (Madrid, 1650), fol. 140.
49. *Comentarios políticos*, pp. 97-98. Let us again note the use of *to suspend.*
50. *Anamorphoses ou magie artificielle des effets merveilleux* (Paris, 1969), p. 12.
51. Ortega related Velázquez's art with this discovery: "Reality differs from myth in that it is incomplete" ("Introducción a Velázquez," in *OC*, vol. 8, 1943, p. 479).
52. "A pretty and completed refinement . . . [is] the typical Spanish taste in painting" (*Historia de la Orden de San Jerónimo*, vol. 12 of NBAE, vol. 2, p. 549).
53. See D. W. Bleznick, *Quevedo* (New York, 1972).
54. *Obras*, vol. I, p. 27. The passage comes from the *Fábula de Leandro y Hero.*
55. G. Díaz-Plaja, *El espíritu del barroco* (Barcelona, 1940).
56. Prologue to the *Obras* of A. Pantaleón de Ribera, in the posthumous edition (Madrid, 1631). I am quoting from the 1944 ed. (Madrid), vol. 1, p. 28.
57. *El español Gerardo*, p. 246.
58. *Libro de la erudición poética*, edited by M. Cardenal Iracheta (Madrid, 1946), pp. 93-94.
59. *Philosophía antigua poética*, vol. 1, p. 154.
60. Prologue to the *Obras de Pantaleón de Ribera*, p. 24.
61. *El discreto*, p. 320.
62. Collard, *Nueva poesía: Conceptismo, culteranismo en la crítica española* (Madrid, 1967), pp. 99ff. The cited work of Menéndez Pidal is "Oscuridad, dificultad entre culteranos y conceptistas," collected in *Castilla, la tradición, el idioma* (Madrid: Col. Austral); the work of F. Lázaro, "Sobre la dificultad conceptista," in *Estudios dedicados a Menéndez Pidal*, vol. 6 (Madrid, 1956).
63. *Cisne de Apolo*, vol. 1, p. 114.
64. *Agudeza y arte de ingenio*, discurso 40.
65. Ibid., discurso 7, p. 266.
66. *La tradición clásica*, 1, p. 256.
67. *Confusión de confusiones*, 1688 (facsimile ed., Madrid, 1958), p. 142.
68. See my "La literatura de emblemas en el contexto de la sociedad barroca," collected in my *Teatro y literatura en la sociedad barroca* (Madrid, 1972).

69. *Obras*, p. 1242.

70. *Cisne de Apolo*, vol. 2, p. 89.

71. See J. Gállego, *Visión y símbolos en la pintura española del Siglo de Oro* (Madrid, 1972).

72. See my *Teoría española del estado en el siglo XVII* (Madrid, 1944), p. 54.

73. *Anales de Madrid*, edited by Fernández Martín (Madrid, 1971).

74. "Machinerie et perspectives curieuses dans leur rapport avec le cartésianisme," *Bulletin de la société d'Etudes sur le XVIIe siècle* (Paris, 1956).

75. See *Anamorphoses ou magie artificielle des effets merveilleux*.

76. See Ramón Ceñal, "La vida, obras e influencia de Emmanuel Maignan," *REP*, no. 46 (1952), and "La filosofía de Emmanuel Maignan," *Revista de Filosofía* 13, no. 48 (1954).

77. *Antiguos y modernos: La idea de progreso en el desarrollo inicial de una sociedad*, p. 574; *Estado moderno y mentalidad social*, vol. 1, pp. 50 and 82.

78. Baltrusaitis, *Le Moyen Age fantastique*, pp. 58-60.

CHAPTER 9. THE SOCIAL ROLE OF ARTIFICE

1. *El español Gerardo*, p. 201.

2. *Cigarrales de Toledo*, p. 173, repeated on p. 263.

3. Suárez de Figueroa, *Varias noticias*, fol. 20.

4. *Rinascimento e barocco*, p. 25n.

5. See my *Antiguos y modernos: La idea de progreso en el desarrollo inicial de una sociedad*, part 1.

6. *La más infame venganza*, in *Desengaños amorosos*, edited by G. de Amezúa (Madrid, 1950), vol. 2, p. 20. In another passage: "Novelties at least possess the quality that although they are not very tasty everybody likes to eat them" (vol. 2, p. 102).

7. *El viaje entretenido*, edited by J. P. Ressot, p. 105; it appears as the work's title.

8. *Avisos*, ed. *Semanario Erudito*, 33, p. 150.

9. BAE, 22, p. 187 (29 May 1658).

10. MHE, 14, p. 339.

11. BAE, 21, p. 46 (19 August 1654).

12. See the great number of similar cases cited in the first chapter. Concerning Adam de la Parra, see J. de Entrambasaguas's preface to de la Parra's *Conspiración herético-cristianísima*, translated by A. Roda (Madrid, 1943).

13. Suárez de Figueroa, *El pasagero*, p. 361.

14. *El mesón del mundo*, p. 68.

15. *El español Gerardo*, p. 193.

16. *Cisne de Apolo*, vol. 1, p. 74.

17. *República original sacada del cuerpo humano* (Barcelona, 1597), the first unnumbered pages.

18. *Genio de la historia* (Vitoria, 1957), p. 331.

19. *De historia, para entenderla y escribirla*, edited by S. Montero Díaz (Madrid, 1948), p. 42.

20. Here I will raise a question that G. M. Foster's interesting suggestion poses for us:

In general, the positive attraction of the new and novel seems to be associated with industrial societies. Whether peoples with the most interest in novelty became the first industrialists because of this interest, or whether an industrial system produces these values, we cannot be sure. I suspect the latter — that aspirations are developed through the opportunity to satisfy them. In any event, the relationship between a productive economy and a tradition for change is so close that it cannot be thought of as being due to chance" (*Traditional Cultures and the Impact of Technological Change*, p. 65).

I believe that in Spain the connection would follow the second direction indicated by Foster: the industrial stagnation of the seventeenth century would produce the limitation or diversion, accordingly, of the taste for novelty, although it would never succeed in suffocating it, and both phenomena depended on the triumph of conservative interests in the seventeenth- and eighteenth-century monarchy.

21. *Paradoxas racionales*. Although the work's permission to be printed dated from 1655, it nevertheless remained unpublished; it was published, with a preliminary study by E. Buceta, in Madrid, 1935 (the quote appears on p. 30).

22. Ibid., pp. 5, 7.

23. *Nueva idea de la tragedia antigua* (Madrid, 1633), pp. 193ff. Concerning González de Salas, it is interesting to consult the pages that A. Vilanova dedicated to him in *Historia de las literaturas hispánicas*, vol. 3, p. 641.

24. Mandrou, "Le baroque européen: Mentalité pathétique et révolution sociale," in *Annales*, 1960, p. 909.

25. Antonio de León Pinelo, *Anales de Madrid, desde el año 447 al de 1658*.

26. Letter 16, p. 300.

27. *Avisos*, ed. *Semanario Erudito*, 32, p. 53 (7 May 1641); further on it relates a supernatural prodigy that defies reason (33, p. 16).

28. BAE, 21, p. 59 (12 September 1654).

29. A curious example of how nature is viewed magically can be seen in the passage where the *Dietari de Jeroni Pujades* recounts a strange phenomenon. A "gran barra bermella" arose from the sea and was seen in the air; it moved and broke into fragments; the parts fought among themselves, disappeared, and appeared again; "se formà como un foch y fum de forn de cals," and in the end it suddenly disappeared; this was reported on 11 December 1625 and repeated more briefly on 21 December (*Dietari*, vol. 3, pp. 237, 241). It appears to be the first mention of a UFO.

30. *Cartas de jesuitas* (16 November 1637), MHE, 14, p. 209.

31. *Au coeur religieux du XVIe siècle* (Paris, 1958). This was not happenstance; it was an attempt to utilize these irrational forces in a blind defense of the existing order.

32. See the two studies of E. Garin included in his *Medioevo e Rinascimento* (Bari, 1954).

33. Suárez de Figueroa recorded the doctrine that habitually circulated in his time: there are two kinds of magic, natural magic and superstitious magic (which turns out to be a recognition of the effective activity of both). "Natural magic . . . views celestial and terrestrial things and considers their advantages and drawbacks, discovering the faculties hidden in nature, and consequently mixes the ones with the others in a necessary proportion and in a certain constellation"; this magic, then, combining the beings' occult properties whose knowledge has been attained, "produces what appears to be unheard-of miracles." The other is superstitious magic: "It is done by invoking evil spirits and is manifest idolatry, always prohibited by well-ordered republics" (*Varias noticias*, fol. 54). The tendency to utilize magical expedients provoked a popular dissemination of the latter.

34. See references in Mandrou, "Le baroque européen." Works by Baissac, Gauzons, Gerhardt, and J. Français are cited in the extensive bibliography of Caro Baroja's book (see n. 37 below).

35. Ever since Burckhardt, the role of magic in the Renaissance has been emphasized. Cassirer granted it a relevant role in the formation of science (*The Individual and the Cosmos in Renaissance Philosophy*, trans. Mario Domandi [New York, 1964]); see the classic work on the subject, Thorndike's *A History of Magic and Experimental Science*, 4 vols. (New York, 1929-34). B. Nardi and E. Garin have made more recent contributions to the theme.

36. "The European Witch-craze of the Sixteenth and Seventeenth Centuries," in his *The Crisis of the Seventeenth Century*, pp. 90-192. The bibliography on the subject of manifestations and surviving remnants of magic in the early modern age continues to grow. Even in the ambit of social groups displaying a bourgeois character — which reveals that the mentality of these bourgeois groups was not as rationalizing as is topically repeated — there has been verified, proportionately speaking, a widespread preservation of a magical mentality. See Dupont, Bouchat, Frijhoff and Muchembled, *Prophètes et sorcières au Pay-Bas; XVIe-XVIIe siècles* (Hachette, 1978). Among others, one might also consult the following studies: D. P. Walker, *Spiritual and Demonic Magic from Ficino to*

Campanella (London, 1958); R. Mandrou, *Magistrats et sorcières en France au XVIIe siècle* (Paris, 1968); S. Anglo, "Melancholia and Witchcraft," in *Folie et déraison à la Renaissance* (Brussels, 1976).
37. See J. Caro Baroja, *Las brujas y su mundo* (Madrid, 1961).
38. "Discurso acerca de los cuentos de las brujas y cosas tocantes a magia," edited by Serrano Sanz, *Revista de Extremadura*, 1900, pp. 289-303 and 337-47; "Segundo discurso acerca de los brujos y de sus maleficios," *RABM*, 3rd epoch, 2, 1906.
39. *Anales de Madrid*, p. 292.
40. *La pensée religieuse française de Charron à Pascal* (Paris, 1933), pp. 351ff.
41. From the sociohistorical point of view, B. W. Wardropper proposed a differentiation between *tragedy* and *comedy* in Spanish baroque theater. According to this distinction, comedy "gives free rein to the antisocial and anarchic impulses of individuals rebelling against society"; "the message of comedy is that individuals have rights to exceed the rights of society. This message was and is revolutionary" (see his study *La comedia española del Siglo de Oro*, published following E. Olson's *Teoría de la comedia* [Barcelona, 1978]; the quotes appear on pp. 231, 235). It seems a suggestive point of view, but one that is difficult to prove.
42. *El pasagero*, p. 207: "The days of men are like hay."
43. *Entretiens sur la vie et sur les ouvrages des plus excellents peintres anciens et moderns*, vol. 2, p. 322 (Trévoux, 1725).
44. *Historia de la orden de San Jerónimo* NBAE, 12, p. 557.
45. *Obras; Prosa*, vol. 1, pp. 120, 169, which correspond to *La vida del Buscón* and *El alguacil endemoniado*, respectively. In the latter he considered that Bosch did not really believe that there were demons but that he went that far in cultivating strangeness for itself.
46. *Epístola sobre la poesía*, in *Obras escogidas*, vol. 2 (Madrid, 1953), p. 933.
47. *Diálogos practicables*, p. 185.
48. *Día y noche de Madrid*, p. 435.
49. *Genio de la historia*, p. 300.
50. *Principes de la tragédie*, p. 37.
51. *Memoriales y discursos*, edited by G. Anes, p. 285 (they are the work's last words).
52. *Anales de Madrid*, pp. 290, 310, 311.
53. See M. Iriarte, *El doctor Huarte de San Juan y su "Examen de ingenios"* (Madrid, 1939).
54. Ibid., pp. 292ff.
55. López Piñero, *Introducción de la ciencia moderna en España* (Barcelona, 1969).
56. *Avisos*, BAE, 22, p. 143 (1658).
57. *Fábrica y uso de varios instrumentos matemáticos* (Madrid, 1675). About the author, see A. Cotarelo, *El P. José de Zaragoza y la astronomía de su tiempo* (Madrid, 1935).
58. *Antiguos y modernos*, pp. 570ff.
59. *Theatro de los dioses de la gentilidad* (Salamanca, 1620), 1, 3, xxii.
60. *Theatro de los theatros*, P. 78.
61. See my *Antiguos y modernos*, 1, ii, and 4, iv. To the data collected there on printing one can add the interesting elegy of Suárez de Figueroa in *Varias noticias*, fols. 232ff.
62. "El desdén del Alameda," in *Historias peregrinas y ejemplares*, p. 115.
63. "Pachecos y Palomeques," ibid., p. 269.
64. Letter 6 (22 October 1621), p. 103.
65. *Anales de Madrid*, pp. 241, 351.
66. BAE, 221, p. 222.
67. *Anales de Madrid*, pp. 247, 300, 312.
68. MHE, 16, pp. 19 and 21 (2 October 1640). Other Jesuits' references to the comedy and fiesta of Cardinal Borja, in MHE, 15, p. 383.
69. *Anales de Madrid*, p. 290.
70. Ibid., p. 318. The wind, however, was responsible for spoiling the production.
71. R. Froldi, *Il teatro valenziano e le origine della commedia barocca* (Pisa, 1962).

72. *Cartas de jesuitas* (22 June 1639), MHE, 15, p. 270. Barrionuevo, BAE, 221, p. 148 (16 June 1655).

73. In his edition of *El mejor alcalde, el rey*, p. 67.

74. BAE, 222, p. 199 (19 June 1658).

75. Ibid., p. 165 (20 February 1658). Similar comments were frequently repeated.

76. BAE, 221, pp. 212, 214.

77. Ibid., p. 148.

78. See the article cited in *Dramaturgie et société*, 1968, p. 7.

79. There were also manifestations of the theater adapting itself to the cruder aspects of baroque sensibility. Pellicer tells us (31, p. 139 [14 February 1640]) that the queen liked to hear hissing at the plays she attended, whether they were good or bad; she was also entertained by women fighting in the galleries and by the fact that mice were let loose. Many years later, Barrionuevo gave a similar report:

His Majesty has ordered that tomorrow only single women without hoopskirts go to the comedy because more will fit that way, and it is said that he and the queen want to view it without being seen and that there are cages with more than a hundred fattened mice ready to be released at the high point of the fiesta; when it happens there will be much to see and much entertainment for their Majesties.

Ultimately such a royally repugnant plan was not carried out (27 February 1656; BAE, 1, p. 250).

80. *Theatro de los theatros*, p. 78.

81. Alewyn, *L'univers du baroque*, French translation (Paris, 1964), p. 71.

82. This final observation is from Alewyn (p. 76), who did not place it in relation with the historical changes but who acutely manifests why it is of interest.

83. BAE, 21, p. 247.

84. *Diálogos practicables*, p. 123.

85. "Annotazioni sull'importanza della festa teatrale per la vita artistica e dinastica nel barocco," in *Retorica e barocco*, p. 235.

86. L. P. Thomas, "Les jeux de scène et l'architecture des idées dans le théatre allégorique de Calderón, in *Homenage a Menéndez Pidal* (Madrid, 1925), 2, pp. 501ff.

87. Quennell, *Shakespeare et son temps* (Paris, 1964), p. 363.

88. See K. Vossler, *Lope de Vega y su tiempo*, p. 222. It is possible that the elements to be manipulated in the scenography of the time were not numerous, as J. Gállego maintained (*Visión y símbolos*, p. 137); yet one need not gauge this merely in terms of real practice, but must also bear in mind the epoch's considerations and reflections. After Lope's death, scenographic means certainly increased greatly, and references — not literary but merely in news items or private or public references — constantly emphasized the great role played by stage machinery.

89. See Hugh A. Rennert, *The Spanish Stage in the Time of Lope de Vega* (New York, 1909; recently republished, n.d.).

90. Rennert, Ibid., pp. 241-42.

91. J. B. Trend ("Escenografía madrileña en el siglo XVII," *RBAM*, 3, 1926, pp. 269-91) gave some interesting information about the representations of comedies organized in honor of Prince Charles (later Charles I of England) in his surprise visit to Madrid. Trend observed a curious correspondence between the development of the theatrical locales in London at the end of the sixteenth and beginning of the seventeenth century and the development taking place in Madrid during the same epoch. And he gave an interesting scenographic sketch of Philip IV's Salón de Comedias that could not be more instructive about what I have called the epoch's "perspectivism."

92. *Cartas de España* (Madrid, 1972), pp. 144ff.

93. See Thomas, "Les jeux de scène," p. 504.

94. *Avisos*, ed. *Semanario Erudito*, 31, p. 142. The Jesuits also prepared them "with awe-inspiring stage machines" (ibid., 30, p. 219).

95. BAE, 221, pp. 106, 121, 141.
96. MHE, 15, p. 414; BAE, 221, pp. 267, 153; BAE, 221, pp. 53, 119, 120, 131, 165.
97. BAE, 221, p. 237.
98. Ibid., p. 242.
99. MHE, 15, pp. 471, 487.
100. Orozco Díaz, *El teatro y la teatralidad del barroco* (Barcelona, 1969), p. 144.
101. *Avisos*, ed. *Semanario Erudito*, 33, p. 112.
102. Rousset, *La littérature de l'âge baroque*, p. 19.
103. See M. N. Grand-Mesnil, *Mazarin et la presse* (Paris, 1967), p. 49.
104. *The Spanish Stage*, pp. 232-33.
105. *El rey se divierte*, 3rd ed. (Madrid, 1964), pp. 149-50.
106. *Die Barocke Freskmalerei in Deutschland* (Munich, 1951).
107. *Cigarrales*, p. 118.
108. The social interpretation of the theater's own technical aspects has to be related to the sociohistorical interpretation that some of us have attempted to carry out and that is being developed in younger writers with interesting results. In relation to Lope de Vega, I have cited Díez Borques's study that precedes his edition of *El mejor alcalde, el rey*. Let us recall M. Sauvage's study, *Calderón: Essai* (Paris, 1973), in which he brought out the dramatic tension and ultimate conformity between morality and order on the level of social responsibility within a mentality proper to estatist society (which characterized seventeenth-century society in all areas).
109. *La época mercantilista* (Mexico, 1943), p. 574.
110. Recently reedited with a preliminary study and notes by Ch. V. Aubrun (Paris, 1965), it constitutes one of the most significant works of the Calderonian baroque.
111. Lope's poem has been reedited by Ch. V. Aubrun and M. Muñoz Cortés, accompanied by their respective studies (Paris, 1962). In addition one can find mention of the myth in Céspedes's *El soldado Píndaro*, p. 308, and in Zayas y Sotomayor's novel *La esclava de su amante* (*Obras*, vol. 2, p. 35). The amusing mention we are referring to is found in Quiñones de Benavente's entremezzo *El sueño del perro*, edited by H. E. Bergman (Salamanca, 1968), p. 102.
112. In Marlowe, *The Tragical History of Dr. Faustus* (1588), which introduced the English baroque; in Calderón, *El mágico prodigioso*.
113. The adamic myth inspired the figure of Andrenio in Gracián's *El criticón* and is found in Milton's *Paradise Lost*; Grotius wrote a tragedy on the subject: *Adamus exil* (1601). For other references, see my study on Gracián, "Las bases antropológicas," pp. 421-22.
114. "Lectura política de Quevedo," *REP*, no. 49, Madrid, 1950.
115. See C.-G. Dubois, *Le baroque*, p. 165: "It was a matter of making an ostentation of possibilities . . . "; that is, of a demonstration, characterized by showing one's fitness for having possessions and power, within the context of a fiesta.
116. *Cigarrales*, p. 156.
117. Letter 12 (15 August 1623), p. 203.
118. *Noticias de Madrid* (June 1622), p. 27. These *Noticias*, motivated by the presence of the Prince of Wales in Madrid, offer an overwhelming and absurd picture of the life of the grandees.
119. *Anales de Madrid*, p. 307.
120. Ibid., pp. 346, 347, 353, passim.
121. BAE, 221, p. 51 (27 December 1656). The Jesuits were more conformist with the regime; years earlier, we read in one of their letters that "those with grand occupations must have some relaxation all year long" (9 February 1638), MHE, 14, p. 317. Nevertheless, even the prudent Pellicer felt indignant because of the senseless squandering of the fiestas.
122. BAE, 221, p. 157 (30 June 1655).
123. MHE, 14, p. 335 (16 February 1638).
124. *Avisos*, ed. *Semanario Erudito*, 32, p. 74 (June 11, 1640).
125. Ibid., pp. 242 and 248.

126. BAE, 222, p. 103 (13 January 1655). "In the direst straits it is only a matter of fiestas" (p. 153).

127. Ibid., p. 39 (27 December 1656).

128. Ibid., p. 124 (12 December 1657).

129. Ibid., p. 148 (9 January 1658).

130. Deleyto Piñuela, *El rey se divierte*, p. 240.

131. Deleyto Piñuela, *También se divierte el pueblo*, 3rd ed. (Madrid, 1966).

132. *La Junta de Reformación*, AHE, pp. 31, 210.

133. *Cartas de jesuitas* (9 February 1638), MHE, 14, p. 320.

134. The greatest wealth of Madrid was found "in the eating houses on the day of the bulls," said F. Santos, *Día y noche de Madrid*, p. 394; "to write [about these fiestas] one needs a paper mill." J. Pellicer had the bad taste to publish a pamphlet entitled *Anfiteatro de Felipe el Grande. Contiene los elogios que han celebrado la suerte que hizo en el toro, en la Fiesta agonal de trece de octubre deste año de MDCXXXI*, printed in Madrid (eighty-seven epigrams of various authors and, at the end, various ballads, *espinelas*, *silvas*, and other verse forms). It is difficult to place admiration for royalty on a lower level, but that corresponded well to the admiring popularity in the baroque.

135. Grand-Mesnil, *Mazarin et la presse*, pp. 47-48.

136. In introducing the edition of *Novelas peregrinas y extraordinarias*, pp. 42-44.

137. Note these two passages from Céspedes in *El español Gerardo* (pp. 142, 181):

A league from the city we had a pretty farm surrounded by charming forests, productive lands and fragrant, well-designed gardens where we, with the peaceful and licentious freedom of its solitudes, spent three or four days with a thousand agreeable delights and ingenious games that the servants, shepherds and rustics made to cheer up our convalescent son.... Gerardo has to remain in the city to gather some things fitting and necessary for the fiestas they were ordering.

Elsewhere Céspedes was one of the propagandists of the fiesta, of diversion and entertainment to alleviate the passions of the soul (p. 214).

138. *Les caractères*, p. 184.

139. *Avisos*, ed. *Semanario Erudito*, 31, p. 36.

140. Barrionuevo, *Avisos*, BAE, 222, pp. 89, 92, 96, 161, and 190. They correspond to the time between July 1657 and June 1658.

141. In his comedy *Las suertes trocadas y torneo venturoso* in *Poetas dramáticos valencianos*, vol. 1, p. 383.

142. Deleyto, *El rey se divierte*, pp. 163ff.

143. *Cigarrales de Toledo*, p. 93.

144. Pp. 28, 78, 91, 166, 222, 245.

145. MHE, 14, p. 18.

146. *Avisos*, ed. *Semanario Erudito*, 31, p. 50; ibid., 33, pp. 194, 215, passim.

147. BAE, 222, pp. 124, 132, 160, 161, passim.

148. *Anales de Madrid*, pp. 173, 311, passim.

149. Cited by G. Gentile, *Il pensiero del Rinascimento* (Florence, 1940), p. 63.

150. *Sucesos y prodigios de amor*, novel 2, p. 73.

151. *Cigarrales de Toledo*, p. 77.

152. *El español Gerardo*, p. 266.

153. P. 55 (April 1623).

154. MHE, 15, p. 144 (December 1638).

155. P. M. Skrine recently called attention to the role of the dazzling, surprising "appearance" that could attract and lock the gaze of the people who did not take part in the wealth of those in power, that could make the people feel subjugated by means of the spectacle offered them by the urban milieus of Versailles, Venice, London, and Madrid (*The Baroque*, pp. 37ff.).

APPENDIX. SOCIOPOLITICAL OBJECTIVES OF THE USE OF VISUAL MEDIA

1. *Principes de la tragédie*, edited by E. Vinaver (Paris, 1951), p. 14.

2. *La Europa de las capitales*, p. 23.

3. See my "La literatura de emblemas en el contexto de la sociedad barroca," published in my *Teatro y literatura en la sociedad barroca* (Madrid, 1972).

4. León Pinelo, *Anales de Madrid*, pp. 172, 181; in the exequies of a royal person there was "a funeral oration and a sermon with thirty-six etched hieroglyphics" (pp. 181, 210, passim).

5. See my "La concepción del saber en una sociedad tradicional," included in my *Estudios de historia del pensamiento español*, ser. 1: *Edad Media*, 2d ed. (Madrid, 1973).

6. Mandrou, *Introduction à la France moderne* (Paris, 1961).

7. *Varias noticias importantes a la humana comunicación*, fol. 244.

8. *Avisos*, ed. *Semanario Erudito*, 31, p. 278.

9. *Cartas de jesuitas*, MHE, 15, p. 313.

10. See A. M. Pollin, "Cithara Jesu: La apoteosis de la música en el *Divino Orfeo* de Calderón," in *Homenaje a Casalduero* (Madrid, 1972); I believe that his erudite and interesting thesis supports my general interpretation.

11. I have indicated that it was remarked upon by preceptists of emblematic literature ("La literatura de emblemas").

12. Francisco de Holanda recalled the value, in this sense, of painting for religion and its utilization by the Church (*Diálogos de la pintura antigua*, edited by E. Tormo [Madrid, n.d.], pp. 31ff.).

13. Weisbach has brought this relationship out in reference to the example of Zuccaro, president of the Academy of San Lucas in Rome and author of a theoretical treatise on painting that is manifestly of baroque inspiration (see *El Barroco, arte de la Contrarreforma*, p. 58).

14. It was reedited in Leipzig, 1910.

15. *Cartas de jesuitas*, MHE, 15, p. 196.

16. Francisco de Villapando, *Tercero y quarto libro de arquitectura de Sebastián de Serlio Bolonés* (Toledo, 1552), collected by Sánchez Cantón in *Fuentes literarias para la historia del arte*, vol. 1, p. 143.

17. See M. Herrero García, *Contribución de la literatura a la historia del arte* (Madrid, 1943), p. 199.

18. The expression "muy a lo pintoresco" is found with this new nuance in Francisco Pacheco, *Arte de la pintura, su antiguedad y grandezas*, edited by Sánchez Cantón (Madrid, 1956), vol. 2, p. 8.

19. Wölfflin, *Rinascimento e barocco*, pp. 37-38.

20. A. M. Boase, "Poètes anglais et poètes français à l'époque baroque," *RSH*, nos. 55-56 (1949), p. 181.

21. See his "Calderón y Velázquez," *Clavileño*, no. 10 (1951), p. 9.

22. *Dialogos de la pintura*, p. 175.

23. See R. Lee, "Ut pictura poesis: The Humanist Theory of Painting," in *Art Bulletin* 22 (1940), pp. 197ff.

24. A perfect example is contained in *La hermosura de Angélica*, cantos 5 and 13, in *Obras escogidas* (Madrid: Aguilar), pp. 513, 556-57, passim.

25. Edited by González Palencia (Madrid: Aguilar), p. 163.

26. This passage is found in his novel *El curioso y sabio Alejandro, fiscal de vidas ajenas*, edited by E. Correa-Calderón, in *Costumbristas antiguos españoles*, vol. 1, p. 145.

27. Louis Richeome, *Tableaux sacrés des figures mystiques . . . de l'Eucaristie* (Paris, 1601).

28. *El mesón del mundo*, p. 78.

29. *Diálogos de la pintura*, edited by Cruzada Villamil (Madrid, 1865), pp. 141, 255.

30. Ibid., appendixes, p. 442.

31. Madrid, 1681. Sánchez Cantón collected some fragments in his *Fuentes literarias para la*

316 □ NOTES TO PP. 257–263

historia del arte (Madrid, 1941), vol. 3; one passage relates the impression that St. Teresa confessed to having experienced once when she was contemplating a painting.

32. *Diálogos de la pintura*, p. 430.

33. Luque Fajardo, among others, tells us: "It is the function of portraits to represent the living image" (*Fiel desengaño contra la ociosidad y los vicios*, edited by M. de Riquer [Madrid, 1955], vol. 2, p. 173).

34. Panofsky has pointed out this antinomic formulation in *Idea: A Concept in Art Theory*, translated by Joseph J. S. Peake (New York, 1968).

35. "The power of making the individual go from the level of nature to the level of the allegorically sublime depends on ornamentation. This latter possesses a magical force that escapes us because we do not believe in it" (Alewyn, *L'univers du baroque*, p. 53).

36. In my *Velázquez y el espíritu de la modernidad* (Madrid, 1960), I wrote about the role of Rembrandt, particularly with regard to his self-portraits, and of Velázquez, with his portraits of a deformed and debilitated humanity. There I put forth my thesis about Velázquez's painting as "painting in the first person," as a testimony of personal experiences concerning things and human beings.

37. See J. Gállego, *Visión y símbolos en la pintura española del Siglo de Oro* (Madrid, 1972).

38. *Genio de la historia*, edited by Higinio de Santa Teresa (Vitoria, 1957), p. 312.

39. Baroque writers called this painting "a lo valiente" or "con valentía," expressions that are found in historians like Sigüenza or J. de San José, in preceptists like Pacheco or Carducho, and in critics like Rodrigo Caro, Quevedo, and Gracián.

40. See my "Las bases antropológicas del pensamiento de Gracián."

41. See my "La pintura como captación de la realidad," in the volume of miscellany *Varia velazqueña* (Madrid, 1960), vol. 1, pp. 48ff.

42. *Le vite dei più eccellenti pittori, scultori ed architetti* (Milan, 1908).

43. *Diálogo entre la naturaleza y las dos artes, pintura y escultura*, BAE, 42, pp. 116-17.

44. Galileo, letter to Ludovico Cigoli (26 June 1612), *Opere*, Edizione nazionale, vol. 11, p. 34 (cited and reproduced in the appendix of Panofsky's *Galileo as a Critic of the Arts* [The Hague, 1954]).

45. Antonio Pérez, *Aforismos de las segundas cartas*, no. 405. I am quoting from the edition of *Las obras y relaciones de Antonio Pérez* (Geneva, 1620), p. 1062.

46. See my *Velázquez y el espíritu de la modernidad* (Madrid, 1960).

47. *The Social History of Art*, vol. 2, p. 200.

48. "Color does much more than straight lines in making a human image appear clearer" (*Tragicomedia de Lisandro y Roselia, llamada Elicia y por otro nombre cuarta obra y Tercera Celestina* [1542; Madrid, 1872], prologue, p. x).

49. An interesting example is found in the prologue to Cristóbal de Virués's *La gran Semíramis*, in *Poetas dramáticos valencianos*, vol. 1, p. 25.

50. *Estudios y ensayos gongorinos* (Madrid, 1955), p. 78.

51. *Diálogo*, p. 117.

52. *Obras*, vol. 1, p. 188.

53. *República literaria*, in *OC*, edited by González Palencia, p. 1144.

Index

Index

José Antonio Maravall was born in Spain in 1911. He holds a chair at the Universidad Complutense in Madrid, is an associate professor at the University of Paris, and is a member of the Spanish Royal Academy of History. He has been a visiting professor at many universities in the United States and Europe, and is the author of more than 30 books and articles. *La cultura del Barroco* was first published in 1975.

Terry Cochran is humanities editor at the University of Minnesota Press.

Wlad Godzich teaches comparative literature at the Université de Montréal and at the University of Minnesota, where he is director of the Center for Humanistic Studies, and is co-editor, with Jochen Schulte-Sasse, of the series Theory and History of Literature.

Nicholas Spadaccini is professor of Spanish and comparative literature at the University of Minnesota. He has co-edited and written several books on the Spanish Golden Age.